HOPI KATSINA SONGS

HOPI KATSINA SONGS

Emory Sekaquaptewa
Kenneth C. Hill
Dorothy K. Washburn

University of Nebraska Press
Lincoln and London

Library of Congress Cataloging-in-Publication Data

Sekaquaptewa, Emory.
Hopi katsina songs / Emory Sekaquaptewa ; Kenneth C. Hill ; Dorothy K. Washburn.
pages i–xii, 1–421   cm
Includes bibliographical references and index.
ISBN 978-0-8032-6288-1 (cloth : alk. paper)—ISBN 978-0-8032-6848-7 (pdf). 1. Songs,
Hopi—Texts. 2. Hopi Indians—Music—History and criticism. 3. Kachinas. 4. Hopi
Indians—Social life and customs. I. Hill, Kenneth Cushman. II. Washburn, Dorothy Koster.
III. Title.
ML3557.s35 2015
782.42162′9745800268—DC23
2014023102

Contents

Preface

This volume contains Hopi transcriptions, English translations, and explanatory commentaries of 150 Hopi katsina songs. One hundred twenty-five are from recordings made throughout the twentieth century from singers from all three Hopi mesas; the other twenty-five are songs contributed by the late Emory Sekaquaptewa. The volume contains the katsina songs in the recorded collections archived at the Library of Congress and the Indiana University Archives of Traditional Music. These recordings, with a very few exceptions, had not been transcribed or translated.

This presentation represents one of Emory Sekaquaptewa's many efforts to provide a written record of portions of the Hopi patrimony. Because he understood how intimately cultural ideas are embedded in language, he devoted much of his lifetime to promoting literacy in Hopi and to creating written materials that would strengthen the language and, in so doing, the lifeway of his people. Similarly, he felt that preparing transcriptions and translations of early recordings of katsina songs would serve to demonstrate the vital continuity of Hopi religious thought and cultural practice since some songs included here were recorded over 100 years ago. In fact, he wanted to include song fragments in the hope that Hopi readers would remember the songs and be able to complete them and, in this way, to continue the creative process of perpetuating the Hopi legacy. As well, he felt that these songs would also be texts that future generations could return to again and again as guideposts while navigating the ups and downs of contemporary life.

In addition to the goal of providing written texts of the songs in Hopi, Emory was concerned that the younger generations were not sufficiently conversant with the ways in which these principles of life, presented as advice from the katsinas, were metaphorically encoded. For this reason he felt that some explication of this material was important for the continued vitality of Hopi religious beliefs and practices. In the spirit of the best anthropological tradition, where the fieldworker takes the role of listener and observer, we chose to listen to Emory, accepting his understanding and interpretation of Hopi concepts. In our view, to have interrupted this flow of ideas and experiences and the referential and metaphoric ways he explained the songs would have been tantamount to questioning his authority on the subject. In this light, this work is neither intended to be a critical commentary on past research nor a literature review of even the major studies about the Hopis. Emory never critiqued anyone else's ideas. That would have been *qa hopi* (not Hopi), for each Hopi is considered to be an individual with the right to act as he or she pleases. He insisted that he spoke only for himself. It is in this spirit that we present this material—the translations, interpretations, and explanations—as representing his point of view.

To this end, this volume contains Emory's interpretations of the meanings of the songs and the metaphors contained therein. It is to be expected, of course, that other Hopis may have their own, somewhat differing interpretations. However, our hope is that we have fairly represented Emory's perspective, insofar as we have understood his teachings and have been able to interpret them accurately in our English discussions of the meanings and metaphors in each song.

Emory provided the vision and guidance for all parts of the study. He transcribed each song in standard Hopi orthography, that of the Hopi Dictionary (Hopi Dictionary Project 1998), and then worked with us to translate them into English. The introduction and individual song commentaries were written by Dorothy Washburn. Kenneth Hill provided the linguistic footnotes, the final forms of the song translations, the appendices and index as well as overall editing.

Above all, this project was sustained by Emory's extraordinary vision and lifetime dedication to the preservation of Hopi language and culture. Emory was our teacher and mentor who guided us as we gained knowledge about the many ways in which katsina song embodies the very heart and soul of the Hopi people. He helped us come to understand and appreciate the integrity of oral tradition as a powerful vehicle that not only conveys cultural truths, but also, in so doing, becomes its own literature that has a rich past and a deserving future. It has truly been a pleasure and a privilege for us to have studied and worked with such a great man. We dedicate this volume to his memory and to his efforts on behalf of his people. Emory passed away December 13, 2007, having approved the song texts and translations in almost their present form. We completed the manuscript in 2008 and it is our great regret that Emory did not live to see his vision realized in print for he so dearly hoped that it would contribute to his life-long effort to vitalize the Hopi language and preserve the traditions contained therein for the Hopi people.

Kenneth C. Hill
Dorothy K. Washburn

Acknowledgments

Toward the goal of making this song material available to the Hopi people as well as to interested scholars and the public at large, the Collaborative Research Division of the National Endowment for the Humanities awarded a 2005–2007 grant to Emory Sekaquaptewa at the Bureau of Applied Research in Anthropology at the University of Arizona for the transcription and translation of seven major collections of Hopi katsina songs housed in the Archives of Traditional Music at Indiana University and in the Library of Congress.

We thank Judith Gray at the American Folklife Center, Library of Congress, and Marilyn Graf at the Archives of Traditional Music, Indiana University, for arranging for CD copies of the song recordings and Program Officer Elizabeth Arndt at the National Endowment for the Humanities for facilitating our grant. We are grateful to the Bureau of Applied Research in Anthropology (BARA),Timothy J. Finan, Director, at the University of Arizona, for sponsoring this project.

We used Sound Forge and Audacity software to clean the recordings of much of their extraneous noise and to adjust the speed of many of the early, wax cylinder recordings to make transcription possible. We thank Falina Enriquez, who was able to recover some additional text for the transcriptions from the recordings. We also thank Delfred Leslie, Alph Secakuku, and Leland Dennis for their participation in this project. Helpful commentary and advice has also been offered by several individuals who have chosen to remain anonymous.

Introduction

Katsinas, Katsina Song, and this Volume

Katsinas (*katsinam*) are perfect life-promoting spirit beings who come to sing and dance in public performances in the Hopi villages during a lengthy period that begins after the Winter Solstice ceremony, *Soyalangw,* and ends in mid-summer at the Home dance, *Nimàntikive.* The katsinas take the people's prayer messages for rain to their spiritual homes and, in answer to these prayers, the katsinas come to the villages with their gift burden of rain. The songs make frequent reference to this reciprocal relationship between the people's prayers and the katsinas' promise to come as rain. They advise people to steadfastly adhere to their daily obligations and responsibilities to members of their communities to which they are connected through kinship, clanship, and ritual society membership. These institutionalized social and ritual relationships, reiterated throughout the katsinas' songs, sustain the Hopi communal corn-based way of life.

The katsina songs make it clear that the cultural values and distinctions of the Western world do not always accurately reflect how the Hopis think about and operate in their world. Many Hopi categories and ways of thinking about the world have no counterparts in cultures outside of Hopi. For this reason, the translations and the meanings of the words and phrases of the songs and the explanations of the ways in which the ideas they convey relate to actual cultural practice have been solely informed by Emory's exegesis. To our knowledge, the only other publication of Hopi songs informed by Hopi singers is the modest privately published collection of songs by Milland Lomakema and Mark Lomayestewa, two singers from the Second Mesa village of Songòopavi (Kabotie 1978).

Katsina songs are publicly performed. The words of the katsinas are intended to be heard by all people; the messages they carry are relevant for all humankind. While they are first sung in the context of a performance, they are intended to be sung by individuals as they go about their daily activities. There is nothing in this volume in the words of the songs or in the explanations provided that divulges restricted knowledge that might compromise the integrity of the katsina rituals as they are practiced in the Hopi community.

Katsinas and Their Role at Hopi

In order to understand katsina songs and the practices they espouse, we review here background information as provided by Emory regarding relevant aspects of Hopi history and culture. The Hopis (*Hopìit*) are a sedentary, corn-farming people, who live today in twelve small communities mainly along the mesa outcroppings at the southern edge of Black Mesa on the Colorado Plateau in northeastern Arizona.

Archaeological research suggests that the domestication and cultivation of corn, which forms the heart of the Hopi lifeway, occurred in Mexico and spread throughout the Americas. This sedentary corn raising lifeway and the practices that supported it diffused northward into the American Southwest thousands of years ago carried by many people seeking lands on which to live and grow this corn. The early travels of these groups are marked by distinctive totems and other representations of their life practices that they carved on rock faces along their migration routes. The present-day Hopis are descendants of these early peoples.

In Hopi belief all the people in the world passed through three previous worlds and eventually emerged into this, the Fourth World. This Emergence is also a description of the arrival of ancestral Hopis from "down below," that is, from areas to the southwest of the Hopi mesas, probably as Uto-Aztecan-speaking farmers (J. Hill 2001). At Emergence, the people encountered Màasaw, the guardian of this world, who offered everyone a choice of lifeway and the tools to pursue that lifeway. Those people that would become the Hopis chose a small, short, plain ear of corn and agreed to plant it with a planting stick, *sooya,* given to them by Màasaw. The intent was that this method of farming would enable each family to assume primary responsibility for sustaining themselves. This household-based self-sufficient mode of subsistence is in distinct contrast to more complex community arrangements wherein some members are farmers who grow crops that others in the community purchase or trade for other kinds of goods that they produce. Today not all Hopis plant all the food that they need to support their families, nor do those who continue to plant necessarily plant with a planting stick. Some, in their innovative adoption of tractors, have modified the planting mechanism to simulate the action of a planting stick. Nevertheless, in all these departures, they have preserved the spirit and intention of family self-sufficiency.

To find the best place to live, groups of people who chose the small ear of corn embarked on a series of migrations marked by movements, settlements, segmentations, and resettlements as they searched for the best places to grow the hardy corn. It should be noted that these groups were not necessarily composed of related people and almost certainly did not represent the relocation of entire communities. During their travels, these migrating groups took on separate identities by choosing totems that reminded them of some significant thing, place or happening that guided them or helped them survive as a group as they moved from place to place. Only after they arrived at Hopi did they coalesce as clans, taking totems as the identifying marker of their common origin. These clans form the basis for the social and ceremonial interrelationships between individuals in each community.

In Hopi belief, all of these groups were predestined to ultimately settle at the mesa area, called *Tuuwanasavi*, where they live today. The word *Tuuwanasavi*, literally "the place in the middle of the land" (*tuuwa* 'sand, land', -*nasa*- 'middle', -*vi* 'place') refers to all the Hopi lands. After the first groups settled around the mesas, many other groups of people came over the years requesting admission to join these original communities. This process is explicitly described in Song 139. To gain admittance, each group had to agree to share with everyone in the community their ritual practices as well as their practical knowledge about growing corn. In addition they had to commit to live by the reciprocity-based social institutions that were necessary to insure the well-being and survival of the community. In this way, many different people became participating members of a community by agreeing to put to rest their separate and independent ways of life.

Some groups were turned away because they did not follow the communal life of corn or would not agree to the precepts of that lifeway. Others were not admitted at first, but only later when they demonstrated that they could contribute something of value to support the Hopi lifeway. For example, oral tradition says that the Badger people (the *Honanngyam*) were rejected on their first request to settle at Orayvi. They made camp in the plains below Orayvi, also sometimes referred to as "*Tuuwanasavi*," and planted corn to show that they had the spiritual capacity to grow the corn and thus deserved to join the community. When the Orayvi elders observed that the corn just planted had grown to maturity overnight, they immediately invited the Badger people to join the village. In this way, the

Badger people brought the *Powamuya* ceremony as well as their skills and rituals concerned with corn germination to Hopi.

Hopi Principles of Life

Hopis believe that their communal farming lifeway was preordained, that is, predetermined by their choice at Emergence of the small humble ear of corn that would grow in fields watered by rain. So committed were these people to living this lifeway that when periods of drought threatened their ability to grow the corn, they moved to other areas that would allow them to continue to pursue this lifeway rather than shift to another mode of subsistence because that would have required them to depart from their sedentary lifeway and develop new social institutions and different kinds of communities. The cosmological foundation of the Hopis as a people with a shared identity is, thus, rooted in their living in small, settled, self-sufficient, communities.

The Hopis conceive of the pristine land into which they emerged as a divine creation. All things on this land were placed there to sustain mankind. In this sense the land is viewed as having a beautiful, reverential quality which is captured in their word for the land, *tuuwapongya,* the "sand altar." It is important to clarify here that the Hopis do not celebrate the land and its natural beauty from the point of view of its *visible beauty,* although it is a beautiful place in Hopi eyes. The point is that the pristine world which the Hopis agreed to care for is beautiful not only because of the chromatic beauty codified in the many words relating to the flowery aspect of the landscape (J. Hill 1992), but also because, in the Hopi mind, this beauty references the original state of nature in which all life flourished as well as the potential for life that such land embodies. In their choice of the humble ear of corn at Emergence, the Hopis agreed to accept the responsibility to live on this land in a way that would preserve its natural bounty.

The common characterization of the Hopi lifeway as the "corn lifeway" or the "life of corn" is, however, somewhat misleading. While corn *is* the central metaphor because it is their main source of subsistence, the essence of Hopi life is the communal way in which everyone participates in raising lives—of both plants and people—so that life will be rejuvenated. It is not so much their dependence on corn as a food, since beans and squash were also adopted long ago as food staples. Indeed, corn is probably the metaphor since it is easy to grow and can be preserved and prepared in many different ways. It is the Hopis' institutionalized dependence on each other as they strive to keep pursuing practices that rejuvenate life (*natwani*) that is central to their survival. The participation of every individual in these interdependent interrelationships insures the survival of a community. These interrelationships have been institutionalized into an intricate network of kinship and clanship responsibilities as well as ritual society obligations that are shared by all members of the community. Corn is simply their principal economic venture. Katsinas spend fully half of each year urging the Hopis to live by the moral imperative to perform obligations so that everyone can enjoy fulfilled lives and live together peacefully.

The Hopi lifeway is not simply one characterized by raising corn by dry farming. Inherently, the process of raising corn is a metaphor about raising Hopi people who are caring, sharing, and self-sufficient. All the practices of raising corn and the stages of corn growth are metaphors about living communally in small nurturing communities. Importantly, the Hopi concept of community involves an *identity* that encompasses all the people who share the ideals and practices that sustain their corn lifeway. Thus, when the katsinas speak of preserving and supporting the community, they are referring to all Hopis including both the people who live in the villages as well as those who live off the Reservation. All of these individuals are considered part of the Hopi community because they share the ideals and practices of living that are in accord with the Hopi lifeway. The Hopi community is not a place; it is an identity.

This concept of community is embodied in the oft-repeated compound song word, *qatsi'nangwa,* translated as the "will to live" (from *qatsi* 'life', *unangwa* 'heart') that carries the idea that the people in the community must put their hearts, minds and efforts together for the well-being of the community. Everyone must be united in their agreement to follow the same body of beliefs and practices; everyone must persist with the determination to live the communal lifeway that entails hard work and self-sacrifice. Only in this way will the Hopi way of life be sustained. Toward this goal, the katsinas use many words to urge all community members to make their prayers (*naawakna*) to the katsinas with sincerity in their hearts (*unangwvàasi*) and with hearts that are free of ill will toward others (*suyanis'unangwa*). Implied in all these words is the message that only when everyone in the community is united in their intentions (*sunsa tunatya*) for the common good, then and only then will their prayers be heard by the katsinas.

The choice of this communal lifeway sustained by corn has shaped the social institutions and activities as well as the ethical principles and ritual practices that must be participated in to sustain these small settled farming communities. Below is a brief review of some of the kin and clan responsibilities and obligations as well as the moral principles that organize and create the numerous reciprocities that interrelate individuals in these communities.

Hopis trace their lineage through the mother's line. Children are born into their mother's clan and, in this way clans perpetuate themselves through the female line. Upon marriage, a girl must take a husband from another clan. The children thus have relationships not only with individuals in their own clan, that is, their mother's clan, but also with those in their father's clan. As individuals grow up and pass through different stages of life, they are supported by and, in turn, obligated to these connections they have with people through the kin and clans of their mothers and fathers. As they marry and have children, they gain more kin and clan connections with individuals in their spouses' families. Further, as individuals are initiated into the many ritual societies, they acquire fictive kinship connections to yet other people. For example, since a man can belong to several ritual societies, he gains a different father–son relationship with each of his ceremonial sponsors in each of the societies he joins. And within each society, a man gains a father–son relationship to all the male members of that society. In sum, while one's clan obligations are created by birth, one's ritual society obligations are created by voluntary membership. Uninitiated Hopis never acquire ritual obligations. While sometimes these are a burden, at other times they are important sources of support and succor.

The anthropological literature has emphasized that the Hopis are not only matrilineal in their lineage affiliation but also matrilocal in their post-marital residence pattern. However, this is an incomplete and somewhat mistaken understanding of how the Hopis view the marriage process, which is really a process of relating members of two clans. As a future bride, a woman goes to live at the home of her future husband. There she grinds corn and prepares food for his family in order to prove her worth as a future wife and mother. During this time the men associated with the groom's family weave her wedding robes that are replete with symbols of procreation as a way of signifying their acceptance of her as a potential mother for the groom's children. These new roles and family obligations are alluded to in several of the songs by the word *mö'wi,* an "in-married woman." Likewise, just as the woman lives briefly in the man's house prior to marriage, he comes to live, temporarily, in her natal house after marriage. However, as soon as the husband is able, he builds a new home for his wife that may or may not be adjacent to her mother's home.

Furthermore, even though inheritance and temporary residence is with the mother's line, the bride takes on the role of *mö'wi* to all the members of her husband's clan. In this relationship, she extends her wifely duties of preparing food and keeping a welcoming household for her husband and her children to all members of his clan, just as she does for members of her clan. For example, if she and her husband go to another village to see a dance and visit his clansmen, she would prepare food and bring it to his clansmen during their visit. In this way the Hopi in-law relationships are much more than titular; they come with definite obligations and responsibilities to provide reciprocities for both sides of the family.

In addition to the social institutions and practices described above, the settled life of raising corn has greatly shaped the ethics and moral principles that each Hopi must accept and follow. Every individual as a participating member of his community is guided by a code of unwritten moral imperatives that obligate him or her to work for the welfare of everyone in the community. Collective adherence to these moral principles is essential to the enduring vitality of the community. While any individual is free to act in any way he or she chooses, in practice one's activities are constrained by an unvoiced set of expectations that demand respect for others coupled with the constant burden of helping and sharing with others.

The moral imperatives that underpin this lifeway are clearly stated in katsina songs. The oral repetition of these ethical ways of living not only preserves these values but also reinforces their continuing relevance in ever changing cultural circumstances. In effect, the katsinas are the bearers of a community's moral conscience. The coming of the katsinas to perform in a community, as beautiful beings with the spiritual countenance (*pitsangwa*) of life, makes a strong impression on every Hopi's conscience. Their presence serves to reaffirm the resolve of the people to live according to these beliefs and practices. In the absence of persons ("headmen" or "leaders") who carry the power to exact obedience to civic duties, only the power of conscience as it is institutionalized at Hopi exists to impel people to carry out their obligations.

From this perspective, an individual Hopi's life requires great personal sacrifice and subordination of personal goals and aspirations. Yet the institutionalized ties to one's kin and clan and ritual societies as well as the strong attachment to one's home and the land that supports one's family brings a sense of fulfillment, well-being, and security that have sustained the Hopis for centuries. The ethical principles of communal cooperation, mutual help, and fidelity to the tenets of the community's social fabric are the Hopis' ways of insuring their survival against adverse conditions in the natural world as well as threats to their continued existence from other peoples. Any understanding of the beliefs and rituals that support the ideology of this lifeway must begin with an appreciation of the power of these moral precepts.

The Corn Metaphor

This communally-sustained lifeway is expressed in ritual song and daily practice by likening the raising of new generations of Hopi to the raising of corn. Corn is not only a food; it is the central metaphor of Hopi life (Black 1984). The land, *tuwapongya,* the "sand altar," as the nurturer of all living things, is personified as *Tuwapongtumsi* 'Sand Altar Woman'. Envisioned to be like a mother who nurtures her children, *Tuwapongtumsi* is generally understood to correspond to the English expression "Mother Earth." Just as the corn plant emerges from Mother Earth so too do human babies emerge from their mother. Just as the cornstalk takes its sustenance from Mother Earth, so too does a young child nurse from its mother. In effect, the corn plants and other natural resources that are sustenance are like the nipples of Mother Earth from which people and all other living things nurse. For example, in Song 132 when the katsinas say that they have brought the different colors of corn to the people, they are referring to the way that their rains nurse the corn so that it will mature for the benefit of the people.

Just as the corn plants await pollination, so too do young Hopi girls, who may be referred to as corn maidens (*qa'ömamant*), await fertilization. This likening of the growing corn plants to growing Hopi girls is referred to in this text as the "maiden metaphor." The growing ears on the corn plants are the plants' children. When the girls become brides, they grind corn for their future in-laws to prove their worth as a wife and mother. The ground cornmeal is likened to raindrops, both of which are the sustenance that, respectively, feeds people and corn plants. Just as corn-stalks bear ears with kernels for the next generation of corn plants, when women marry they have the obligation of bearing and nurturing new generations. Perfect, mature ears of corn, "corn mothers" (*totsmingwu*), are given to individuals at birth, naming, and initiation rituals that mark their passage into different stages of their lives. For example, the corn mothers given to infants at birth are thought of as metaphorically nursing the infants with sustenance so that they will grow up to lead a perfect, fulfilled life. Likewise when an individual is initiated into a ritual society he is considered to be a fledgling to be nursed by the corn mother with knowledge about his future roles within the community. Those individuals who are not initiated essentially remain children for they do not gain in knowledge and thus do not become fully integrated members of the community. This same concept of rebirth and nurturing at each new stage of life is also embedded in the songs with the metaphorical use of corn maidens as metaphors for women who will nature new life.

Just as a deceased person is laid to rest in the earth, after the cobs are harvested, the cornstalk is pushed over onto the earth. Both the remains of a deceased person's body and the remains of the cornstalks after the harvest are referred to as *qatungwu*, that which has borne life. This return to the earth of deceased corn plants and people carries the implication that they will nurture new growth in new generations.

Living a life sustained by this corn is the Hopi life plan (*hopivöts-kwani*). The values of *naavaasi*, caring for one another, *naatatami*, self-lessness and self-sacrifice for the well-being of all, and *naakyaptsi*, mutual respect—paramount in the small communally organized communities of the Hopi—are continually being voiced by the katsinas.

Naavaasqatsi is a life of mutual caring that obligates everyone to help one another because of one's kin, clan, and community relationships. In Song 142, the people are urged to become caring of one another, *naavaa-stoti*, with the implication that if they do, the perfect life will be theirs—the rains will come from every direction and the lands will be bright with flowering plants that are signs of life to come.

Nami'nangwa, mutual care for one another's welfare, involves the practice of *na'qalànpi*, giving each other mutual encouragement and support. In fact, because almost everyone at Hopi is related to almost every other Hopi either through kinship or clanship or by ceremonial association, the obligations to render assistance, *naava'angwa*, to anyone who is deserving are constant and inescapable. If individuals fail to attend to this fundamental imperative, they risk being ignored and excluded at some later time when they may need help.

Adherence to these principles of sharing, helping and caring while practicing one's daily activities and ritual obligations is considered to be work (*tumala*) to be undertaken in humility. Whether it is planting and weeding a field of corn, having sex for procreation, or endowing prayer feathers (*paaho*) with prayers for rain, all these traditional life-promoting practices (*natwani*) are work that is essential for the rejuvenation of life. In practicing this work, Hopis are taught to accept whatever life brings and to strive to overcome the trials that cross one's path as one performs this work. Although the obligation to help others often becomes burdensome (*maqsoni*), Hopis accept these sacrifices in return for the security of being part of their community. The value placed on one's persistence in following the tenets of Hopi life and one's courage in the face of adversity and personal and physical hardship (*taqa'nangwa*) carries Hopis through difficult times and enables them to see beyond temporary obstacles in order to continue following the practices that make a fulfilled life.

This work ethic is the cornerstone of viable Hopi communities. It is often recalled in katsina songs. In Song 118, Spider Boy is cast as a humble plain looking man. The message in this song is that people should not ignore men with unassuming looks because such men are hard working and will provide for their families. In Song 93, the katsinas are reminding women that they should be choosing such humble men for they are the ones who will be willing to put in the hard work necessary to grow this corn and thereby provide for their families. In Song 147, the Pot Carrier katsinas, by teaching the girls how to properly prepare cornmeal, are reinforcing the virtues of the hard work that wives and mothers do every day to prepare the corn that is their basic food.

This united life of work is their plan of life (*qatsivötskwani*); it sustains their communal lifeway. Living this lifeway requires everyone's heartfelt devotion to and acceptance of the ethical practices that maintain this lifeway. The importance of the power of moral conscience in making individuals adhere to these shared beliefs and practices cannot be overstated. If a person strays from living this path and instead asserts himself and attempts to manipulate others so that the integrity of the community is compromised, then life in the community becomes morally corrupt (*koyaanisqatsi*), the community must be dissolved to cleanse itself of these divisive elements, and a new community created so that the people can once again live in harmony (*suyanisqatsi*).

While the unspoken power of these moral imperatives sustains the performance of the many institutionalized reciprocities, there is, in every community a village "chief," the *kikmongwi,* as well as leaders, *momngwit* (singular, *mongwi*), of the different ritual societies who direct the ceremonies that are held throughout the year. These individuals are respected as leaders because they have the knowledge, experience and moral integrity gained through living their lives in selfless humility, *na'okiwqatsi.* However, the moral leadership possessed by these individuals does not correspond to persons with actual powers of compliance that characterize "leaders" in other societies, for these latter persons lead by powers other than by conscience and example. *Naakyaptsi,* mutual respect, describes the way that individuals without knowledge should defer to those with knowledge. These individuals with knowledge preserve and maintain the integrity of all rituals that hand down words of wisdom (*wukwlavayi*), the oral tradition (*wukwnavoti*) and teachings (*wukwtutavo*) (cf. Glowacka 1998).

The Hopi goal in life is fulfillment, that is, a life of happiness, health and security that will be enjoyed by everyone in the community (*naavokyawintiwa*). In Song 129, this life of fulfillment is referred to as the good life (*qatsi lolma*). However, this does not refer to a life of pleasure, fancy living, and self indulgence, but rather to a life of living according to the moral imperatives that bring the rewards of happiness, health and freedom from want and suffering. Furthermore, the Hopi life path assures fulfillment at every stage in one's life, not simply at the end of life as is the way in many Western societies where fulfillment is associated with retirement and relaxation that comes in old age only after a life of work. By mutually helping and sharing and respecting everyone at every stage of one's life, the Hopis believe that such behavior will bring contentment and peace of mind throughout one's life. In Song 124, Wùutaqkatsina, the Old Man katsina, reminds the people that, as they grow old, they are as if dressed with the countenance of the crook. The crook, while a symbolic representation of people in old age, has the countenance of health, happiness and freedom from suffering and hunger. That is why at the Winter Solstice (*Soyalangw*), people pass by the Tawkiva and momentarily grasp the crook (*ngölöshoya*) at the hatchway of the kiva to capture this fulfillment that one hopes to experience into old age.

The ultimate goal in all Hopi communities is their survival as a people. The yearly cycle of katsina rituals is designed to insure that the rains arrive to bring plentiful harvests that, in turn, will provide the food to nourish new generations. For such a fulfilled life, Hopis are said to be happy in their hearts, *hàalay'unangwa* (happy hearts). The katsinas promise in their songs that, in return for the people's sincere prayers and moral living, they will come as clouds, thunder, lightning and rain. By this means, the planted fields of the people will bloom, the yellowjackets and butterflies will flutter about pollinating the flowers, and the people will sing and dance with happiness at these signs of the promise of new life.

This life of plenty (*kuwan'èwqatsi*) is often described metaphorically in the songs as fields shimmering and glistening with puddles of water after a rain, expanses of blooming plants covering the land, and corn plants with four ears on each stalk. These descriptive song phrases describe the results of the hard summer thunderstorms that are the object of the Hopis' prayers. These rainstorms bring quantities of water over very short periods. Some of this rainwater stands in shallow puddles and sheets of water that glisten and sparkle in the sun after these afternoon storms. The compound word *paatàlpuva* (along a land glistening with water) used to describe these sparkling pools of water. The root *taala* (*-tal-*), which refers to the light of a new day, is thus a reference to the new life that comes with rain, and thus *paavatalawna,* making things glisten with water, is a metaphorical reference to the rebirth of life that comes with the light of each new day.

Other rainwater moves down the slopes and along the washes. It is referred to as runoff water, *muunangw* (flowing water). Hopis locate their fields strategically on the alluvial fans that form at the mouths of the washes so that the runoff water will spread among the plants. The Hopis are heartened (*kuwan'ew'unangwa*) by the vitality they see in these rain-waters because they bring the promise that their corn will mature (*uymuk-ti*) and provide for them. This sight of flourishing life—when corn plants are growing and children are thriving—makes the people deeply thankful in their hearts (*kwakwha'unangwa*). For a Hopi, this is the "good life" (*lomaqatsi*). Living such a fulfilled life is their life plan (*hopivötskwani*).

The destiny of the Hopis, that is, their spiritually preordained life plan, *tiingavi,* is to survive as a people by their chosen lifeway of corn farming. Once this lifeway was chosen at Emergence, it became the inherited duty of every Hopi in every generation to fulfill this preordained life (*qatsimkiwa*) by adhering to a series of life-promoting practices (*natwani*) that embody the humble mind-set and physical hard work necessary to live according to this life plan. Continual performance of these practices is essentially a testing of one's belief in the preordained path of life and whether one has the will, that is, determination to live (*qatsi'nangwa*) according to this path. In Hopi belief, the constant practicing of these ways of living will bring a fulfilled life to each individual as well as to the community as a whole. This ideal lifeway and the precepts that define it are learned by every generation through their daily participation in the practices that support and sustain this lifeway. The preservation and transfer to succeeding generations of the principles of this lifeway reverberate throughout every katsina song.

Hopi Katsinas

When an individual passes on, his spirit becomes a cloud, that is, a katsina who lives in the next, the Fifth World. As perfected spirit beings of the Fifth World katsinas are typically described in song as clouds who come from their homes in the four cardinal directions—northwest, southwest, southeast and northeast—that represent the four corners of their world. In each of these cardinal directions is a shrine. The most frequently mentioned shrines are at *Kawestima* (the archaeological site of Betatakin) in the northwest, *Nuvatukya'ovi* (the San Francisco Peaks) in the southwest, *Weenima* in the southeast, and *Kìisiw* (Shadow Springs) in the northeast. Each direction is associated with a directional color: northwest is yellow (*sikya-*), southwest is blue/green (*sakwa-*), southeast is red (*pala-*), and northeast is white (*qöya-*). Typically in song the directions are named in opposite pairs: northwest and southeast, and southwest and northeast (Song 19), but they can be invoked separately or in any combination. They are always named moving in a counterclockwise direction beginning with the northwest direction. A Kooyemsi ("Mudhead" katsina) song recorded by Helen Roberts (Song 52) is a good example of the repetitive but beautiful way that the clouds are described as arriving from all four cardinal directions in this sequence.

In their songs the katsinas refer to people of the village as their mothers and fathers. This may appear counterintuitive to a non-Hopi person but consider that we, who are living in this world, call those who lived before us our ancestors. Likewise, because the katsinas live in the next, the Fifth World, and the Hopi people live in this, the Fourth World, the people are the ancestors of the katsinas. By the same logic, the katsinas address the people in song as their mothers and fathers.

To correct a common misunderstanding about katsinas and what they do, in Hopi belief, the katsinas do not *bring* the rain; they *are* the rain. Upon the sincere prayerful request of the people (Song 15), they travel from their homes in the four cardinal directions to the people's lands. Their concern is to sustain the lives of all people and all creatures of the natural world with rain and other good things of life. Their gifts are thought of as gift burdens (*na'mangwu*) that are the people's due in return for their fervent, heartfelt prayers and right living. This is the reciprocal conditional relationship between the katsinas and the people—if/when the people proffer prayers with unified hearts and with intentions of right living, the katsinas will come as rain. Through the admonitions, advice, and encouragement that fill their songs, the katsinas revitalize and reinspire the people's faith in their preordained corn way of life (*qatsimkiwa*). Song after song embodies these messages. Sometimes they are stated directly (Songs 7, 127); always they are there by implication.

The katsinas prepare themselves at their homes in the four directions by adorning themselves with rain (Song 23). They then travel to the Hopi lands, usually described in the songs as "starting on a journey as rain," *yoynànkwusa.* The arrival of the katsinas is usually described as descending as rain, but on occasion it is described as descending as clouds (Song 94). Their arrival is presaged with thunder and lightning, two aspects of rain that are frequently described in song. Sometimes the thunder is likened to the beating of the wings of nighthawks (Song 32). At other times the strikes of lightning (Songs 33, 133, 144) and sounds of thunder rumbling along the lands are highlighted (Songs 131, 133) as ways to emphasize how the rain arrives and moves along across the land.

When rain first starts to descend, it appears as visible lines of rain, described as "rain lines," *yoyleki.* As the rain splashes in the puddles, each drop makes a little column of water, a "water pillar," *paamotoro,* literally water (*paa-*) stalactites (*motoro*), that rebound vertically, *hoohongva,* and create circular "water shields," *paatuwvota* (from *paa-* 'water' and *tuwvota* 'shield'). The word *paatuwvota* compares the idea of the concentric ripples that form around each raindrop to the rings of a coiled plaque, *poota* (Songs 47, 99, 122). In yet another song (Song 104), the katsinas describe the way that they have created mud in the aftermath of their driving rains by describing how the rainwater has splashed mud on the plants and animals.

In ceramic designs, the lines of rain (*yoyleki*) are represented as series of parallel lines and the clouds as stepped units. Likewise, in the prehistoric murals from the sites of Awat'ovi and Kawàyka'a on Antelope Mesa, rain is imaged in numerous ways. One particularly beautiful representation is projected in an image of seated figures holding trays into which particulate matter is falling, as if both rain and, metaphorically, cornmeal are descending to the Hopi people. This metaphor of rain as particulate cornmeal is almost identically expressed in the late twentieth century Song 138, thus demonstrating the longevity and constancy of the fundamental ideas and metaphors that express the Hopi way of life (see also Sekaquaptewa and Washburn 2004).

To Hopis, the katsinas have the countenance (*pitsangwa*) of the perfect life to which everyone aspires. The expression *lolmat pitsangwa'yta* (have as a beautiful countenance) refers to the way that a given entity manifests its essence. In songs katsinas arrive bearing this countenance in the form of rain and, by implication, the new life that their rains bring (Song 1). In this way the katsinas "wear their world," meaning that they are adorned spiritually in their countenance and, in performance to the way their dress is covered with symbols of their gifts. In a highly creative depiction of the countenance of rain (Song 31), the *Hòo'e* katsinas ask the people to look into their eyes, cast as dark holes (*suqömkoro*), for they represent the dark clouds of a much desired all-night rain.

Hopis send their prayers embedded in prayer feathers to the katsinas hoping for their beneficence. They ask them to visit their villages and hear their prayers. The katsinas describe their preparations to respond to these prayers as dressing themselves or adorning themselves with clouds and rain. The verb *yuwsina* in everyday usage means clothe someone, get someone dressed, but in ceremonial contexts it is used metaphorically to mean clothe or adorn with beneficent powers. It does not refer to the dressing of the katsinas for their performance in the plaza. Likewise, just as katsinas adorn themselves metaphorically with rain, so too do people adorn prayer feathers by imbuing them with their purest thoughts and most heartfelt hopes. Thus, clothing (*yuwsina*) the prayer feathers with spiritual powers, makes reference to the way the people say their prayers from the "bottom of their hearts." This metaphorical clothing addresses the beauty of one's heart rather than the outward beauty of the prayer feather itself.

If the katsinas deem the people deserving, they acknowledge the sincerity of the people's prayers and their continuing efforts at right living with their gift of rain and other things that bring health, happiness and well-being. Even though in most cases it does not rain during the katsinas' physical presence at the villages, in Hopi belief their presence is a *promise* of rain, just as the blooming plants in the fields and the pollinating butterflies and yellowjackets are promises of food and thus fulfillment. This promise is encapsulated in words expressed in the future tense—for example, that the katsinas will (-*ni*) come as rain, *yoy'ökini.*

Many signs of the beneficent presence of the katsinas are described in the songs. Building stacks of clouds (Songs 24, 133), descending columns of rain lines (Songs 44, 52), lightning flashing and thunder booming (Song 49) are all animate presences of the katsinas. Likewise, fields of blooming plants (Song 53), the pollinating activity of the butterflies (Song 14) and yellowjackets amidst these fields of flowering plants (Song 10) as well as the tasseling corn and descending corn silk on the new ears (Song 25) are all signs that the katsinas have placed their gifts along the landscape. All of these processes nurture the people and in this way are not seen as purely biological events (e.g., pollination), but as representatives of the on-going processes that give them sustenance.

To Hopis, katsinas are nurturing, beneficent beings who sustain all life with their life-giving rain. But, in order for the katsinas to bring these gifts, the people must reciprocate with their most heartfelt efforts to live by their preordained path. Having the will to live (*qatsi'nangwa*) according to the moral precepts required by the corn farming lifeway, is central to whether the people are deserving of the gifts of the katsinas. The katsinas, as perfect beings who have the countenance of this lifeway, are thus able to advise and encourage the people about how to live and in this way keep them on the path toward that lifeway.

Katsina Performances

There are hundreds of different katsinas; the Hopi Dictionary (1998) lists 316 distinct katsinas and that listing omits many First and Second Mesa katsinas. Some katsinas appear more frequently than others; some appear only at designated times; some no longer appear. They arrive at the Hopi villages in public performances that begin in late January that lead, around February, to the *Powamuya* ceremony, commonly referred to as the Bean dance. At this time it is cold and often still snowing on the mesas, but the people have already turned their attention to preparing for the coming growing season. *Powamuya* is focused on ritual efforts to insure the germination of the crops that will be planted in the coming spring months.

After this event, katsinas appear in nighttime dances in the kivas during the cold months and, when the weather ameliorates, in daytime performances in the plaza. They end their assistance to the people in late July at *Nimàntikive,* commonly referred to as the Home dance, before they return to their homes in the four cardinal directions.

The katsinas come only if the people proffer their most sincere and heartfelt prayers. It is this prayers-for-rain exchange that is at the core of the reciprocal relationship between the people and the katsinas. Many preparations take place in the village, with men, referred to in the songs as "the fathers" or those in "leadership positions," spending much time in the kiva praying and ritually smoking. These individuals are the heads of the ritual societies who plan the performance and prepare their hearts for the coming of the katsinas. They are referred to as *momngwit* (singular, *mongwi*). They are in "control" of activities in the village for the duration of the ceremony. After that time, the general moral leadership of the village reverts to the *kikmongwi,* commonly referred to as the "village chief."

The heartfelt nature of the preparations by the ceremonial leaders that take place in the days prior to the public performance is fundamental to their efficacy. Not only must the prayers be from their hearts; they must be proffered in the metaphorical heart of the kiva, that is, the center, where life-promoting and life-restoring rituals are performed. Many of the songs detail some of the ritual practices that take place in the kiva prior to the performance. The preparation of the prayer feathers, that is, imbuing them with prayers for rain, is a metaphorical adornment of them with the prayers proffered by the ceremonial leaders as they smoke over them (Song 78). These preparations begin when midnight passes and the actual day of the public performance begins (Song 134). Sitting in the center of the kiva, the ceremonial fathers pass around the tray of prayer feathers and repeatedly smoke and pray over them for the benefit of all the people. The pipe smoking is referred to as *oomawlawa* (be making clouds) or *oomawvoyanta* (be cloud blowing). The pipe is an *oomàwtapi,* a "cloud maker." In this way by smoking they send their prayers.

The day that has been scheduled for the public performance is the "set date," *tokila* (Songs 68, 126). If the katsinas appear very early in the morning when most people are still asleep, the katsina father (*katsinmuy na'am*), who later directs the katsinas as they perform, greets them and implores them to stay to inspire the people with their performances throughout the day. At other performances the katsinas make their first appearance in the village later in the morning. The arrival of the katsinas with their beautiful singing and dancing is an event that brings great pleasure to the people. In addition, it is a metaphor for the coming of a new day, as each new day brings the promise of new life and the happiness that comes with new life.

Because katsinas are spirit beings, they travel from their homes in the four directions to the villages along a path that has been sanctified with prayers to the place where they will perform. They enter this performance place along a path that has been sanctified with cornmeal and prayer feathers, the *pòòtavi*. This path is also a metaphor for the path of life, *pötskwani*, as laid out by Màasaw at Emergence. In daily life this dance place is called the plaza, *kiisonvi*. During a ceremony, when this plaza area has been sanctified, it is known as the dance-display place, *tivongyapavi*.

The katsinas perform four dance sets in the plaza before noon and four dance sets in the afternoon before the sun sets (Song 49), a time determined by when the sun is observed to be striking the rooftops. Between dance sets they refresh themselves at the katsina resting place, *katsìnki*, usually located outside the village. Throughout the day the katsina father "feeds" the katsinas by sprinkling each one with a pinch of cornmeal that embodies the people's prayers. To correct a common misconception, the katsinas are not being "blessed" with this cornmeal; this is a Christian concept and interpretation. At the end of the dance, as the katsinas are ready to leave along their consecrated path, they each receive a prayer feather and cornmeal from the katsina father that embodies the prayers of the people (Songs 4, 5, 56). If the people's prayers that are taken home by the katsinas are given with their utmost earnestness of intent and determination to live according to the Hopi way, the katsinas promise that they will come to their fields as rain, *yoy'ökini* '[we] will arrive, come as rain'. This promise is usually voiced in the songs in future tense—that rain will come from all four directions and life will be rejuvenated (Song 24).

The katsinas' appearance to dance in the village (*tiikive*) is not to be understood simply as entertainment. It is a ritual performance that is to be observed attentively. The word *tiitayawna* (gladden with a performance) describes the heartening nature of these dance day performances for the people. The katsinas, dressed in clothing covered with symbols of rain, corn and other features are visual metaphors of life. Some songs describe in detail how aspects of their clothing metaphorically recall their essence.

For example in Song 144, the Corn Boy katsinas wear cloud feather headdresses comprised of down feathers fastened to the top of their heads that bounce up and down as they dance, as if these feathers are the clouds moving in rain.

Katsina Song

In Hopi belief, katsina songs are understood as made by katsinas; no mortal being is the composer. The words of these songs are essentially archaic Hopi, that is, they are the words of the Ancients who developed the social institutions and the ritual practices that were best suited to organizing and sustaining small sedentary communities of corn farmers. Over the centuries these ideas have become codified in special words and phrases that are endlessly different because they are the product of individual creativity. They describe the core beliefs of the Hopi lifeway and how they should be followed. This process of creating and performing the oral tradition that represents the people's lifeway continues today as new song words and phrases are constantly being invented to describe the same fundamental concepts in endlessly different ways.

These concepts are not only expressed in katsina and other ritual songs, but they are also embedded visually in images and symbols on ritual paraphernalia, baskets, textiles and pottery. Song, dance, ritual paraphernalia and all objects imbued with the countenance of life are integral and inseparable parts of their oral tradition. In this way ritual song is just one part of an integrated package of media that transmits the ideals of life from generation to generation. Individuals learn the words from hearing them at a performance and then commit them to memory by singing them every day as they work. But since, like the game of telephone, it is the nature of orally preserved "texts" to change over time, the song texts may have changed over the years as they are passed from one individual to another. Thus, the reader will find songs in this volume that are very similar, some being only slightly different versions of the same song. However, remarkably, despite such minor changes, essentially the same song with the same core ideas has been preserved and passed along through many generations. Although recordings have preserved only songs from the twentieth century, it must be noted that many songs recorded at the beginning of the century were those remembered by individuals who learned them from their fathers and grandfathers, making those songs representatives of the ideals of a life that was practiced well before the advent of recording equipment.

Although katsina songs are part of the Hopi oral tradition, they are neither historical nor mythological narratives, nor are they celebrations of historical or mythological personages. Rather they are concerned with delineating a way of life, the moral imperatives that define that way of life, and the appropriate practices of living that will preserve and protect that way of life for future generations. These principles of living are centered around a collective, communal resolve to adhere to the practices that bring the rain that nurtures the corn that sustains communities of people who share and help each other (*nami'nangwa*). These basic themes and concepts are virtually omnipresent, either explicit or implied, in every katsina song.

Katsina songs are not prayers, but admonitions that remind the members of the community to follow the moral imperatives of mutual care and help that underlie communal living. Their words recall the pristine life of the past when people lived by these tenets (Song 125). With steady all-night rain, the flowers bloomed and all the creatures were fulfilled (often described as giving their cries of happiness) (Song 130). In fact, such songs that recall the pristine beauty of the land and all that it provides are sometimes called songs that soothe (*ñitapta*) because, as positive inspirational reassurances, they are designed to calm the troubled hearts of the people and help them rise above their daily travails. The intent in all songs is to revitalize the people and reenergize their efforts to accept the obligations and responsibilities that come with living a communal lifeway.

Katsina songs are also designed to be instructional. Although some readers may be confused by the intent of songs sung today that hark back to traditional practices, such as grinding cornmeal on a stone metate, the intent of singing about these traditional practices is not that women should revert to such practices on a daily basis. Rather, the katsinas sing about these practices because they are a way of talking about the wisdoms of the past that embody the ideals of humility, mutual care, and mutual respect that should guide life at all times. For example, in a song recorded by Robert Black in the 1950s (Song 61), the katsinas, using butterfly maidens as stand-ins for young Hopi girls, remind the girls that when they visit the homes of others, they should make themselves useful and help grind corn. This practice of helping others and learning the roles that they will per-form as adults is constantly being championed by the katsinas. In another example, while Hopis today no longer hunt much for food, this practice symbolizes the same kinds of metaphorical relationships—that people, corn and rabbits all nurse from Mother Earth. Thus, it is not what the people are hunting (i.e., antelope or rabbits), but whether they are practicing hunting at all because it is symbolic of taking sustenance from the earth.

Several songs recall traditional practices that are hallmarks of the Hopi lifeway that are being lost through lack of practice (Songs 102, 103, 123). Grinding corn, hunting, running in the morning to greet the sun, wearing the proper hairstyles that indicate an individual's stage in life, and engaging in appropriate courting behavior all reference traditional practices of communal living that insure community solidarity and survival. The katsinas also lament that the Hopi farmers are not caring for the lands, allowing them to become eroded, by metaphorically describing them as looking like the incised lines of petroglyphs (*tutuven 'iwyungwa*).

In some cases katsina songs contain pointed reproofs of behavior counter to a community's well-being by rhetorically asking, for example, whether the people think they are living a moral life (Songs 1, 2, 3, 67). In Song 128, the katsinas challenge the people to assume the duties of their generation as a way of reminding the adults that they should be performing their responsibilities and obligations to the community. In Song 139, the katsinas prod the people, asking them what they intend to do about their present errant ways, lamenting that gossip and self-serving actions have prevailed over concerns for the whole community's well-being. They predict that people will forget their duties to care for their crops and their children and so will have no fulfillment in old age. In Song 102, the katsinas pointedly suggest that while the people say they are Hopis, actually they are only pretending to live the Hopi lifeway while ignoring their communal obligations. Finally we have included some songs, even when we have not been able to completely translate them, because they are examples of the way that the katsinas admonish deviant sexual activities (Songs 34, 35, 51) that are destructive to community harmony.

Nevertheless, even the katsinas' admonitions always end on a positive note of encouragement by assuring the people that, if they mend their ways and unite their hearts in prayer, they will come as rain. To emphasize the positive nature of their message, the katsinas often close their songs with the observation that after they have come descending as rain on the land, the people will go about their blooming fields with happy hearts, *hàalay'unangway,* sing and dance, *taatawtimani,* to express their grateful happiness at seeing the rain and the signs of new life that the rain brings.

Once publicly performed, these songs are available to everyone. Hopis are expected to sing them as they carry out their daily tasks. Through repeated singing of these songs, the ideals of Hopi life that are spelled out in the words and phrases sink into their minds and hearts. Learning about katsinas, participation in their performances, and continually singing these songs begins at a very early age. After performances children can be seen singing and dancing as they play katsina. Indeed, it is the continuous use of these song words and phrases that enables us to trace the history of Hopi ritual thought and practice back to the beginning of the twentieth century in recorded song and then back to the fourteenth century (Sekaquaptewa and Washburn 2004, 2006) where the correlates of the concepts voiced in the song words are found imaged in kiva murals and pottery design.

Songs of different katsinas are recognizable by differences in vocable phrases, tempo, pitch and melody. The songs usually begin with vocables characteristic of the katsinas performing. These vocables are in turn followed by introductory words, often the vocative *haw,* which is intended to gather the attention of those attending the performance. *Haw* also appears in other forms, such as *haw'o, ha'o, haa'o.* We translate the vocative particle as "hark" or simply "o." The katsinas address the people as *haw íngumu* 'hark my mothers', *haw ínamu* 'o my fathers'. It is customary that when both the mothers and the fathers are addressed, the katsinas address the mothers first. Some songs have this reversed. Emory said these are mistakes, although it should be noted here that the songs as recorded are not from actual katsina performances and thus perhaps the reversal was deliberate because they were being sung out of context. The second section of the song is often introduced by *hapi me. Hapi* is a particle indicating a degree of certainty and *me* is a particle to call attention. These particles can be translated in various ways, such as as "listen, truly, all right, let it be that way." We translate *hapi me* as "listen, there is more." In performance, a complete katsina song has the structure AABBA, A and B each being a separate verse. We have not labeled the verses in this way because none of the recordings represent complete performances of songs. As well, on Emory's suggestion, we have omitted from the transcription the verses that were repeated in the recordings.

With our focus on song content, we have found that the katsina songs are endlessly varied voicings of advice, admonition and encouragement.

Metaphorical Presentation of the Song Message

Katsinas convey their messages through both everyday words and special song words and phrases. Some of this ritual language is composed of juxtaposed everyday words; others are specially created compound word forms. In a new word creatively composed or in a few words creatively juxtaposed into a phrase, whole complexes of ideas about Hopi life are brought to mind. These song words and phrases are, in effect, succinct messages to Hopi listeners who, by virtue of their lifelong participation in Hopi life, only need these shorthand reminders because they know all the associated implications and references contained in them. In their evocative state, they also augment the whole effect of the performance by bringing to mind the sights and sounds of things and activities central to Hopi life and its continual rejuvenation.

Metaphor, words and ideas from one domain that clarify or illuminate the essence of another domain, is a communicative device that the Hopis use in song as well as in object decoration and image depiction to stimulate vivid mental images of their message. When words are used as metaphors in song, they are powerful communicative devices because they economically and poignantly evoke mental images and ideas fundamental to the purpose and perpetuation of Hopi life. For example, song metaphors capture the intimate associations Hopis have with the rain, their cornfields, and all the things in the natural world which they see as essential to enabling their lifeway.

Hopi song word metaphors, however, are far more than ornamental figures of speech. In katsina song these metaphorical words reinforce the ideas behind daily and ritual practices that the people need to follow in order to maintain their communities. In particular, metaphor is the perfect vehicle to capture their belief in the animate nature of all living things. The maiden metaphor is a ritual reference to all animate entities that are associated with the procreative process. Thus, corn plant maidens (*humi-'uyimamant*) are plants in the fields that are going through the process of growing themselves up just as young children go through the process of growing up and gaining knowledge as they move from one life stage to the next. The maiden metaphor is so deeply embedded in the language that the word for young corn plants, *paavönmamant,* includes the element for "maidens," -*mamant.* In contemporary language *paavönmamant* is the everyday word for young corn plants. There exists a longer, related from, *paavönyevewmamant* (Song 84), which we have translated as "young corn plant maidens." The Hopi Dictionary includes another frozen form, *tuvevolmamant,* as a song language form meaning "cornstalks." But in the songs in the present study, the word *tuvevolmamant* is used to refer to "butterfly maidens of various colors." (See the appendix of compounds.)

There are many examples where metaphor is used to promote the focus on the way rain brings life to the people. The clouds, as cumulus cloud maidens (*tukwunangwmamant*), come from the four cardinal directions to the Hopi land. As animate beings, they show themselves to the people, that is, they peek over the horizon (*kuukuyva*) or as we might say, they come into view (Song 19). In Song 107, the katsinas wear their clouds tied on the sides of their heads, metaphorically likening the way cumulus clouds mound up before a rain to the rounded hairbuns, *naasomi,* worn on the sides of the heads by prepubescent girls. By this metaphor the katsinas are saying that both cumulus rain clouds and these side hairbuns are visible signs of the promise of future life. In Song 126, the brides of the past year are referred to as white cloud maidens (*qöya'omawmamant*) thus metaphorically equating the potential life bringing powers of the clouds with those of the brides as mothers-to-be. In Song 149, the Turtle Boy katsinas have "made their breath into clouds," a highly metaphoric way to depict the condensation of moisture into clouds. In Song 144, the katsinas metaphorically liken the swaying of the down feathers they wear on their heads (*oomaw'inakwa*) to the movement of the clouds as they gather before a rainstorm. And finally in an early turn-of-the-twentieth-century song (Song 15), the clouds are characterized as dark billowing cloud boys (*toko'omawtotim*) who are practicing making rain by making lightning in the early morning hours.

In katsina song, animals take on human personae with spiritual powers. In the Fourth World of the people, maternal uncles are the advisors and disciplinarians of their sisters' children. In some katsina songs, toads assume this kin relationship and in this way they can admonish the people as well as encourage them to live by the moral imperatives that sustain the communal lifeway. In other songs, the appearance of the toad after a rain is used as a metaphor for the renewal of life that comes with rain. Just as toads emerge from the earth after a rain and go along making their calls of happiness (Song 138), so too do people sing and dance in their fields in happiness after the rain (Song 117). Badgers, believed to be beings with spiritual healing powers, are sometimes called upon in song to cleanse a village of errant practices that have led the people astray from their preordained lifeway. In Song 140, Old Man Badger, representing the healing powers of the Badger clan, has been asked to come sing his purifying songs at the village of Kiqötsmovi. In Song 116, Old Man Badger is advising his nephews, other Badger katsinas, to adorn themselves with rain and go in performance to the people, presumably to sing their healing songs.

All of the lands that sustain the Hopi people, both the fields that are planted and the lands where wildflowers grow, greens are gathered, and animals are hunted, are given spiritual powers and are cast reverentially as the "sand altar," *tuuwapongya*. For Hopis, the land circumscribed within the four cardinal directions marked by shrines in the four corners of their universe is a sacred place with spiritual qualities. These lands are seen as the mother of all life. It is in this sense that the land is regarded as "Mother Earth." In this vast space the nurturing rain moves along the land renewing all life. Plants, animals and people who live on this land nurse, that is, take their sustenance, from it. In these ways, metaphorical comparisons between the Hopi people and the animate beings and places in their universe are not only powerful poetic vehicles, but they are also highly appropriate ways of conceptualizing the animate nature of all life in their universe.

Importantly, it is the people's perception of the similarities suggested in these metaphors tempered by knowledge about these things in cultural context that creates meaningful and powerful metaphors. Indeed, sometimes, the physical thing that is referenced may not be the real object of the metaphor, although it gathers the listeners' attention to think about the connection of that something with a quality, idea or function that is the essential point of the metaphor. For example, the song phrase *itamu 'ova 'a oomawvawikyam puyayatani,* that translates as "along above us the cloud ducks will go along fluttering and fluttering" (Song 62), appears to make little sense until one recognizes that the critical entity is not the ducks, but the water that drops from their feet when they take off from a body of water. The katsinas use this image to refer to the rain that descends from the clouds. Here, flying ducks stand for clouds above the village laden with water. Just as drops of water fall from the ducks' feet as they take off from a body of water, so too do drops of water fall from the clouds when it rains.

Finally, it is important to distinguish the Hopi use of metaphor from the Western concepts of symbolism, that is, with attempts to make equivalent links between ritual objects and what they appear to stand for. The Hopis' general metaphorical association of things is rooted in their premise that there is no one thing in nature that has such great significance that it can stand alone as *the* symbolic equivalent of some thing or some idea. In ritual, any one of a number of things can be used to stand for many other things with the same meaning. For example, blue/green (*sakwa*) is a significant color because it is the color of plants and thus symbolic of growth as well as because it is the color of water and thus symbolic of rain. It is also the color associated with the southwest cardinal direction. In this way the Hopis see the color blue/green in terms of its general association with many things in nature that are significant to the Hopi way of life. Likewise, because other growing plants can stand for corn as a metaphor for sustenance, the katsinas distribute bean sprouts (*haaru*) raised in the kivas to families at *Powamuya* with the understanding that the bean sprouts "stand for" all things that nourish the people. Similarly, although the songs often mention mariposa lilies and blue asters when referrring to the promise of life, in fact, any plant that blooms represents the promise of life. One kind of blooming plant is no more important than any other in the way it countenances new life. All flower references have to do with the ideal world of nature where every living being is enjoying health, happiness and prosperity. This is the world that is the object of every Hopi's prayers to the katsinas for the gifts of rain and other good things of life.

Project History

This project had its genesis in two earlier initiatives related to the preservation and revitalization of Hopi language and culture. The first was a ten-year endeavor that culminated in 1998 with the publication of the *Hopi Dictionary/Hopìikwa Lavàytutuveni, a Hopi-English Dictionary of the Third Mesa Dialect* compiled by Kenneth C. Hill, Emory Sekaquaptewa, and Mary E. Black at the University of Arizona, and Ekkehart Malotki and Michael Lomaway'ma at Northern Arizona University, with input from the Hopi Health Department and numerous other contributors, including 44 Hopi language consultants. The Dictionary was funded by the National Endowment for the Humanities, Research Materials Division, as well as many other public and private agencies and foundations. It is a comprehensive and systematic reference for word meanings and for the principles of spelling for the Hopi language. Extensive entries include sentence examples that convey information about cultural meaning and usage in numerous contexts. Though the dictionary is based on Third Mesa Hopi, the orthography accommodates First and Second Mesa speech. Also included is a brief overview of the rules of Hopi grammar, a pronunciation guide, and an English-Hopi word finder. The Dictionary has been adopted by the Hopi Tribe as the guide for the teaching of the Hopi language in the Hopi schools.

Work on the Dictionary has formed the cornerstone for the linguistic analysis found in the footnotes in this volume. These footnotes reflect forms and the definitions of the words in their everyday usage, as found in the Hopi Dictionary. In contrast, Hopi ritual songs, of which katsina songs form a subset, are composed of both everyday words and what we have termed "song words" (Sekaquaptewa and Washburn 2004). Many song words are special combinations of everyday words which highlight Hopi principles of life, practices of living, and important features in the Hopi world that recall the essential role of rain and corn in Hopi life. These song words and their meanings are the focus of this volume.

The second initiative that preceded this project began in 1999 with a joint Harvard University, Peabody Museum/Museum of Northern Arizona/ Hopi Cultural Preservation Office agreement to reanalyze the fourteenth and fifteenth century kiva mural images from Awat'ovi and Kawàyka'a preparatory to a traveling exhibit of these images and associated objects. Emory proposed that, given the stability of Hopi beliefs related to katsinas, new understandings of the murals beyond the identification of the symbols therein (cf. Smith 1952) could be achieved by studying the content of twentieth century katsina songs. Key to this approach was the recognition not only that these songs, in conjunction with other aspects of katsina performance, are metaphorical voicings of the principles and practices of Hopi life, but also that they are an important mode of oral transmission of cultural traditions.

For this study, Emory transcribed and translated over 100 ritual songs that had been recorded by Samuel Barrett in 1911, by Robert Black in the 1950s, as well as those known by Emory from his lifetime as an active participant of the Third Mesa Hopi community. It was found that the metaphors in the words from late twentieth century songs not only characterize practices fundamental to the Hopi lifeway, but also that these *same* concepts were visually depicted in the fourteenth and fifteenth century mural images as well as in associated ritual paraphernalia and ceramic and textile design (Sekaquaptewa and Washburn 2004, 2006). This research was supported by the John Paul Getty Grant Program (1999–2001) as part of the joint museum project as well as by a Research Fellowship to Washburn from the National Endowment for the Humanities (2001).

In the course of locating recorded songs for this study, many substantial collections of katsina songs were discovered, almost all of which had neither been transcribed into written Hopi nor translated into English. They spanned the entire period of recorded song, from the earliest recordings made on wax cylinders at the turn of the twentieth century to those made on cassette tape as late as the 1980s (see summary in Kinkade and Mattina 1996). Emory determined that transcriptions and translations of the katsina songs from these collections would be an important contribution to a Hopi literature for the benefit of the Hopi people.

Recordings of Indigenous Song

At the turn of the twentieth century, sound was recorded with a stylus on rotating wax cylinders. Jesse Walter Fewkes used these wax cylinders to record native songs, first among the Passamaquoddies in the Bay of Fundy in 1889, then among the Zunis in 1890, and among the Hopis in 1891. However, these devices had many limitations. It was difficult to maintain a constant recording speed; each cylinder could record only five to seven minutes of music; and the cylinders, being of malleable wax, were easily damaged. Nevertheless, throughout the twentieth century, researchers made recordings of music and song from many North American tribes on wax cylinders as well as a variety of other media. These have lain largely unconserved and unappreciated in the archives of various university departments and museums. In many cases, especially for songs recorded on wax cylinders, the condition of the matrix and thus the recording quality has degraded over the years so that, in some cases, the songs are now unintelligible. In 1981 the Federal Cylinder Project was organized to locate and list the extant wax cylinder recordings (Brady et al. 1984). As a result of this project, many institutions turned their recorded song collections over to the Library of Congress where they were remastered in reel-to-reel tape format. However, magnetic tape, while greatly improving field recording and storage technology, has proven to be a similarly impermanent medium since the tape becomes brittle over time. Digitizing these recordings is the current industry standard.

There are three principal repositories of Native American song recordings: the American Folklife Center at the Library of Congress, the Archives of Traditional Music at Indiana University, and the Phoebe Hearst Museum, University of California Berkeley. The holdings of native music at the Library of Congress can be accessed at the web site www.loc.gov/folklife. The holdings of the Archives of Traditional Music at Indiana University can be accessed at the web site www.Indiana.edu/~libarchm. The holdings of the Hearst Museum can be found in Keeling (1991). Specific to the Indiana University Archives is a catalog prepared by Dorothy Lee (1979) of recordings on different media made between 1893 and 1976, as well as a catalog by Seeger and Spear (1987) listing only their cylinder holdings from 1893 to 1938. A recent annotated bibliography and introductory historical essay by Keeling (1997) surveys work related to native North American music.

It should be noted that there have been a number of phonographic records available to the public that were mastered by RCA Victor, Gennett Records, Folkways Records and the Library of Congress Archive of American Folk Song from some of these original recordings of American Indian music (cf. Rhodes 1952). All of our analyses with one exception were taken from the original cylinder or tape recordings that have not been published elsewhere. The exception is the recordings that Fewkes made in 1926 that were previously remastered by Gennett Records (5757–5761).

The focus of all this recording activity was the preservation of native music and this, perforce, included the recording of song. However, most of the analyses of this material have focused on the nature of the music itself (cf. Roberts 1933, 1936; Merriam 1964) and of the dance performances that the music was designed to accompany (Kurath 1970, Frisbie 1980, Sweet 1985) rather than on the songs or their content. Frances Densmore (1950: 450) noted that despite a half century of study, most attention had been given to the structure of the melodies and the form of the songs as well as the contexts of their uses rather than to the meaning of the words of the songs. She rightly observed that the words of many songs, properly translated, contain poetry, humor, historical references as well as an appreciation of the beauty of nature and mention of contacts with the supernatural.

Indeed, in reviews of the research literature it is distressing to find that the field of ritual performance has been analytically separated into domains (Murphy 1978, Keane 1997, Bauman and Briggs 1990) such as dance (Kaeppler 1978, Reed 1998), music (Rhodes 1952, McLeod 1974), and performance (Beeman 1993), despite the fact that all the components of a ritual performance are thought of by native practitioners as an inseparable complex. Only one overview touched to any degree on song, but the focus of most of the song studies reviewed was on the structure of the texts and their presentation, rather than on the content of the songs (Feld and Fox 1994). We note in passing that songs were collected by H.R. Voth at Orayvi for which he gave transcriptions and translations (Voth 1912), but these were not katsina songs. Miller (1996: 225) avers that few have systematically explored how song language differs from everyday speech, an issue that we hope to rectify in this volume.

Some of the reason for the paucity of extensive analyses of song content and cultural meaning undoubtedly lies in the lack of appropriate linguistic competence, especially of ritual song language, by non-native anthropologists and ethnomusicologists who record and study this material. Furthermore, the special nature of ritual song words requires an understanding of the cosmological principles underlying the culture as well as the metaphorical nature of the song words that convey these principles. For this reason, we have attempted to faithfully express Emory's exegesis of general Hopi cultural principles and their metaphorical expressions in the introduction and then how they are expressed in katsina song in the commentaries that follow each song.

One of the most difficult problems—and the central issue in ritual song—is capturing and linguistically representing the cultural *values* of one culture with conceptual words from another language (see also Swann 1987, Krupat 1992). Indeed, as Karl Kroeber argues, "It is our scholarship, not Indian literature, which is primitive or undeveloped" (1981: 9) because we are generally ignorant of the culture of which the literature, both oral and written, is a part. Always sensitive to the Other, Umberto Eco cuts to the essential issue. "In order to translate, one must know a lot of things, most of them independent of mere grammatical competence" (Eco 2003: 17–18). It is in this sense that Emory has gone beyond the dictionary definitions of daily word usage to carefully choose words that explain the song words and metaphors that evoke the cosmological world of the Hopis.

It should be noted that most songs were not sung in their entirety, that is, in the full AABBA verse sequence, during the recording session. In most cases only the A verse was sung and often only once. Sometimes the B verse, after *hapi me,* was sung, but usually only once. This is because they were recordings made on request of a researcher, not recordings of a performance. They represent the recollections, however complete or incomplete, of the singers. In addition, because of the degraded condition of the recordings, it is possible that Emory may not have heard all the words and/or may not have heard them correctly. In this volume, we have not repeated verses when they are identical within a given song.

Emory did not endeavor to fully transcribe the vocables, that is, the non-word sounds that are sung at the beginning, end, and between sections of the song. Most of the repeated lines of these vocables are omitted from the song transcriptions. The significance and form of these so-called "nonsense syllables" have been the subject of a number of studies of song (Densmore 1943, Halpern 1976, Frisbie 1980, Hinton 1989, Powers 1992). These researchers found that vocables function in a number of ways to enhance the melodic line, sound quality, and aesthetics of a song. In Hopi katsina songs, they are typically used to reinforce the content of the song. Vocables often mimic the sounds of grinding or thunder booming. They can also be calls peculiar to a katsina, words or word sounds from another language, or merely sounds to fill out a melodic line. These latter may be formulaic, for example, being similar to English expressions such as *tra-la-la.* We have indicated where they fall in the text since, in performance, they not only mark pauses between song sections, but also, in this way, provide time for the katsinas to change position, make hand gestures, or engage in other ritual practices that would have occurred during a performance.

Finally, it was Emory's decision not to address the issue of the music that accompanied the song when it was sung in performance by a group of singers with the full accompaniment of musical instruments. In the first place, the songs were not recorded as they were sung in performance but rather were sung by a solo singer without musical accompaniment. In the second place, while new pieces of music are constantly being created as new songs are composed, contrary to the claim that no new pieces of music are currently being added to the Hopi musical tradition (McLeod 1974: 107), there exists no standardized writing system for transcribing all styles of music. George List's attempts to score Hopi melodic lines within the existing Western notation were not successful because he found that Hopi music is not based on the notes of the Western scale (List 1985). For these reasons we have left the study of the musical accompaniment to the expertise of other scholars. Emory's focus here is a transcription, translation, and explication of the song texts.

The Katsina Song Collections

For this volume Emory transcribed into written Hopi and then translated into English the katsina songs collected by Natalie Curtis (Burlin) (1903), Samuel Barrett (1911), Helen Roberts (late 1920s), Jesse Walter Fewkes (1926), Ernest and Pearl Beaglehole (ca. 1934), Robert Black (1957–59) and George List (1960). It should be noted that each recorded collection also contains songs of ritual societies, social songs, lullabies, and other kinds of chants and oral announcements. However, the material presented in this volume is restricted to the katsina songs. In addition to the recorded collections we include twenty-five songs contributed by Emory.

The song collections have been arranged by collector, beginning with the earliest work in 1903 by Curtis. Within each collection the songs are grouped by the katsina who sang the song. Each song is referred to by its original cylinder or tape and track number. Overall the 150 songs have been given a sequential number, 1–150. It should be noted that some of the songs recorded by Barrett and Black and all of the songs contributed by Emory are also referred to in the Table of Contents and in the heading of the relevant songs by another number series (numbers 1–125), such as, for example, "Barrett Song 28." These are the numbers originally assigned during the mural study. Since these numbers have been referred to in previous publications (cf. Sekaquaptewa and Washburn 2004), we have included them here as a cross-reference for reader convenience. In this introductory section, however, we reference the songs by the 1–150 number sequence in which they are listed in this volume.

Emory attempted to transcribe the songs Fewkes collected in 1891 and 1898 as well as the songs recorded by Inez Barrington in 1927. The sound quality of the Fewkes songs was too degraded to allow study beyond recognition of the identity of the katsina singing the song and a few vocables and words. In fact, some were not Hopi songs, or, if they were Hopi songs, they were either not katsina songs or they were katsina songs with the words sung in another language. The songs recorded by Barrington were either not Hopi songs or, if they were Hopi songs, they were apparently not sung by a Hopi because of mistakes in verse order that would not have been made by a Hopi singer.

Based on Emory's identifications, we have compiled new listings of the songs in the Library of Congress and Indiana University collections that he reviewed, correcting errors of song identification and other matters. These new listings, combined with his transcriptions and translations and copies of the songs cleaned of much of the background noise and rerecorded on audio disks are on deposit at the Archives of Traditional Music at Indiana University and the American Folklife Center at the Library of Congress.

The Natalie Curtis Burlin Collection

Natalie Curtis (later Natalie Curtis Burlin), by training a musician, undertook the task of salvaging the music of many Native American groups. This work is preserved in her *The Indians' Book* (Curtis 1907). As part of this project, she recorded ten cylinders of songs from nine elderly men at Orayvi in 1903 who she thought were the "least corrupted" by European life. Although subsequent researchers have questioned her motives (Clements 1996) and the accuracy of her translations (Shaul 1992, 1994), the song recordings she made on the wax cylinders were sufficiently intelligible to enable Emory to make transcriptions. Since Fewkes's earlier recordings cannot be discerned, Curtis's 1903 recordings stand as the oldest Hopi katsina song recordings extant today. They were transferred to the Library of Congress from the collections of the Museum of the American Indian, Heye Foundation. The Archives of Traditional Music at Indiana University lists other cylinders of Hopi songs collected by Curtis Burlin, some deposited from the American Museum of Natural History and others from the Field Museum of Natural History, but these principally contain songs of other tribes in addition to Hopi social songs, lullabies, and songs from non-katsina societies that we did not include in this study.

The Samuel Barrett Collection

In 1911, Samuel Barrett, an ethnologist, spent eight months at Hopi. During that period he made 98 wax cylinder recordings of Hopi songs, with one to three songs recorded on each cylinder. Recordings 1–43 were made at Musangnuvi and recordings 44–98 were made at Orayvi. Barrett produced a typescript for the Milwaukee Public Museum that presents general observations on Hopi katsinas and songs and a brief description of each song recorded (Barrett 1946). This typescript and the taped recordings of these songs are archived at both the Library of Congress and the Indiana University Archives of Traditional Music.

The Jesse Walter Fewkes Collection

The archaeologist Jesse Walter Fewkes first recorded Hopi songs in 1891. However, some of these songs were either not Hopi songs or were Hopi songs that were not katsina songs. Of the Hopi katsina songs some were largely composed of vocables and others were songs with a few phrases repeated over and over. Other songs had words but they were not discernable. Benjamin Ives Gilman made musical transcriptions of these songs (1908). The 1926 recordings that we transcribed and translated were made by Fewkes, with J.P. Harrington's assistance, at a public performance by Hopi singers from Wàlpi at the El Tovar Hotel, Grand Canyon National Park, Arizona. These songs have been previously published in record format by Gennett Records (5757–5761) with an accompanying text by Fewkes explaining Hopi music and the relationship of the songs to Hopi culture (Fewkes 1926).

The Helen Roberts Collection

The exact dates of anthropologist Helen Roberts's field work or where she made her recordings are unknown. Most of her publications focus on the structure and form of Native American music (1932, 1936). In an editorial note by Marta Weigle (1989) concerning J.P. Harrington's work at Picuris in the 1920s, where he collected songs that Roberts then studied, she noted that Roberts made field trips to the Southwest in 1929 and 1930 to study Pueblo music. Prior to this time, in 1924, she was a research assis-

tant at Yale where she worked on music from the Southwest and California, among other areas. She wrote a brief overview article of field recordings made in the Southwest (1927) but that article does not mention her
Hopi work. We presume that she made the recordings of Hopi music
sometime during the 1920s. Catalog information from the Federal Cylinder Project indicates that Roberts used an Edison Home Phonograph with
electric pickup to make the recordings. The material was originally on
deposit at the School of American Research, Santa Fe.

The Beaglehole Collection

The anthropologist Ernest Beaglehole and his wife Pearl spent the summer
of 1934 at Musangnuvi and Supawlavi researching several topics with
three consultants (Beaglehole and Beaglehole 1935). In a separate
publication (Beaglehole 1937) Ernest reported on fieldwork completed
during the summers of 1932 and 1934 using the same informants.
Although there was no mention of making song recordings during any of
this fieldwork, we presume that during these two summers these recordings were made. Catalog information from the Federal Cylinder Project
indicates that Beaglehole used an Edison Home Phonograph with electric
pickup to make the recordings. The material was originally on deposit at
the School of American Research, Santa Fe.

The Robert Black Collection

Between 1957 and 1959 Robert Black, an anthropologist, recorded singers
at Zuni and Hopi villages as well as Hopi singers in Flagstaff and in 1965
he recorded songs sung by six singers at Hotvela, Orayvi, Kiqötsmovi
("New Oraibi"), and Sitsom'ovi. Black's research focus, however, was on
chants—secular announcements of work parties for cleaning ditches,
planting, harvesting, roasting, grinding and hunting, invitations to feasts
and trading events, and grievances. They were the subject of his dissertation (1965) and two later articles (1967a,b). The songs he recorded have
never been fully translated and studied. They are on deposit at the Library
of Congress and at the Archives of Traditional Music at Indiana University accompanied by his typed listings and short description of each
song (Black 1959).

The George List Collection

During the summer of 1960, George List, an ethnomusicologist, collected song recordings from ten singers from Wàlpi. Each song recording is either prefaced by or followed by a taped discussion between List, his wife, and the singer concerning the meaning of the song and other related topics. In some cases he asked the singer to "say the words of the song," but the singer often misunderstood and simply summarized what the song was about. In our re-listing of these songs, we have corrected errors of song identification and some misunderstandings of the explanations offered to List about song form and content.

List wrote a number of articles about this recorded material (1962, 1985, 1987, 1993, 1997). His particular interest was to follow up on the early observation of Gilman that Hopi music was without a scale (1908). List found that it is, indeed, "impossible to translate them [the songs] into the discrete pitches of our Western notation system," concluding that the "Hopis must conceive their melody as a series of contours rather than a series of discrete pitches" (1985: 144). In this project we have made no attempt to resolve this musicological issue and have limited our work to the transcription and translation of the words of the songs and a discussion of their meaning and content as they relate to Hopi ideals and values. These songs are reproduced here through the courtesy of George List and with the condition that they be used only for Hopi and scholarly use.

Songs Contributed by Emory Sekaquaptewa

As is the experience of all Hopis who participate in the ritual life of their community, Emory had learned a great many katsina songs over his lifetime. Some of these are included in the text here.

Guidelines for Reading this Volume

The Hopi transcriptions are in the orthography of the Hopi Dictionary (1998), which has been adopted by the Hopi Tribe. Some of the songs were obtained from singers from First and Second Mesa and where dialect differences in spelling and meaning occur, they are noted.

The transcription is accompanied by footnotes that translate each word at its first appearance in the song. This translation is the everyday usage of the word, much as found in the Hopi Dictionary definitions. When a word in the song is pronounced differently from the way it would appear in the Third Mesa spelling of the Hopi Dictionary, the footnote begins with an equals sign (=) signaling the equivalence. The footnotes also provide comments when song usage differs from the everyday usage. In addition, the footnotes include important grammatical and linguistic information that is crucial to an understanding of the nuanced usage of these words in context. Though the same word may be translated differently in different contexts, an effort has been made to keep the translation very close to the wording of the Hopi language original. While a Hopi word may appear to a native speaker to have a constant meaning in its different contexts, the way to express this meaning in translation is not a constant. An example is the word *maana,* which in the songs translates variously as "girl," "young woman," and "maiden." Given the right context, *maana* would also translate as "virgin." It is a truism regarding translation that in every language words have ranges of meaning and that the range of meanings of a word in one language hardly ever corresponds to exactly the same range of meaning in another language, especially in an unrelated and culturally distant language. Also it should be noted that inserted material is indicated by square brackets, [], and explanatory material by parentheses, ().

The transcription and associated footnotes are followed by a line-by-line translation of the song, which in turn is followed by a discussion of the song content and meaning. The discussion includes an explanation, where appropriate, of the metaphors that embody the critical principles of Hopi life as they are embedded the words of the song. The discussion also touches on the cultural beliefs and practices alluded to that must be understood in order to appreciate the fuller implications of the song and its message. Much of this background cultural information is discussed at greater length in the Introduction. The non-Hopi reader should review the introductory material first before proceeding to the song explanations in order to fully appreciate the more abbreviated reference to this material in the discussion of each song.

There are three appendices. The first is a discussion of the relevant features of the Hopi language, the second is an analytic listing of the compound Hopi words found in this volume, and the third is a glossary of the words found in the songs and discussions. In Appendix 2 Emory has added some untranslated comments in Hopi for the Hopi reader about some of the compound words.

For a proper understanding of these songs, it is important that the reader attend to both the footnotes and the descriptive explanations that accompany each song, as well as make reference to the appendices to more fully understand grammatical issues and the structure of the compounds found in the songs. All of these parts have been designed to complement and enhance each other.

This is intended as a reference volume, rather than a volume to be read from the beginning to the end. For this reason, the explanations of the meanings and metaphors in each song are complete for each song. Thus, while overall, the explanations are somewhat repetitive since similar songs will be given similar treatment, the explication of each song can stand alone. Readers unfamiliar with Hopi culture should preface their use of a given song with a reading of the material in the Introduction.

Songs Recorded by Natalie Curtis in 1903

Part I: Indiana University Archives of Traditional Music (IUATM)

1. Angaktsìntawi*₁*
(Curtis Burlin 391, Cylinder 3671, Track 18; IUATM)

Haa'o,*₂* haa'o, haw*₃* íngumu.*₄*
Haa'o, haa'o, haw ínamu.*₅*
Itam*₆* pew*₇* umumi*₈* yooya'öki,*₉*
péwi'i.*₁₀*
Umùu'uyinawita*₁₁* oo'omawutuy*₁₂* ökinayani,*₁₃*
taawanawita.*₁₄*
Yaantaniqat*₁₅* itam yep*₁₆* naawakinaya,*₁₇*
haa'o ínamu.
Lee lehe la.
Ha'óo*₁₈* íngumu,

1. *angaktsìntawi* 'Long-Hair katsina song'.
2. *haa'o,* vocative particle.
3. *haw,* vocative particle.
4. = *ingum* 'my mothers'.
5. = *inam* 'my fathers'.
6. *itam* 'we'.
7. *pew* 'toward here, coming this way'.
8. *umumi* 'to you (plural)'.
9. = *yoy'öki* 'arrive, come as rain'.
10. = *pew'i,* pausal form of *pew* 'toward here, coming this way'.
11. = *umùu'uyinawit* 'along your planted fields'.
12. = *oo'omàwtuy,* object form of *oo'omawt* 'clouds'.
13. *ökinayani* 'will make several come (plural)'.
14. = *taawanawit* 'all day long'.
15. = *yantaniqat* 'for it to be this way', object form of *yantaniqa* 'one that will be this way'.
16. *yep* 'here'.
17. = *naanawakna* 'pray, want (plural)'.
18. *ha'óo,* vocative particle.

hin pa[19] uma[20] yep lolmat[21] yeese,[22]
yeepe'e.[23]
Pay[24] kur[25] uma yep lolmat yeese,
ha'o[26] ínamu.
Pantaqw[27] ítamu[28] oo'omawutu[29] hàalay'unangway[30] naayuwasinayata'a,[31]
angqw[32] pew yoynaanakwusa,[33]
péwi'i.
Umùu'uyiy[34] ang[35] yookinaya.[36]
Hiy'a hiy'a.
Haqami[37] taawanawita.
"Ókiwa[38] ura[39] nu'[40] yangqö[41] haqami waymakyango[42] taatawyuuyuwinti-
*   ma.[43]"*
Hay'a hiy'ay.
Ítamu lolmat[44] pitsangwa'ykyango[45] pew umumi yooya'öki.

19. *hin pa* 'I wonder how'.
20. *uma* 'you (plural)'.
21. *lolmat* 'beautifully, well, properly'.
22. *yeese* 'live, dwell (plural)'; *lolmat yeese,* 'live in accord with Hopi teachings (plural)'.
23. = *yep'e,* pausal form of *yep* 'here'.
24. *pay,* expressive particle.
25. *kur,* modal of inference.
26. *ha'o,* vocative particle.
27. *pantaqw* 'if/when it is that way'.
28. = *itam* 'we'.
29. = *oo'omawt* 'clouds'.
30. *hàalay'unangway* 'with happy hearts, with beneficent intentions'.
31. = *naayuwsinayat* 'after clothing selves'.
32. *angqw* 'from it, from there'.
33. = *yoynànkwusa* 'start on a journey as rain'.
34. *umùu'uyiy,* object form of *umùu'uyi* 'your (plural) planted fields'.
35. *ang* 'along there, in that area, in several places'.
36. = *yoknaya* 'make it rain (plural)'.
37. = *aqwhaqami* 'throughout'.
38. = *okiw* 'humbly, pitifully'.
39. *ura,* modal of recollection: 'as I recall, as you'll recall'.
40. *nu'* 'I'.
41. = *yangqw* 'from here'.
42. = *waymakyangw* 'while walking along'.
43. = *taatawyuyuwintima* 'go along dancing and singing songs'.
44. *lolmat,* object form of *lolma* 'beautiful, good, proper'.
45. = *pitsangwa'ykyangw* 'while having a countenance'.

Hark, hark, o my mothers.
Hark, hark, o my fathers.
We are coming to you as rain,
coming this way.
Along your planted fields, we will make the clouds come
all day long.
We want it to be this way here,
o my fathers.
(Vocables.)
O my mothers,
we wonder if your life is in accord with Hopi teachings
here.
Perhaps you are living here in accord with Hopi teachings,
o my fathers.
If it is that way, then we clouds, with happy hearts, after clothing our-
selves,
start out coming from there on a journey as rain,
coming this way.
Along your planted fields [we] make it rain.
(Vocables.)
Throughout, all day long.
"Just think, I used to go along humbly singing and dancing while I walked
along from here all along the way."
(Vocables.)
Having a beautiful countenance, we come to you as rain.

The katsinas begin their song by calling for the attention of the mothers
and fathers of the village. This is not a reference to the people of the village as biological mothers and fathers of their children, but to the people
as mothers and fathers of the katsinas. The people live in this present
world, the Fourth World, and the katsinas, who are individuals who have
passed on, inhabit the next world, the Fifth World. From this perspective,
the people are their mothers and fathers. In their songs when the katsinas
address the people, it is traditional for them to address the mothers first
and then the fathers. By addressing the women first, the katsinas acknowledge their pivotal importance in procreation and thus in the continued
survival of the people. However, in many of the recorded songs in this
volume, this custom is not always followed. Sometimes only the fathers
are addressed and sometimes the fathers are addressed before the mothers.

The katsinas announce that they are coming as rain to the people: "We are coming to you as rain, coming this way." The katsinas are, of course, the rain. They live in their homes in the four cardinal directions as clouds and, when summoned by the prayers of the people, come as rain to the Hopi lands. In this song the katsinas sing about how they are going to come as clouds all day long, indicating that it is going to be an all-day rain. The katsinas' statement "We want it to be this way here" means that they have deemed the people deserving of their rain and thus they are coming with beneficent intentions to nurture the people and their planted fields with their rain. The planted fields are to be understood as including all crops—corn, beans, melons, and anything else the people plant, tend and harvest.

However, after some vocables, the katsinas pause to wonder if the people are living their lives according to the principles and practices they accepted at Emergence when they agreed to live by the humble ear of corn. This is a mild indirect admonition to the people that, if they have strayed from adhering to the moral imperatives that sustain communal living, they should rededicate themselves to this life. But then they tell the people, if you are living according to Hopi teachings, then they (the clouds) will be happy to clothe themselves, adorning themselves with rain, and journey to the planted fields with their gift of rain. This is the reciprocal relationship between the people and the katsinas. When the people live by the tenets of the Hopi lifeway, the katsinas will come to sustain them with rain. Since the clouds are animate, indeed they are katsinas, their coming is described as a journey.

The katsinas then sing as if they are the people who are reminding themselves that in the past when they lived humbly, the rains came regularly and they were happy. As if confirming this sentiment, the katsinas respond that they are coming as rain with a beautiful countenance (*lolma pitsangwa'yta*). Their beautiful countenance is the rain, and by implication, all the good things that the rain brings—a life fulfilled with health, happiness, and the freedom from want.

2. Angaktsìntawi[1]

(Curtis Burlin 391, Cylinder 3652, Track 3; IUATM)

Haw'o,[2] ha'o,[3] haw[4] íngumu.[5]
Itam[6] pew[7] umumi[8] yooya'öki,[9]
péwi'i.[10]
Umùu'uyinawita[11] oo'omawutu[12] yookinayani,[13]
taawanawita.[14]
Yantaniqat[15] itam yep[16] naawakinaya,[17]
haw'o ínamu.[18]
Ha'óo[19] íngumu,
hin pa[20] úma'a,[21]
lolmat[22] yeese,[23]
yépe'e.[24]
Pay[25] sen[26] uma[27] yep lólomat[28] yeese,

1. *angaktsìntawi* 'Long-Hair katsina song'.
2. *haw'o*, vocative particle.
3. *ha'o*, vocative particle.
4. *haw*, vocative particle.
5. = *ingum* 'my mothers'.
6. *itam* 'we'.
7. *pew* 'toward here, coming this way'.
8. *umumi* 'to you (plural)'.
9. = *yoy'öki* 'arrive, come as rain'.
10. = *pew'i*, pausal form of *pew* 'toward here, coming this way'.
11. = *umùu'uyinawit* 'along your planted fields'.
12. = *oo'omawt* 'clouds'.
13. = *yoknayani* 'will make it rain (plural)'.
14. = *taawanawit* 'all day long'.
15. *yantaniqat* 'for it to be this way', object form of *yantaniqa* 'one that will be this way'.
16. *yep* 'here'.
17. = *naanawakna* 'want (plural)'.
18. = *inam* 'my fathers'.
19. *ha'óo*, vocative particle.
20. *hin pa* 'I wonder how'.
21. *úma'a*, pausal form of *uma* 'you (plural)'.
22. *lolmat* 'beautifully, well, properly'.
23. *yeese* 'live, dwell (plural)'; *lolmat yeese*, 'live in accord with Hopi teachings (plural)'.
24. = *yep'e*, pausal form of *yep* 'here'.
25. *pay*, expressive particle.
26. *sen* 'perhaps'.
27. *uma* 'you (plural)'.
28. = *lolmat* 'beautifully, well, properly'.

haa'o$_{29}$ ínamu.
Pantaqw$_{30}$ ítamu$_{31}$ oo'omawutu hàalay'unangway$_{32}$ naayuwasinayata$_{33}$
angqw$_{34}$ pew yoynaanakwusa,$_{35}$
péwi'i.$_{36}$
Umùu'uyiy ang$_{37}$ yookinayani,
taawanawita.
Hii'aa hii'a.
Hapi me.$_{38}$
Haqami$_{39}$ taawanawita.
"Ókiwa$_{40}$ ítamu yangqö$_{41}$ haqami waymakyango$_{42}$ taatawyuuyuwintima."$_{43}$
Hii'a aya hii.

Hark, hark, o my mothers.
We are coming to you as rain,
coming this way.
Along your planted fields, the clouds will make it rain
all day long.
We want it to be this way here,
o our fathers.
O my mothers,
we wonder how you
are living in accord with Hopi teachings
here.
Perhaps you are living here in accord with Hopi teachings,
o my fathers.

29. *haa'o,* vocative particle.
30. *pantaqw* 'if/when it is that way'.
31. = *itam* 'we'.
32. *hàalay'unangway* 'with happy hearts, with beneficent intentions'.
33. = *naayuwsinayat* 'after clothing selves'.
34. *angqw* 'from it, from there'.
35. = *yoynànkwusa* 'start on a journey as rain'.
36. = *pew'i,* pausal form of *pew* 'toward here, coming this way'.
37. *ang* 'along it, along there, in that area, in several places'.
38. *hapi me,* formulaic expression introducing the song's second part, *oomi* 'upward'.
39. = *aqwhaqami* 'throughout'.
40. = *okiw* 'humbly, pitifully'.
41. = *yangqw* 'from here'.
42. = *waymakyangw* 'while walking along'.
43. = *taatawyuyuwintima* 'go along dancing and singing songs'.

If it is that way, then we clouds, with happy hearts, after clothing ourselves,
start out coming from there on a journey as rain,
coming this way.
Along your planted fields [we] will make it rain
all day long.
(Vocables.)
Listen, there is more.
[We will make it rain] throughout,
all day long.
"We used to go along humbly dancing and singing songs while we were
walking along from here and all along the way."
(Vocables.)

This song is similar to Song 1 with minor differences in wording and
structure. These differences illustrate the way tradition, passed along
orally, results in variation. Though different individuals may remember a
song slightly differently, the intent and message of the different versions
remains the same.

3. *Angaktsìntawi$_1$*
(Curtis Burlin 393, Cylinder 3720, Track 16; IUATM)

Haa'o$_2$ haa'o haa'o íngumu.$_3$
Itam$_4$ pew$_5$ umumi$_6$ yooya'öki,$_7$
péwi'i.$_8$
Umùu'uyinawita$_9$ oo'omawutu$_{10}$ yookinayani,$_{11}$

1. *angaktsìntawi* 'Long-Hair katsina song'.
2. *haa'o,* vocative particle.
3. = *ingum* 'my mothers'.
4. *itam* 'we'.
5. *pew* 'toward here, coming this way'.
6. *umumi* 'to you (plural)'.
7. = *yoy'öki* 'arrive, come as rain'.
8. = *pew'i,* pausal form of *pew* 'toward here, coming this way'.
9. = *umùu'uyinawit* 'along your planted fields'.
10. = *oo'omawt* 'clouds'.
11. = *yoknayani* 'will make it rain (plural)'.

taawanawita.$_{12}$
Yantaniqat$_{13}$ *itam*$_{14}$ *yep*$_{15}$ *naawakinaya,*$_{16}$
haa'o ínamu.$_{17}$
Haa'o íngumu,
hin pa$_{18}$ *úma'a,*$_{19}$
lolmat$_{20}$ *yeese,*$_{21}$
yépe'e.$_{22}$
Pay$_{23}$ *kur*$_{24}$ *uma*$_{25}$ *yep lolmat yeese,*
ha'óo$_{26}$ *ínamu.*
Pantaqw$_{27}$ *ítamu*$_{28}$ *oo'omawutu hàalay'unangway*$_{29}$ *naayuwasinayata'a,*$_{30}$
angqw$_{31}$ *pew yoynaanakwusa,*$_{32}$
péwi'i.
Umùu'uyiy$_{33}$ *ang*$_{34}$ *yookinayani,*
taawanawita.
Hiy'aa hiy'aa hay'a.
Haqami$_{35}$ *taawanawita.*

12. = *taawanawit* 'all day long'.
13. *yantaniqat* 'it to be this way', object form of *yantaniqa* 'one that will be this way'.
14. *itam* 'we'.
15. *yep* 'here'.
16. = *naanawakna* 'pray, want (plural)'.
17. = *inam* 'my fathers'.
18. *hin pa* 'I wonder if'.
19. *úma'a,* pausal form of *uma* 'you (plural)'.
20. *lolmat* 'beautifully, well, properly'.
21. *yeese* 'live, dwell (plural)'; *lolmat yeese* 'live in accord with Hopi teachings (plural)'.
22. = *yep'e,* pausal form of *yep* 'here'.
23. *pay,* expressive particle.
24. *kur,* modal of inference.
25. *uma* 'you (plural)'.
26. *ha'óo,* vocative particle.
27. *pantaqw* 'when it is that way'.
28. = *itam* 'we'.
29. *hàalay'unangway* 'with happy hearts, with beneficent intentions'.
30. = *naayuwsinayat* 'after clothing selves'.
31. *angqw* 'from it, from there'.
32. = *yoynànkwusa* 'start on a journey as rain'.
33. *umùu'uyiy,* object form of *umùu'uyi* 'your (plural) planted fields'.
34. *ang* 'along it, along there, in that area, in several places'.
35. = *aqwhaqami* 'throughout'.

Ókiwa₃₆ uma pi yangqö₃₇ haqami waymakyango₃₈ taatawyuuyuwintima.₃₉

Hark, hark, o my mothers.
We are coming to you as rain,
coming this way.
Along your planted fields, the clouds will make it rain
all day long.
We want it to be this way here,
o my fathers.
O my mothers,
we wonder if you are
living a life in accord with Hopi teachings
here.
Apparently you are living in accord with Hopi teachings here,
o my fathers.
If it is that way, then we clouds, with happy hearts, after clothing ourselves,
start out coming from there on a journey as rain,
coming this way.
Along your planted fields [we] will make it rain
all day long.
(Vocables.)
[We will make it rain] all throughout,
all day long.
May you also humbly go along dancing and singing songs while walking
along from here all along the way.

This is a third version of Songs 1 and 2, with very minor differences from
Song 2.

---

36. = *okiw* 'humbly, pitifully'.
37. = *yangqw* 'from here'.
38. = *waymakyangw* 'while walking along'.
39. = *taatawyuyuwintima* 'go along dancing and singing songs'.

4. *Angaktsìntawi*[1]
(Curtis Burlin 393, Cylinder 3711, Track 7; IUATM)

Haa'o[2] *haa'o haw*[3] *íngumu.*[4]
Haa'o haa'o haw ínamu.[5]
Inumi[6] *hoomat*[7] *óya'a.*[8]
Inumi yoynawakina'a.[9]
Lee lehe la.
Oo owa eehe heelo.

Hark, hark, o my mothers.
Hark, hark, o my fathers.
Hand me the consecrated cornmeal.
Pray to me for rain.
(Vocables.)

This is the final song of the day at a performance. At this time the katsina father instructs the katsinas to line up facing him and he places a prayer feather and pinch of cornmeal in the left hand of each katsina. Then the katsinas turn and exit the plaza one behind the other along a path of consecrated cornmeal. In these prayer feathers are the prayers of the people that the katsinas take with them on their journey to their homes in the four cardinal directions. In this song the katsinas direct the katsina father to hand them consecrated cornmeal. The prayer feathers are mentioned only implicitly, because the injunction to "pray to me for rain" (*yoynawakna'a*) implies that, on this last opportunity before the katsinas leave, the people will be sending their most humble and pleading prayers to them via the prayer feathers placed in their hands.

1. *angaktsìntawi* 'Long-Hair katsina song'.
2. *haa'o,* vocative particle.
3. *haw,* vocative particle.
4. = *ingum* 'my mothers'.
5. = *inam* 'my fathers'.
6. *inumi* 'to me'.
7. *hoomat,* object form of *hooma* 'consecrated cornmeal'.
8. *óya'a,* imperative form of *oya* 'hand (to), hand out, deposit, place, put, set (several) in a particular position'.
9. = *yoynawakna'a,* imperative form of *yoynawakna* 'pray for rain'.

5. *Angaktsìntawi[1]*

(Curtis Burlin 394, Cylinder 3724, Track 2; IUATM)

Aahaa iihii.
Haa'o[2] haw[3] haw íngumu.[4]
Haa'o haw haw ínamu.[5]
Inumi[6] hooma'oya'a.[7]
Inumi yoynaawakina'a.[8]
Lee lehe la.
Ooho oho oho ha ehe eelo.
Aa aha.

(Vocables of the sound of singing.)
Hark, hark, o my mothers.
Hark, hark, o my fathers.
Hand me the consecrated cornmeal.
Pray to me for rain.
(Vocables.)

This is almost identical to Song 4.

6. *Angaktsìntawi[1]*

(Curtis Burlin 391, Cylinder 3662, Track 10; IUATM)

Sikya'omaw[2] umumi[3] kuuyiva.[4]
Sakwa'omawmanatu,[5]

1. *angaktsìntawi* 'Long-Hair katsina song'.
2. *haa'o,* vocative particle.
3. *haw,* vocative particle.
4. = *ingum* 'my mothers'.
5. = *inam* 'my fathers'.
6. *inumi* 'to me'.
7. *hom'oya'a,* imperative form of *hom'oya* 'hand out consecrated cornmeal'.
8. = *yoynawakna'a,* imperative form of *yoynawakna* 'pray for rain'.

1. *angaktsìntawi* 'Long-Hair katsina song'.
2. *sikya'omaw* 'yellow cloud'.
3. *umumi* 'to you (plural)'.
4. = *kuyva* 'appear, come into sight'.
5. = *sakwa'omawmamant* 'blue/green cloud maidens'.

umumi kuukuyivani.$_6$
Yooki- yookinayani.$_7$
Lee lehe la.
(*Vocables to end of song.*)

The yellow cloud made its appearance to you.
The blue/green cloud maidens,
they will make their appearance to you.
They will make it rain.
(Vocables.)

The katsinas are describing the appearance of clouds from two of the four
cardinal directions. They are named in counterclockwise order beginning
with the yellow clouds from the northwest that have apparently already
appeared. The katsinas promise that the blue/green clouds will appear
from the southwest. The blue/green clouds are metaphorically specified
as maidens because both rain clouds and young women bear the promise
of future life.

7. *Angaktsìntawi*$_1$
(Curtis Burlin 392, Cylinder 3682, Track 8; IUATM)

Ha'óo$_2$ *uma*$_3$ *ínamu.*$_4$
Uma yep$_5$ *inumi*$_6$ *naawakinaya.*$_7$
Umùupahoyu$_8$ *ákwa'a,*$_9$
inumi naawakinaqw'ö,$_{10}$

6. = *kuukuyvani* 'will appear, come into sight (plural)'.
7. = *yoknayani* 'will make it rain (plural)'.

1. *angaktsìntawi* 'Long-Hair katsina song'.
2. *ha'óo,* vocative particle.
3. *uma* 'you (plural)'.
4. = *inam* 'my fathers'.
5. *yep* 'here'.
6. *inumi* 'to me'.
7. = *naanawakna* 'pray, want (plural)'.
8. = *umùupahoy,* object form of *umùupaho* 'your prayer feathers'.
9. *ákwa'a,* pausal form of *akw* 'using it, by means of it, with it'.
10. = *naanawaknaqw,* subordinate clause form of *naanawakna* 'pray, want (plural)'.

yangqw₁₁ pew₁₂ naanan'ivaqö₁₃
oo'omawutu₁₄ pew yoynaanakwusa,₁₅
taawanawita.₁₆
Lee lehe la.
Yan₁₇ uma tsootsong.yakyangw₁₈ naawakina,₁₉
yépe'e.₂₀
Oowa eelo.

Hark, my fathers.
You here(a) prayed to me.
When with your prayer feathers,
you prayed to me,
[then] from here(b), coming from the different directions around,
the clouds started out coming on their journey as rain,
all day long.
(Vocables.)
This is what you were praying for while you were smoking
here(a).
(Vocables.)

The katsinas begin by addressing the people as their fathers, who have
prayed to them with their prayer feathers. This is a reference to activities
that have taken place prior to the day of the performance. A katsina
performance requires much preparation on the part of those who are
sponsoring the dance. For four days prior to their appearance in the plaza,
these elder leaders make prayer feathers and smoke and pray over them
in the kiva. The prayers infused in these prayer feathers are the fervent
hopes of the people that the katsinas will come with their gift burden of
rain and other good things of life.

11. *yangqw* 'from here'.
12. *pew* 'toward here, coming this way'.
13. = *naanan'ivaqw* 'from the different directions around'.
14. = *oo'omawt* 'clouds'.
15. = *yoynànkwusa* 'start on a journey as rain'.
16. = *taawanawit* 'all day long'.
17. *yan* 'like this, in this way, thus'.
18. *tsootsong.yakyangw* 'while smoking (plural)'.
19. = *naawakna* 'pray, want'.
20. = *yep'e,* pausal form of *yep* 'here'.

Then, in the reciprocity that is fundamental to the relationship between the katsinas and the people, the katsinas say that after the people "here$_{(a)}$," meaning where the people are, prayed, the clouds started on their journey from "here$_{(b)}$," meaning where the katsinas are in the four cardinal directions, and journey toward "here$_{(a)}$," meaning, again, where the people are. They remind the people that this coming of the rain is what they have been praying for as they were smoking over the prayer feathers in the kivas. During their ritual preparations the elders sit in a circle in the kiva and pass the smoking pipe from one to another, each man taking a puff and making his prayer. The smoke symbolizes the clouds that will come as rain.

8. Angaktsìntawi$_1$
(Curtis Burlin 393, Cylinder 3717, Track 13; IUATM)

Humisimanatuy$_2$ uuyive$_3$ amunawita$_4$ tuvevolimanatu$_5$ naangöyimani.$_6$
Taatawyuyuwinani.$_7$
Lee lehe la.
Aahaa yoowi aha ha.

Along the corn blossom maidens in the planted field, the butterfly
    maidens of various colors will go along chasing one other.
[You] will be dancing and singing songs.
(Vocables.)

The song describes a primary Hopi concern, the pollination of flowers so that plants will produce sustenance for the people. Here the butterflies are pollinating the corn. Both the corn blossoms and the butterflies are metaphorically likened to maidens, that is, young women, since they both hold the promise of future life. The katsinas imply that this pollinating activity will prompt the people to sing and dance in happiness over these signs of

---

1. *angaktsìntawi* 'Long-Hair katsina song'.
2. = *humisimamàntuy,* object form of *humisimamant* 'corn blossom maidens'.
3. *uuyive* 'at the planted field'.
4. = *amunawit* 'along them, along their course'.
5. = *tuvevolmamant* 'butterfly maidens of various colors'.
6. = *naangöytiwwisni* 'will be going along chasing one other'.
7. *taatawyuyuwinani* 'will be dancing and singing songs'.

new life to come. The description of the butterflies as of various colors emphasizes their beauty and recalls the pristine vitality and ideal life of the past Uto-Aztecan world where everyone lived right and enjoyed fulfillment.

9. *Korowistakatsìntawi₁*
(Curtis Burlin 391, Cylinder 3649, Track 1; IUATM)

Polisimanatuy₂ amunawita,₃
taatangayatu₄ tiitiwungwintani.₅
Ahaa ihii.
Umu'uyiyu₆ aw₇ yoy- yoy'umumutimani,₈
taawanawita.₉
Hay'aa.
Umu'uyiyu aw yoyhoyoyotimani,₁₀
taawanawita.
Hay'aa.
Yowi'aha aa yahi aa.
Aaha.
Yahiy aayaw linayaw linayaw.

Among the evening primrose maidens,
the yellowjackets will be repeatedly nurturing them.
(Vocables.)
[We] will go along thundering toward your planted fields
all day long.
(Vocable.)
[We] will go moving along as rain toward your planted fields
all day long.

1. *korowistakatsìntawi* 'Korowista katsina song'.
2. = *poñisimamàntuy,* object form of *poñisimamant* 'evening primrose maidens'.
3. = *amunawit* 'along them, along their course'.
4. = *taatangayt* 'yellowjackets', plural of *taatangaya.*
5. *tiitiwungwintani* 'will be nurturing offspring repeatedly'.
6. = *umùu'uyiy,* object form of *umùu'uyi* 'your (plural) planted fields'.
7. *aw* 'to it, to there'.
8. *yoy'umumutimani* 'will go along thundering'.
9. = *taawanawit* 'all day long'.
10. *yoyhoyoyotimani* 'will be moving along as rain'.

(Vocables.)

The katsinas are describing how the vitality of the beautiful evening primrose maidens is being enhanced by the pollination activities of the yellowjackets. Characterizing the evening primroses (*poñisi*) as maidens metaphorically likens them to young girls that are growing in the beauty of their capacity to make life. The pollination process is described as "nurturing offspring repeatedly" (*tiitiwungwinta,* from *tihu* 'child' [-*ti*-] and *wúngwinta* 'be raising, nurturing, making grow'; the initial reduplication, *tii-,* indicates that it is happening repeatedly). This conveys the idea that just as the yellowjackets nurture the evening primroses, so parents nurture their children. While many plants and creatures could be used as metaphors for this nurturing process, the colorful beauty of the evening primroses and yellowjackets is an effective way to create a mental image of the perfect world where people care for each other and thus life flourishes. The katsinas promise to go along thundering and moving as rain along the planted fields all day long. Thunder is often mentioned in katsina songs because it accompanies the heavy summer rainstorms that bring the corn to maturity.

10. *Korowistakatsìntawi*[1]
(Curtis Burlin 391, Cylinder 3665, Track 13; IUATM)

Sikyavolimu,[2] *humisimanatuy*[3] *talasiyamuyu*[4] *pitsangwatimakyango*[5] *tuve-naangöyintani.*[6]
Ahaa ihii.
Sakwavolimu,[7] *morisimanatuyu*[8] *talasiyamuyu pitsangwatimakyango tuve-naangöyintani.*
Oho ew heway eehe eelo.

1. *korowistakatsìntawi* 'Korowista katsina song'.
2. = *sikyavolim* 'yellow butterflies'.
3. = *humisimamàntuy,* object form of *humisimamant* 'corn blossom maidens'.
4. = *talasiyamuy,* object form of *talasi'am* 'their pollen'.
5. = *pitsàngwtimakyangw* 'while going along adorning the face with'.
6. = *tuvenangöytani* 'will be chasing one other colorfully'.
7. = *sakwavolim* 'blue/green butterflies'.
8. = *morisimamàntuy,* object form of *morisimamant* 'bean blossom maidens'.

The yellow butterflies will be chasing one other about colorfully as they go along adorning their faces with the pollen of the corn blossom maidens.
(Vocables.)
The blue/green butterflies will be chasing one other about colorfully as they go along adorning their faces with the pollen of the bean blossom maidens.
(Vocables.)

This song describes the promise of new life as represented by a field of blossoming corn plants and bean plants that are being pollinated by the butterflies. The yellow butterflies will be pollinating the corn blossoms and the blue/green butterflies will be pollinating the bean blossoms. The maiden metaphor is used to describe both plants. The description of the pollination process as "adorning their faces with pollen," can be understood to mean that the blossoms are metaphorically taking on the countenance of future life. The song creates an image of colorful butterflies flitting about covered with pollen. By describing the butterflies as being of two of the directional colors, yellow associated with the northwest and blue/green with the southwest, the katsinas remind the people of the rain that comes from these two directions.

11. *Korowistakatsìntawi₁*
(Curtis Burlin 394, Cylinder 3723, Track 1; IUATM)

Sikyavolimu₂ humisimanatuyu₃ talasiyamuyu₄ pitsangwatimani.₅
—(inaudible)— -yang wunimani.₆
Aaha iihii.
Sakwavolimu₇ humisimanatuyu talasiyamuyu pitsangwatimani.
—(inaudible)—
Oho howa ee elo hiy'a aya hiy.

1. *korowistakatsìntawi* 'Korowista katsina song'.
2. = *sikyavolim* 'yellow butterflies'.
3. = *humisimamàntuy,* object form of *humisimamant* 'corn blossom maidens'.
4. = *talasiyamuy,* object form of *talasi'am* 'their pollen'.
5. = *pitsàngwtimani* 'will go along adorning the face with'.
6. *wunimani* 'will be dancing'.
7. = *sakwavolim* 'blue/green butterflies'.

The yellow butterflies will go along adorning their faces with the pollen
from the corn blossom maidens.
—(*inaudible*)— will be dancing.
(Vocables.)
The blue/green butterflies will go along adorning their faces with the
pollen of the corn blossom maidens.
—(*inaudible*)—
(Vocables.)

This song is like Song 10 except that bean blossom maidens are not
included and there is mention of dancing, presumably by the people. It is
always a happy sight to see the butterflies pollinating the plants for it por-
tends future sustenance. In many songs, the katsinas describe how such a
sight prompts people to go along dancing in their fields.

12. *Masawkatsìntawi₁*
(Curtis Burlin 392, Cylinder 3698, Track 19; IUATM)

Naanawiniwa.₂
Uma₃ ikwatshòoyam₄ mamanhoyamu,₅
uma umunay₆ uuyiyat₇ áwi'i.₈
Aw₉ úmuyu₁₀ őkiqw'ö,₁₁

1. *masawkatsìntawi* 'Màasaw katsina song (*masawkatsìntawi*)'.
2. = *nanawiniwa* 'it is being planned'.
3. *uma* 'you (plural)'.
4. = *ikwatshòoyam* 'my little friends' (plural of *ikwatshoya*).
5. = *mamanhòoyam* 'little girls' (plural of *manàwya*).
6. *umunay*, object form of *umuna* 'your (plural) father'.
7. *uuyiyat*, object form of *uuyi'at* 'his planted field'.
8. = *aw'i*, pausal form of *aw* 'to it, to there'.
9. *aw* 'to it, to there'.
10. = *umuy*, object form of *uma* 'you (plural)'. This is the subject of the following verb (*öki*) but is in object form because of the adverbial status of the clause, "when you get there."
11. *őkiqw'ö*, subordinate clause pausal form of *öki* 'arrive, come, get there, reach a destination (plural)'.

pàapu'uuyi'ata,$_{12}$ kawayvatnga,$_{13}$ melooni$_{14}$ naakyasoniwa.$_{15}$
Pu'$_{16}$ kur$_{17}$ hapi$_{18}$ tawaktsi'uyi'ata,$_{19}$ kokom'uyiyata$_{20}$ nuvawvaqòltiqö'ö,$_{21}$
ang$_{22}$ uma hàalaykyangw$_{23}$ yaayatimani,$_{24}$
tuvevoli- -volimanatu.$_{25}$
Ahaa iihiiy.
Mee, meey aa'a aa ahay'a.
Hay'a hay'a hay'aa haay'a.

It is being planned.
You, my little friends, little girls,
you go to your father's planted field.
When you get there,
his pod bean plants, watermelons, and muskmelons look reticent.
Then it turns out that his sweet corn and dark red corn plants have
    become an area of mature corn,
and you will go along it frolicking happily,
you butterfly maidens of various colors.
(Vocables of the sound of singing.)

The Màasaw katsinas (*Masawkatsinam*) appear after the Home dance
(*Nimàntikive*), when the fruits of the field are beginning to ripen. In this
song the katsinas are talking to the girls, telling them that plans are being
made for them to go to their father's fields. There they will see that the
pod bean plants, the watermelons, and the muskmelons look reticent, a
way of saying that they are only in a nascent stage of growth. In contrast,
they observe that the sweet corn and dark red corn plants already have

---

12. = *pàapu'uyi'at* 'his pod bean plants'.
13. *kawayvatnga* 'watermelon'.
14. *melooni* 'muskmelon' (from Spanish *melón*).
15. *naakyasoniwa* 'look reticent, reserved'.
16. *pu'* 'now, then'.
17. *kur,* modal of inference.
18. *hapi* 'truly, surely, certainly'; *kur hapi* 'it turns out that'.
19. = *tawaktsi'uyi'at* 'his sweet corn plants'.
20. = *kokom'uyiyat,* object form of *kokom'uyi'at* 'his dark red corn plants'.
21. = *nuvawvaqòltiqw'ö,* subordinate clause pausal form of *nuvawvaqòlti* 'become an area of mature corn'.
22. *ang* 'along it, along there, in that area, in several places'.
23. *hàalaykyangw* 'while being happy, happily'.
24. *yaayatimani* 'will go along teasing, frolicking'.
25. = *tuvevolmamant* 'butterfly maidens of various colors'.

mature ears on them. The katsinas predict that this sight will make the girls go among the plants joyfully.

It is notable that the songs mention plants in various stages of growth. Hopis celebrate the passage from one stage of growth to another, from birth, through adolescence, to adulthood and old age. The early developing stages of life, as shown by the buds on these bean and melon plants, portend the promise of new life. The stage of mature, ripe corn is a sign of sustenance assured. The katsinas call the girls butterfly maidens of various colors, metaphorically suggesting that they are like the growing plants, beautiful with the signs of vitality and the promise of future life.

13. *Qöqlökatsìntawi$_1$*
(Curtis Burlin 392, Cylinder 3687, Track 13; IUATM)

Haa'o,$_2$ haa'o ínamu.$_3$
Yep$_4$ uma,$_5$
yep uma sonwakw$_6$ pitsangwat$_7$ natwanlawu,$_8$
ínamu.
Piw$_9$ ayó$_{10}$ talvewi$_{11}$ pöötavit$_{12}$ puuhutaqö'ö,$_{13}$
put$_{14}$ ánawit$_{15}$ wuupat$_{16}$ qatsi'nangwat$_{17}$ naavokyawintiwni.$_{18}$

1. *qöqlökatsìntawi* 'katsina song of the Qööqöqlöm'. The Qööqöqlöm are the katsinas who open the kivas for katsinas at the time of the Winter Solstice ceremony (*Soyalangw*).
2. *haa'o,* vocative particle.
3. = *inam* 'my fathers'.
4. *yep* 'here'.
5. *uma* 'you (plural)'.
6. *sonwakw,* object form of *sonway* 'beautiful'.
7. *pitsangwat,* object form of *pitsangwa* 'countenance'.
8. = *natwanlawu* 'keep pursuing life-promoting practices, customs related to the rejuvenation of life'.
9. *piw* 'also, too, again'.
10. = *ayó'* 'to, toward over there'.
11. *talvewi* 'toward the direction of the sunrise'.
12. *pöötavit,* object form of *pöötavi* 'consecrated path'.
13. = *puuhutaqw'ö,* subordinate clause pausal form of *puuhuta* 'renew'.
14. *put,* object form of *pam* 'that, that one, he, she, it'.
15. *ánawit* 'along its course'.
16. *wuupat,* object form of *wuupa* 'long, tall'.
17. *qatsi'nangwat,* object form of *qatsi'nangwa* 'will to live'.
18. *naavokyawintiwni* 'fulfillment will be enjoyed by all'.

Piw hapi₁₉ paavönmanatuy₂₀ tímokimuyatuy₂₁ naavokyawintiwni.
Yansa₂₂ ùu'unangwvasiy₂₃ yuuyahiwa,₂₄
yánga'a.₂₅
Pew₂₆ umumi₂₇ kuukuyivani,₂₈
oomawutu.₂₉
Yoo- yoyhoyoyotani.₃₀
Yoo- yoy'umumutani,₃₁
humi'uyisonaqa.₃₂
Amunawita₃₃ paatalawvaqö'ö,₃₄
hàalay'unangway₃₅ taayimuyiwni.₃₆
Aa haay aa aahay a'haha iihii hii.

Hark, o my fathers.
Here you,
here you keep practicing the rejuvenation of life for a beautiful countenance,
my fathers.
Also when you renew the consecrated path toward the direction of the
sunrise,
along that, there will be fulfillment of the will to live a long life to be
enjoyed by all.

19. *hapi* 'truly, surely, certainly'.
20. = *paavönmamàntuy*, object form of *paavönmamant* 'young corn plants'.
21. *tímokimuyatuy*, object form of *tímokimat* 'their young corn ears on the stalk'.
22. *yansa* 'only in this way'.
23. = *ùu'unangwvàasiy*, object form of *ùu'unangwvàasi* 'your heartfelt wish, hope, prayer'.
24. *yuuyahiwa* 'have been dressed as for a ceremony, be adorned (plural)'. Here this word
    means 'practice', with 'your prayers' as object.
25. = *yang'a*, pausal form of *yang* 'here, along here'. In this context *yang* refers to keeping
    on doing something season to season.
26. *pew* 'toward here, coming this way'.
27. *umumi* 'to you (plural)'.
28. = *kuukuyvani* 'will appear, come into sight (plural)'.
29. = *oo'omawt* 'clouds'.
30. *yoyhoyoyotani* 'will be moving as rain'.
31. *yoy'umumutani* 'will be thundering'.
32. = *humi'uysonaq* 'throughout the midst the area(s) planted with corn'.
33. = *amunawit* 'along them, along their course'.
34. = *paatalawvaqw'ö*, subordinate clause pausal form of *paatalawva* 'come to glisten with
    water'.
35. *hàalay'unangway* 'with happy hearts, with beneficent intentions'.
36. *taayimuyiwni* 'will look in awe'.

The ears on the stalks of the young corn plants will also be a fulfillment
    to be enjoyed by all.
Only in this way do you practice your heartfelt prayers
from season to season.
Toward here for you the clouds will make their appearance.
They will be moving as rain, as rain.
They will be thundering, thundering,
throughout the midst of the corn-planted fields.
When it glistens with water along their course,
[you] will look in awe with happy hearts.
(Vocables of the sound of singing.)

This is a particularly poignant song, full of advice and encouragement
from the *Qöqlöm,* who open the kivas for the katsinas at the Winter
Solstice ceremony (*Soyalangw*). Their caring tone sets the stage for the
katsinas to return to help the people during a new agricultural season. The
katsinas observe that the people have been praying earnestly and living
right, following all the daily and ritual practices that contribute to the
survival of their community. All of these principles of moral living and
sharing and caring activities are embodied in *natwani,* the life-promoting
practices related to the rejuvenation of life. Such renewal does not simply
occur with pollination, procreation and growth to maturity. It also has to
do with having the moral fiber to suffer through adversity and to work
hard and persist in accepting the burden of the roles and responsibilities
to kin and clan that every individual acquires through birth as well as
through membership in religious societies. The essence of such a life plan,
preordained at Emergence, has a beauty of purpose and vitality that is
metaphorically described as having the countenance of blooming plants,
growing children, fluttering butterflies, flowing corn silk, and thundering
rain. This state of pristine perfection is not primarily an outward quality,
but rather an inner state of fulfillment that one attains when one practices
all the beliefs, teachings and rituals of the Hopi lifeway.

The katsinas promise that when the fathers renew the consecrated
path in the direction of the sunrise, everyone will enjoy the fulfillment of
life. In most songs the consecrated path refers to the path of consecrated
cornmeal and prayer feathers along which the katsinas enter and exit the
village. However, in this song, it refers to the path of a life lived by corn.
Those who have dedicated themselves to live by this path constantly strive
to practice the daily obligations and religious rituals that maintain this life.

The katsinas come to encourage the people to constantly strive to reenergize their commitment to live the communal corn-based lifeway. Thus in this song, renewing the consecrated path toward the direction of the sunrise refers to the necessity for everyone to give constant attention to practices that renew life. Every dawn (*taalawva*) of a new day is metaphorically a rebirth of life. When people live by the principles and practices that lead to the continual revitalization of life, the katsinas promise that everyone will have a fulfilled life. The katsinas then metaphorically describe this fulfillment. The ears on the stalks of the young corn plants are metaphors for the new life that will come when the young girls, who are blossoming with the promise of motherhood, grow to maturity and have children of their own.

The katsinas then enjoin the people to make sincere and heartfelt prayers for the rain, for only in this way will the rain come that will enable everyone to enjoy fulfillment. The song ends with the katsinas' promise, implicit but clear, that when the people live by the tenets of the Hopi lifeway, the clouds will arrive thundering in rain. They will provide their gift of water that will make the planted fields glisten, a sight that will make the people deeply thankful.

14. Sa'lakwmanàwyat₁ Taawi'am₂
(Curtis Burlin 392, Cylinder 3686, Track 12; IUATM)

Aaha iihi.
Ítamu₃ naatuwanlawu,₄
ayám₅ atkya₆ Tuuwanasave'e.₇

1. *Sa'lakwmanàwyat* '(two) little Sa'lako maidens'.
2. *taawi'am* 'their song'.
3. = *itam* 'we'.
4. = *natwanlawu* 'keep pursuing life-promoting practices, customs related to the rejuvenation of life'.
5. *ayám* 'over there'.
6. *atkya* 'down, down there, down below'.
7. *Tuuwanasave'e,* pausal form of *Tuuwanasave* 'at *Tuuwanasavi* (the Hopi lands)'.

Tuvevolimanatu$_8$ nana'löngöt$_9$ qaaqa'öt$_{10}$ síngumanyuuyuwinaya.$_{11}$
Nana'alöngöta$_{12}$ oomawuy$_{13}$ yooyangwuy$_{14}$ talawiptuveniy$_{15}$ umungem$_{16}$
naatuwanlawu.$_{17}$
Suvuyoysonaqa$_{18}$ paavönmanatu$_{19}$ oomi$_{20}$ naawungwina,$_{21}$
péwi'i.$_{22}$
Mee aayay holi holi holiwliyawiy'aa.

(Vocables of the sound of singing.)
We keep practicing rejuvenation of life
over there down below at *Tuuwanasavi.*
The butterfly maidens of various colors dance with the pollen of the
different kinds of corn.
[We] keep doing life-sustaining practices for you with the different kinds
of clouds, rain, and depictions of lightning.
In the gentle rain, the young corn plants are making themselves grow
upward,
coming this way.
(Vocables.)

This song is sung during the performance of two marionette Sa'lako katsina maidens at a night dance in the kiva during the winter months after
Powayuma, the Bean dance. The katsinas begin by saying that they are rejuvenating life at *Tuuwanasavi,* which, in this song, refers to all the Hopi
lands—lands for cultivation as well as lands for gathering and hunting.

8. = *tuvevolmamant* 'butterfly maidens of various colors'.
9. *nana'löngöt,* object form of *nana'löngö* 'of different kinds'.
10. *qaaqa'öt,* object form of *qaaqa'ö* 'different kinds of dry ears of corn'. This is the
    distributive of *qaa'ö* 'corn, dry ear(s) of corn'.
11. = *síngumanyuyuwinaya* 'be dancing with pollen (plural)'.
12. = *nana'löngöt,* object form of *nana'löngö* 'of different kinds'.
13. *oomawuy,* object form of *oomaw* 'cloud'.
14. *yooyangwuy,* object form of *yooyangw* 'rain'.
15. = *itàatalwiptutuveniy,* object form of *itàatalwiptutuveni* 'our depictions of lightning'.
16. *umungem* 'for you (plural), for your benefit'.
17. = *natwanlawu* 'keep pursuing life-promoting practices, customs related to the
    rejuvenation of life'.
18. = *suvuyoysonaq* 'in the steady drizzle, through the gentle rain'.
19. = *paavönmamant* 'young corn plants'.
20. *oomi* 'upward'.
21. = *naawungwnaya* 'make selves grow'.
22. = *pew'i,* pausal form of *pew* 'toward here, coming this way'.

The katsinas describe this rejuvenation in terms of the pollinating activities of the butterflies, described as butterfly maidens of various colors (*tuvevolmamant*). The flitting of the butterflies from flower to flower is described as dancing with the pollen (*síngumanyuyuwinaya*) of the different kinds of corn (*nana'löngö qaaqa'ö*), a reference to corn of different colors. The mention of color emphasizes the beauty that characterizes the perfect pristine life to which everyone aspires. It also may relate to the reference to the different kinds of clouds, rain, and lightning mentioned in the next line. This implies that the rain is coming from the different cardinal directions, each of which is associated with a different color.

The katsinas reiterate that they are doing life-sustaining practices with clouds, rain, and lightning to nourish the plants and people. In Hopi belief, lightning fertilizes everything it strikes. In the fifteenth century murals from Awat'ovi and Kawàyka'a, zigzag lines of lightning are depicted vertically striking the "sand altar" (*tuuwapongya*) as well as tops of corn ears "planted" in it (Smith 1952: Figs. 81b and 76a respectively). All of these fertilizing and nourishing practices are understood to be life-sustaining. They are the gifts of the katsinas in return for right living and heartfelt prayers on the part of the people.

The katsinas close mentioning the gentle rain that comes in the early spring and summer to nurture the young corn plants. As volitional beings, the corn plants are taking the rain and making themselves grow upward.

15. *Si'ohemiskatsìntawi,*
(Curtis Burlin 392, Cylinder 3699, Track 20; IUATM)

Ítamu₂ tiitiwuniwa,₃
ayo'o.₄
Naalönaanan'ivo₅ omaw'inakway₆ yoywawayitiwa,₇

1. *si'ohemiskatsìntawi* 'Zuni Hemiskatsina song'.
2. = *itam* 'we'.
3. *tiitiwuniwa* 'have been asked to (come and) dance'.
4. *ayo'o*, pausal form of *ayó'* 'to, toward over there'.
5. = *nalönanan'ivo* 'to the four directions'.
6. = *oomaw'inakway*, object form of *oomaw'inakwa* 'the down feathers worn on my head'.
7. *yoywangwaytiwa* 'have been earnestly requesting (them) to come as rain'.

sakwavaahomanatu.[8]
Aahaa ihiiy.
Puma[9] *pew*[10] *námura*[11] *yoo- yoy'umumutoyani,*[12]
péwi'i.[13]
Uuyisonaqa[14] *yánga'a,*[15]
paavataalawinani,[16]
tuu- tuuwapongyanawita.[17]
Paatuwataviyani.[18]
Haa haa ha'ay aaha iihii.
Hapi me.[19]
Toko'omawtiyotu[20] *talawipiy*[21] *yoynanatuwniwa;*[22]
ayangqö[23] *tuuwaytalawvangaqö,*[24]
aaha iihii,
paatuwataviyani.

We have been asked to come and dance
(from) over there.
To the four directions, the blue/green prayer feather maidens
are calling for the down feathers worn on my head to come as rain.
(Vocables of the sound of singing.)
Let them come making it thunder
coming this way.
In the midst of the planted fields along here,
they will make it glisten with puddles of water

8. = *sakwavahomamant* 'blue/green prayer feather maidens'.
9. *puma* 'they'.
10. *pew* 'toward here, coming this way'.
11. *námura* 'let it be so'.
12. = *yoy'umumutoynani* 'will make it be thundering'.
13. = *pew'i,* pausal form of *pew* 'toward here, coming this way'.
14. = *uysonaq* 'throughout the midst of the planted area(s)'.
15. = *yang'a,* pausal form of *yang* 'here, along here, in these places, in this area'.
16. = *paavatalawnani* 'will make it glisten with puddles of water'.
17. = *tuuwapongyanawit* 'along the land'.
18. = *paatuwatapyani* 'will lay water on the land (plural)'.
19. *hapi me,* formulaic expression introducing the song's second part, *oomi* 'upward'.
20. = *toko'omawtotim* 'dark billowing cloud boys'.
21. = *talwipiy,* object form of *talwipi'am* 'their lightning'.
22. = *yoynanatuwniwa* 'be practicing the skill of rain'.
23. = *ayángqw* 'from over there'.
24. = *tuuwaytalawvangaqw* 'from where the first light of day is still out of sight'.

along the land.
They will lay water on the land.
(Vocables of the sound of singing.)
Listen, there is more.
The dark billowing cloud boys are rehearsing their rain skills by flashing
    lightning
over there where the first light of day is still out of sight,
(vocables of the sound of singing),
and they will lay water upon the land.

The katsinas describe how they have been asked to come perform "over there" at some unspecified village. They describe how the people have invested their blue/green prayer feather maidens, that is, their prayer feathers, with fervent prayers for rain that they have sent to the katsinas in the four cardinal directions. They liken the down feathers tied to the tops of their head (*oomaw'inakwa*) that bounce up and down as the katsinas dance to the movement of the clouds as they build and travel to the planted fields. The katsinas predict (*námura* 'let it be so') that, if the people's prayers are deserving, the clouds will make it thunder as it rains along the planted fields, making them glisten with puddles of water. The word *paavatalawna* (from *paahu* 'water' and *taala* 'light') focuses on the sense of sparkling brightness that one sees on looking at the puddles on the land after a rain, likening this to the light of a new day that brings new life. The word for the land, *tuuwapongya,* "sand altar," emphasizes the reverence and respect with which the Hopis regard the land.

After formulaic *hapi me,* the katsinas describe how the billowing clouds, *toko'omawtotim,* the "cloud boys," are making rain and lightning. The fact that they are rehearsing suggests that the clouds are repeatedly making lightning. *Talwìipi* 'for lightning to flash' is literally "fling out (*-wìipi*) light (*tal-*)." This idea is created visually in the performance by accordion-like lightning frames that are shot out by a katsina. All this activity of making lightning is said to be happening out of sight, that is, before dawn, as expressed by the word *tuuwaytalawvangaqw* 'from where the first light of day is still out of sight' (*tuuwayi* 'a place out of sight' [*tuuway-*], *taalawva* 'become light' [*-talawva*], *-ngaqw* 'from'). The katsinas close by promising that the clouds will lay water on the land.

16. Si'ohemiskatsìntawi$_1$
(Curtis Burlin 392, Cylinder 3680, Track 6; IUATM)

Ítamu$_2$ tiitiwuniwa,$_3$
ayo'o.$_4$
Nalönaanan'ivo'o,$_5$
oomaw'inakway$_6$ yoywawayitiwa,$_7$
sakwavahomanatu.$_8$
Aahaa iihii.
Puma$_9$ pew$_{10}$ námura$_{11}$ yoo- yoy'umumutoyani,$_{12}$
péwi'i.$_{13}$
Uuyisonaqa$_{14}$ yánga'a,$_{15}$
paavataalawinani'i,$_{16}$
tuuwapongyanawita.$_{17}$
Aahayii aaha iihii aaha iihi.
Hapi me.$_{18}$
Toko'omawtiyotu$_{19}$ yoytalawipiy$_{20}$ yoynanatuwtiwa,$_{21}$
ayangqö$_{22}$ kuwantalawvangaqö.$_{23}$

1. *si'ohemiskatsìntawi* 'Zuni Hemiskatsina song'.
2. = *itam* 'we'.
3. *tiitiwuniwa* 'have been asked to (come and) dance'.
4. *ayo'o,* pausal form of *ayó'* 'to, toward over there'.
5. = *nalönanan'ivo'o,* pausal form of *nalönanan'ivo* 'to the four directions'.
6. *oomaw'inakway,* object form of *oomaw'inakwa* 'the down feathers worn on my head'.
7. = *yoywangwaytiwa* 'be earnestly requesting (them) to come as rain'.
8. = *sakwavahomamant* 'blue/green prayer feather maidens'.
9. *puma* 'they'.
10. *pew* 'toward here, coming this way'.
11. *námura* 'let it be so'.
12. = *yoy'umumutoynani* 'will make it be thundering'.
13. = *pew'i,* pausal form of *pew* 'toward here, coming this way'.
14. = *uysonaq* 'throughout the midst of the planted area(s)'.
15. = *yang'a,* pausal form of *yang* 'here, along here, in these places, in this area'.
16. = *paavatalawnani* 'will make it glisten with puddles of water'.
17. = *tuuwapongyanawit* 'along the land'.
18. *hapi me,* formulaic expression introducing the song's second part, *oomi* 'upward'.
19. = *toko'omawtotim* 'dark billowing cloud boys'.
20. = *yòytalwipiy,* object form of *yòytalwipi'am* 'their lightning in the rain'.
21. = *yoynanatuwniwa* 'be practicing the skill of rain'.
22. = *ayángqw* 'from over there'.
23. = *kuwantalawvangaqw* 'from the colorful beginning of the day (dawn)'.

We have been asked to come and dance
(from) over there.
To the four directions,
the blue/green prayer feather maidens
are calling for the down feathers worn on my head to come as rain.
(Vocables of the sound of singing.)
Let them come thundering,
coming this way.
In the midst of the plantings along here,
they will make it glisten with puddles of water
along the land.
(Vocables of the sound of singing.)
Listen, there is more.
The dark billowing cloud boys are practicing their skills of making rain
 and flashing lightning,
from the colorful beginning of the day.

This is almost the same song as Song 15 except that it is less complete
and has a few word changes. It was recorded earlier than Song 15. Perhaps after the singer sang it, he was able to remember more of the words
and so asked to sing it again. The more complete version, Song 15, is the
result.

17. *Kur Himuwa Katsìntawi*[1]
(Curtis Burlin 391, Cylinder 3666, Track 14; IUATM)

Sikyavoĺimanatu,[2] *sakwavoĺimanatu,*[3]
puma[4] *yang*[5] *heesita,*[6] *tsorosita*[7] *sìiqölöva*[8] *puyayatani.*[9]
Haay ahaa haay'a.

1. *kur himuwa katsìntawi* 'don't-know-which-one katsina song'. The katsina who performed
   this song has not been identified.
2. = *sikyavolmamant* 'yellow butterfly maidens'.
3. = *sakwavolmamant* 'blue/green butterfly maidens'.
4. *puma* 'they'.
5. *yang* 'here, along here, in this area'.
6. = *heesit*, object form of *heesi* 'mariposa lily/lilies'.
7. = *tsorosit*, object form of *tsorosi* 'blue aster(s)'.
8. = *sìiqòlpa* 'in, along the flowery expanse(s)'.
9. *puyayatani* 'will be flapping, fluttering'.

Kaway'uyita$_{10}$ *sìiqölnawita*$_{11}$ *kuwanvuyayatani,*$_{12}$
tuvevolimanatu.$_{13}$
Melon'uyita$_{14}$ *sìiqölnawita kuwanvuyayatani,*
tuvevolimanatu.

The yellow butterfly maidens and the blue/green butterfly maidens,
they will be fluttering along here in the flowery expanse of mariposa lilies
and blue asters.
(Vocables.)
The butterfly maidens of various colors
will be fluttering colorfully along the flowery expanse of watermelon
plants,
The butterfly maidens of various colors
will be fluttering colorfully along the flowery expanse of muskmelon
plants.

This song celebrates the pristine beauty of the ideal world where all life
flourishes. This idea is represented by the yellow butterfly maidens and
the blue/green butterfly maidens who are fluttering about among the fields
of mariposa lilies and blue asters, as well as among the planted fields of
flowering watermelon and muskmelon plants. The butterflies are cast as
colorful maidens to enhance the reference to young girls who are growing
in beauty as they grow in the potential to produce new life. The reference
to many colors acknowledges the colors of the four directions from which
the rains come to nurture this new life. The pollination activity as the
butterflies move from flower to flower is a metaphor for the renewal of
life.

10. = *kaway'uyit*, object form of *kaway'uyi* 'watermelon plant(s)'.
11. = *sìiqölnawit* 'along the flowery expanse'.
12. *kuwanvuyayatani* 'will be flapping, fluttering colorfully'.
13. = *tuvevolmamant* 'butterfly maidens of various colors'.
14. = *melon'uyit*, object form of *melon'uyi* 'muskmelon plant(s)'.

18. *Kur Himuwa Katsìntawi*[1]
(Curtis Burlin 393, Cylinder 3710, Track 6; IUAT1M)

Sikyavolimanatu,[2] sakwavolimanatu,[3]
puma[4] yang[5] heesit[6] tsorosita[7] síqölöva[8] puyayatani.[9]
Mee.[10]
Ahay haa'ay yahiy'a.
Kaway'uyita[11] sìiqölnawita[12] kuwanvuyayatani,[13]
tuvevolimanatu.[14]
Melon'uyita[15] sìiqölnawita kuwanvuyayatani,
tuvevolimanatu.
Mee.
Ahay haa'ay yahiy'a.

The yellow butterfly maidens and the blue/green butterfly maidens,
they will be fluttering along here in the flowery expanses of mariposa
lilies and blue asters.
Listen,
(Vocables of the sound of singing.)
The butterfly maidens of various colors,
will be fluttering colorfully along the flowery expanses of watermelon
plants.
The butterfly maidens of various colors,
will be fluttering colorfully along the flowery expanses of muskmelon
plants.

1. *kur himuwa katsìntawi* 'don't-know-which-one katsina song'. The katsina who performed this song has not been identified.
2. = *sikyavolmamant* 'yellow butterfly maidens'.
3. = *sakwavolmamant* 'blue/green butterfly maidens'.
4. *puma* 'they'.
5. *yang* 'along here, in this area'.
6. *heesit,* object form of *heesi* 'mariposa lily/lilies'.
7. = *tsorosit,* object form of *tsorosi* 'blue aster(s)'.
8. = *sìiqòlpa* 'in, along the expanse(s) of flowers'.
9. *puyayatani* 'will be flapping, fluttering'.
10. = *me* 'listen', a particle to direct the attention.
11. = *kaway'uyit,* object form of *kaway'uyi* 'watermelon plant(s)'.
12. = *sìiqölnawit* 'along the flowery expanse(s)'.
13. *kuwanvuyayatani* 'will be fluttering colorfully'.
14. = *tuvevolmamant* 'butterfly maidens of various colors'.
15. = *melon'uyit,* object form of *melon'uyi* 'muskmelon plant(s)'.

Listen.
(Vocables of the sound of singing.)

This is the same as Song 17 except for some differences in vocables.

19. *Kur Himuwa Katsìntawi$_1$*
(Curtis Burlin 391, Cylinder 3661, Track 9; IUATM)

Sikya'oomaw,$_2$ pala'omaw'u,$_3$
puma$_4$ pew$_5$ kuukuyivani.$_6$
Sakwa'omaw,$_7$ qöya'omaw'u,$_8$
puma pew kuukuyivani.
Puma pew yoynaanakwusani,$_9$
pew yoo- yoyhoyoyotani.$_{10}$
"Uuyisonaqa$_{11}$ yooki.$_{12}$
"Aa ayahi aa ayahi."

The yellow clouds and red clouds,
they will make their appearance coming this way.
The blue/green clouds and white clouds,
they will make their appearance coming this way.
They will start coming this way on their journey as rain,
and will come moving as rain.
[You'll be saying,] "It rained in the midst of the planted fields.
"(Vocables of the sound of singing.)"

---

1. *kur himuwa katsìntawi* 'don't-know-which-one katsina song'. The katsina who performed this song has not been identified.
2. = *sikya'omaw* 'yellow cloud'. The words for the clouds in the song are in singular form but represent many clouds in a collective sense.
3. *pala'omaw'u,* pausal form of *pala'omaw* 'red cloud'.
4. *puma* 'they'.
5. *pew* 'toward here, coming this way'.
6. = *kuukuyvani* 'will appear, will make their appearance, will come into view'.
7. *sakwa'omaw* 'blue/green cloud'.
8. *qöya'omaw'u,* pausal form of *qöya'omaw* 'white cloud'.
9. = *yoynànkwusani* 'will start on a journey as rain'.
10. *yoyhoyoyotani* 'will be moving as rain'.
11. = *uysonaq* 'throughout the midst of the planted area(s)'.
12. *yooki* 'rain' (verb).

This song celebrates the rain that comes from the four cardinal directions by describing how the clouds of all colors are making their appearance and moving "this way" toward the villages. The verb *kuukuyva* 'emerge, come into view' is used in song to convey the idea that as the clouds appear over the horizon, they are showing themselves to the people. The people anxiously await the first appearance of the clouds because they portend the rain that will follow.

The colors are named in opposite pairs and are enumerated in counterclockwise fashion beginning with the northwest. Thus the yellow clouds from the northwest are paired with the red clouds from the southeast and the blue/green clouds from the southwest are paired with the white clouds from the northeast. When all this rain appears, the katsinas, speaking as if for the people, comment that they will observe that it rained throughout their planted fields.

Part II: Library of Congress (LoC)
(Identified as "Natalie Curtis Burlin 1903 Songs 8708.")

20. *Kookopòltawi*[1]
(Curtis Burlin 286, Track 21; LoC)

Kookopölölö,
Kookopölölö siwahopmangu'iwta.[2]
Nu'[3] *ókiwa.*[4]
Haqaqw[5] *nu' alòngkingaqw*[6] *—(inaudible)— qatsit*[7] *tunatyawta.*[8]
Yan[9] *nu' ókiwa tunatyawkyango*[10] *nu' tuutunopnangwu.*[11]
Haa yaa loloosi.

1. *kookopòltawi* 'Kookopölö song'.
2. *siwahopmangu'iwta* 'be tired of bachelorhood'.
3. *nu'* 'I'.
4. = *okiw* 'humbly, pitifully'.
5. *haqaqw* 'from/inside somewhere'.
6. *alòngkingaqw* 'from or inside a house belonging to someone who is not a relative'.
7. *qatsit*, object form of *qatsi* 'life'.
8. *tunatyawta* 'nurture hope for'.
9. *yan* 'like this, in this way, thus'.
10. = *tunatyawkyangw* 'while nurturing hope'.
11. *tuutunopnangwu*, habitual tense form of *tuutunopna* 'be feeding the spirits'.

Kookopölö,
Kookopölö is tired of being a bachelor.
Poor me!
In someone else's house somewhere I nurture hope for —(*inaudible*)—
life.
Thus while I humbly nurture hopes, I feed the spirits.
(Vocables.)

The Kookopölö katsina is chiding those men who remain single. In Hopi practice, men continue to live in their mother's house until they marry. In this song, the katsina represents a man who, tired of being single, is hoping to move to a house that does not belong to one of his clan relatives, that is, a house that is not his mother's house or one of his clan sisters' houses. This refers to the Hopi stipulation that you do not marry someone of your own clan. However, while he is still living at a house belonging to someone of his own clan, he "feeds the spirits" (*tuutunopna*), perhaps meaning that by this practice he will find someone to marry. The practice of *tuutunopna* refers to the custom of putting aside a pinch of food from one's plate as a prayer before eating.

21. *Palhikwmamantuy*₁ *Taawi'am*₂
(Curtis Burlin 286, Track 29; LoC)

*Itam*₃ *yuuyahiwa,*₄
*ayamo.*₅
Itam yuuyahiwa,
ayamo,
*ayám*₆ *taavang*₇ *omàwkive'e.*₈
—(*inaudible*)—

1. *Palhikwmamantuy,* object form of *Palhikwmamant* 'Moisture Drinking Maidens'.
2. *taawi'am* 'their song'.
3. *itam* 'we'.
4. *yuuyahiwa* 'have been dressed as for a ceremony, be adorned (plural)'.
5. *ayamo,* pausal form of *ayám* 'over there'.
6. *ayám* 'over there'.
7. *taavang* 'in the southwest'.
8. *oomàwkive'e,* pausal form of *oomàwkive* 'at the dwelling place of the clouds'.

We have been adorned,
over there.
We have been adorned,
over there,
over there at the dwelling place of clouds in the southwest.
—(*inaudible*)—

This song fragment is sung by katsinas who are Moisture-Drinking Maidens, metaphors for butterflies that drink the nectar from the flowers as they pollinate them. The katsinas say they have been adorned over at their cloud homes in the southwest, meaning that they have received the people's prayers.

22. *Kur Himuwa Katsìntawi*₁
(Curtis Burlin 286, Track 18; LoC)

Pay₂ sonway₃ taalawkuyiva.₄
Angwu₅ huvam₆ talahoyiwa,₇
tootimu.₈

A beautiful new day has made its appearance.
Boys,
wake up, in anticipation.

This song fragment describes the dawning of a beautiful new day. The katsinas direct the Hopi boys to wake up, presumably so that they will run to greet the dawn.

1. *kur himuwa katsìntawi* 'don't-know-which-one katsina song'. The katsina who performed this song has not been identified.
2. *pay,* expressive particle.
3. *sonway* 'beautiful'.
4. = *taalawkuyva* 'for daylight to make its appearance'.
5. *angwu* 'in anticipation of, beforehand, ahead of time'.
6. *huvam,* hortative particle.
7. *talahoyiwa* 'awaken for the new day'.
8. = *tootim* 'boys'.

Songs Recorded by Samuel Barrett in 1911

23. *Angaktsìntawi*[1]
(Barrett Song 26, 8901, Track 2; LoC)

Soosonkiwa.[2]
Aayamo[3] *taavang*[4] *oomawkiva 'a,*[5]
yuuyahiwa.[6]
Puma[7]*pew*[8]*kwakwha 'unangway*[9]*taayimakyangw*[10]*yooynaanakwusaani.*[11]
Yooki,[12] *yooki.*
Antsa[13] *uma*[14] *yang*[15] *töötökimakyangw*[16] *sonkiwa.*[17]

Pleasing things have been going on.
Over there in the southwest, along the dwelling place of the clouds,
they have been adorned.
With tranquil hearts, coming with anticipation, they will set out on their
   journey as rain.
It rains and rains.
Truly you are pleased while going along here shouting for joy.

1. *angaktsìntawi* 'Long-Hair katsina song'.
2. = *sosonkiwa* 'be pleasing'.
3. = *ayám* 'over there'.
4. *taavang* 'in the southwest'.
5. = *oomàwkiva 'a,* pausal form of *oomàwkiva* 'along the dwelling place of the clouds'.
6. *yuuyahiwa* 'have been dressed as for a ceremony, be adorned (plural)'.
7. *puma* 'they'.
8. *pew* 'toward here, coming this way'.
9. *kwakwha 'unangway* 'with tranquil hearts, with beneficent intentions'.
10. = *taymakyangw* 'while going along looking'. The combination *pew tayma* means 'be coming with anticipation, expectation, intention'.
11. = *yoynànkwusani* 'will start on a journey as rain'.
12. *yooki* 'rain' (verb).
13. *antsa* 'truly, really, indeed'.
14. *uma* 'you (plural)'.
15. *yang* 'along here, in these places, in this area'.
16. *töötökimakyangw* 'while going along making calls, sounds'.
17. = *sosonkiwa* 'be pleasing'.

The katsinas are describing how the clouds have been adorned with the essence of rain in their dwelling place in the southwest. They describe these preparations as pleasing, for the katsinas are looking forward to journeying to the Hopi villages with their gift of rain. The katsinas assure the people that the clouds are coming with tranquil hearts because they have been "going along looking," monitoring the people's behavior to be certain that the people deserve their gifts. The katsinas describe the results of the coming of the clouds: "It rains and rains." Then, the katsinas describe how the people will be happy because they have come as rain. It should be noted that many of the practices and details of the reciprocal practices of the people and the gifts of the katsinas often remain implied and unstated in song since every Hopi knows what is expected of him.

24. *Angaktsìntawi*$_1$
(Barrett 8901, Tracks 5–6; LoC)

Nalönaanan 'ivaqö,$_2$—
Ínamu,$_3$
úma 'a,$_4$
yep$_5$ *tapkinaya.*$_6$
Taaqavaahomongwitu,$_7$
ínamu,
úma 'a,
yep naawakinaya.$_8$
Naalönaanan 'ivaqö$_9$ *qöyapaw 'oomaw*$_{10}$ *umumi,*$_{11}$

1. *angaktsìntawi* 'Long-Hair katsina song'.
2. = *nalönanan 'ivaqw* 'from the four directions'. This word is apparently a false start; it correctly begins a later part of the song.
3. = *inam* 'my fathers'.
4. *úma 'a,* pausal form of *uma* 'you (plural)'.
5. *yep* 'here'.
6. *tapkinaya* 'make it to the end of the day (plural)'.
7. = *taqvahomomngwit* 'men who make the prayer feathers'.
8. = *naanawakna* 'pray (plural)'.
9. = *nalönanan 'ivaqw* 'from the four directions'.
10. = *qöyapaw 'omaw* 'low-lying white cloud(s)'.
11. *umumi* 'to you (plural)'.

kwaakwaviwmakyango$_{12}$ yang$_{13}$ yookinayani.$_{14}$
Ang$_{15}$ taatawyuuyuwimani.$_{16}$
Ohowa ehelo.
Hapi me.$_{17}$
Paasanawita$_{18}$ paavopkomatu$_{19}$ töökiyuuyuwinani.$_{20}$
Paasanawita tuvevolmanatu$_{21}$ töökiyuuyuwinani,
taawanawita.$_{22}$
Naalönaanan'ivaqö qöyapaw'oomaw umumi,
kwaakwaviwmakyango yang yookinayani.
Ang taatawyuuyuwimani.
Ohowa ehelo.

My fathers,
you,
you have reached the end of the day here.
You,
the men who make the prayer feathers
my fathers,
you pray here.
From the four directions toward you, the low-lying white clouds,
as they go along stacked up, they will make it rain along here.
[You] will go along there singing and dancing.
(Vocables.)
Listen, there is more.
Along the planted fields, the water creatures will dance and make their
    calls.
Along the planted fields, the butterfly maidens of various colors will
    dance and make their calls,
all day long.

12. = *kwaakwap'iwmakyangw* 'as (they) go along stacked up in several stacks'.
13. *yang* 'along here, in this area'.
14. = *yoknayani* 'will make it rain (plural)'.
15. *ang* 'along it, along there, in that area, in several places'.
16. = *taatawyuyuwmani* 'will go along dancing and singing songs'.
17. *hapi me,* formulaic expression introducing the song's second part, *oomi* 'upward'.
18. = *paasanawit* 'along the fields'.
19. = *paavopkomat* 'water creatures'.
20. = *töökiyuyuwinani* 'will be dancing while making characteristic calls'.
21. = *tuvevolmamant* 'butterfly maidens of various colors'.
22. = *taawanawit* 'all day long'.

From the four directions toward you, the low-lying white clouds,
as they go along stacked up, they will make it rain along here.
[You] will go along there singing and dancing.
(Vocables.)

The katsinas address the fathers, in this case, the men who have prepared
the prayer feathers for the katsinas, telling them that the end of the day
has come, that is, that this is the last dance of the day. At the completion
of this song, the katsina father will place a prayer feather and pinch of
cornmeal in the left hand of each katsina as they take their leave from the
dance plaza. Embedded in these prayer feathers are the final prayers of the
people that the katsinas will take with them back to their homes. The
katsinas, implicitly acknowledging that the elders in charge of the
ceremony have prayed earnestly, say that the clouds from all the directions will come as rain. They describe the low-lying white clouds (*qöyapaw 'omaw*) as going along stacked up (*kwaakwap 'iwma*), a description of
the way clouds build themselves up before a storm. The katsinas predict
that these rainstorms will reenergize the people to sing and dance in their
happiness for the renewed vitality that all this rain will bring.

In the second section of the song the katsinas make it clear that all
beings that depend on water for life, here referred to as water creatures
(*paavopkomat*), will make their calls of happiness as they enjoy the effects
of the rain throughout the planted fields. These creatures include the
butterflies ("butterfly maidens"), whose various colors are a reminder of
the beauty of new life. By invoking the maiden metaphor, the katsinas
liken the pollinating activities of butterflies with the future procreating
abilities of young girls who will grow up to become the mothers of new
generations. Finally, though butterflies do not make perceptibly audible
calls, the katsinas are using poetic license in order to express the sentiment of joy that living beings have with the coming of the rain. The
katsinas live in the perfect world and they are enjoining the people to
strive to live in a perfect way, even though in everyday life such a life can
only be metaphorically envisioned.

25. Angaktsìntawi,

(Barrett Song 29, 8902, Track 4; LoC)

Umungem$_2$ sonwakw$_3$ tal'angwyookvaqe'e,$_4$
úmuyu$_5$ lolmata.$_6$
Nuwu pa$_7$ umuu'uyiy$_8$ tala'amu$_9$ súmaatsiwyungwa.$_{10}$
Nuwu pa amunawit$_{11}$ siwi'amu$_{12}$ síwukiwyungwa.$_{13}$
Amunawit yowi'amu$_{14}$ síwukiwyungwa.
Yan$_{15}$ nu'$_{16}$ umungem naawakina.$_{17}$
Yan uma$_{18}$ naawakinaya,$_{19}$
ínamu.$_{20}$
Uní,$_{21}$ uní, uní.
Nuwu pa umuutimu$_{22}$ noonovani.$_{23}$
Nuwu pa öö'öyani.$_{24}$
Nuwu pa uma soosoyam$_{25}$ noonovani.
Ya'i hiina.
Aaho ahowiiya'a.

1. angaktsìntawi 'Long-Hair katsina song'.
2. umungem 'for you (plural), for your benefit'.
3. sonwakw 'beautifully', adverbial or object form of sonway 'beautiful'.
4. = tal'angwyokvaqe'e, subordinate clause pausal form of tal'angwyokva 'rain during the summer'.
5. = umuy, object form of uma 'you (plural)'.
6. lolmata 'beautify, restore beauty, improve the looks'.
7. nuwu pa 'just think, at last'.
8. = umùu'uyiy, object form of umùu'uyi 'your (plural) plants, planted fields'.
9. = tala'am 'their tassels'.
10. = súmatsiwyungwa 'be quite visible (plural)'.
11. amunawit 'along them, along their course'.
12. = siwi'am 'their tendrils'.
13. síwukiwyungwa 'be cascading (plural)'.
14. = yoowi'am 'their corn silk'.
15. yan 'like this, in this way, thus'.
16. nu' 'I'.
17. = naawakna 'want'.
18. uma 'you (plural)'.
19. = naanawakna 'pray (plural)'.
20. = inam 'my fathers'.
21. uní 'how delightful'.
22. = umùutim 'your (plural) children'.
23. noonovani 'will be eating (plural)'.
24. öö'öyani 'will become satiated with food or drink, get full (plural)'.
25. = sòosoyam 'all, all of them'.

Umuu'uyinawita,$_{26}$
yaani,$_{27}$
yaanita.$_{28}$

When it rains beautifully during the summer for you,
it restores your beauty.
Just think, at last the tassels of your corn plants are quite visible.
Just think, their "tendrils" are cascading down along them.
Along them their corn silk is cascading down.
I want it this way for you.
This is what you are praying for,
my fathers.
How delightful, delightful, delightful.
Just think, at last your children will be eating.
Just think, at last they will get full.
Just think, at last all of you will be eating.
(Vocables.)
Along your planted fields,
in this way,
it is this way.

The katsinas are reminding the people about the beautiful results of the rain and, by implication, of the necessity to pray for rain so that they will receive these gifts from the katsinas. Here rain is specifically described as a vitalizing and restorative force that, in rejuvenating life, brings beauty to the land. Beauty is referred to with two words, *sonway,* a form restricted to feminine speakers in everyday speech, and *lolma,* a form restricted to masculine speakers in everyday speech. However in songs, many of these gender-specific usage restrictions are often suspended.

The beauty here is not visible glamour, but the beauty of life itself. The katsinas then point to some of the visible essences of this beauty—the corn plant tassels and silk, both of which are signs of developing ears of corn. Metaphorically the katsinas compare the falling corn silk to tendrils that cascade down from plants, both being signs of the future life that will be produced by the plants. The katsinas' phrase "I want it this way for

26. = *umùu'uyinawit* 'along your planted fields'.
27. = *yan* 'like this, in this way, thus'.
28. = *yanta* 'be this way, be like this'.

you" is their hope that these signs of growth will happen. That is what the people have been praying for.

The katsinas reflect that it will be really delightful for the people to have enough food to feed their children, indeed, enough for everyone so that the whole community will be free from hunger. The implication is that, with this food, everyone will have a fulfilled life. They end their song with some words of musing about the fields. Implied here is an encouraging reminder to the people that, if they work hard in their fields, they will be rewarded with plentiful sustenance for their families.

26. Angaktsìntawi$_1$
(Barrett Song 30A, 8902, Track 9; LoC)

Yuuyahiwa,$_2$
ayamo.$_3$
Taalaw'oomawkiva'a,$_4$
yuuyahiwa.
Puma$_5$ pew$_6$ kwakha'unangwat$_7$ taayimakyang,$_8$
yoynaanakwusani.$_9$
Lee lehe la.
Iitsi'i.$_{10}$
Yooki,$_{11}$
tuukwi'ova.$_{12}$
Yang$_{13}$ tuukwiva$_{14}$ sonkiwa.$_{15}$
Oho wa eehe heelo.

1. *angaktsìntawi* 'Long-Hair katsina song'.
2. *yuuyahiwa* 'have been dressed as for a ceremony, be adorned (plural)'.
3. = *ayám* 'over there'.
4. = *taalaw'omàwkiva'a,* pausal form of *taalaw'omàwkiva* 'along the dwelling place of the clouds in the direction of the sunrise'.
5. *puma* 'they'.
6. *pew* 'toward here, coming this way'.
7. = *kwakwha'unangwat* 'with tranquil hearts, with beneficent intentions'.
8. = *taymakyangw* 'while going along looking'.The combination *pew tayma* means 'be coming with anticipation, expectation, intention'.
9. = *yoynànkwusani* 'will start on a journey as rain'.
10. *iitsi'i* 'make haste', imperative form of *iits* 'soon, early'.
11. *yooki* 'rain' (verb).
12. = *tukwi'ova* 'up along the mesa(s)'.
13. *yang* 'along here, in this area'.
14. *tuukwiva* 'along the mesa(s)'.
15. *sonkiwa* 'sound pleasing, for there to be pleasing sounds'.

[They] have been adorned,
over there.
Along the dwelling places of the clouds in the direction of the sunrise,
[they] have been adorned.
With tranquil hearts, coming with intention,
they will set off on their journey as rain.
(Vocables.)
Make haste.
It is raining
up along the mesas.
Along the mesa here, there are pleasing sounds.
(Vocables.)

The katsinas describe how they have been adorned over at their cloud dwelling place in the direction of the sunrise. They agree to begin their journey as rain with thankfulness in their hearts, an implicit reference to the fact that they have observed that the people are deserving of their gift of rain. Thus, thankful that the people are living right, they come with the full intention to bestow their gifts of rain. Then they tell the people to hurry, suggesting that they are already at the villages by alluding to the pleasing sounds that their thunder makes as it reverberates along the mesa walls.

27. *Haw'okatsìntawi$_1$*
(Barrett Song 42, 8908, Track 3; LoC)

Haa'o.$_2$
Haalay'unangway$_3$ naawakinaya,$_4$
haa'a haw$_5$ ínamu.$_6$
Úma'a'aa'a,$_7$

1. *haw'okatsìntawi* 'Haw'o katsina song'.
2. *haa'o,* vocative particle.
3. = *hàalay'unangway* 'with happy hearts, with beneficent intentions'.
4. = *naanawakna* 'pray (plural)'.
5. *haw,* vocative particle.
6. = *inam* 'my fathers'.
7. = *úma'a,* pausal form of *uma* 'you (plural)'.

it$_8$ uma$_9$ umuutimuy$_{10}$ haalayyaniqw'ö,$_{11}$
ayó$_{12}$ taatö$_{13}$ Kowaawaayvami'i,$_{14}$
itamuy$_{15}$ naawakinayaqö'ö,$_{16}$
it$_{17}$ iitam$_{18}$ qööqöngpit$_{19}$ yuuyahiwvata'a,$_{20}$
umuukisoonaqa$_{21}$ kiiskyava'a,$_{22}$
qatsi'nangwat$_{23}$ siwi'ytaniqatni,$_{24}$
uumungemi.$_{25}$
Yay'i ay hii ay hii.
Antaniqat$_{26}$ umuungem$_{27}$ yuuyahiwva,$_{28}$
péwi'i.$_{29}$

Hark.
You are praying with happy hearts,
o my fathers.
You,

8. *it*, object form of *i'* 'this'.
9. *uma* 'you (plural)'.
10. = *umùutimuy*, object form of *umùutim* 'your (plural) children'.
11. = *hàalayyaniqw'ö*, subordinate clause pausal form of *hàalayyani* 'will be happy (plural)'.
12. = *ayó'* 'toward over there'.
13. *taatö* 'to the southeast'.
14. = *Kowawayvami'i*, pausal form of *Kowawayvami* 'to Kowawayva', a spring. This is probably the same place as the Zuni *Kolhuwala:wa*, "Kachina Village," the home of the Zuni katsinas, located about seventy-five miles southwest of Zuni Pueblo. The names *Kolhuwala:wa* (= *Kowawayva*) and *Weenima*, the katsina dwelling place of the southeast, may be for the same place.
15. *itamuy* 'us', object form of *itam* 'we'.
16. = *naanawaknaqw'ö*, subordinate clause pausal form of *naanawakna* 'pray (plural)'.
17. *it*, object form of *i'* 'this'.
18. = *itam* 'we'.
19. = *qööqòngpit*, object form of *qööqòngpi* 'things used as though racing stones (*qööqöngö*)', a reference to solid clay objects that tumble along in streams of runoff water.
20. = *yuuyahiwvat'a*, pausal form of *yuuyahiwvat* 'after having come clothed, adorned (plural)'.
21. = *umùukisonaq* 'through the middle of your (plural) village'.
22. = *kiskyava'a*, pausal form of *kiskyava* 'along the passageway(s), in the passageways'.
23. *qatsi'nangwat*, object form of *qatsi'nangwa* 'will to live'.
24. *siwi'ytaniqatni* 'will have that which will have vitality', cf. *siwi* 'tendrils'.
25. = *umungem* 'for you (plural), for your benefit'.
26. *antaniqat*, object form of *antaniqa* 'that which will be right'.
27. = *umungem* 'for you (plural), for your benefit'.
28. *yuuyahiwva* 'come dressed, adorned (plural)'.
29. = *pew'i*, pausal form of *pew* 'toward here, coming this way'.

when you pray for us [to come]
so that these children of yours will be happy,
[sending your prayers] over there to the southeast to Kowawayva,
after we have come along the passageways in the middle of your village
adorned with these things like racing stones,
[then] there will be that which will have the vitality of the will to live,
for you.
(Vocables of the sound of singing.)
We have come adorned with that which will be right for you,
coming this way.

The katsinas observe that the people are praying with happy hearts for them to come from their home in the southeast at *Kowawayva*, a spring which may be the same place as the Zuni Kachina Village (*Kolhuwa-la:wa*) and the Hopi katsina home at *Weenima* (Stevenson 1904: 33). They comment that the people are praying so that their children will be happy, implying that if the katsinas come as rain in return for their prayers, the plants in their fields will mature themselves and the children will have food to eat.

The katsinas then describe their entrance into the village. As the katsinas enter the village along the consecrated cornmeal path, they pass through a covered passageway (*kiskya*) into the plaza (*kiisonvi*). In this way the katsinas come with their vitalizing gift of rain to the heart of the village. As they enter the plaza, the katsinas say that they are adorned with "things like racing stones" (*qööqòngpi*), referring to the clay, sticks, and stones that accumulate into ball-shaped masses as they are pushed down the washes by the rushing runoff water. These balls of debris are likened to the racing stones that the men kick in races in a symbolic effort to bring the rain. In this song it is a creative way to describe how the katsinas are coming with their rain. The katsinas remind the people that this rain will revive their will to live (*qatsi'nangwat*) by giving them new vitality (*siwi'ytaniqat*). They compare this vitality to plants with tendrils that have been nourished by their rain. The katsinas close by reminding the people how they have come adorned with their gift of rain, describing it as a benefit, "that which will be right for you."

28. Hemiskatsìntawi*~1~*

(Barrett Song 41, 8908, Track 1; LoC)

Húvamu~2~ ínamu~3~ paahoomongwitu,~4~
pumuy~5~ uma~6~ naanaan'ivo',~7~
oomaw'oyaqw'ö,~8~
piw~9~ tuwaati'i,~10~
naanan'ivaqö~11~ oo'oomawtu~12~ kuukuyivani,~13~
taawaanawita.~14~
Hii hihila.
Uuyisonaqa~15~ umuumuutimani.~16~
Tayaayaatimani.~17~
Ahay'a hiihii'a.
Hihii hay'aa hay'aa.

My fathers, the prayer feather leaders,
when you place them (the prayer feathers),
as clouds in the different directions around,
then the clouds, for their part, will also
make their appearance from the different directions around,
all day long.
(Vocables.)
They will go along booming throughout the midst of the planted areas.
They will go along quaking.

1. *hemiskatsìntawi* 'Hemiskatsina song'.
2. = *huvam,* hortative particle.
3. = *inam* 'my fathers'.
4. = *pahomomngwit* 'prayer feather leaders'.
5. *pumuy* 'them', object form of *puma* 'they'.
6. *uma* 'you (plural)'.
7. = *naanan'ivo',* pausal form of *naanan'ivo* 'to the different directions around'.
8. *oomaw'oyaqw'ö,* subordinate clause pausal form of *oomaw'oya* 'place as clouds'.
9. *piw* 'also, too, again'.
10. *tuwaati'i,* pausal form of *tuwat* 'in turn, for (one's) part'.
11. = *naanan'ivaqw* 'from the different directions around'.
12. = *oo'omawt* 'clouds'.
13. = *kuukuyvani* 'will appear, will make their appearance, will come into view'.
14. = *taawanawit* 'all day long'.
15. = *uysonaq* 'throughout the midst of the planted area(s)'.
16. = *umumutimani* 'will go along booming'.
17. = *tayayatimani* 'will go along trembling, shaking, quaking'.

(Vocables.)

This song voices the quintessential reciprocal relationship between the katsinas and the people. The katsinas address the fathers who made the preparations for the performance as the prayer feather leaders, *pahomom-ngwit*. As part of their preparations, they made the prayer feathers and imbued them with prayers for the katsinas to come. In this song the prayer feathers are likened to clouds that are created symbolically as the men smoke over them while making their prayers. In response to these prayers, the katsinas, as clouds, say they will make their appearance from all four directions throughout the day. They promise to come with thunder that will make the earth tremble and shake as they move throughout the planted fields.

29. *Hemiskatsìntawi₁*
(Barrett Song 50, 8911, Track 5; LoC)

Paavönmanaatuy₂ síqölööva'a,₃
oo'oomawutu₄ yooki- yookinayani,₅
taawaanawita.₆
Pew₇ yoo'oo- yoki,₈
yookii'i.₉
Paasatuwanit₁₀ síqölööva'a,
paatuwatavini.₁₁
Paayoywuutayu₁₂ siitalawvatayu,₁₃

1. *hemiskatsìntawi* 'Hemiskatsina song'.
2. = *paavönmamàntuy,* object form of *paavönmamant* 'young corn plants'.
3. = *sìiqòlpa'a,* pausal form of *sìiqòlpa* 'along the flowery expanses'.
4. = *oo'omawt* 'clouds'.
5. = *yoknayani* 'will make it rain (plural)'.
6. = *taawanawit* 'all day long'.
7. *pew* 'toward here, coming this way'.
8. = *yooki* 'rain' (verb).
9. = *yooki* 'rain' (verb).
10. *paasatuwanit,* object form of *paasatuwani* 'the expanse of all the fields'.
11. *paatuwatavini* 'will lay water on the land'.
12. = *paayoywutay,* object form of *paayoywuta'am* 'their poured-out rainwater, the rainwater they pour out'.
13. = *sìitalawvatay* 'after it has come to be bright with flowers' (object form).

ang₁₄ siipuyaayatani.₁₅

Along the flowery expanses of young corn plants,
the clouds will make it rain,
all day long.
It comes raining,
raining.
Along the flowery expanses of all the fields,
they will lay water on the land.
Along where it has come to be bright with flowers from the rainwater
     they poured out,
the flowers will be opening out.

This is a rasping song (*rukùntawi*) performed by katsinas standing in a line facing the people with katsina maidens kneeling in front of them rasping with scapulae on notched sticks. The song describes how the clouds will lay their water along the fields of young corn plants all day long. The result of this promised all-day rain will a land bright with blooming flowers. Notably the katsinas emphasize the great quantity of rain they will provide by describing it as their "poured-out rainwater" (*paayoy-wuta'am*). The katsinas then describe the spectacle of blooming flowers by describing how they are opening up after having been nurtured by their rainwater.

30. *Hòo'ekatsìntawi₁*
(Barrett 8901, Track 9; LoC)

Ura,₂ itam₃ taatawita,₄
ura,₅ itam naatayawisa.₆

14. *ang* 'along it, along there, in that area, in several places'.
15. = *sìipuyayatani* 'will be opening out as flowers'.
1. *hòo'ekatsìntawi* 'Hòo'e katsina song'.
2. *uma* 'you (plural)'.
3. *itam* 'we'.
4. = *taatawit*, object form of *taatawi* 'songs'.
5. *ura*, modal of recollection.
6. = *naatayawnawisa* 'go to make selves feel glad'.

"Itam itaamö'wimuy$_7$ wik.yaqö'ö,$_8$
"ephaqam$_9$ itamungem$_{10}$ maphenlawni."$_{11}$
Yanhaqam$_{12}$ naangemintani.$_{13}$
[Keresan *Siiwayna, henat'isi$_{14}$ kaatsa'anoma.* Keresan]
Yan$_{15}$ uma umuukiy$_{16}$ ánga'a,$_{17}$
yoknaye'e,$_{18}$
angq$_{19}$ pew$_{20}$ paatalnawita$_{21}$ muumunangsonaqa,$_{22}$
töökiwawayni.$_{23}$
Hapi me.$_{24}$
Kaway'uyisonaqa,$_{25}$ melon'uyisonaqa,$_{26}$
taatangayatu$_{27}$ töökilawni.$_{28}$
[Keresan *Siiwayna, henat'isi kaatsa'anoma.* Keresan]

Remember how we, with songs,
remember how we go to make ourselves feel glad with them.
"If we take our in-married women along,
"they will be doing domestic chores there for us."
In this way they will be inviting their in-married women to come along.
(Keresan words with reference to clouds.)

7. = *itàamö'wimuy,* object form of *itàamö'wim* 'our in-married women'.
8. *wik.yaqö'ö,* subordinate clause pausal form of *wik.ya* 'take along (plural)'.
9. *ephaqam* 'there, at an unspecified place'.
10. *itamungem* 'for us, for our benefit'.
11. *maphenlawni* 'will be doing domestic chores'.
12. *yanhaqam* 'in approximately this way'.
13. *naangemintani* 'will be inviting each other'.
14. *henat'isi* represents a Keresan word for 'clouds', cf. Santa Ana *hénaⱨ* (Davis 1964: 166), *-ši* 'plural subject' (*id.*: 179).
15. *yan* 'like this, in this way, thus'.
16. = *umùukiy,* object form of *umùuki* 'your (plural) houses, dwelling places'.
17. = *ang'a,* pausal form of *ang* 'along it, along there, in that area, in several places'.
18. *yoknaye'e,* pausal form of *yoknaye'* 'if (you) make it rain, get rain'.
19. = *angqw* 'from it, from there'.
20. *pew* 'toward here, coming this way'.
21. = *paatalnawit* 'along where it is glistening with water'.
22. = *muumunangwsonaq* 'in the midst of streams of runoff water'.
23. = *töökiwangwayni* 'there will be shouting of joy'.
24. *hapi me,* formulaic expression introducing the song's second part, *oomi* 'upward'.
25. = *kaway'uysonaq* 'throughout the midst of the area(s) planted with watermelons'.
26. = *melon'uysonaq* 'throughout the midst of the area(s) planted with muskmelons'.
27. = *taatangayt* 'yellowjackets'.
28. = *töötöqlawni* 'will keep making characteristic calls, sounds'.

In this way at your houses,
if you get rain,
from there toward here there will be shouting of joy
along where it is glistening with water and amidst streams of runoff
    water.
Listen, there is more.
Throughout the midst of the areas planted with watermelons and with
    muskmelons,
the yellowjackets will keep making their characteristic sounds.
(Keresan words with reference to clouds.)

The katsinas are recalling among themselves how they used to make themselves happy with song as a way to remind the people how song raises ones spirits and energizes people to live according to the tenets of the Hopi way of life. They metaphorically reference this perfect life by casting it in the Hopi institution *mö'wi,* a role a woman takes on once married. As a wife and mother she has the pivotal responsibility of performing all the culturally prescribed duties and practices that make her household the center of cultural activities for her children as well as for her clan relatives. In this song the katsinas, who have families just as people do, are talking about taking along their *möömö'wit,* perhaps to the people's villages. In this way they hope that their *möömö'wit* will be inspiring role models, reminding the women of the village of all the requisite traditional chores that represent the way Hopi women are supposed to live in order to sustain the Hopi lifeway.

Then, after some words in Keresan, the katsinas muse about how nice it will be for the people to have the rain come to their houses, meaning to the village and the lands all around the village. Indeed, when the people see the glistening puddles of water and the streams of runoff water—which implies that there will have been a great quantity of rain—they will be shouting with joy. The katsinas observe that the yellowjackets will be making their characteristic sounds, that is, they will be buzzing about throughout the fields of watermelon and muskmelon plants. The implied reminder here is that the pollination of the melon plants by the yellowjackets cannot occur without the coming of the rain that nourishes the plants into the flowering stage.

31. *Hòo'ekatsìntawi*[1]

(Barrett Song 49, 8911, Track 9; LoC)

Haalay'unangway[2] *itamuy*[3] *tiitii'ayalawu,*[4]
peewi'i.[5]
Ayám[6] *wukotupqave'e,*[7]
itam[8] *yuuyahiwvata'a,*[9]
angqw[10] *pew*[11] *umumi*[12] *yoynaanakwusaani.*[13]
Ahaa'ay.
Waykolölö sii aahaa haay'aa.
Hapi me.[14]
Ivosmiq[15] *taayungwa*[16] *huuvamu.*[17]
Pam[18] *hapi*[19] *yooyangwuyu*[20] *tokyeptatoqat*[21] *tu'awi'ytaqe'e,*[22]
suqömkoro'ta.[23]
Haalayya,[24]
ínamu[25]

1. *hòo'ekatsìntawi* 'Hòo'e katsina song'.
2. = *hàalay'unangway* 'with happy hearts, with beneficent intentions'.
3. *itamuy* 'us', object form of *itam* 'we'.
4. = *tiiti'ayalawu* 'be asking others to perform'.
5. = *pew'i*, pausal form of *pew* 'toward here, coming this way'.
6. *ayám* 'over there'.
7. *wukotupqave'e*, pausal form of *wukotupqave* 'at the big canyon', a reference to the Grand Canyon, *Ôngtupqa* (literally 'salt canyon').
8. *itam* 'we'.
9. *yuuyahiwvata'a*, pausal form of *yuuyahiwvat* 'after having come to be clothed, adorned (plural)'.
10. *angqw* 'from it, from there'.
11. *pew* 'toward here, coming this way'.
12. *umumi* 'to you (plural)'.
13. = *yoynànkwusani* 'will start on a journey as rain'.
14. *hapi me*, formulaic expression introducing the song's second part, *oomi* 'upward'.
15. *ivosmiq* 'into my eye'.
16. *taayungwa* 'look (plural)'.
17. = *huvam*, hortative particle.
18. *pam* 'that, that one, he, she, it'.
19. *hapi* 'truly, surely, certainly'.
20. = *yooyangwuy*, object form of *yooyangw* 'rain'.
21. *tokyeptatoqat*, object form of *tokyeptatoqa* 'one that goes to do s.th. all night'.
22. *tu'awi'ytaqe'e*, subordinate clause pausal form of *tu'awi'yta* 'have a message, signify, represent'.
23. *suqömkoro'ta* 'be a dark hole'.
24. = *hàalayya* 'be happy (plural)'.
25. = *inam* 'my fathers'.

Ivosmiq taayungwa huuvamu.
Pam hapi yooyangwuyu tokyeptatoqat tu'awi'ytaqe'e,
suqömkoro'ta.
Haalayya,
ínamu.

[You] have been asking us with happy hearts to perform
coming this way.
Over there at the big canyon,
after having come to be adorned,
we will start out coming from there on our journey as rain to you.
(Vocables.)
Listen, there is more.
Look in my eye.
Because it really represents an all-night rain,
so it is a dark hole.
[You] are happy,
my fathers.
Look in my eye.
Because it really represents an all-night rain,
so it is a dark hole.
[You] are happy,
my fathers.

Ths song describes how the people have been praying with hearts full of tranquility and good intentions so as to persuade the katsinas to come to come to perform at their village. The katsinas say that after they have adorned themselves with rain and all the good things of life at their home in the big canyon, presumably the Grand Canyon, they will begin their journey as rain from there to you, the people, here, that is, where the people are in their village.

In the next part of the song the katsinas command the people "Look in my eye." The word *suqömkoro'ta,* to be a dark hole, refers to the particular shape of the eyes of these katsinas that, in their darkness, recalls nighttime rainstorms that are particularly intensified by dark clouds. The dark eyes of the katsinas are cast as metaphors for all-night rains. In this symbolic way, the katsinas remind the people that katsinas wear all things of the world, that is, they are endowed with the essence of all the benefits of a fulfilled life, one of which is rain. When the people realize the benefits of an all-night rain, they will be happy.

32. Hootetawi$_1$ / Soyohìmkatsinmuy$_2$ Taawi'am$_3$
(Barrett Song 28, 8901, Track 10; LoC)

Yoyaavikwaatu$_4$ yoy'umukiy$_5$ sosonkiwyani,$_6$
taawanawiita.$_7$
Pew$_8$ yoyhoyoyotani.$_9$
Yoy'umumutani.$_{10}$
Humi'uuyita$_{11}$ síqölönawita,$_{12}$
pumuy$_{13}$ amuunawit$_{14}$ yang$_{15}$ taatawyuuyuwinani.$_{16}$
Aha aa'aha.
Pew yoyhoyoyotani.
Yoy'umumutani.
Humi'uuyita síqölönawita,
pumuy amuunawit yang paatuwataviyani.$_{17}$
Aha aa'aha iihi ii.
Hapi me.$_{18}$
Humi'uyita síqölönawita,
paatuwataviyani.
Pew yoyhoyoyotani.
Yoy'umumutani.
Humi'uuyita síqölönawita,
pumuy amuunawit yang paatuwataviyani.
Aha aa'aha iihi ii.

1. *hootetawi* 'Hoote song '. Hoote is a katsina whose characteristic cry is *hoote* or *áhoote.*
2. *soyohìmkatsinmuy,* object form of *soyohìmkatsinam* 'all kinds of katsinas, mixed katsinas'.
3. *taawi'am* 'their songs'.
4. = *yoyvivìikwam* 'nighthawks'.
5. = *yoy'umukiy,* object form of *yoy'umuki'am* 'their thunder'.
6. *sosonkiwyani* 'will be pleasing (plural)'.
7. = *taawanawit* 'all day long'.
8. *pew* 'toward here, coming this way'.
9. *yoyhoyoyotani* 'will be moving as rain'.
10. *yoy'umumutani* 'will be thundering'.
11. = *humi'uyit,* object form of *humi'uyi* 'corn plant(s)'.
12. = *sìiqölnawit* 'along the flowery expanses'.
13. *pumuy* 'them', object form of *puma* 'they'.
14. = *amunawit* 'along their course'.
15. *yang* 'along here, in this area'.
16. = *taatawyuyuwinani* 'will be dancing and singing songs'.
17. = *paatuwatapyani* 'will lay water on the land (plural)'.
18. *hapi me,* formulaic expression introducing the song's second part, *oomi* 'upward'.

The nighthawks will be pleasing with their thunder,
all day long.
[We] will come moving as rain.
[We] will be thundering.
Along the flowery expanses of corn plants,
they (the people) will be singing and dancing along their course here.
(Vocables of the sound of singing.)
Rain will be moving toward here.
Along the flowery expanses of corn plants,
[we] will lay water on the land along their course here.
(Vocables of the sound of singing.)
Listen, there is more.
Along the flowery expanses of corn plants,
[we] will lay water on the land.
[We] will come moving as rain.
[We] will be thundering.
Along the flowery expanses of corn plants.
[we] will lay water on the land along them here.
(Vocables of the sound of singing.)

In this song the thunder, *yoy'umuki*, that accompanies the rain is associated with the sound of the beating wings of nighthawks (*yoyvivìikwam*) who appear and swoop down over bodies of water to feed on the insects that are stirred up by the winds that precede a rain. To the Hopi ear, the booming sound that results when the nighthawks flap their wings very fast resembles thunder. This metaphor recalls part of the process of the coming of rain—the sounds of thunder that are most pleasing and welcome to the people. The katsinas promise to lay their waters along the fields of flowering plants and, in return, the people will be singing and dancing with joy at this sight. Several conventions appear here, as in many songs. Fields of corn plants are understood to encompass all plants, and corn flowers are understood to mean corn tassels.

33. Kookopö̀ltawi₁

(Barrett Song 45, 8908, Track 8; LoC)

Aa'haaha ii'ihiihi.
Inumi₂ naawakinaaya.₃
Inumi yooynaawakinayaqö,₄
ínamu,₅
aahay'a,
yoo- yoy'umuuki₆ yooy'umumuta.₇
Haqami₈ paatuwataviyani.₉
Himu₁₀ pay₁₁ tayma,₁₂
iitaamu,₁₃
umungem₁₄ paataalawnaqö'ö.₁₅
"Pu₁₆ pas₁₇ pay iitaamu!
"Yan₁₈ nu'₁₉ lavaaytiqe'e,₂₀
"himuwya'iwnuma.₂₁
"Yaaha haa.
"Ayahii aaha iihii."

1. *Kokopö̀ltawi* 'Kookopölö song'.
2. *inumi* 'to me'.
3. = *naanawakna* 'pray (plural)'.
4. = *yoynanawaknaqw*, subordinate clause form of *yoynanawakna* 'pray for rain (plural)'.
5. = *inam* 'my fathers'.
6. = *yoy'umuki* 'thunder'.
7. = *yoy'umumuta* 'be thundering'.
8. = *aqwhaqami* 'throughout'.
9. = *paatuwatapyani* 'will lay water on the land (plural)'.
10. *himu*, indefinite pronoun: 'something, what, one, you'.
11. *pay*, expressive particle.
12. *tayma* 'go along looking, seeing, watching'.
13. = *itam* 'we'.
14. *umungem* 'for you (plural), for your benefit'.
15. = *paatalawnaqw'ö*, subordinate clause pausal form of *paatalawna* 'make it glisten with water'.
16. = *pu'* 'now, then'.
17. *pas* 'very'.
18. *yan* 'like this, in this way, thus'.
19. *nu'* 'I'.
20. = *lavàytiqe'e*, subordinate clause pausal form of *lavàyti* 'speak'.
21. = *himùwya'iwnuma* 'go around feeling proud'.

Hapi me.$_{22}$
—(*inaudible*)—
Yan'i:$_{23}$
"*Ítamu*$_{24}$ *siwawaytimani.*"$_{25}$
Umumi$_{26}$ *uuyisonaqa*$_{27}$ *oovi*$_{28}$ *qöyavoli- voliwmanatu.*$_{29}$

(Vocables of the sound of singing.)
You pray to me.
When you pray to me for rain,
my fathers,
(vocable of the sound of singing),
the thunder is thundering.
We will lay water on the land throughout.
You had best go along looking,
my fathers,
when we make it glisten with water for you.
"Just think, it was really us!
"So say I,
"as I go around feeling proud.
"(Vocables of the sound of singing)."
Listen, there is more.
—(*inaudible*)—
[And] like this:
"We will be going along joyfully."
[And] that's why the white butterfly maidens [will sing] to you in the
    midst of the planted areas.

The katsinas observe that when the people pray to them for rain, it comes
thundering (*yoy'umumuta*), laying its water throughout the land. Rain does
not "fall" on its own; it is placed on the land by the katsinas. This sentiment is suggested by the word *paatuwatavi* 'lay water on the land', which
is derived from *paahu* 'water' (*paa-*), *tuuwa* 'sand' (*-tuwa-*) and *tavi* 'put'.

22. *hapi me,* a formulaic expression introducing the song's second part, *oomi* 'upward'.
23. *yan'i,* pausal form of *yan* 'like this, in this way, thus'.
24. = *itam* 'we'.
25. *siwawaytimani* 'will be going along in joy, in happiness'.
26. *umumi* 'to you (plural)'.
27. = *uysonaq* 'throughout the midst of the planted area(s)'.
28. *oovi* 'that's why'.
29. = *qöyavolmamant* 'white butterfly maidens'.

(The word *tuuwa* 'sand' is used metaphorically for the land portion of the earth.) The katsinas recommend that the people go to see the results of the rain—glistening puddles of water on the land. Then the katsinas report on some comments by people who are pleased that their heartfelt prayers have caused the rain to come. "Just think, it was really us!" they say. They predict that they will be walking about their fields joyfully. The song closes with mention of the white butterflies, here represented as white butterfly maidens, who are appearing in the midst of the fields as a sign of purity and fertility.

34. *Kookopöltawi₁*
(Barrett 8909, Track 13; LoC)

Haa'o₂ haa'o haw'a₃ haa₄ imankwatsi.₅
Haa'o haa'o haw'a haa imankwatsi.
Itam₆ kuyvato,₇
ayó₈ Siwukvami,₉ Kivokvami₁₀ tuyqat₁₁ aw₁₂ imankwatsi.
Itamuy₁₃ aw waymaqö'ö,₁₄
soosonlavayiy₁₅ ang₁₆ pa₁₇ naakopantiwa.₁₈

1. *kookopöltawi* 'Kookopölö song'.
2. *haa'o,* vocative particle.
3. *haw'a,* vocative particle.
4. *haa,* vocative particle.
5. = *imànkwatsi* 'my girl friend'.
6. *itam* 'we'.
7. *kuyvato* 'go check on, get up early to go run and pray'.
8. = *ayó'* 'toward over there'.
9. *Siwukvami* 'to *Siwukva*'. *Siwukva* is a spring on Third Mesa.
10. *Kivokvami* 'to *Kivokva*'. *Kivokva* is an unidentified spring.
11. *tuyqat,* object form of *tuyqa* 'point, projecting point of a mesa, external corner of a structure'.
12. *aw* 'to it, to there'.
13. *itamuy* 'us', object form of *itam* 'we' (as subject of adverbial clause).
14. = *waymaqw'ö,* subordinate clause pausal form of *wayma* 'walk along'.
15. = *sosonlavayiy,* object form of *sosonlavayi'at* 'his pleasing speech'.
16. *ang* 'along it, along there, in that area, in several places'.
17. *pa* 'possibly'.
18. *naakopantiwa* 'have been leaving to go away voluntarily'.

—(unintelligible)—$_{19}$ yaayatima.$_{20}$
Aha aa.
Aha aa.
Aha aa.
Yaayatima.
Iihii.
Talavay$_{21}$ iihii.
Aaha iihii.
Aaha iihii.
Hapi me.$_{22}$
Talavayi,$_{23}$
talavayi taalawkuyiva.$_{24}$
Niikyango$_{25}$ kuyva.$_{26}$
Hakii$_{27}$ vii$_{28}$ púma'a,$_{29}$
tuutu'awnaya,$_{30}$
Isiwatunikyango$_{31}$
—(unintelligible)—
yani$_{32}$ puma$_{33}$ taw$_{34}$ ikwatsi$_{35}$ —(unintelligible)—
Niikyangw$_{36}$ —(unintelligible)— puyayata.$_{37}$
Hapi$_{38}$ töqtini.$_{39}$

19. From this point on, the recording of this song is extremely hard to hear.
20. yaayatima 'go along teasing, frolicking'.
21. talavay 'in the morning'.
22. hapi me, a formulaic expression introducing the song's second part, oomi 'upward'.
23. = talavay 'in the morning'.
24. = taalawkuyva 'for daylight to make its appearance'.
25. = niikyangw 'however, but'.
26. kuyva 'come into sight, appear'.
27. = hakiy, object form of hak 'who'.
28. = viy, an unexplained particle occurring in the expression hakiy viy 'I wonder who'.
29. púma'a, pausal form of puma 'they'.
30. = tutu'awnaya 'be informing others of the meaning of something (plural)'.
31. = isiwamniikyangw 'even though they are my younger sisters'.
32. = yan 'like this, in this way, thus'.
33. puma 'they'.
34. taw is not identified. It may be misheard or it may be a word partial, the rest of the word being inaudible in the recording.
35. ikwatsi 'my friend'.
36. niikyangw 'however, but'.
37. puyayata 'be flapping, fluttering'.
38. hapi 'truly, surely, certainly'.
39. töqtini 'will shout, make a characteristic call'.

Hapi töqtini.
Hapi me, hapi me.[40]
Tala eloo.
Tala eloo.
—*(unintelligible)*—
tíwungniitiyotu.[41]
Iihii.
Aaha iihii.

Hark, hark, hark, o my girl friend.
Hark, hark, hark, o my girl friend.
We were going to go check on things,
over to Siwukva, and to Kivokva, to the point, my girl friend.
While we went walking along to there,
[we saw that others] had left the village perhaps by sweet talk.
—(unintelligible)— go along teasing.
(Vocables.)
[They] go along teasing.
(Vocable.)
In the morning (vocable).
(Vocables.)
Listen, there is more.
In the morning,
In the morning daylight makes its appearance.
However, he/she (?) makes his/her (?) appearance.
I wonder who they are that
are informing others about what it means.
Even though they are my younger sisters
—(unintelligible)—
like this they (unknown element) my friend —(unintelligible)—
However —(unintelligible)— they are fluttering.
Truly it will give its cry.
Truly it will give its cry.
Listen, there is more, there is more.

---

40. *Hapi me* usually occurs at only one place in a song, to introduce the song's second part, *oomi* 'upward'. In this song *hapi me* appears unexplainedly yet again here, and doubled.
41. = *tíwungwnitiyot,* song form of *tíwungwnitotim* 'boys being raised'.

(Vocables.)
—(unintelligible)—
boys being raised.
(vocables.)

The Kookopölö katsina describes how he took his girl friend to two springs, Siwukva and Kivokva, and to a point of a mesa, presumably as places to engage in visits with her. They tease each other about the excitement they might have there. On their way they notice that others have left the village, presumably to have a rendezvous there also. Much of the remainder of the song is unintelligible but it seems to describe events of the next morning.

35. *Kwikwilyaqat Taawi'at₁*
(Barrett Song 44, 8908, Track 5; LoC)

Tsootsvala,₂ tsootsvala, tsootsvala,
yongyaywuutit₃ kiiyat₄ aw'i.₅
Yoongyaymoomooyamu₆ tsootsvala,
antsa₇ puma₈ tsovaltiqe'e,₉
laavaytaqe'e,₁₀
"Himu₁₁ as₁₂ um₁₃ uukongyaayu₁₄ hoonata'a,₁₅

1. *Kwikwilyaqat taawi'at* 'Stripe Nose's song'.
2. = *tsotsvala* 'be gathered in assembly'.
3. = *yongyaywùutit*, object form of *yongyaywùuti* 'adulterous woman'.
4. *kiiyat*, object form of *kii'at* 'her house'.
5. *aw'i*, pausal form of *aw* 'to it'.
6. = *yongyaymomoyam* 'adulterous women'.
7. *antsa* 'truly, really, indeed'.
8. *puma* 'they'.
9. = *tsovàltiqe'e*, subordinate clause pausal form of *tsovàlti* 'gather, assemble'.
10. = *lavaytaqe'e*, subordinate clause pausal form of *lavayta* 'be talking about, telling about'.
11. *himu*, indefinite pronoun: 'something, what, one, you'.
12. *as* 'presumably': something is claimed to be so without full evidence. *Himu as* means something like "should, I wish you would."
13. *um* 'you'.
14. = *ùukongyay*, object form of *ùukongya* 'your husband'.
15. *hoonata'a*, pausal form of *hoonat* 'after sending away'.

"imuy$_{16}$ taahayamuy$_{17}$ amum$_{18}$ qatuptuni.$_{19}$
"Noqw$_{20}$ pas$_{21}$ iitam$_{22}$ suupa 'iwtani,$_{23}$
"pas.
"Itam$_{24}$ ung$_{25}$ hin$_{26}$ kwangwamö 'wi 'yungwni. "$_{27}$
Yan$_{28}$ ura$_{29}$ lavaytaqe 'e,$_{30}$
"Antsa amum qaatuptuqö 'ö,$_{31}$
"yaasavo$_{32}$ hakim$_{33}$ kwangwamö 'wi 'yungngwu. "$_{34}$
Hak$_{35}$ pay$_{36}$ mootiwat$_{37}$ koongyay$_{38}$ uu 'naqe 'e,$_{39}$
antsa pitsinaqe 'e,$_{40}$
qa$_{41}$ hintiqey$_{42}$ tunatyawkyangw$_{43}$ tookyep$_{44}$ ura naatsoptangwu.$_{45}$

16. *imuy,* object form of *ima* 'these'.
17. *taahayamuy,* object form of *taaha 'am* 'their maternal uncle'.
18. *amum* 'with him/her'.
19. *qatuptuni* 'will sit down, cohabit'.
20. *noqw* 'but, whereas, and so'.
21. *pas* 'very'.
22. = *itam* 'we'.
23. = *su 'pa 'iwtani* 'will be showing kindness, friendship'.
24. *itam* 'we'.
25. *ung,* object form of *um* 'you'.
26. *hin* 'in some way, somehow, how'.
27. = *kwangwamö 'wi 'yyungwni* 'will have as a pleasant in-married woman (plural)'.
28. *yan* 'like this, in this way, thus'.
29. *ura,* modal of recollection: 'as I recall, as you'll recall'.
30. *lavaytaqe 'e,* same-subject subordinate clause pausal form of *lavayta* 'be talking about, telling about'.
31. = *qatuptuqw 'ö,* subordinate clause pausal form of *qatuptu* 'sit down'.
32. = *yàasavo* 'to this length or distance, as far as this; to this present time only, until this time (and no longer)'.
33. *hakim* 'some people, who (plural)'.
34. = *kwangwamö 'wi 'yyungngwu,* habitual tense form of *kwangwamö 'wi 'yyungwa* 'have a pleasant in-married woman (plural)'.
35. *hak* 'someone, who'.
36. *pay,* expressive particle.
37. = *mòotiwat,* object form of *mòotiwa* 'previous, last, from the time before'.
38. *koongyay,* object form of *koongya 'at* 'her husband'.
39. = *u 'naqe 'e,* same-subject subordinate clause pausal form of *u 'na* 'remember'.
40. *pitsinaqe 'e,* same-subject subordinate clause pausal form of *pitsina* 'get someone to come'.
41. *qa* 'not'.
42. *hintiqey* 'to happen, occur'.
43. *tunatyawkyangw* 'while nurturing hope for'.
44. *tookyep* 'all night long'.
45. *naatsoptangwu,* habitual tense form of *naatsopta* 'be having sex with each other'.

"Alíi.$_{46}$
"Alí,$_{47}$ *kwangwalöw'inöma,*$_{48}$ *kwangwakwas'ikongya*$_{49}$ *puye'em*$_{50}$ *ura um
yanta.*$_{51}$
"Tarukop'öqaqa."$_{52}$
Yan uma$_{53}$ *hingqaqwangwu.*$_{54}$
tasaphonaqmomoyamu.$_{55}$
Paantaq'ö,$_{56}$
oovi$_{57}$ *tuuwingaq*$_{58}$ *lööwaawaqaaqa.*$_{59}$
Puma tuupkiwta.$_{60}$
Alíi.
Alíi, "taaqa"$_{61}$ *angwu*$_{62}$ *tuuwati,*$_{63}$
amumiq$_{64}$ *yomiimiitoya.*$_{65}$
Kyapi$_{66}$*paas*$_{67}$ *ima*$_{68}$ *soosokmuy*$_{69}$*hiituyu*$_{70}$*koongtotaniiqey*$_{71}$ *naanawakna-
qöö'ö,*$_{72}$

46. = *alí,* exclamation of pleasure.
47. *alí,* exclamation of pleasure.
48. *kwangwalöw'inöma* 'my wife with the pleasant vulva'.
49. *kwangwakwas'ikongya* 'my husband with the pleasant penis'.
50. *puye'em,* adverb meaning approximately 'have a feeling or hunch, suspect'.
51. *yanta* 'be this way, be like this'.
52. *tarukop'öqaqa* '(one) that has an erection as hard as a bone'.
53. *uma* 'you (plural)'.
54. = *hìngqaqwangwu,* habitual tense form of *hìngqaqwa* 'say something (plural)'.
55. = *tasaphonaqmomoyam* 'women who are crazy for Navajo men'.
56. = *pantaqw'ö,* subordinate clause pausal form of *panta* 'be that way, be like that'.
57. *oovi* 'that's why'.
58. = *tuuwingaqw* 'from the cliff ledge, from the terrace', a reference to the upper kiva floor
    which cannot be seen from the lighted portion of the kiva down below. In the song, which
    is sung in the kiva, this term is used metaphorically to mean someplace out of sight just
    as that part of the kiva is out of sight.
59. = *löwawaqaqa* 'squishy sounds of sexual activity'.
60. = *tupkiwta* 'be hidden, concealed, kept secret'.
61. *taaqa,* literally 'man', but here 'husband'.
62. *angwu* 'in anticipation of, beforehand, contrary to expectation: but, and yet'.
63. = *tuwat* 'for one's part'.
64. *amumiq* 'at them'.
65. = *yomimitoyna* 'be thrusting the hips rapidly against'.
66. *kyapi* 'I guess'.
67. = *pas* 'very'.
68. *ima* 'these'.
69. = *sòosokmuy,* object form of *sòosoyam* 'all of them, every one of them'.
70. = *hìituy,* object form of *hìitu,* plural of *himu* 'something, what'.
71. = *kongtotaniqey* 'for them to take husbands'.
72. = *naanawaknaqw'ö,* subordinate clause pausal form of *naanawakna* 'want (plural)'.

Oovi nu'$_{73}$ yep$_{74}$ Kwiikwilyaqanikyaango$_{75}$ nuutum$_{76}$ umuy$_{77}$ höölömnata-
qe,$_{78}$
pas nu' haalayi.$_{79}$
—(inaudible)— hay'iiyee.
Aaha iihiihi.
Aaha iihiihi.

They are gathering, gathering, gathering,
at the adulterous woman's house.
The adulterous women are gathering,
really, [after] they had gathered,
they were talking.
"After you send your husband away,
"you should cohabit with the maternal uncle of these.
"Then indeed we will be on friendly terms,
"indeed.
"We will have you as a very pleasant in-married woman."
In this way, you'll recall, they would be talking.
"Truly when she cohabits with him,
"up to this time only we would have a pleasant in-married woman."
When she remembers the previous husband,
and in fact has him come,
and while acting as though she did not do anything wrong,
she hopes, you'll recall, to have sex with him all night long.
"How nice!
"How nice, my wife with a pleasant vulva, my husband with a pleasant
penis!
"I recall that you are like this.
"[You are] one with an erection like a bone."
Like this you would be talking,
[you] Navajo men-craving women.

73. *nu'* 'I'.
74. *yep* 'here'.
75. = *Kwikwilyaqaniikyangw* 'while being Stripe Nose'.
76. = *nùutum* 'with others'.
77. *umuy,* object form of *uma* 'you (plural)'.
78. = *hölömnataqe,* subordinate clause form of *hölömnata* 'uncover one at a time'.
79. = *hàalayi* 'be happy'.

That's the way it is,
[and] that's why there are squishy sounds of vulvas as if from the back of
    the upper kiva floor.
They are hidden in there.
How nice!
How nice, you "man," in anticipation, for your part,
to be thrusting your hips rapidly at them.
I guess all of them
want to take husbands of all kinds of people.
That's why I, Stripe Nose here, such as I am, with others, have uncovered
    you one by one,
and I am very happy.
(Vocables of the sound of singing.)

The Striped Nose katsina, or Stripe Nose, is exposing the adulterous behavior of women who seek sexual favors with Navajo men while still pretending to live with their husbands. It is a song of admonition that concerns traditional values regarding social interchange with non-Hopi people. Although Stripe Nose usually appears with clowns (*tsutskut*) who instruct people through bad example, here he apparently performs alone.

36. *Kwivikatsìntawi*₁
(Barrett Song 43, 8908, Track 4; LoC)

Oho hoo ihi hii hii.
*Yooy'umumutani.*₂
*Yoyhoyoyotani.*₃
*Yooytöökiy*₄ *yuuyuuwinani.*₅
[Keresan? *Hee awina ho.*
Aawina hoowi ohooho iihihi. Keresan?]
*Hapi me.*₆

---

1. *kwivikatsìntawi* 'Vain katsina song'.
2. = *yoy'umumutani* 'will be thundering'.
3. *yoyhoyoyotani* 'will be moving as rain'.
4. = *yòytötökiyam*, object form of *yòytötöki'am* 'their rain sounds'.
5. = *yuuyuwinani* 'will be making dance'.
6. *hapi me,* formulaic expression introducing the song's second part, *oomi* 'upward'.

[Keresan *Ita siiwayna hawwirayna.* Keresan]

(Vocables.)
They will be thundering.
They will be moving as rain.
They will be making their rain sounds dance.
(Vocables or possibly Keresan words.)
Listen, there is more.
(Keresan words.)

This is a song about the katsinas coming as a summer thunderstorm. The sounds of the rain are poetically described as dancing, *yooytöökiy yuuyuuwinani* 'they will be making their rain sounds dance'. Much of the song is in Keresan.

37. Ma'lokatsìntawi*₁*
(Barrett 8908, Track 6; LoC)

Heesita,₂ tsorosita₃ síqölöva₄ yang₅ tayimuyiwni.₆
Aa'aha ii'ihi.

In the expanses of mariposa lilies and blue asters along here, they will
    look in awe.
(Vocables of the sound of singing.)

This song draws the attention of the people to the beauty the fields of yellow mariposa lilies and blue asters. The katsinas remark that people will be looking at them, presumably not only because of their beauty, but also because they are reminders of the perfection of the ideal world to which everyone aspires.

1. *ma'lokatsìntawi* 'Ma'lo katsina song'.
2. = *heesit*, object form of *heesi* 'mariposa lily/lilies'.
3. = *tsorosit*, object form of *tsorosi* 'blue aster(s)'.
4. = *sìiqölpa* 'in, along the expanse(s) of flowers'.
5. *yang* 'along here, in this area'.
6. = *taayimuyiwni* 'will look in awe'.

38. Sa'lakwmanatuy Taawi'am$_1$
(Barrett Song 33, 8907, Track 2; LoC)

Haw'o,$_2$
qöyaviqaa'ö$_3$ tsootsoomingwu$_4$ íngu'u.$_5$
Puma$_6$ yev$_7$ itamuy$_8$ tiitiiwungwina.$_9$
Pumuy$_{10}$ itam$_{11}$ pitsaangwayamuy$_{12}$ sínevela'iikyang$_{13}$ umumi$_{14}$ tiitiiwu-
   nima;$_{15}$
tuuhiiyongwaya,$_{16}$
tivoongyapave'e.$_{17}$
Aha yaha mee.
Aayaw liihi liiho liiho liinayee.
Ayaw linoye.

Hark.
The perfect ear of glossy-kerneled corn is my mother.
They (the perfect ears of corn) are nurturing us (all the people) like chil-
dren here.

1. *Sa'lakwmanatuy taawi'am* 'song of the two Sa'lako maidens'. The Sa'lako maidens
   always come as a pair.
2. *haw'o,* vocative particle.
3. = *qöyapqa'ö* 'corn with glossy kernels'.
4. = *tsotsmingwu* 'perfect ear of white corn with kernels all the way to the tip'. This is
   sometimes referred to as a "corn mother". The word *tsotsmingwu* contains the root *tsomi-*
   as found in the verb *tsómikiwta* 'be bunched up'. The initial *tso-* is a reduplicative prefix,
   the root is reduced to *-tsmi-*, and the final *-ngwu* is an ending that derives nouns. (This
   complex word is not a compound—it contains only the single root *tsomi-* —so it is not
   listed in the appendix of compounds.)
5. *íngu'u,* pausal form of *íngu* 'my mother'.
6. *puma* 'they'.
7. *yev* 'here', Second Mesa pronunciation equivalent of Third Mesa *yep*.
8. *itamuy* 'us', object form of *itam* 'we'.
9. = *tiitiwungwna* 'raise children, nurture like children'.
10. *pumuy* 'them', object form of *puma* 'they'.
11. *itam* 'we'.
12. = *pitsangwayamuy,* object form of *pitsangwa'am* 'their countenance'.
13. = *sínevela'ykyangw* 'while having perfection as their due', a reference to the perfect,
    heartfelt prayers that the katsinas, as perfect beings, deserve.
14. *umumi* 'to you (plural)'.
15. = *tiitiwunima* 'be dancing in performance'.
16. = *tùuyongwaya* 'delight others (plural)'.
17. = *tivongyapave'e,* pausal form of *tivongyapave* 'at/in the dance-display place'.

Having their countenance as the perfection that is due us, we are dancing
    and singing songs for you,
and thereby delight you,
in the dance-display place.
(Vocables.)

This song is sung by katsinas in performance with two *Sa'lako* maiden
katsina marionettes in night dances in the kiva during the winter months
after *Powamuya,* the Bean dance. The katsinas are speaking to the people,
telling them that perfect ears of corn are their metaphorical mothers. Perfect ears of corn, *tsotsmingwu,* called "corn mothers," are corn ears that
have mature full kernels all the way to the tip. White corn mothers are
given to babies as symbols of purity and hope that the child will have a
perfect life, as well as to other individuals as they pass into different
stages of their lives. Metaphorically, such corn represents sustenance and
in this sense corn is understood as a mother that nurtures the people from
birth to old age.

    The katsinas remind the people that such perfect corn has the counte-
nance of perfection. With their choice at Emergence of the short ear of
corn, the people agreed to follow a lifeway based on ethical and moral
principles that would sustain the community. All of these ideas are embodied in *pitsanagwa,* the countenance of corn. Then the katsinas use the
perfection of corn as a metaphor to emphasize their own perfection, and,
for this reason, the necessity for the people to proffer to them their most
heartfelt, sincere and perfect prayers. This is what is meant by "the perfection that is due us." In return for these sincere prayers, the katsinas
have come to dance and sing in performance for the people. The katsinas,
for their part, hope that they delight the people with their essence of
perfect beauty as they perform in the plaza, *tivongyapavi,* the dance-
display place.

39. Si'ohemiskatsìntawi$_1$
(Barrett 8900, Track 2; LoC)

Ayamo$_2$ tatkya$_3$ Kowawayvave'e,$_4$
Kooyemsitu.$_5$
Tuhpevuyu,$_6$ somivikiyu,$_7$ tsukuvikita$_8$ umungem$_9$ kivaya.$_{10}$
"Ta'a$_{11}$ pew$_{12}$ haani'i,$_{13}$
"tootimhoyamu.$_{14}$
"Ahaa ihii.
"Wáriku'u,$_{15}$ wáriku'u.
"Koona$_{16}$ pantsana.$_{17}$
"Wáriku'u, wáriku'u.
"Kìisa,$_{18}$
"kìisa pantsana.
"Aha aha.
"Yan$_{19}$ pi$_{20}$ nu'$_{21}$ naawakina."$_{22}$

1. *si'ohemiskatsìntawi* 'Zuni Hemiskatsina song'.
2. = *ayám* 'over there'.
3. *tatkya* 'in the southeast'.
4. *Kowawayvave'e,* pausal form of *Kowawayvave* 'at *Kowawayva*', a spring. This is probably the same place as the Zuni *Kolhuwala:wa* 'Kachina Village', the home of the Zuni katsinas, located about seventy-five miles southwest of Zuni Pueblo.
5. = *Kookoyemsim* 'Mudhead katsinas'.
6. = *tùupevuy,* object form of *tùupevu'am* 'their roasted sweet corn'.
7. = *somivikiy,* object form of *somiviki'am* 'their *somiviki*'. *Somiviki* is blue corn pudding boiled or steamed in a corn husk wrapper, tied at both ends.
8. = *tsukuvikit,* object form of *tsukuviki.* *Tsukuviki* is blue corn pudding wrapped into a crescent shape in a green corn leaf and boiled or steamed.
9. *umungem* 'for you (plural), for your benefit'.
10. *kivaya* 'bring many things (plural)'.
11. *ta'a* 'all right'.
12. *pew* 'toward here, coming this way'.
13. *haani'i,* imperative form of *haani* 'descend (plural)'.
14. = *totimhòoyam* 'little boys, young boys', plural of *tiyòoya.*
15. *wáriku'u,* imperative form of *wari* 'run'.
16. *koona* 'tree squirrel'.
17. *pantsana* 'do that to (it)'.
18. *kìisa* 'chicken hawk'.
19. *yan* 'like this, in this way, thus'.
20. *pi* 'truly'.
21. *nu'* 'I'.
22. = *naawakna* 'want'.

Yan ura₂₃ Kooyemsi₂₄ nuutumi₂₅ hingqawkyangw₂₆ wukokuriy₂₇ palalata-
   ngwuy,₂₈
—*(inaudible)*—,
tivongyapave'e.₂₉
Ahaa aha.
Ahaa iihiyi.

Over in the southeast at *Kowawayva*,
[there live] Mudhead katsinas.
They have brought [from there] their roasted sweet corn, their *somiviki,*
   and the *tsukuviki* for you.
"All right, climb down here,
"little boys.
"(Vocables.)
"Run, run.
"The tree squirrel does that to it.
"Run, run.
"The chicken hawk,
"the chicken hawk does that to it.
"(Vocables.)
"Truly I want it to be like this."
In this way you recall the Mudhead katsina, as he says it to others in this
   way, he would pat his big buttocks
—*(inaudible)*—
in the dance-display place.

The katsinas begin their song by describing how the Mudhead katsinas
have come from their home at *Kowawayva*. This is a spring southwest of
Zuni Pueblo. It may be the same place as Zuni *Kolhuwala:wa*, the home
of the Zuni katsinas, as well as *Weenima*, the home of Hopi katsinas in the
southeast direction (Stevenson 1904: 33). The Mudheads are bringing
tùupevu, fresh sweet corn steamed overnight in a pit oven, *somiviki*, blue

23. *ura*, modal of recollection: 'as I recall, as you'll recall'.
24. *Kooyemsi* 'Mudhead katsina'.
25. = *nùutumi* 'to others'.
26. = *hìngqawkyangw* 'while saying'.
27. *wukokuriy*, object form of *wukokuri'am* 'their big buttocks'.
28. = *palalatoynangwu*, habitual tense form of *palalatoyna* 'be patting'.
29. *tivongyapave'e*, pausal form of *tivongyapave* 'at the dance-display place'.

corn flour tied in a corn husk wrapper and boiled, and *tsukuviki,* blue corn flour batter boiled in a crescent-shaped corn leaf wrapper for the benefit of the people. These foods are examples of traditional corn-based foods that are exchanged on specific occasions. For example, girls make *somiviki* as gifts to boys in return for the rabbits they kill on the hunt and brides make *tsukuviki* for those weaving her wedding robes. These foods form an integral part of the communal system of reciprocities that the katsinas are encouraging the people to maintain. These foods represent all the obligations that involve the kinds of practices such as sharing, providing help, and participating in the religious rituals that underpin Hopi society. By bringing these foods to the people "for your benefit," *umungem,* the Mudheads are reminding the people of their responsibilities to others.

Then the Mudheads begin a conversation with the little boys of the village as a way of reminding them of their responsibilities. They call to the boys, who are presumably watching the performance from the roofs of the houses that border the plaza, to climb down into the plaza. They instruct them to run, just as the tree squirrel does, that is, quickly, to chase the chicken hawk from ravaging the crops. In this way the Mudheads remind the boys of their responsibility to watch over the young plants in the fields so that predators do not eat them before they mature. The Mudheads' comment that "I want it to be like this" is their way of saying that they want boys to learn their responsibilities as members of the Hopi community. In effect, this song is reminding all Hopis of all generations to continue to perform such traditional activities because they represent the humble, hardworking lifeway that was chosen at Emergence that will lead to a fulfilled life.

40. *Wakaskatsìntawi,*
(Barrett 8911, Track 8; LoC)

Yoyhaniy.,
Yoyhaniya.,

---

1. *wakaskatsìntawi* 'Cow katsina song'.
2. *yoyhaniy,* expressive form of *yoyhani* 'descend as rain'.
3. *yoyhaniya,* expressive form of *yoyhani* 'descend as rain'.

Uyisonaqa₄ paavataalawintani.₅
Yoowi'aha,₆ yoowi'aha.
Hiy'a yayho yayho howina.
Hapi me.₇
Sikya'oo'omawutu₈ yoyhaniya.₉

Rain descends.
Rain descends.
It will glisten with puddles of water in the planted fields.
(Vocables.)
Listen, there is more.
The yellow clouds descend as rain.

The song focuses on the object of Hopi prayers—rain. Here rain is descending and descending, making the planted fields glisten with puddles. In the second section of the song, the yellow clouds, from the northwest cardinal direction, are descending as rain.

41. *Kur Himuwa Katsìntawi₁*
(Barrett 8900, Track 1; LoC)

Haa'a,₂ haw₃ ínamu.₄
Nana'alöngöta₅ qaa'ömanatuy,₆
itamuy₇ yuuwasinani.₈

4. = *uysonaq* 'throughout the midst of the planted area(s)'.
5. = *paavatalawintani* 'will be making it glisten with puddles of water'.
6. The vocable *yoowi'aha* is reminiscent of *yoowi* 'corn silk'.
7. *hapi me,* formulaic expression introducing the song's second part, *oomi* 'upward'.
8. = *sikya'o'omawt* 'yellow clouds'.
9. Barrett writes: "Last few words of Part 3 are lost on this Rec[ording]" (Barrett 1946: 59).

1. *kur himuwa katsìntawi* 'don't-know-which-one katsina song'. The katsina who performed this song has not been identified.
2. *haa'a,* vocative particle.
3. *haw,* vocative particle.
4. = *inam* 'my fathers'.
5. = *nana'löngöt,* object form of *nana'löngö* 'different kinds of'.
6. = *qa'ömamàntuy,* object form of *qa'ömamant* 'corn maidens'.
7. *itamuy* 'us', object form of *itam* 'we'.
8. = *yuwsinani* 'will clothe, adorn'.

Oho howa eehelo, aa'aa ahawiy aa.
Hapi me.$_9$
Nalönangwmongwitu$_{10}$ paavönmanatuy$_{11}$ hiikyangwintani,$_{12}$
tal'angwnawita.$_{13}$
Oho howa eehelo, aa'aa ahawiy aa.

Hark, o my fathers.
The corn maidens of the different kinds,
you will adorn us with them.
(Vocables.)
Listen, there is more.
The Four-Directional Cloud Chiefs will be vitalizing the young corn
    plants
all summer long.
(Vocables.)

The katsinas direct the people to adorn them, the katsinas, with corn maidens "of the different kinds," meaning the different colors of corn. This is a metaphorical way of referring to the process by which the fathers infuse prayer feathers with the people's prayers. The reference to different colors of corn maidens is a reference to the yellow, blue, red, and white colors of Hopi corn as well as to the four cardinal directions and the rain that comes from those directions.

    In the second section, after *hapi me,* the katsinas assure the people that the Four-Directional Cloud chiefs, meaning the clouds from all four cardinal directions, will be coming all summer long with their rain to vitalize the young corn plants who are implicitly growing Hopi girls. Because Hopis see the stages of human life as metaphorically analogous to that of corn plants, the reference to vitalizing here means that just as corn plants produce mature ears of corn with seeds for the next genera-tion, so too do Hopi girls grow up and become mothers with the power of procreation. The verb *hiikyangwinta,* song language for revitalizing and renewing life, reflects the idea that the rain coming from the four direc-tions will rejuvenate the plants as well as, by implication, the people.

---

9. *hapi me,* formulaic expression introducing the song's second part, *oomi* 'upward'.
10. = *Nalönangwmomngwit* 'Four-Directional Cloud Chiefs'.
11. =*paavönmamàntuy,* object form of *paavönmamant* 'young corn plants'.
12. *hiikyangwintani* 'will be vitalizing'.
13. = *tal'angwnawit* 'all summer long'.

42. Kur Himuwa Katsìntawi[1]
(Barrett 8909, Track 3; LoC)

Taayiyungwa[2] húvamu.[3]
—(inaudible)—qö,[4]
uma[5] pew[6] inumi,[7] tiimaynaanakwusani.[8]
Talasiyalaha'iqöma[9] umumi[10] sosonkiwyani,[11]
yépe'e.[12]
Hayaw loloo loloo loloosi.
Hayaw loloo loloo loloosi.
Hayaw loloo loloo loloosi.
Yanhaqamo,[13]
yanhaqam,[14]
ítamu[15] umumi tiitiwunima;[16]
haqami[17] tiitimuyiwa.[18]
Hii nini hiiyay a.

You, look!
When —(inaudible)—,
you should come to me to see the dance.
My face painted with pollen with sparkles in it will be pleasing to you,
here.

1. *kur himuwa katsìntawi* 'don't-know-which-one katsina song'. The katsina who performed this song has not been identified.
2. = *taayungwa* 'look (plural)'.
3. *húvamu*, pausal form of *huvam*, hortative particle for second person dual and plural.
4. = *-qw*, subordinating suffix, the only element identifiable in this line. The line probably had to do with the prayers of the people.
5. *uma* 'you (plural)'.
6. *pew* 'toward here, coming this way'.
7. *inumi* 'to me'.
8. = *timaynànkwusani* 'will set out on a journey to watch a performance'.
9. *talasiyalaha'iqöma* 'my face painted with pollen with sparkles in it'.
10. *umumi* 'to you (plural)'.
11. *sosonkiwyani* 'will be pleasing (plural)'.
12. = *yep'e,* pausal form of *yep* 'here'.
13. = *yanhaqam* 'in approximately this way'.
14. *yanhaqam* 'in approximately this way'.
15. = *itam* 'we'.
16. *tiitiwunima* 'be dancing in performance'.
17. = *aqwhaqami* 'throughout'.
18. *tiitimuyiwa* 'be caught up in dancing'.

(Vocables.)
This is the way,
this is the way
we are going along dancing dances for you,
[and] are caught up in dancing throughout.
(Vocables.)

The katsinas tell the people to watch them, recommending that they come to see them dance. They then describe how their faces are painted with pollen that sparkles. The pollen represents the Hopi focus on fertility and new life and so is a pleasing sight. Performing with this countenance of life, the katsinas say they are dancing pleasingly for the people. They describe how they are thoroughly engrossed in performing for the people.

Songs Recorded by
Jesse Walter Fewkes in 1926

43. *Hemiskatsìntawi₁*
(Fewkes 18991, Track 10; IUATM)

Aa, haw₂ ínamu,₃
paahoy₄ tuutuvenaya.₅
Okiw₆ pew₇ yokva,₈
námura.₉
Yan₁₀ uma naawakinaya.₁₁
Hoopaq₁₂ oongaq₁₃ muunang₁₄ hoyoyotimani.₁₅
Paavataalawiyungni.₁₆
Ahaa iihii.
Me.₁₇
Yoyhoyoyotimani.₁₈
Uuyisonaqa₁₉ paavataalawiyungni.
Aaha iihii.

Oh, hark my fathers,
you are marking your prayer feathers.

1. *hemiskatsìntawi* 'Hemiskatsina song'.
2. *haw*, vocative particle.
3. = *inam* 'my fathers'.
4. *paahoy*, short for *umùupahoy*, object form of *umùupaho* 'your prayer feathers'.
5. = *tutuvenaya* 'be marking (plural)'.
6. *okiw* 'humbly, pitifully'.
7. *pew* 'toward here, coming this way'.
8. *yokva* 'rain' (verb).
9. *námura* 'let it be so'.
10. *yan* 'like this, in this way, thus'.
11. = *naanawakna* 'pray (plural)'.
12. = *hoopaqw* 'from the northeast'.
13. = *oongaqw* 'from above'.
14. = *muunangw* 'flowing water, runoff water'.
15. *hoyoyotimani* 'will be moving along'.
16. = *paavatalawyungwni* 'will be glistening with puddles of water in several places'.
17. *me* 'listen', a particle to direct the attention.
18. *yoyhoyoyotimani* 'will be moving along as rain'.
19. = *uysonaq* 'throughout the midst of the planted area(s)'.

Humbly may it rain here,
let it be so.
In this way you pray.
From up in the northeast the runoff water will move along.
Water will be glistening all around.
(Vocables of the sound of singing.)
Listen.
Rain will be moving along.
Throughout the planted fields, there will be glistening puddles of water.
(Vocables of the sound of singing.)

The katsinas note that the people are marking their prayer feathers, meaning that they are figuratively imbuing them with their most heartfelt prayers for rain. They are humbly praying that it will rain here, that is, on their planted fields. In response to these heartfelt prayers, the katsinas promise that runoff water will move from the northeast throughout their planted fields. The puddled water in the fields will be glistening with the promise of the new life that results from this rain.

44. Koyemsitawi$_1$
(Fewkes 18987, Track 2; IUATM)

(For a fuller version of this song, see Song 52: Roberts Cylinder 28, Track 2.)

Tootiiya ona maa yee.
Kwiningyaqö$_2$ sikya'omaw$_3$ kuukuyivani.$_4$
Angq$_5$ pew$_6$ yooyhaahawimani.$_7$
Sikyayoyaleki$_8$ hoohoongivani.$_9$
[lines missing from performance]
Sakwayoyaleki$_{10}$ hoohoongivani.

1. koyemsitawi 'Mudhead katsina song'.
2. = kwiningyaqw 'from the northwest'.
3. = sikya'o'omawt 'yellow clouds'.
4. = kuukuyvani 'will appear, will make their appearance, will come into view'.
5. = angqw 'from it, from there'.
6. pew 'toward here, coming this way'.
7. = yoyhahawtima 'go along descending as rain'.
8. = sikyayoyleki 'yellow rain lines'.
9. = hoohongvani 'will stand up (in several places)'.
10. = sakwayoyleki 'blue/green rain lines'.

Paatuwataviyani,₁₁
humi'uyit₁₂ síqölönawita.₁₃
Aaha iihi, aaha iihi.

(Vocables.)
The yellow clouds will make their appearance from the northwest.
From there they will come descending as rain.
The yellow rain lines will stand up.
[*missing lines mentioning the blue/green clouds of the southwest*]
The blue/green rain lines will stand up.
They will lay water on the land,
along the expanses of flowering corn plants.
(Vocables of the sound of singing.)

The Mudhead katsinas are singing about the coming of the rains from the northwest and southwest directions. In naming the cardinal directions, the northwest is the first named, and then the others follow in a counterclockwise direction. In this song only the first two directions and the associated clouds and rain are mentioned. However, since this appears to be a song fragment, perhaps the other two directions were mentioned in the complete song, as is the case in a very similar song recorded by Helen Roberts, Song 55.

The katsinas describe how yellow clouds from the northwest make their appearance and descend as rain, characterizing the rain as "yellow rain lines [that] will stand up," *sikyayoyleki hoohongni.* Then the blue/green rain lines from the southwest are mentioned. During summer thunderstorms, cells of descending rain move across the land. Seen from a distance, this rain appears as vertical lines of rain, *yoyleki.* This rain is often imaged on textiles as a motif of three stacked clouds with vertical lines extending from their base. There are apparently missing lines that would repeat this sentiment for the clouds from the southwest direction. The katsinas comment that they will lay their water on the land, throughout the fields of flowering corn plants. Of course, there are other kinds of food plants in the fields besides the corn plants that are flowering. However, this general reference to corn plants is used because corn is seen as

11. = *paatuwatapyani* 'will lay water on the land (plural)'.
12. *humi'uyit,* object form of *humi'uyi* 'corn plant'.
13. = *sìiqölnawit* 'along the flowery expanses'.

the primary subsistence staple and thus is understood here to encompass all kinds of plants that flower and produce sustenance for the people.

45. Ma'lokatsìntawi$_1$
(Fewkes 18279, Track 7; IUATM)

Aaha aahay.
Sonway$_2$ talti,$_3$
ayangqö.$_4$
Sonway talti,
hoopaq$_5$ ayangqö.
Kisiwuvangaqö$_6$ qöya'omawt$_7$ kuukuyivani.$_8$
Umumutima,$_9$
naanan'ivaqö$_{10}$ péwi'i.$_{11}$
Pewya,$_{12}$
umumi'i.
Hoyoyotimani,
uyisonaqa.$_{13}$
Aa aa'a yahi aa'hay aa.

(Vocables.)
It becomes beautiful daylight
from over there.
It becomes beautiful daylight
from over there in the northeast.
The white clouds will make their appearance coming from Shadow Spring.

1. *ma'lokatsìntawi* 'Ma'lo katsina song'.
2. *sonway* 'beautiful'.
3. = *tàlti* 'become daylight'.
4. = *ayángqw* 'from over there'.
5. = *hoopaqw* 'from the northeast'.
6. = *Kisiwvangaqw* 'from Shadow Spring'.
7. = *qöya'o'omawt* 'white clouds'.
8. = *kuukuyvani* 'will appear, will make their appearance, will come into view'.
9. *umumutima* 'go along booming'.
10. = *naanan'ivaqw* 'from the different directions around'.
11. = *pew'i*, pausal form of *pew* 'toward here, coming this way'.
12. *pewya* 'come here (plural)', plural predicate form of *pew* 'toward here, coming this way'.
13. = *uysonaq* 'throughout the midst of the planted area(s)'.

They will come along booming
from the different directions around.
They come toward here,
to you.
They will move along
throughout the midst of the planted fields.
(Vocables of the sound of singing.)

The katsinas are singing of the beautiful light that comes with the dawn of a new day. This is metaphorically compared to the new life that results from the coming of rain. From the northeast direction, from Shadow Spring, the white clouds will appear and come along with thunder booming. Then the katsinas say that clouds are coming from all directions and will be moving throughout the planted fields.

46. *Ma'lokatsìntawi$_1$*
(Fewkes 18279, Track 8; IUATM)

Ayám$_2$ paave'e,$_3$
oo'omawutu$_4$ yoytokilayu$_5$ naanawinaya,$_6$
taawanawita;$_7$
puma$_8$ pew$_9$ umumi$_{10}$ yawi$_{11}$ Tuwanasave'e,$_{12}$
sonwakw$_{13}$ qátsita$_{14}$ yangqw$_{15}$ yoywunuto;$_{16}$
naatayawinaya.$_{17}$

1. *ma'lokatsìntawi* 'Ma'lo katsina song'.
2. *ayám* 'over there'.
3. *paave'e,* pausal form of *paave* 'at the spring'.
4. = *oo'omawt* 'clouds'.
5. *yòytokilay,* object form of *yòytokila'am* 'the date they set for rain'.
6. = *nanawinya* 'be making plans (plural)'.
7. = *taawanawit* 'all day long'.
8. *puma* 'they'.
9. *pew* 'toward here, coming this way'.
10. *umumi* 'to you (plural)'.
11. = *yaw,* quotative particle.
12. = *Tuuwanasave'e,* pausal form of *Tuuwanasave* 'at *Tuuwanasavi* (the Hopi lands)'.
13. *sonwakw,* object form of *sonway* 'beautiful'.
14. = *qatsit,* object form of *qatsi* 'life'.
15. *yangqw* 'from here, in here'.
16. *yoywunuto* 'go/come stand as rain'.
17. = *naatayawnaya* 'make feel good about each other (plural)'.

Aa aho aa ha ee ehe eelo.

Over there at the spring,
the clouds are making plans for when it is to rain
all day long,
for when they are to come to you at *Tuuwanasavi*
and stand as rain for a beautiful life here,
for when they make the people feel good about each other.
(Vocables.)

The katsinas describe how the clouds, who are the katsinas, are making plans over at the spring, a reference to a spring in one of the four cardinal directions where they live. They are planning to come on the date that has been set for rain (*yòytokila*). This refers to the date established earlier for their performance in the village. The katsinas say that when they come and stand as rain, they will make life beautiful, *sonway qatsi*, meaning that the coming of the rain will refresh and revitalize life.

    Tuuwanasavi refers to all the lands used by the Hopi people, whether for hunting, gathering wild greens, or raising plants in a planted field. In this song the storm cells that move across the land are described as "standing as rain" in order to suggest the vertical nature of the descending rain. The katsinas say that when such rain rejuvenates life so that it is beautiful, the people will feel encouraged and will rededicate their efforts to live right. In this way are able to feel good about each other.

47. *Soyohìmkatsinmuy₁ Taawi'am₂*
(Fewkes 18989, Track 5; IUATM)

Aaha ha iihi.
Naanakwusiwa.₃

---

1. *soyohìmkatsinmuy,* object form of *soyohìmkatsinam* 'all kinds of katsinas, mixed katsinas'.
2. *taawi'am* 'their song'.
3. = *nànkwusiwa* 'for a journey by several to have begun'.

Ayangqö$_4$ Kisiwvangaqö$_5$ wuuwukmuyu$_6$ pöötapyamuy$_7$ ánawit$_8$ ítamu$_9$
umumi$_{10}$ naanakwusa,$_{11}$
péwi'i.$_{12}$
Paatuwvootay$_{13}$ taalawinaya,$_{14}$
paamotoro$_{15}$ ang$_{16}$ hoohongivani.$_{17}$
Putak$_{18}$ itam$_{19}$ umumi yooya'öki,$_{20}$
péwi'i.
Aha aa iihi.
Angq$_{21}$ pútakwa$_{22}$ námura$_{23}$ umu'uyi$_{24}$ naawungwinayani.$_{25}$
Angq pútakwa námura umu'uyimanatu$_{26}$ naatukwsintani.$_{27}$
Oo'ohoy ooho wa e'he'eelo.

(Vocables of the sound of singing.)
The journey has begun.
From over at Shadow Spring, along the elders' consecrated path, we have
    set out on our journey to you,
coming this way.
We make the water shields glisten.

4. = *ayángqw* 'from over there'.
5. = *Kisiwvangaqw* 'from Shadow Spring'.
6. = *wuuwukwmuy*, object form of *wuuwuyom* 'elders'.
7. = *pöötapyamuy*, object form of *pöötavi'am* 'their consecrated path'.
8. *ánawit* 'along its course'.
9. = *itam* 'we'.
10. *umumi* 'to you (plural)'.
11. = *nànkwusa* 'start on a journey (plural)'.
12. = *pew'i*, pausal form of *pew* 'toward here, coming this way'.
13. = *paatuwvotay*, short for *itàapatuwvotay*, object form of *itàapatuwvota* 'our water shields, rings of ripples in water'.
14. = *taalawnaya* 'make glisten (plural)'.
15. *paamotoro* 'water pillars, splashes of raindrops'.
16. *ang* 'along it, along there, in that area, in several places'.
17. = *hoohongvani* 'will stand up repeatedly (plural)'.
18. = *putakw* 'with that, by means of that, using that'.
19. *itam* 'we'.
20. = *yoy'öki* 'arrive, come as rain'.
21. = *angqw* 'from it, from there'.
22. = *putakw* 'with that, by means of that, using that'.
23. *námura* 'let it be so'.
24. = *umùu'uyi* 'your (corn) plants'.
25. = *naawungwnayani* 'will make selves grow'.
26. = *umùu'uyimamant* 'your (corn) plant maidens'.
27. *naatukwsintani* 'will be making selves mature'.

The water pillars will repeatedly stand up along there.
With that (the rain), we come to you as rain,
coming this way.
(Vocables of the sound of singing.)
From there with that, let it be that your plant maidens will make them-
selves grow.
From there with that, let it be that your plant maidens will be making
themselves mature.
(Vocables.)

This is the same song as Song 99 recorded by Robert Black in the 1950s
and Song 122 recorded by George List in 1960. Given that Fewkes
recorded this song in 1926, we can surmise that it was known and performed for at least 50 years. The high degree of similarity in these
versions indicates the retentive power of oral tradition.

The katsinas announce that they have begun their journey, coming
from their home at Shadow Spring in the northeast direction. They are
traveling along a consecrated path that is a virtual path of prayer from
their homes but becomes an actual path of sprinkled cornmeal as the
katsinas enter the village and pass into the plaza. This path was laid out
by the elders who planned and made the preparations for the performance.
Although unstated, the katsinas are coming as rain, which will make the
water shields glisten and the water pillars stand. The "water shields"
(*paatuwvota*) are the concentric ripples formed in puddles of rainwater
when raindrops strike the surface and the "water pillars" (*paamotoro*) are
the little rebounds that occur when drops strike the surface of a puddle.
By means of this rain, the katsinas say, the corn plants, metaphorically
referred to as plant maidens, will make themselves grow up.

Songs Recorded by Helen Roberts
in the 1920s

48. *Angaktsìntawi$_1$*
(Roberts Cylinder 8, Tracks 3–4; LoC)

Haw'o$_2$ ínamu,$_3$
uma$_4$ yep$_5$ kwakwha'unangway$_6$ oomawnaawakinayaqö'ö',$_7$
pu'$_8$ tuwat$_9$ oo'omawutu$_{10}$ kwakwha'unangway oomi$_{11}$ kuukuyivani.$_{12}$
Angqw$_{13}$ pew$_{14}$ yoyhaahawimani;$_{15}$
oomi kuukuyivani.
Angqw pew yoynaanakwusani.$_{16}$
Owí$_{17}$ uma yep inumi$_{18}$ yoynawakinayaqö'ö,$_{19}$
péwi'i,$_{20}$
antsa$_{21}$ naanan'ivaqw$_{22}$ oo'omawutu pew umumi$_{23}$ yoyhoyoyotani,$_{24}$
péwi'i.

1. *angaktsìntawi* 'Long-Hair katsina song'.
2. *haw'o*, vocative particle.
3. =*inam* 'my fathers'.
4. *uma* 'you (plural)'.
5. *yep* 'here'.
6. *kwakwha'unangway* 'with tranquil hearts, with beneficent intentions'.
7. = *oomawnanawaknaqw'ö*, subordinate clause pausal form of *oomawnanawakna* 'pray for clouds (plural)'.
8. *pu'* 'now, then'.
9. *tuwat* 'in turn, for (one's) part'.
10. = *oo'omawt* 'clouds'.
11. *oomi* 'upward'.
12. = *kuukuyvani* 'will appear, will make their appearance, will come into view'.
13. *angqw* 'from it, from there'.
14. *pew* 'toward here, coming this way'.
15. = *yoyhahawtimani* 'will go along descending as rain'.
16. = *yoynànkwusani* 'will start on a journey as rain'.
17. *owí* 'yes'.
18. *inumi* 'to me'.
19. = *yoynanawaknaqw'ö*, subordinate clause pausal form of *yoynanawakna* 'pray for rain (plural)'.
20. = *pew'i*, pausal form of *pew* 'toward here, coming this way'.
21. *antsa* 'truly, really, indeed'.
22. *naanan'ivaqw* 'from the different directions around'.
23. *umumi* 'to you (plural)'.
24. *yoyhoyoyotani* 'will be moving as rain'.

Ooho way, eehe loy.
Ooho wa haa'wi'a.
*Hapi me.*₂₅
Owí, uma yep inumi yoynawakinayaqö'ö,
péwi'i,
antsa naanan'ivaqw oo'omawutu pew umumi yoyhoyoyotani.

Hark, my fathers,
you have prayed here for clouds with tranquil hearts,
and for their part the clouds, with tranquil hearts, will make their appear-
    ance up above.
Coming from there, they will be descending as rain;
they will make their appearance up above.
Coming from there, they will start on their journey as rain.
Yes, when you here pray to me for rain,
coming this way,
truly from the different directions around, the clouds, coming toward you,
    will be moving as rain,
coming this way.
(Vocables.)
Listen, there is more.
Yes, when you here send me prayers for rain,
coming this way,
truly from the different directions around, the clouds, coming toward you,
    will be moving as rain.

The katsinas address the people, acknowledging their prayers for rain,
here described as clouds. They describe their prayers as being made with
tranquil hearts (*kwakwha'unangway*), meaning that the people have sent
their prayers free from ill will and selfish goals. To receive the gifts of the
katsinas, the people must pray with hearts united for the well-being of all
members of the community and with hearts untroubled with thoughts of
individual desires that might conflict with the overall good of the community. The goal of Hopi life is community survival. All prescribed practices
and activities are designed to achieve that end. The Hopi lifeway relies on
voluntary cooperation, with everyone participating actively and selflessly
for the good of the whole. These ideas are unstated but embodied in the

25. *hapi me,* formulaic expression introducing the song's second part, *oomi* 'upward'.

various ways that making prayers with the necessary beneficent intentions are described in katsina songs.

If the people pray with these sincere intentions, the katsinas promise that, from their homes, they will come with tranquil hearts, that is, with good intentions. They will make their appearance as clouds, appearing above the horizon, and then journey, that is, move toward the villages and fields, building and descending as rain. The word *yoynànkwusa* 'start on a journey as rain' includes the idea that the clouds, as animate beings, can deliberately choose to make a journey somewhere. The clouds will come from all directions, that is, from the katsinas' homes in all four cardinal directions. This sentiment is repeated.

49. *Angaktsìntawi$_1$*
(Roberts Cylinder 27, Track 1; LoC)

Ha'o$_2$ ha'o haw$_3$ itanamu.$_4$
Itamuyu$_5$ yuuwasinaya.$_6$
Paahomanatuy$_7$ itamuyu yaawitoyaqw'ö.$_8$
pay$_9$ nuwu$_{10}$ yàasatiqw'ö,$_{11}$
taawa$_{12}$ pakima.$_{13}$
Itamu$_{14}$ naakwusani,$_{15}$
atkyami$_{16}$ Móngwivami'i.$_{17}$

1. *angaktsìntawi* 'Long-Hair katsina song'.
2. *ha'o*, vocative particle.
3. *haw*, vocative particle.
4. = *itanam* 'our fathers'.
5. = *itamuy* 'us', object form of *itam* 'we'.
6. = *yuwsinaya* 'clothe, adorn (plural)'.
7. = *pahomamàntuy*, object form of *pahomamant* 'prayer feather maidens'.
8. = *yawtoynaqw'ö*, dependent clause pausal form of *yawtoyna* 'put something in someone's hand to hold'.
9. *pay*, expressive particle.
10. *nuwu* 'even now'.
11. = *yàasattiqw'ö*, subordinate clause pausal form of *yàasatti* 'become this time'.
12. *taawa* 'sun'.
13. *pakima* 'sink, go down out of sight, set'.
14. = *itam* 'we'.
15. = *nàakwustani* 'will be setting out on a journey (as one group after another)'.
16. *atkyami* 'downwards', a reference to the southwest.
17. = *Mongvami'i*, pausal form of *Mongvami* 'to Leadership Spring'.

—*(inaudible)*— *aw$_{18}$ uma$_{19}$ kawayota$_{20}$ meloonit$_{21}$* —*(inaudible)*— *-mana-tuy$_{22}$ naawakinani.$_{23}$*
—*(inaudible)*—
Pew$_{24}$ yooy- yoytalawiptimani;$_{25}$
hoyoyotimani.$_{26}$
Pew yooy- yoy'umumutimani;$_{27}$
tayayatimani.$_{28}$
Yoytökiyamuy$_{29}$ naahiyongwani.$_{30}$
Hapi me.$_{31}$
Pew yooy- yoytalawiptimani;
hoyoyotimani.
Pew yooy- yoy'umumutimani;
tayayatimani.
Yoytökiyamuy naahiyongwani.

Hark, hark, o our fathers.
You have adorned us (with your prayers).
You have put the prayer feather maidens in our hands,
it has become this time now,
and the sun is going down.
We will set out on our journey
to Leadership Spring down below (to the southwest).

18. *aw* 'to it, to there'.
19. *uma* 'you (plural)'.
20. = *kawayot,* object form of *kawayo,* which is short for *kawayvatnga* 'watermelon', literally "horse squash" (*-vatnga* is from *patnga* 'squash'); *kawayo/kaway-* is from Spanish *caballo* 'horse'.
21. *meloonit,* object form of *melooni* 'muskmelon' (from Spanish *melón*).
22. = *-mamàntuy* '-maidens'. The first part of the compound cannot be identified in the recording.
23. = *naawaknani* 'will pray'.
24. *pew* 'toward here, coming this way'.
25. = *yòytalwiptimani* 'will go along as rain with lightning flashing'.
26. *hoyoyotimani* 'will be moving along'.
27. *yoy'umumutimani* 'will go along thundering'.
28. *tayayatimani* 'will go along trembling, shaking, quaking'.
29. = *yòytötökiyamuy,* object form of *yòytötöki'am* 'their rain sounds', a reference to everything that makes a sound when it rains.
30. = *nàayongwani* 'will delight in'.
31. *hapi me,* formulaic expression introducing the song's second part, *oomi* 'upward'.

To —(*inaudible*)— you will pray for watermelons, muskmelons and
—(*inaudible*)—.
—(*inaudible*)—.
They will be coming along with lightning flashing in the rain;
they will be moving along.
They will be coming along thundering;
they will go along shaking the earth.
There will be delight in their rain sounds.
Listen, there is more.
They will be coming along with lightning flashing in the rain;
they will be moving along.
They will be coming along thundering;
they will go along shaking the earth.
There will be delight in their rain sounds.

This is the last song of the day. The sun is going down; it is time for the katsinas to return to their homes. At the end of the last dance, the katsinas line up facing the people and the katsina father goes down the line, placing a prayer feather and pinch of cornmeal in the left hand of each katsina. Then the katsinas turn and file out of the plaza. In this song the katsinas acknowledge this process by describing how the fathers have adorned them with their prayers. They say they will be returning to their homes at Leadership Spring in the southwest direction as indicated by the expression "down below."

In return for their prayers, the katsinas promise that the rain will come with lightning flashing and thunder booming. These sights and sounds of rain are delightful to all who await them. Lightning and thunder are characteristic of the hard late summer rainstorms that move across the land, depositing the much prayed for water that will bring their crops to maturity.

50. Hehey'akatsìntawi$_1$
(Roberts Cylinder 2, Track 15; LoC)

Yaahiya yaahiya yaahiya hiniiniyay'a.
Itanam,$_2$ itangum,$_3$
itamuy$_4$ naawakinaya,$_5$
ayó$_6$ taatö,$_7$ hoopo,$_8$ oo'omawkimi'i.$_9$
Ev$_{10}$ itam$_{11}$ umungem$_{12}$ paayoysingumannaayuwasina,$_{13}$
péwi'i.$_{14}$
Ii aahawi aahawi aa ii aa niiya.
Hapi me.$_{15}$
Naanan'ivaqö$_{16}$ oo'omawutu$_{17}$ pew$_{18}$ yooyanaanakwusani.$_{19}$

(Vocables.)
Our fathers, our mothers,
you are sending us prayers
over to the southeast, to the northeast, to the dwelling places of the
  clouds.
There we adorn ourselves for you with rainwater pollen,
coming this way.
(Vocables.)

1. *hehey'akatsìntawi* 'Hehey'a katsina song'.
2. *itanam* 'our fathers'.
3. *itangum* 'our mothers'.
4. *itamuy* 'us', object form of *itam* 'we'.
5. = *naanawakna* 'pray (plural)'.
6. = *ayó'* 'toward over there'.
7. *taatö* 'to the southeast'.
8. *hoopo* 'to the northeast'.
9. = *oo'omàwkimi'i*, pausal form of *oo'omàwkimi* 'to the dwelling places of the clouds (in different directions)'.
10. *ev* 'there'. This is the Second Mesa form of Third Mesa *ep*. Syllable-final *v* in Second Mesa pronunciation regularly corresponds to Third Mesa *p*, and vice versa.
11. *itam* 'we'.
12. *umungem* 'for you (plural), for your benefit'.
13. = *paayoysingumannayuwsina* 'adorn self with rainwater pollen'.
14. = *pew'i*, pausal form of *pew* 'toward here, coming this way'.
15. *hapi me*, formulaic expression introducing the song's second part, *oomi* 'upward'.
16. = *naanan'ivaqw* 'from the different directions around'.
17. = *oo'omawt* 'clouds'.
18. *pew* 'toward here, coming this way'.
19. = *yoynànkwusani* 'will start on a journey as rain'.

Listen, there is more.
From the different directions around, the clouds will start coming on their
journey as rain.

The katsinas acknowledge that the people, here addressed as fathers and
mothers, are sending their prayers to them at their cloud homes in the
southeast and northeast directions. They respond to these heartfelt prayers
by adorning themselves with rain so that they can come as rain as their
gift. They promise to begin their journey coming from all directions.
Likening the particulate nature of raindrops to pollen, the rain is
described as rainwater pollen, *paayoysingumni*. This word appears in its
combining form *paayoysinguman-* in the compound *paayoysingumannayuwsina*[20] 'adorn selves with rainwater pollen'. Pollen in ritual contexts
has sanctified powers. It is part of the consecrated path along which the
katsinas travel into the village. Its use here may be to acknowledge this
role as well as to metaphorically create an image of the particulate nature
of rain. A similar metaphoric likening of rainwater to ground cornmeal on
a tray appears in Song 138.

51. *Kookopòltawi*[1]
(Roberts Cylinder 15, Track 10; LoC)

Haa'o[2] *haw*[3] *haa'o iwuuti.*[4]
Pay[5] *um*[6] *ingu*[7] *kítikyango*[8]
i'unngway[9] *hovalanta,*[10]

---

20. *-nayuwsina* is from *naayuwsina* 'dress, adorn selves'.

1. *kookopòltawi* 'Kookopölö (katsina) song'.
2. *haa'o,* vocative particle.
3. *haw,* vocative particle.
4. = *iwùuti* 'my woman, my wife'. Grave-accented vowels are not distinguished in the pronunciation of the Second Mesa villages of Supawlavi (Shipaulovi) and Songòopavi
   (Shungopavi). This song is from one of those villages.
5. *pay,* expressive particle.
6. *um* 'you'.
7. *ingu* 'my mother'.
8. = *kítikyangw* 'while saying'.
9. = *i'unangway,* object form of *i'unangwa* 'my heart'.
10. *hovalanta* 'be disheartening'.

pay nu'$_{11}$ naav$_{12}$ i'unngwayniiqö'ö,$_{13}$
lavay'aysakwita,$_{14}$
amum$_{15}$ nu' qatuvtuqe'e.$_{16}$
Aw$_{17}$ nuy$_{18}$ wuuwantaqö'ö,$_{19}$
piw$_{20}$ pay haqami$_{21}$ tuungeminta.$_{22}$
Ayó$_{23}$ kwiniwi$_{24}$ naawiki'maqö'ö,$_{25}$
i'unang$_{26}$ tuutuya.$_{27}$
Yan,$_{28}$
yanhaqamo$_{29}$ "hahaymumuy$_{30}$ talaymumuy$_{31}$" lavaysakwiqatsilvayiyata,$_{32}$
kwangwa'iwta.$_{33}$

11. *nu'* 'I'.
12. = *naap* 'by oneself'. Syllable-final *-v* (as in *naav*), regularly appears in place of *-p* in Second Mesa pronunciation.
13. = *i'unangwayniqw'ö*, subordinate clause pausal form of *i'unangway* 'my heart' (object form). *Naap unangway* 'one's own fault, one's own doing'.
14. = *lavay'aysakwit*, object form of *lavay'aysakwi* 'gossip, one who gossips'.
15. *amum* 'with her'.
16. *qatuvtuqe'e*, subordinate clause pausal form of *qatuvtu* 'marry' (with *amum*). The corresponding Third Mesa pronunciation is *qatuptu*.
17. *aw* 'to it, to there'.
18. *nuy* 'me', object form of *nu'* 'I'. *Nuy* serves as subject of *wuuwanta;* it is in the object form because of the adverbial status of the subordinate clause.
19. = *wuuwantaqw'ö*, subordinate clause pausal form of *wuuwanta* 'be thinking'.
20. *piw* 'also, too, again'.
21. = *aqwhaqami* 'throughout'.
22. *tuungeminta* 'be inviting someone else to go/come along'. This is the "unspecified object" form of *ngeeminta* 'invite to go/come along'.
23. = *ayó'* 'to, toward over there'.
24. *kwiniwi* 'toward the northwest'.
25. = *naawiki'ymaqw'ö*, subordinate clause pausal form of *naawiki'yma* 'go along escorting one another'.
26. = *i'unangwa* 'my heart'.
27. *tuutuya* 'be sick, ill, aching, hurting, in pain'.
28. *yan* 'like this, in this way, thus'.
29. = *yanhaqam* 'in approximately this way'.
30. *hahaymumuy*, an example of a kind of usage characteristic of certain people.
31. *talaymumuy*, another example of such usage. *Hahaymumuy* (previous note) and *talaymumuy* seem to be object forms, in agreement with the object form of the next word (see next note).
32. = *lavaysakwiqatsilvayiyat*, object form of *lavaysakwiqatsilvayi'at* 'the worn-out words of the language of her way of life'.
33. *kwangwa'iwta* 'remain with something that is attractive or irresistible'.

Nam₃₄ yépe'e;₃₅
taq₃₆ nu' ókiwni.₃₇
Nu' pa₃₈ yánga'a,₃₉
ayah ii aa haay aa aha.₄₀
Okiw₄₁ nu' tooki₄₂ qaatsiptiqe'e,₄₃
wuuwanlawu,₄₄
hal₄₅ pay tatami.₄₆
Hapi me.₄₇
[part of song missing]

Hark, hark, o my wife.
Although you keep saying you're my mother,
you dishearten me,
though it was my own fault,
[because] I married
the gossip.
While I'm thinking about her,
she is asking people to go somewhere again.
When they go with each other over to the northwest,
my heart aches.
In this way,
in this way she stays attracted to
the yackety-yack worn-out words of the language of her way of life.
Let it be, here,
even though I'll be miserable.
Just think, I'm here [saying],

34. *nam* 'may it, let it be so', impersonal hortative particle.
35. = *yep'e,* pausal form of *yep* 'here'.
36. *taq* 'for, seeing that, since, because, despite the fact, notwithstanding, even though', a conjunction that contrasts a previous statement with its logical consequence.
37. *ókiwni* 'will be humble, pitiful'.
38. *pa,* particle used to indicate wonder, awe, surprise, doubt.
39. = *yanga',* pausal form of *yang* 'here along here, in these places, in this area'.
40. *ayah ii aa haay aa aha* are sounds of emotional distress.
41. *okiw* 'humbly, pitifully'.
42. *tooki* 'last night, last evening'.
43. = *qaatsiptuqe'e,* subordinate clause pausal form of *qaatsiptu* 'lie down'.
44. *wuuwanlawu* 'keep thinking, worrying'.
45. *hal* 'but then, well', a particle of concession.
46. *tatami,* an expression of resignation to a situation.
47. *hapi me,* formulaic expression introducing the song's second part, *oomi* 'upward'.

(vocables of emotional distress).
Poor me when I lay down last night
I kept thinking,
well, let it go ahead and be like that.
Listen, there is more.
[*missing lines*]

The Kookopölö katsina is singing the laments of a lovelorn man who is distressed by the wayward activities of his wife. He addresses her as his mother, reflecting the Hopi idea that when a man marries, his wife takes on the nurturing role formerly provided by his mother. The man admits that he married a gossip who he says is always luring people to go with her to the northwest, presumably a good place to gossip. He laments that she seems to be captivated by this apparently exciting life of talking about others behind their backs. He resigns himself to being miserable and declares that he is going to let her continue this kind of life. Gossip has no constructive place in a communal society. By singing about such persons, the katsinas are admonishing this type of behavior. The message is that persons who live for their own interests and enjoyment are ultimately destructive to the harmony and well-being of a small community.

52. *Koyemsitawi,*
(Roberts Cylinder 28, Track 2; LoC)

(For an abbreviated version of this song, see Song 44: Fewkes 18987, Track 2.)

Tootiiya ona maa yee.
Kwiningyaqö$_2$ sikya'o'omawt$_3$ kuukuyivani.$_4$
Angqw$_5$ pew$_6$ yooy- yoyhaahawiwmani.$_7$
Sikyatalawipiy,$_8$
yooy- yoyhoohongimani.$_9$

1. *koyemsitawi* 'Mudhead katsina song'.
2. = *kwiningyaqw* 'from the northwest'.
3. *sikya'o'omawt* 'yellow clouds'.
4. = *kuukuyvani* 'will appear, come into sight'.
5. *angqw* 'from it, from there'.
6. *pew* 'toward here, coming this way'.
7. = *yoyhahawiwmani* 'will go along descending as rain'.
8. = *sikyatalwìipikiy,* object form of *sikyatalwìipiki'am* 'their yellow lightning'.
9. = *yoyhohonginmani* 'will go along repeatedly making (them) stand in the rain'.

Sikyayoyalekiy,[10]
haahawiwmani.[11]
Paatuwataviyani,[12]
humi'uyisiqölönawita.[13]
Taavangqö[14] *sakwa'oomawt*[15] *kuukuyivani.*
Angqw pew yooy- yoyhaahawiwmani.
Sakwatalawipiy,[16]
hoohongimani.[17]
Sakwayoyalekiy,[18]
haahawiwmani.
Paatuwataviyani.
hum'iuyisiqölönawita.
Tatkyaqö[19] *pala'oomaw*[20] *kuukuyivani.*
Angqw pew yooy- yoyhaahawiwmani.
Palatalawipiy,[21]
hoohongimani.
Palayoyalekiy,[22]
haahawiwmani.
Paatuwataviyani,
humi'uysiqölönawita.
Aaha iihi.
Hoopaqö[23] *qöya'omaw*[24] *kuukuyivani.*
Angqw pew yooyoyhaahawiwmani.

10. = *sikyayoylekiy,* object form of *sikyayoyleki'am* 'their yellow rain lines'. Though in object form, this word is the subject of the verb in the next line.
11. = *haahawiwmani* 'will go/come along descending'.
12. = *paatuwatapyani* 'will lay water on the land (plural)'.
13. = *humi'uyisìiqölnawit* 'along the flowery expanse(s) of corn plants'.
14. = *taavangqw* 'from the southwest'.
15. = *sakwa'o'omawt* 'blue/green clouds'.
16. = *sakwatalwìipikiy,* object form of *sakwatalwìipiki'am* 'their blue/green lightning'.
17. = *hoohonginmani* 'will go along making stand'.
18. = *sakwayoylekiy,* object form of *sakwayoyleki'am* 'their blue/green rain lines'. Though in object form, this word is the subject of the verb in the next line.
19. = *tatkyaqw* 'from the southeast'.
20. = *pala'omaw* 'red cloud(s)'.
21. = *palatalwìipikiy,* object form of *palatalwìipiki'am* 'their red lightning'.
22. = *palayoylekiy,* object form of *palayoyleki'am* 'their red rain lines'. Though in object form, this word is the subject of the verb in the next line.
23. = *hoopaqw* 'from the northeast'.
24. = *qöya'omaw* 'white cloud(s)'.

Qöyatalawipiy,[25]
hoohongimani.
Qöyayoyalekiy,[26]
haahawiwmani.
Paatuwataviyani,
humi'uysiqölönawita.
Aaha iihi.
—*(inaudible)*—[27]

(Vocables of the Mudhead katsina.)
The yellow clouds will make their appearance from the northwest.
Coming from there, they will go along descending as rain.
Their yellow lightning,
they will go along repeatedly making it stand in the rain.
Their yellow rain lines,
will go along descending.
They will lay water on the land,
along the expanses of flowering corn plants.
The blue/green clouds will make their appearance from the southwest.
Coming from there, they will go along descending as rain.
Their blue/green lightning,
they will go along repeatedly making it stand.
Their blue/green rain lines,
will go along descending.
They will lay water on the land,
along the expanses of flowering corn plants.
The red clouds will make their appearance from the southeast.
Coming from there, they will go along descending as rain.
Their red lightning,
they will go along repeatedly making it stand.
Their red rain lines,
will go along descending.
They will lay water on the land,

25. = *qöyatalwìipikiy,* object form of *qöyatalwìipiki'am* 'their white lightning'.
26. = *qöyayoylekiy,* object form of *qöyayoyleki'am* 'their white rain lines'. Though in object form, this word is the subject of the verb in the next line.
27. Considering the completeness of the audible parts of this song, it seems fair to conclude that the inaudible portion consisted only of material like vocables and vocative expressions.

along the expanses of flowering corn plants.
(Vocables of the sound of singing.)
The white clouds will make their appearance from the northeast.
Coming from there, they will go along descending as rain.
Their white lightning,
they will go along repeatedly making it stand.
Their white rain lines,
will go along descending.
They will lay water on the land,
along the expanses of flowering corn plants.
(Vocables of the sound of singing.)
—(*inaudible*)—

This song describes the coming of the rains from all four directions in the complete counterclockwise ceremonial circuit beginning with the northwest, followed by the southwest, southeast, and finally the northeast. Each direction is associated with a color. Thus the clouds, lightning, and descending rain lines of the northwest are yellow, of the southwest blue/green, of the southeast red, and those of the northeast are white. The same song phrases are repeated to describe the rain from each direction, beginning with the clouds that make their appearance and go along descending as rain, to the lightning that repeatedly stands, that is, strikes the land vertically, to the rain lines that go along laying their water on the land along the fields of flowering corn plants. The clouds, lightning, and rain lines are all animate beings that are intentionally delivering their water to the fields. The plants are indicated as corn plants, but this mention is generally understood to encompass all plants.

The repetition of the coming of the rain from the homes of the katsinas in the four cardinal directions is intended to evoke a beautiful sight in the minds of the listeners of plentiful rain and, by implication, bountiful harvests that will bring food for the sustenance of the community. It is unusual to have such a complete song cycle preserved in a recording. In performance this complete directional circuit would be voiced, but when the songs were recorded from individuals singing into a microphone, the singers often did not sing all the verses and repeats of the songs. The completeness of the song in this recording is a rare treasure.

53. *Ma'lokatsìntawi₁*
(Roberts Cylinders 17–18, Tracks 11–12; LoC)

Qöya'omaw₂ umungem₃ námura,₄
humisi'uyita,₅ morisi'uyita₆ paayoyangwuy₇ tu- tuuwatavini,₈
taawanawita.₉
Kaway'uyit₁₀ sìiqölönawita úma'a,₁₁
taatawtimani,₁₂
siwawaytimakyang₁₃ kwiyavasnawita.₁₄
Paypu,₁₅
paypu námura.
Oo'o oo owa ee ahaa iihi ihi.
Hapi me.₁₆
Kaway'uyi sìiqölönawita úma'a,
taatawtimani,
siwawaytimakyang kwiyavasnawita.
Paypu,
paypu, námura.

Let it be that the white cloud, for your benefit,
will place rainwater on the land of blossoming corn plants and blossoming
    bean plants,
all day long.
Along the flowery expanses of watermelon plants
you will go singing songs
while enjoying yourselves along the fields with windbreaks.

1. *ma'lokatsìntawi* 'Ma'lo katsina song'.
2. *qöya'omaw* 'white cloud'.
3. *umungem* 'for you (plural), for your benefit'.
4. *námura* 'let it be so'.
5. = *humisi'uyit*, object form of *humisi'uyi* 'blossoming corn plants'.
6. = *morisi'uyit*, object form of *morisi'uyi* 'blossoming bean plants'.
7. *paayoyangwuy*, object form of *paayoyangw* 'rainwater'.
8. = *tuuwatavini* 'will place on the land'.
9. = *taawanawit* 'all day long'.
10. *kaway'uyit*, object form of *kaway'uyi* 'watermelon plant(s)'.
11. *úma'a*, pausal form of *uma* 'you (plural)'.
12. *taatawtimani* 'will go along singing songs'.
13. = *siwawaytimakyangw* 'while going along in joy, in happiness'.
14. = *kwiyavasnawit* 'along fields with windbreaks constructed on them'.
15. = *paapu* 'nowadays, anymore, now'.
16. *hapi me*, formulaic expression introducing the song's second part, *oomi* 'upward'.

Now,
let it be so now.
(Vocables of the sound of singing.)
Listen, there is more.
Along the flowery expanses of watermelon plants
you will go singing
whiie going in joy along the fields with windbreaks.
Now,
let it be so now.

This song describes how it will come to pass that the white clouds of the northeast will place their rainwater on the blossoming corn plants and blossoming bean plants all day long. The hope is that the rain will nurture the blossoming plants so that they will fruit and produce sustenance for the people. Then the katsinas sing how the people will go walking among their fields of watermelon plants, enjoying the sight of flourishing plants. This will prompt them to sing in happiness. They mention that the melon fields have windbreaks. These are rows of brush piled along the windward side of the field to protect the young plants from being covered by blowing sand.

54. *Si'ohemiskatsìntawi*₁
(Roberts Cylinder 32, Track 6; LoC)

EPTAWI

Itam₂ umumi₃ kwangwatu'awva,₄
atkyaqw₅ suvuyoyangw₆ itamuy₇ ngöytaqe'e,₈

1. *si'ohemiskatsìntawi* 'Zuni Hemiskatsina song'.
2. *itam* 'we'.
3. *umumi* 'to you (plural)'.
4. *kwangwatu'awva* 'come with a pleasant message, pleasant news'.
5. *atkyaqw* 'from below, from down there', a reference to the southwest direction.
6. *suvuyoyangw* 'steady drizzle, gentle rain'.
7. *itamuy* 'us', object form of *itam* 'we'.
8. *ngöytaqe'e,* subordinate clause pausal form of *ngöyta* 'be pursuing, following'.

yang$_9$ puma$_{10}$ umungem$_{11}$ sumi'nangwat$_{12}$ pasiwnayani.$_{13}$
Yan$_{14}$ uma$_{15}$ naawakinaya.$_{16}$
Ahaa iihii.
Itam umumi kwangwatu'awva,
atkyaqw tokyepyoyangw$_{17}$ itamuy ngöytaqe'e,
yang puma umungem sumi'nangwat pasiwnayani.
Yan uma naawakinaya.
Aaha iihi.
Oho oho oho yahiy aa.
Wi'a haay haawi'a haay aaha iihi.

RUKÙNTAWI

Aaha iihi' aaha iihi'.
Katsina, qa$_{18}$ um$_{19}$ pítuni,$_{20}$
qöyaviqaa'öy$_{21}$ yawmani?$_{22}$
Musangnuve'e,$_{23}$
maana$_{24}$ askwallawni,$_{25}$
Pikmokiy$_{26}$ tsootsona'a.$_{27}$

9. *yang* 'along here, in this area'.
10. *puma* 'they', 'it' in this context. Liquids (the gentle rain) have plural grammatical agreement in Hopi.
11. *umungem* 'for you (plural), for your benefit'.
12. *sumi'nangwat* 'together in intentions, united in endeavors, in unanimity'.
13. *pasiwnayani* 'will set out the intent (plural)'.
14. *yan* 'like this, in this way, thus'.
15. *uma* 'you (plural)'.
16. = *naanawakna* 'pray (plural)'.
17. *tokyepyoyangw* 'all-night rain'.
18. *qa* 'not'.
19. *um* 'you (singular)'.
20. *pítuni* 'will arrive, come, get there, reach a destination'.
21. = *qöyapqa'öy*, short for *ùuqöyapqa'öy*, object form of *ùuqöyapqa'ö* 'your ear of white corn'.
22. *yawmani* 'will be carrying by hand, taking, bringing'.
23. *Musangnuve'e*, pausal form of *Musangnuve* 'at Musangnuvi', a Second Mesa village.
24. *maana* 'girl, young unmarried woman, maiden'.
25. *askwallawni* 'will be thanking' (female speaker).
26. *pikmokiy*, object form of *pikmoki'at* 'her bundle of piki'.
27. = *tsòotsona'a*, pausalized form of *tsòotsona* 'kiss'.

Kwakhá$_{28}$ *oovi*$_{29}$ *um*$_{30}$ —(*inaudible: damaged recording*)—.
Aaha.

IN-PLACE SONG

We come to you with pleasant news
that from down below, a long gentle rain is following us,
and along here, for your benefit, it (the rain) will set out with the intent
    [that you should be] united in endeavors.
Thus you pray.
(Vocables of the sound of singing.)
We come to you with pleasant news
that from down below, an all-night rain is following us,
and along here, for your benefit, it will set out with the intent [that you
    should be] united in endeavors.
Thus you pray.
(Vocables and vocables of the sound of singing.)

RASPING SONG

(Vocables of the sound of singing.)
Katsina, will not you (be the one to) come,
bringing your white corn?
At Musangnuvi,
the maiden will be saying thank you,
and she kisses her bundle of piki.
It's a good thing therefore that you —(*inaudible*)—.
(Vocable.)

This song is a performed in two parts. The first section is sung by katsinas
singing in a line; the second as they are accompanied by katsina maidens
rasping scapulae on notched sticks. In the first part, the katsinas announce
that they are bringing pleasant news of a gentle drizzling all-night rain
coming from "down below," meaning the southwest direction. You are
praying for this, the katsinas say, meaning a long, steady rain that deeply

28. = *kwakwhá* 'thank you (masculine-speaker form), it's a good thing'.
29. *oovi* 'that's why'.
30. *um* 'you'.

waters the planted fields. The words *sumi'nangwat pasiwnayani* express the idea that the rain will cause the people to unite their hearts, meaning that it will bring them together in their intentions to live in harmony.

In the second section, in a rhetorical conversation, the katsina is bringing white corn to a girl at Musangnuvi. She thanks him for the piki, kissing it. The rest of the song is lost, but it seems that the corn from the katsina, implicitly grown by the gift of their rain, will be ground by the maiden to make piki. The white color of the corn is an allusion to the pristine purity of the life that the people agreed to at Emergence when they chose this corn. Piki is a paper-thin preparation of corn flour baked quickly on a hot stone. It is rolled or folded depending on the occasion. Because it is prepared for all ceremonial contexts as well as for daily consumption, it represents the fundamentally important role of corn in Hopi life.

55. Soyohìmkatsinmuy₁ Taawi'am₂
(Roberts Cylinder 26, Track 20; LoC)

Ha'óo₃ íngumu.₄
Ha'óo ínamu.₅
Uma₆ ayó₇ paytuukwimi'i.₈
Námusa₉ móngwitu₁₀ paas₁₁ namuy(?) -yamutu(?)₁₂ taawaniikyango₁₃

1. *soyohìmkatsinmuy,* object form of *soyohìmkatsinam* 'all kinds of katsinas, mixed katsinas'.
2. *taawi'am* 'their song'.
3. *ha'óo,* vocative particle.
4. = *ingum* 'my mothers'.
5. = *inam* 'my fathers'.
6. *uma* 'you (plural)'.
7. = *ayó* 'toward over there'.
8. = *pàytukwimi'i,* pausal form of *pàytukwimi* 'to the triple peaks', a description of *Nuvatukya'ovi,* the San Francisco Peaks, as seen from the Hopi mesas.
9. *námusa* 'let it be so'.
10. = *momngwit* 'leaders'.
11. = *pas* 'very', or perhaps *paas* 'carefully'.
12. What was heard as *namuy -yamutu* has not been identified.
13. = *taawaniikyangw* 'the sun/day however'. Whether *taawa* here should be construed as 'sun' or 'day' is unclear because of the unintelligibility of the material preceding this word.

natwantaqö'ö,$_{14}$
angqw$_{15}$ *puma*$_{16}$ *oomi*$_{17}$ *kuukuyivani.*$_{18}$
Kaway'uynawita$_{19}$ *taatangayatu*$_{20}$ *naangöyimani.*$_{21}$
Aaha aha aa'aaha.
Yoo oo wi'a nii.
Hapi me.$_{22}$
Piw$_{23}$ *tuwat*$_{24}$ *ayangqö*$_{25}$ *naanan'ivaqö*$_{26}$ *oo'omawutu*$_{27}$ *yoyhoyoyotani.*$_{28}$
Aaha aha aa'aaha.

Hark, my mothers,
Hark, my fathers.
Go over there to the triple peaks.
Let it be that while the leaders —(*unintelligible*)— the sun/day(?) however,
pursue life-promoting practices,
from there they will make their appearance coming up.
The yellowjackets will go chasing one other along the watermelon plantings.
(Vocables.)
Listen, there is more.
Also, for their part, the clouds will be moving as rain from over there, from the different directions around.
(Vocables.)

14. = *natwantaqw'ö,* subordinate clause pausal form of *natwanta* 'pursue life-promoting practices, practice customs related to the rejuvenation of life'.
15. *angqw* 'from it, from there'.
16. *puma* 'they'.
17. *oomi* 'upward'.
18. = *kuukuyvani* 'will appear, will make their appearance, will come into view'.
19. = *kaway'uynawit* 'along the watermelon plantings'.
20. = *taatangayt* 'yellowjackets'.
21. = *naangöymani* 'will go along chasing one other'.
22. *hapi me,* formulaic expression introducing the song's second part, *oomi* 'upward'.
23. *piw* 'also, too, again'.
24. *tuwat* 'in turn, for (one's) part'.
25. = *ayángqw* 'from over there'.
26. = *naanan'ivaqw* 'from the different directions around'.
27. = *oo'omawt* 'clouds'.
28. *yoyhoyoyotani* 'will be moving as rain'.

The katsinas are directing the people, here addressed as mothers and fathers, to look at the San Francisco Peaks. In the song they are described as the "triple peaks" (*pàytukwi*) because of the three peaks that are clearly visible from the Hopi mesas. They are usually labeled collectively as *Nuvatukya'ovi,* the "place of the high snowy peaks." These mountains are the home of the katsinas in the southwest direction and are, as well, an important place for gathering Douglas fir branches and other items for ceremonial use. It may be that the line with missing words refers to activities related to rejuvenation at the peaks by the leaders responsible for the dance, as well as to activities by the clouds who are preparing themselves to come to make their appearance to the people and their plants.

Then, as if the katsinas are now in the planted fields, they comment that the yellowjackets are chasing one other among the watermelon plants—an observation that emphasizes the process of pollination and growth with the promise of future sustenance. At the close, the katsinas repeat that the clouds will be moving as rain to the fields from all directions.

56. Soyohìmkatsinmuy$_1$ Taawi'am$_2$
(Roberts Cylinder 30, Track 4; LoC)

Haa'o$_3$ haw$_4$ íngumu.$_5$
Ha'óo$_6$ ha'óo ínamu.$_7$
Uma$_8$ itamuy$_9$ umuupahoy$_{10}$ yaawitoyaqw'ö,$_{11}$

1. *soyohìmkatsinmuy,* object form of *soyohìmkatsinam* 'all kinds of katsinas, mixed katsinas'.
2. *taawi'am* 'their song'.
3. *haa'o,* vocative particle.
4. *haw,* vocative particle.
5. = *ingum* 'my mothers'.
6. *ha'óo,* vocative particle.
7. = *inam* 'my fathers'.
8. *uma* 'you (plural)'.
9. *itamuy* 'us', object form of *itam* 'we'.
10. = *umùupahoy,* object form of *umùupaho* 'your (plural) prayer feathers'.
11. = *yaawitoynaqw,* subordinate clause form of *yaawitoyna* 'put something customary to hold in the hand'. The plural form *yaawitoynayaqw* would expected in this context.

*itam*₁₂ *ayó'*₁₃ *hoopo*₁₄ *Kisiwvami'i.*₁₅
*Umuulavayiyu*₁₆ *tuu'awimakyango*₁₇ *angqw*₁₈ *itam naanakwusani.*₁₉
*Pew*₂₀ *yooy- yoyhoyoyotani;*₂₁
*yooy- yoy'umumutani,*₂₂
*uuyisonaqa.*₂₃
Oho oowa eelo aha aha.
*Hapi me.*₂₄
*Hapi*₂₅ *ayangqö,*₂₆
*naanan'ivaqö,*₂₇
*oo'omawutu*₂₈ *yoyhaahawiwmani.*₂₉
Pew yooy- yoyhoyoyotani;
yooy- yoy'umumutani,
uuyisonaqa.

Hark, o my mothers.
Hark, o my fathers.
When you put your prayer feathers in our hands
we [will] go over to the northeast to Shadow Spring.
We will start our journey from there carrying your message along.
[We] will come moving as rain
and will be thundering
throughout the midst of the planted fields.
(Vocables.)

12. *itam* 'we'.
13. *ayó'* 'toward over there'.
14. *hoopo* 'to the northeast'.
15. *Kisiwvami'i*, pausal form of *Kisiwvami* 'to Shadow Spring'.
16. = *umùulavayiy*, object form of *umùulavayi* 'your (plural) speech'.
17. = *tuu'awmakyangw* 'while taking a message along'.
18. *angqw* 'from it, from there'.
19. = *nànkwusani* 'will start on a journey (plural)'.
20. *pew* 'toward here, coming this way'.
21. *yoyhoyoyotani* 'will be moving as rain'.
22. *yoy'umumutani* 'will be thundering'.
23. = *uysonaq* 'throughout the midst of the planted area(s)'.
24. *hapi me*, formulaic expression introducing the song's second part, *oomi* 'upward'.
25. *hapi* 'truly, surely, certainly'.
26. = *ayángqw* 'from over there'.
27. = *naanan'ivaqw* 'from the different directions around'.
28. = *oo'omawt* 'clouds'.
29. = *yoyhahawiwmani* 'will have gone along descending as rain'.

Listen, there is more.
Truly from over there,
from the different directions around,
the clouds will have come descending as rain.
[They] will come moving as rain
and will be thundering
throughout the midst of the planted fields.

This is the final song of the day. The katsinas, addressing their mothers
and fathers, say that when they place their prayer feathers in their hands
(of the katsinas), the katsinas will depart and return to their home in the
northeast at Shadow Spring. They say that they will be carrying the
people's messages which are their prayers for rain. Then, in return, the
katsinas promise that they will come moving as rain and will be thundering throughout the planted fields.

    The song succinctly states the reciprocal relationship between the
people and the katsinas—if the people pray in sincerity and with united
hearts, the katsinas promise to arrive as rain. It is notable that in this song,
like so many, emphasis is placed on how it rains on the fields (*uysonaq*
'throughout the midst of the planted area(s)'). This is an example of how
songs contain information about Hopi farming practices. In this case, it
alludes to the way that farmers locate their fields on slopes and at the
mouth of washes so as to receive the runoff water. This is of great
concern to the farmer who wishes to take advantage of slope and velocity
of moving water in order to spread the water throughout the field among
all his plants. For a description of Hopi farming techniques in some detail,
see Hack (1942).

57. Tasapkatsìntawi,
(Roberts Cylinder 34, Track 8; LoC)

Haalay'unangway$_2$ naanawiniwa,$_3$
Payaayavu,$_4$ ína'a.$_5$

---

1. *tasapkatsìntawi* 'Navajo katsina song'.
2. = *hàalay'unangway* 'with happy hearts, with beneficent intentions'.
3. = *nanawiniwa* 'it is being planned'.
4. *Payaayavu* seems to be a word from some other language, perhaps a Keresan language.
5. *ína'a,* pausal form of *ina* 'my father'.

Tivongyapave'e,₆
itam₇ tiitiwunima,₈
taawanasave'e.₉
Iyahi oo iyahi oo.
Me.₁₀
[Keresan *Ayawina.*
Yoyhala'iniwa.
Hawiwee.
Siiwane'ee haawiranee'e₁₁ naaya.₁₂ Keresan]
Iyahi oo iyahi oo.

It is being planned with happy hearts,
Payaayavu, my father.
At the dance-display place
we are dancing in performance
at midday.
(Vocables.)
Listen,
(Keresan words.)
(Vocables.)

The katsinas announce to the people that, with happy hearts, they are planning to dance in performance at midday in the plaza, *tivongyapavi,* the dance-display place. Much of this song is in Keresan. Such inclusion of words from other Pueblo languages is the result of much visiting among villages where dances are seen and songs are heard and memorized.

6. *tivongyapave'e,* pausal form of *tivongyapave* 'at the dance-display place'.
7. *itam* 'we'.
8. *tiitiwunima* 'be dancing in performance'
9. *taawanasave'e,* pausal form of *taawanasave* 'at midday, at noon'.
10. *me,* particle to direct another's attention. This may be an abbreviation of the formulaic *hapi me* 'listen, there is more', the introducer of the second part of a song.
11. *haawiranee'e* seems to be Keresan for 'stalk' (as 'cornstalk'), cf. Santa Ana *háwiẓana* (Davis 1964 166).
12. *naaya* seems to be Keresan for 'mother', cf. Santa Ana *-nâ·ya* 'mother, aunt' (Davis 1964: 172).

Songs Recorded by Ernest and Pearl Beaglehole in the 1930s

58. Hemiskatsìntawi[1]
(Beaglehole Cylinder 2, Track 10; LoC)

Ahaa iihii.
Haa'o[2] haa'o haw[3] ínamu.[4]
Paahomanatuy[5] itamuy[6] yuuwasinaya.[7]
Aa hay'a aahaay aay.
Hapi me.[8]
Haa'o haw ínamu,
itamuy yuuwasinaya.
Aa hay'a aahaay aay.

(Vocables.)
Hark, hark, o my fathers.
You have adorned us with the prayer feather maidens.
(Vocables.)
Listen, there is more.
Hark, o my fathers,
you have adorned us.
(Vocables.)

This is the last song of the day. The katsinas acknowledge that the fathers of the village have adorned them with prayer feather maidens, meaning that they have given the katsinas prayer feathers imbued with the people's prayers that they will take with them when they return to their cloud homes. The word *yuwsina* 'clothe, adorn' includes the idea that the

1. *hemiskatsìntawi* 'Hemiskatsina song'.
2. *haa'o,* vocative particle.
3. *haw,* vocative particle.
4. = *inam* 'my fathers'.
5. = *pahomamàntuy,* object form of *pahomamant* 'prayer feather maidens'.
6. *itamuy* 'us', object form of *itam* 'we'.
7. = *yuwsinaya* 'clothe, adorn (plural)'.
8. *hapi me,* formulaic expression introducing the song's second part, *oomi* 'upward'.

preparation of prayer feathers means getting them dressed *for a journey.*
Prayers are always sent *somewhere.* Invoking the maiden metaphor that
expresses, for example, corn plants as corn plant maidens and here prayer
feathers as prayer feather maidens, emphasizes the importance that growing female entities have in the rejuvenation of life.

59. *Hewtokatsìntawi₁*
(Beaglehole Cylinder 3, Track 11; LoC)

Ítamu₂ tiitiwayiwa.₃
Ítamu tiitiwayiwa,
ayó₄ Weenimay₅ áwi'i.₆
Itam₇ (words in Zuni).
Lii laa.
Yoo'oo wiiyahiina.
Hapi me.₈
[Zuni *Elóo hleekya owanami awihlóoyan₉ hliiton'iyahani.* Zuni]

We have been invited to dance.
We have been invited to dance,
[with requests sent to us] over to *Weenima.*
We (words in Zuni).
(Vocables.)
Listen, there is more.
(Zuni words with reference to clouds.)

The katsinas state that they have received an invitation at their home at
Weenima in the southeast direction to dance. The rest of this song frag-

1. *hewtokatsìntawi* 'Hewto katsina song'.
2. = *itam* 'we'.
3. = *tiitiwayakniwa* 'have been invited to dance'.
4. = *ayó'* 'toward over there'.
5. *Weenimay,* object form of *Weenima,* the southeast katsina home.
6. = *aw'i,* pausal form of *aw* 'to it, to there'.
7. *itam* 'we'.
8. *hapi me,* formulaic expression introducing the song's second part, *oomi* 'upward'.
9. *awihlóoyan* corresponds to Zuni *awehluyan* 'cumulonimbus cloud' (Eriacho 1998: 131).

ment is in Zuni. Cumulonimbus clouds are mentioned but the other Zuni words remain unidentified.

60. Tasapkatsìntawi$_1$
(Beaglehole Cylinder 1, Track 9; LoC)

Haa'o$_2$ haw$_3$ ínamu,$_4$
uma$_5$ pew$_6$ naawakinaya.$_7$
Naanan'ivaqö$_8$ yooyangwtiniqat$_9$ uma naawakinaya.
Piw$_{10}$ hapi$_{11}$ uuyimanatuy$_{12}$ sìitalawvaniqata$_{13}$ naawakinaya.
Mee aa aa aay ayahiy aa.
Yang$_{14}$ yoyngyàlpuva,$_{15}$
yang paatalnawita$_{16}$ taayimuyiwni.$_{17}$

Hark, o my fathers,
you come praying.
You are praying that it will rain from the different directions around.
Also truly you are praying for the plant maidens that will become bright
    with flowers.
(Vocables.)
In the postlude of the rain here,
[you] will be looking in awe here along a land glistening with water.

1. tasapkatsìntawi 'Navajo katsina song'. The Navajo katsina (Tasapkatsina) is a Hopi katsina that represents Navajos as seen by Hopis.
2. haa'o, vocative particle.
3. haw, vocative particle.
4. =inam 'my fathers'.
5. uma 'you (plural)'.
6. pew 'toward here, coming this way'.
7. = naanawakna 'pray (plural)'.
8. = naanan'ivaqw 'from the different directions around'.
9. = yooyàngwtiniqat, object form of yooyàngwtiniqa 'that which will become rain'.
10. piw 'also, too, again'.
11. hapi 'truly, surely, certainly'.
12. uuyimamàntuy, object form of uuyimamant '(corn) plant maidens'.
13. = sìitalawvaniqamuy, object form of sìitalawvaniqam 'those which will become bright with flowers'.
14. yang 'here, along here, in this area'.
15. yoyngyàlpuva 'in the postlude of the rain, during the time after it has stopped raining'.
16. = paatalnawit 'along where it is glistening with water'.
17. taayimuyiwni 'will look in awe'.

The katsinas acknowledge that the fathers of the village have been praying for rain to come from all directions. They are praying for the rain that will bring their corn plants, here referred to as plant maidens, to tassel, here described as becoming bright with flowers. After the rain stops, the katsinas predict that the people will look in awe at the land glistening with the watery gifts of the katsinas. The word *yoyngàlpuva* (in the postlude of the rain) directs attention to the period immediately after it stops raining when the fields are covered with puddles and plants are dripping with water. At this time all the land seems to be glistening.

Songs Recorded by Robert Black
between 1957 and 1965

61. *Angaktsìntawi₁*

(Black Song 52)

Tuuqayyungwa'a,₂
péwi'i.₃
Uma₄ yep₅ itàatawiyu₆ taawi'yvayaqw'ö,₇
íma'a,₈
tuuvevolmanatu₉ akw'a,₁₀
ngúmantani.₁₁
Pas₁₂ kur₁₃ antsa₁₄ yaayanhaqam₁₅ qatsi₁₆ yeesiwa.₁₇
Maana₁₈ alòngkimi₁₉ wuuve'e,₂₀
maataqölöva'a,₂₁
qaa'ömanatuyu₂₂ heehe heehe.₂₃

1. *angaktsìntawi* 'Long-Hair katsina song'.
2. *tuuqayyungwa'a,* imperative form of *tuuqayyungwa* 'listen (plural)'.
3. = *pew'i,* pausal form of *pew* 'toward here, coming this way'.
4. *uma* 'you (plural)'.
5. *yep* 'here'.
6. = *itàatawiy,* object form of *itàatawi* 'our song'.
7. *taawi'yvayaqw'ö,* subordinate clause pausal form of *taawi'yvaya* 'learn a song (plural)'.
8. *íma'a,* pausal form of *ima* 'these'.
9. = *tuvevolmamant* 'butterfly maidens of various colors'.
10. *akw'a,* pausal form of *akw* 'using, by means of it, with it'.
11. *ngúmantani* 'will be grinding fine, grinding into flour'.
12. *pas* 'very'.
13. *kur,* modal of inference.
14. *antsa* 'truly, really, indeed'.
15. *yaayanhaqam* 'in approximately these ways'.
16. *qatsi* 'life'.
17. *yeesiwa* 'be in place, exist'.
18. *maana* 'girl, young unmarried woman, maiden'.
19. *alòngkimi* 'to a house belonging to someone who is not a relative'.
20. *wuuve'e,* pausal form of *wuuve'* 'if, when (sg. subj.) climbs up', from *wuuvi* 'climb up, ascend' plus subordinator *-e'* 'if, when'.
21. = *mataqlöva* 'in grinding bins'.
22. = *qa'ömamàntuy,* object form of *qa'ömamant* 'corn maidens'.
23. *heehe heehe,* vocables of the sound of grinding, functioning here as a verb governing the object *qa'ömamàntuy.*

Ooho ooho ooho oohoowa ee'ee hee lo.
Hapi me.$_{24}$
Qatsi naatuwaniwa,$_{25}$
aye'e,$_{26}$
alòngkiva'a.$_{27}$

Listen
this way.
When you learn our song,
these,
the butterfly maidens of various colors, should, using it (singing it),
grind corn.
It seems clear that life is lived in many ways like this.
If a girl enters a house not of a relative,
she goes to the grinding bin
and grinds and grinds corn.
(Vocables.)
Listen, there is more.
Life is being rejuvenated
over there
in houses belonging to other people.

The katsinas open this song with an imperative to the people to pay attention to the song they are about to sing. The song concerns the proper behavior of young girls, who are referred to metaphorically as butterfly maidens of various colors (*tuvevolmamant*), when they visit a house that does not belong to a relative (*alòngkimi*). Traditionally, the women of each household ground corn every day preparatory to make their families' meals. Thus, when anyone visits a house of an unrelated person, she should help the woman she visits grind her corn at one of the bins arranged in a row along the wall. The moral imperative is that when you visit another, you do not simply sit and gossip but make yourself useful. A model Hopi woman should always be doing something for others. In this song the katsinas are reminding the girls of this traditional work ethic.

24. *hapi me,* formulaic expression introducing the song's second part, *oomi* 'upward'.
25. = *natwaniwa* 'be undertaken as life-promoting practices, practices related to the rejuvenation of life'.
26. = *ayé'e,* pausal form of *ayé'* 'along over there'.
27. = *alòngkiva* 'in/at houses belonging to someone who is not a relative'.

The use of the verb *wuuvi* 'climb up' recalls the traditional houses that were entered by ladders to the second floor. This directive to climb up into the house is retained today even though houses are entered through doors on the first floor. The word *mataqlöva* refers to the presence of several (*-qlö* 'cluster, group of') grinding stones (*mata*), with the diffusive suffix *-va* indicating that there are several places on which the corn maidens (*qa'ömamant*), who are, metaphorically, the corn kernels, will be ground. Corn, in all its forms, from seed kernels to mature ears, plays a metaphorical role in instructing the people how to follow the life-promoting practices (*natwani*), that insure the people's survival. Here the corn kernels to be ground are referred to as corn maidens in order to call to mind the idea that just as young women are future mothers, so too are the corn kernels future sustenance.

The katsinas close the song with the reminder that when people practice these traditional roles, the lifeway that sustains the Hopi communities will be rejuvenated and thus endure.

62. *Angaktsìntawi₁*
(Black Song 55)

Hapi₂ Orayave'e,₃
itanamu₄ talasiyalahay₅ pöötavilawu,₆
umumi₇ péwi'i.₈
Pantaqat₉ ánawit₁₀ itam₁₁ öki,₁₂
yépe'e.₁₃
Supawlave'e,₁₄

1. *angaktsìntawi* 'Long-Hair katsina song'.
2. *hapi* 'truly, surely, certainly'.
3. *Orayve'e,* pausal form of *Orayve* 'at Orayvi'.
4. = *itanam* 'our fathers'.
5. *talasiyalahay,* object form of *talasiyalaha'am* 'their pollen with sparkles in it'.
6. = *pöötaplawu* 'keep laying out a consecrated path'.
7. *umumi* 'to you (plural)'.
8. = *pew'i,* pausal form of *pew* 'toward here, coming this way'.
9. *pantaqat,* object form of *pantaqa* 'one that is like that'.
10. *ánawit* 'along its course'.
11. *itam* 'we'.
12. *öki* 'arrive, come, get there, reach a destination (plural)'.
13. = *yep'e,* pausal form of *yep* 'here'.
14. *Supawlave'e,* pausal form of *Supawlave* 'at Supawlavi'.

itangum,$_{15}$ itanam$_{16}$ itamuyu$_{17}$ paas$_{18}$ oo 'oyaqö 'ö,$_{19}$
paypu ókiwa,$_{20}$
itamu 'ova 'a,$_{21}$
oomawvawikyam$_{22}$ puyayatani.$_{23}$
Yahiya yahiy yahiy aaha hahaa.
Aaha ii'ihiihi.

Truly at Orayvi,
our fathers kept laying out their glittering pollen as a consecrated path
to you here.
Along that way we came
here.
At Supawlavi,
when our mothers and fathers receive us with great care,
may it be
that above us,
the cloud ducks will flap their wings.
(Vocables.)
(Vocables of the sound of singing.)

The katsinas are describing how they traveled along a consecrated path of glittering pollen from Orayvi to dance in the village of Supawlavi. This follows the practice where groups of katsinas from one village are often invited to perform in other villages. *Talasiyalaha,* a compound composed of *talasi* 'pollen' and *yalaha* 'specular hematite', embodies the sense of the glittering brightness of the spiritual path along which the katsinas travel. As well, in association with the word *pöötavilawu,* keep laying out the path, it connotes the repeated prayers that are needed to encourage the

15. *itangum* 'our mothers'.
16. *itanam* 'our fathers'.
17. = *itamuy* 'us', object form of *itam* 'we'.
18. *paas* 'thoroughly, completely, carefully'.
19. = *o 'yaqw 'ö* 'when they receive (us)', subordinate clause pausal form of *o 'ya,* the plural of *oya* 'hand (to), hand out, deposit, place, put, set (several) in a particular position'; here the word is used in a social sense, 'receive'.
20. *paypu ókiwa* 'let it be so'.
21. *itamu 'ova 'a,* pausal form of *itamu 'ova* 'along above us'.
22. = *oomawvawikyam* 'cloud ducks'.
23. *puyayatani* 'will be flapping, fluttering'.

katsinas to come. Finally, as the katsinas approach the village, they move along an actual path of consecrated cornmeal and pollen into the plaza.

Then the katsinas say that when they are received by the people of Supawlavi with great care, that is, made welcome with pure hearts, then the katsinas will come with their rain. This is a reminder that one of the moral imperatives of Hopi life is to always be welcoming and hospitable. When the katsinas observe that the people are practicing this virtue, they will be willing to come and bestow their gift of rain. This moral lesson is couched in a metaphor. If the people follow traditional practices and receive the katsinas with pure hearts, the rain will descend from the clouds just as drops of water fall from the feet of ducks as they flap their wings and take off from a body of water.

63. Angaktsìntawi₁
(Black Song 58)

Itam₂ hapi₃ ayamo,₄
ayám₅ Weenimay₆ épe'e.₇
Ep₈ ítamu₉ naatuwanlawu,₁₀
pew'i.₁₁
Uma₁₂ itamuy₁₃ naawakinaya.₁₄
Haa'o,₁₅ haw₁₆ ínamu.₁₇

1. *angaktsìntawi* 'Long-Hair katsina song'.
2. *itam* 'we'.
3. *hapi* 'truly, surely, certainly'.
4. = *ayám* 'over there'.
5. *ayám* 'over there'.
6. *Weenimay*, object form of *Weenima*, the southeast katsina home.
7. = *ep'e*, pausal form of *ep* 'there, at it'.
8. *ep* 'there, at it'.
9. = *itam* 'we'.
10. = *natwanlawu* 'keep pursuing life-promoting practices, customs related to the rejuvenation of life'.
11. *pew'i*, pausal form of *pew* 'toward here, coming this way'.
12. *uma* 'you (plural)'.
13. *itamuy* 'us', object form of *itam* 'we'.
14. = *naanawakna* 'pray (plural)'.
15. = *haa'o*, vocative particle.
16. *haw*, vocative particle.
17. = *inam* 'my fathers'.

Lehe la.
Tuma₁₈ ítamu.
Tuma aa'ayo'o,₁₉
ayóo₂₀ tivongyapami.₂₁
Salavimanatuyu₂₂ itamuy nùutayta,₂₃
lolmat₂₄ pitsangwa'ikyango.₂₅
Put₂₆ hapi àapiy₂₇ pòötavilawu,₂₈
ínamu.₂₉
Pantaqat₃₀ ánga'a,₃₁
ítamu umumi₃₂ yooya'ökini.₃₃
Aa haa haa haa haay.
Aa haa haa haa haa haay.

We, truly, are over there,
over there at *Weenima.*
There we keep doing life-sustaining practices,
coming this way.
You pray for us.
Hark, o my fathers.
(Vocables.)
Let's go.
Let's go over there,
over to the dance-display place.
The Douglas Fir maidens are awaiting us

18. = *tum* 'let's, let's go'.
19. *ayo'o,* pausal form of *ayó'* 'toward over there'.
20. = *ayó'* 'toward over there'.
21. *tivongyapami* 'to the dance-display place'.
22. = *Salapmamàntuy,* object form of *Salapmamant* 'Douglas Fir maidens', a reference to the Douglas fir branches ceremonally placed in the dance-display place.
23. *nùutayta* 'be awaiting'.
24. *lolmat,* object form of *lolma* 'beautiful, good, proper'.
25. = *pitsangwa'ykyangw* 'while having a countenance'.
26. *put,* object form of *pam* 'that, that one, he, she, it'.
27. *àapiy* 'away from it'.
28. *pòötaplawu* 'keep laying out a consecrated path'.
29. = *inam* 'my fathers'.
30. *pantaqat,* object form of *pantaqa* 'one that is like that'.
31. = *ang'a,* pausal form of *ang* 'along it, along there, in an area, in several places'.
32. *umumi* 'to you (plural)'.
33. = *yoy'ökini* 'will arrive, come as rain'.

with beautiful countenance.
[You] truly keep laying out a consecrated path from there,
my fathers.
Along one [laid out] like that,
we will come to you as rain.
(Vocables.)

The katsinas are at *Weenima,* their home in the southeast cardinal direction, making preparations to come to the Hopi villages. There they are continually preparing themselves in beneficent ways with life-promoting practices (*natwani*), that will lead to the rejuvenation of life. The implication is that the katsinas have been adorning themselves with rain and all the other good things of life. Similarly, prayers are understood to be life-sustaining practices because they serve to bring the rain. The statement of the katsinas, "You pray for us," is referring to these prayers.

In anticipation of the people's prayers, the katsinas go to the *tivongya-pavi,* the dance-display place, where the Douglas Fir maidens await them. The Douglas Fir maidens are branches of Douglas fir trees which have been "planted" at the shrine in the plaza. Usually this happens only at *Nimàntikive,* the Home dance. These maidens are described as having a beautiful countenance, meaning that they are replete with spiritual power. The katsinas instruct the fathers to continue laying out the consecrated pollen path and along that path, the katsinas say, they will come as rain.

64. *Angaktsìntawi*$_1$
(Black Song 100)

Itam$_2$ *hapi*$_3$ *ayamo,*$_4$
ayám$_5$ *Weenimay*$_6$ *épe'e.*$_7$

1. *angaktsìntawi* 'Long-Hair katsina song'.
2. *itam* 'we'.
3. *hapi* 'truly, surely, certainly'.
4. = *ayám* 'over there'.
5. *ayám* 'over there'.
6. *Weenimay,* object form of *Weenima,* the southeast katsina home.
7. = *ep'e,* pausal form of *ep* 'there, at it'.

Ep$_8$ ítamu$_9$ naatuwanlawu,$_{10}$
péwi'i.$_{11}$
Uma$_{12}$ itamuy$_{13}$ naawakinaya.$_{14}$
Haa'ó$_{15}$ haw$_{16}$ ínamu.$_{17}$
Le lehe la.
Tuma$_{18}$ ítamu.
Tuma aa'aa'a-$_{19}$ awya,$_{20}$
ayó$_{21}$ tivongyapami'i.$_{22}$
Salavimanatuyu$_{23}$ itamuy nùutayta,
sonwakw$_{24}$ pitsangwa'ikyango.$_{25}$
Put$_{26}$ hapi$_{27}$ àapiy$_{28}$ pöötavilawu,$_{29}$
ínamu.
Pantaqat$_{30}$ ánga'a,$_{31}$
ítamu$_{32}$ umumi$_{33}$ yooya'ökini.$_{34}$
Haw haw haw haw hay.

8. *ep* 'there, at it'.
9. = *itam* 'we'.
10. = *natwanlawu* 'keep pursuing life-promoting practices, customs related to the rejuvenation of life'.
11. = *pew'i*, pausal form of *pew* 'toward here, coming this way'.
12. *uma* 'you (plural)'.
13. *itamuy* 'us', object form of *itam* 'we'.
14. = *naanawakna* 'pray (plural)'.
15. *haa'ó*, vocative particle.
16. *haw*, vocative particle.
17. = *inam* 'my fathers'.
18. = *tum* 'let's, let's go'.
19. *aa'aa'a-*, anticipation of the initial *a* of the following word.
20. *awya* 'go there (plural)'.
21. = *ayó'* 'toward over there'.
22. *tivongyapami'i*, pausal form of *tivongyapami* 'to the dance-display place'.
23. = *Salapmamàntuy*, object form of *Salapmamant* 'Douglas Fir maidens'.
24. *sonwakw*, object form of *sonway* 'beautiful'.
25. = *pitsangwa'ykyangw* 'while having as a countenance'.
26. *put*, object form of *pam* 'that, that one, he, she, it'.
27. *hapi* 'truly, surely, certainly'.
28. *àapiy* 'away from'.
29. = *pöötaplawu* 'keep laying out a consecrated path'.
30. *pantaqat*, object form of *pantaqa* 'one that is like that'.
31. = *ang'a*, pausal form of *ang* 'along it, along there, in that area, in several places'.
32. = *itam* 'we'.
33. *umumi* 'to you (plural)'.
34. = *yoy'ökini* 'will arrive, come as rain'.

Aa'aw yoy haw haw.

We, truly, are over there,
over there at *Weenima*.
There we keep doing life-sustaining practices,
coming this way.
You pray for us.
Hark, hark, my fathers.
(Vocables.)
Let's go,
let's go there,
over to the dance-display place.
The Douglas Fir maidens await us,
with beautiful countenance.
[You] truly keep laying out a consecrated path from there,
my fathers.
Along that way (laid out),
we will come to you as rain.
(Vocables.)

This song is almost identical to Song 63.

65. *Angaktsìntawi₁*
(Black Song 60)

Uma₂ itamuy₃ naawakinaya,₄
ínamu.₅
Uma itamuy naawakinaya,
ayó₆ taatö₇ oomawkimi'i,₈

1. *angaktsìntawi* 'Long-Hair katsina song'.
2. *uma* 'you (plural)'.
3. *itamuy* 'us', object form of *itam* 'we'.
4. = *naanawakna* 'pray (plural)'.
5. = *inam* 'my fathers'.
6. = *ayó* 'toward over there'.
7. *taatö* 'to the southeast'.
8. = *oomàwkimi'i,* pausal form of *oomàwkimi* 'to the dwelling place of the clouds'.

Weenimay$_9$ áwi'i.$_{10}$
Lee lehe la.
Yep$_{11}$ uma itamuy nuutayilawu,$_{12}$
ínamu.
Lee lehe la.
Is uní.$_{13}$
Yang$_{14}$ uymuktiqö'ö,$_{15}$
ang$_{16}$ uma tawmakyango$_{17}$ taayimaqö'ö,$_{18}$
aqhaqami'i,$_{19}$
sóniwaya.$_{20}$
Oho hoo'oway.
Ehe hee'e heeloy.

You pray for us,
my fathers.
You pray for us
over to the southeast dwelling place of the clouds,
to *Weenima.*
(Vocables.)
Here you keep waiting for us,
my fathers.
(Vocables.)
How nice!
When the plants become thriving in full growth along here,
when you go along there looking as you go along singing;
throughout,

9. *Weenimay,* object form of *Weenima,* the southeast katsina home.
10. = *aw'i,* pausal form of *aw* 'to it, to there'.
11. *yep* 'here'.
12. = *nùutaylawu* 'keep awaiting, be waiting and waiting for'.
13. *is uní* 'how nice!'.
14. *yang* 'along here, in this area'.
15. = *uymuktiqw'ö* 'when (they) become thriving in full growth', subordinate clause pausal form of *uymukti* 'become thriving in full growth'.
16. *ang* 'along it, along there, in that area, in several places'.
17. = *tawmakyangw* 'while going along singing'. The plural form, *tawwiskyangw,* would be expected.
18. = *taymaqw'ö,* subordinate clause pausal form of *tayma* 'go along looking, seeing, watching'. In everyday speech this word would be in its plural form, *taywisqw'ö.*
19. = *aqwhaqami'i,* pausal form of *aqwhaqami* 'throughout'.
20. = *sosniwa* 'be beautiful (plural)'.

things are beautiful.
(Vocables.)

The song begins with the katsinas speaking to the people, my fathers, telling them to pray to them at their home at *Weenima* in the southeast. The southeast, *Weenima*, and the dwelling place of the clouds, *oomàwki*, all refer to where the katsinas live. After a series of vocables, the katsinas, now speaking from inside the dance plaza referred to as "here" (*yep*), remark that the people have been waiting for them to come. The verb *nùutaylawu* 'be waiting and waiting' expresses the anxious expectation that the people have at this time as they await the coming of the rains that will bring their crops to maturity.

Following another series of vocables, the katsinas remark on how nice it would be to see a field of flourishing plants that, by implication, are thriving because they, the katsinas, have come with their rain. In effect the katsinas are creating a fantasy world in the minds of the prople of a perfect life in order to inspire them to be earnest in their prayers and humble and hard working in their practices of living.

66. Angaktsìntawi$_1$
(Black Song 67)

Uu'unangwvàasi'ilawu,$_2$
ínamu,$_3$
"Ta'a$_4$ okiw$_5$ ii'itsi$_6$ yooyokvani."$_7$
Yan$_8$ okiw naawakinaya,$_9$
taawanawita.$_{10}$
Lee lehe la.
Uu'unangwvàasi'ilawu,

1. *angaktsìntawi* 'Long-Hair katsina song'.
2. = *u'nangwvaslawu* 'keep praying repeatedly in a heartfelt manner for good results'.
3. = *inam* 'my fathers'.
4. *ta'a* 'okay, all right, I agree'.
5. *okiw* 'humbly, pitifully'.
6. = *ii'its* 'promptly, soon, early'.
7. *yooyokva* 'rain in several places and/or at several times'.
8. *yan* 'like this, in this way, thus'.
9. = *naanawakna* 'pray (plural)'.
10. = *taawanawit* 'all day long'.

ínamu,
"Ta'a okiw ii'itsi yooyokvani."
Yan okiw naawakinaya,
taawanawita.
Lee leehee la.
"Tá'a'a,$_{11}$
"ii'itsi haani'i."$_{12}$
Yoyhaniwa.$_{13}$
Haaniwa$_{14}$ *hi.*$_{15}$
Yoyhaniwa.
Haaniwa hi.
Yang$_{16}$ *uuyisonaqa*$_{17}$ *muumunangwtotiqw'ö,*$_{18}$
hàalay'unangway$_{19}$ *taatawyuuyuwintani.*$_{20}$
Hiiniya hiiniiya hiiniya hi.
Hiiniya hiiniya hiiniya hi.
Haayo haayo haayo ohaayo.

You keep praying in a heartfelt manner,
my fathers,
"All right, may it soon rain repeatedly."
In this way you humbly pray
all day long.
(Vocables.)
You keep praying in a heartfelt manner,
my fathers,
"All right, may it soon rain repeatedly."
In this way you humbly pray
all day long.
(Vocables.)

11. *tá'a'a,* pausal form of *ta'a* 'okay, all right, I agree'.
12. *haani'i,* imperative form of *haani* 'descend (plural)'.
13. *yoyhaniwa* 'be a descent of rain'.
14. *haaniwa* 'for there to be a descent'.
15. *hi,* a meaningless syllable inserted to maintain the rhythmic pattern of the line.
16. *yang* 'along here, in this area'.
17. = *uysonaq* 'throughout the midst of the planted area(s)'.
18. *muumunangwtotiqw'ö,* pausal subordinate clause form of *muumunangwtoti* 'become runoff water in several places'.
19. *hàalay'unangway* 'with happy hearts, with beneficent intentions'.
20. = *taatawyuyuwintani* 'will be dancing and singing songs'.

"All right,
"hurry and come down."
There is a descent of rain.
There is a descent.
There is a descent of rain.
There is a descent.
When it becomes runoff water throughout the midst of the planted areas
    along here,
[you] will be singing and dancing with happy hearts.
(Vocables.)

The katsinas are advising the people, addressed as "my fathers," to keep praying in a heartfelt manner for the rain to come. The katsinas quote the prayers of the people, indicated with quotation marks in the transcription. The katsinas observe that this is the way the people are humbly and fervently praying throughout the day. This sentiment is repeated and then, after a series of vocables, the katsinas repeatedly describe how it is raining. In Hopi belief, rain, because it is animate, does not passively "fall"; it "descends," as though coming down a ladder.

The repetitive mention of the way it is raining highlights the kind of rain that is most desirable—a constant, long rain that thoroughly vitalizes all living things. In fact, rains of some duration produce excess water that does not immediately soak into the ground. This is expressed in the song by the word *muumunangwtotiqw* (when it becomes runoff water in several places). Hopis plant on slopes to receive this runoff water which then flows to all the plants in the field. The katsinas close by predicting that when the runoff water comes and nourishes the fields, the people will be so grateful that they will sing and dance with gladness in their hearts.

67. *Angaktsìntawi*[1]
(Black Song 68)

(This song is a combination: Emory Sekaquaptewa provided the first part from memory, the Robert Black recording has the second part [after *hapi me*].)

Haw[2] *uma*[3] *ìngumu,*[4] *ìnamu.*[5]
Uma itamuy[6] *paahoyaawitoyaqw'ö,*[7]
itam[8] *naanakwusa,*[9]
ayo'o,[10]
Weenimay[11] *oomàwkimi'i.*[12]
Yeep[13] *úma'a,*[14]
hàalaykyango[15] *umùuqatsiyu*[16] *naavokyawintani,*[17]
ha'óo[18] *ìnamu.*
Lee lehe laa.
Yani[19] *ìtamu*[20] *na'qalayaqö'ö,*[21]
yooyangw[22] *haahawiwmani.*[23]

1. *angaktsìntawi* 'Long-Hair katsina song'.
2. *haw*, vocative particle.
3. *uma* 'you (plural)'.
4. = *ingum* 'my mothers'.
5. = *inam* 'my fathers'.
6. *itamuy* 'us', object form of *itam* 'we'.
7. = *pahoyàwtoynaqw'ö*, subordinate clause pausal form of *pahoyàwtoyna* 'place a prayer feather in a katsina performer's hand during a dance to hold'.
8. *itam* 'we'.
9. = *nànkwusa* 'start on a journey (plural)'.
10. *ayo'o*, pausal form of *ayó'* 'toward over there'.
11. *Weenimay*, object form of *Weenima*, the southeast katsina home.
12. *oomàwkimi'i*, pausal form of *oomàwkimi* 'to dwelling place of the clouds'.
13. = *yep* 'here'.
14. *úma'a*, pausal form of *uma* 'you (plural)'.
15. = *hàalaykyangw* 'while being happy, happily'.
16. = *umùuqatsiy*, object form of *umùuqatsi* 'your lives'.
17. *naavokyawintiwni* 'fulfillment should be enjoyed by all'.
18. *ha'óo*, vocative particle.
19. = *yan* 'like this, in this way, thus'.
20. = *itam* 'we'.
21. = *na'qalayaqw'ö*, subordinate clause pausal form of *na'qalaya* 'encourage selves'.
22. *yooyangw* 'rain'.
23. *haahawiwmani* 'will go/come along descending'.

Ang₂₄ haani.₂₅
Ang hani.₂₆
Ang hani.
Aahaa iihii hii hii hii.
Hapi me.₂₇
Hin pa₂₈ lolmat₂₉ úma'a,₃₀
yeese.
[Tewa *Sengkiri po'me.₃₁* Tewa]
Yan₃₂ itam na'qalayaqö'ö,
yooyangw haahawiwmani'i.
Lee lehe laa.
Yani ítamu na'qalayaaqö'ö
yooyangw haahawiwmani.
Ang haani.
Ang hani.
Ang hani.
Aahaa iihii'ii hii hii hii.

Hark, you, my mothers and my fathers.
You have provided us with prayer feathers to carry in the hand,
[and] we start on our journey
over to there,
to the cloud dwelling place of *Weenima.*
Here you
should keep on enjoying your lives to the fullest in happiness,
o my fathers.
(Vocables.)
When we (all people and katsinas) encourage ourselves in this way,
the rain will go along descending.

24. *ang* 'along it, along there, in that area, in several places'.
25. *haani* 'descend (plural)'.
26. = *haani* 'descend (plural)'.
27. *hapi me,* formulaic expression introducing the song's second part, *oomi* 'upward'.
28. *hin pa* 'I wonder if'.
29. *lolmat* 'beautifully, well, properly'.
30. *úma'a,* pausal form of *uma* 'you (plural)'.
31. *sengkiri po'me* appears to relate to Tewa *seŋgiriho'o* 'good-bye' (Harrington 1907–1908: 484). It seems reasonable to assume that when Tewas say good-bye, they express some sort of beneficent wish and that wish appears to be incorporated in this song.
32. *yan* 'like this, in this way, thus'.

It descends along there.
It descends along there.
It descends along there.
(Vocables.)
Listen, there is more.
We ask ourselves how good (morally upright) a life
you are living.
(Tewa words.)
When we encourage ourselves in this way,
the rain will have gone along descending.
(Vocables.)
It descends along there.
It descends along there.
It descends along there.
(Vocables.)

When Emory listened to the tape recording that Robert Black made of this song, he realized that this was a song he knew, except that the recording had preserved only the second half of the song. Apparently the singer could only remember the second half. Emory then recalled the first section. We present the song here with the first section being that recalled by Emory, and the second section, after *hapi me,* being that recorded by Black. This is an excellent example of how songs, once performed, are committed to memory by those who hear them. They are remembered for many years and can be recalled, as in the recording sessions, because they are sung repeatedly as individuals go about their daily lives. In this way songs from long ago are retained, although sometimes with slightly different wording, depending on how the listener remembered what he heard.

This is the last song of the day. The katsinas describe how they have received a prayer feather to carry in their hand as they start out on their journey back to their cloud home at *Weenima.* Unsaid but implied is the fact that the prayer feathers are imbued with the people's prayers for rain. The katsinas remind the people that even after they depart, they should continue to perform the practices that bring rejuvenation and thus fulfillment to their lives. In short, they are reminding the people that even though the katsinas have left, they must be ever mindful of the moral imperatives that underpin their communities. They must continue to live humble, hard-working lives, accepting and cheerfully performing their responsibilities and obligations to everyone in the community. The katsinas then emphasize that when both they and the people strive to live such perfect lives, then it will rain repeatedly.

In the second section of the song, the katsinas are musing whether or not the people are indeed living moral lives. Implicitly, the katsinas are wondering whether the people are deserving of their rain. Nevertheless, they close with the assurance that if everyone helps each other to live right, the rains will repeatedly descend.

68. Angaktsìntawi₁
(Black Song 69)

Haa'ó,₂ haa'ó, ha'áa',₃ haw₄ ínamu.₅
Qaa'ömongwit,₆
ínamu,
tokilayamuy₇ àasa'₈ taalawvaqö'ö,₉
sakwavahoy₁₀ yuuwasinaqö'ö,₁₁
pu'₁₂ túwaati,₁₃
taaha'am₁₄ paakwa₁₅ itamuy₁₆ paahovenayani.₁₇
Lee he laa.
Pu' nu'₁₈ túwati,₁₉

1. *angaktsìntawi* 'Long-Hair katsina song'.
2. *haa'ó,* vocative particle.
3. *ha'áa',* vocative particle.
4. *haw,* vocative particle.
5. =*inam* 'my fathers'.
6. = *qa'ömomngwit* 'corn leaders'.
7. *tokilayamuy,* object form of *tokila'am* 'their set date, the date they set'.
8. *àasa'* 'as often as, the right number of times'.
9. = *taalawvaqw'ö,* subordinate clause pausal form of *taalawva* 'dawn, become light, a new day'.
10. *sakwavahoy,* object form of *sakwavaho'am* 'their blue/green prayer feathers'.
11. = *yuwsinaqw'ö,* subordinate clause pausal form of *yuwsina* 'clothe'.
12. *pu'* 'now, then'.
13. = *tuwat* 'in turn, for (one's) part'.
14. *taaha'am* 'their maternal uncle'.
15. *paakwa* 'toad'.
16. *itamuy* 'us', object form of *itam* 'we'.
17. = *pahovenayani,* future plural form of *pahovena* 'mark prayer feathers'.
18. *nu'* 'I'.
19. = *tuwat* 'in turn, for (one's) part'.

i'uyiy$_{20}$ ang$_{21}$ nu' waynumaqe'e,$_{22}$
nu' ang taatawtinuma.$_{23}$
Hàalaykyangw$_{24}$ wunimantinuma.$_{25}$
Inu'ove$_{26}$ tsukumaana$_{27}$ töötöqa.$_{28}$
Siiyahay eeloyaa, nayahay eeloyaa.
Siiyahay eeloyaay aahay.

Hark, hark, hark, o my fathers.
The corn leaders,
my fathers,
it has dawned the right number of times to reach the date they set,
and they have adorned us with their blue/green prayer feathers,
and now for their part,
they and their maternal uncle the toad will mark the prayer feathers for
   us.
(Vocables.)
Now I, for my part,
I am walking around in my planted fields,
going around there singing songs.
Happily I am going around dancing.
Above me the coot is giving its calls.
(Vocables.)

The katsinas, addressing the fathers as corn leaders (*qa'ömomngwit*),
announce that the day (*tokila*) that was set some time ago for the performance has arrived. This process is expressed as "it has dawned the right
number of times," meaning the right number of days has passed in
preparation for the ceremony.$_{29}$ The katsinas remark that the fathers have

---

20. *i'uyiy*, object form of *i'uyi* 'my planted plant(s), planted field'.
21. *ang* 'along it, along there, in that area, in several places'.
22. *waynùmqe'e*, subordinate clause pausal form of *waynuma* 'be walking around'.
23. *taatawtinuma* 'go around singing songs'.
24. *hàalaykyangw* 'while being happy, happily'.
25. *wunimantinuma* 'be going around dancing'.
26. *inu'ove* 'above me'.
27. = *tsukumana* 'coot', a water bird.
28. *töötöqa* 'be making characteristic calls, sounds'.
29. The third day before the day of the ceremony is *suus qa himu* 'not something once' or
   suus taala 'light once' (*suus* is 'once'); the sceond day before the ceremony is *komok-
   totokya* 'wood gathering eve' or *piktotokya* 'piki eve'; the day of the ceremony is *tiikive*.

adorned them with blue/green prayer feathers, that is, with their prayers. Blue/green is the color associated with the southwest, the direction from which come most of the late summer rainstorms that bring the crops to maturity.

The katsinas then invoke the toad (*paakwa*) as their maternal uncle (*taaha'am*) in a metaphoric way in order to address the importance of a traditional Hopi institution, that of the role of a maternal uncle. In Hopi families, a woman's brother is the primary individual responsible for advising, disciplining and transmitting cultural knowledge and ritual practices to his sister's children. In this song the toad is likened to one of the corn leaders. He is carrying out his responsibilities by imbuing the prayer feathers with the people's prayers. The metaphor here is that the toad is marking the prayer feathers as if he is marking the katsinas with the people's prayers. In this sense, he is giving life to the prayer feathers so that they become katsinas.

There is apparently a line missing after the vocables before the line "Now I, for my part." This section is expressing the reciprocal relationship between the katsinas and the people. The activities of the katsinas are missing. The recorded song resumes with the people speaking, but in the singular. A man describes how he is walking about his planted fields happily singing and dancing because the rains have come and given vitality to his plants. The last line, which describes how the coot (*tsukumana*) is giving its calls, that is, singing its happiness, also indicates that the katsinas have come with their rain. Coots are water birds that come to the shallow ponds of water that form after a rain. Thus, the presence of the coot is a sign that the prayers of the people have been answered and that it has rained in such quantities that pools of water have formed across the land.

69. *Angaktsìntawi*₁

(Black Song 70)

*Ítamu,*₂
*itam*₃ *yuuyahiwa,*₄
*ayám*₅ *tatkya*₆ *Weenimay*₇ *ep'e.*₈
*Ep*₉ *ítamu nana'alöngöta*₁₀ *qaa'ömanatuyu,*₁₁
*nana'löngöt*₁₂ *yooyalekit*₁₃ *itam naayuuwasina.*₁₄
*Angqw*₁₅ *itam umumi*₁₆ *pew*₁₇ *tiiti'ökiwa.*₁₈
Lee lehe la.
[Zuni? *Ho'nawantaatsoo teliikinantii'a,*
awtoowa yaniki anloy'aa. Zuni?]
Oohoo oo oohoo hoowa.
Ee'he eeheloy.

We,
we have been prepared
over there in the southeast at *Weenima*.
There we adorned ourselves with the corn maidens of the different kinds
and with the different kinds of rain lines.
From there we have come in dance to you.
(Vocables.)

1. *angaktsìntawi* 'Long-Hair katsina song'.
2. = *itam* 'we'.
3. *itam* 'we'.
4. *yuuyahiwa* 'have been prepared for a ceremony, be adorned (plural)'.
5. *ayám* 'over there'.
6. *tatkya* 'in the southeast'.
7. *Weenimay*, object form of *Weenima*, the southeast katsina home.
8. *ep'e*, pausal form of *ep* 'at it, there'.
9. *ep* 'there, at it'.
10. = *nana'löngöt*, object form of *nana'löngö* 'different kinds of'.
11. = *qa'ömamàntuy*, object form of *qa'ömamant* 'corn maidens'.
12. *nana'löngöt*, object form of *nana'löngö* 'different kinds of'.
13. = *yoylekit*, object form of *yoyleki* 'rain lines, rain descending in lines as seen from a distance'.
14. = *naayuwsina* 'clothe oneself, get dressed'.
15. *angqw* 'from it, from there'.
16. *umumi* 'to you (plural)'.
17. *pew* 'toward here, coming this way'.
18. *tiiti'ökiwa* 'have come in dance (and thereby to soothe)'.

(Words in some other language, perhaps Zuni.)
(Vocables.)

The katsinas describe how they have been preparing themselves over at their home in the southeast direction at *Weenima* before they travel to perform at a Hopi village. They describe how they have adorned themselves with corn maidens of different kinds, that is, of different colors, and with the different kinds of rain lines, a reference to rain lines of the different colors associated with the different directions. That they are said to come from all four directions emphasizes the full extent of the katsinas' benevolence. The katsinas close with the promise that, from their home, dressed in corn and rain from all directions, they have come to dance for the people.

70. Angaktsìntawi₁

(Black Song 72)

Haqami₂ yang₃ umùupasanawita₄ paavönmanatu₅ talasimasay₆ puyayatota.₇
Puma₈ yang oomi₉ naawungwinani.₁₀
Aw₁₁ yuuyaha,₁₂
aw yuuyahay,₁₃
paasami₁₄ paavönmanatuy₁₅ aw yuuyaha 'ay,₁₆

1. *angaktsìntawi* 'Long-Hair katsina song'.
2. = *aqwhaqami* 'throughout'.
3. *yang* 'along here, in this area'.
4. = *umùupasanawit* 'along your (plural) fields'.
5. = *paavönmamant* 'young corn plants'.
6. *talasimasay*, object form of *talasimasa 'am* 'their pollen-laden wings'.
7. *puyayatota* 'be flapping, fluttering (plural)'.
8. *puma* 'they'.
9. *oomi* 'upward'.
10. = *naawungwnayani* 'will make selves grow'.
11. *aw* 'to it, to there'.
12. *yuuyaha* 'dress, prepare for a ceremony, adorn selves'.
13. *yuuyahay*, expressive form of *yuuyaha* 'dress, prepare for a ceremony, adorn selves'.
14. = *pasmi* 'to the field(s)'.
15. = *paavönmamàntuy*, object form of *paavönmamant* 'young corn plants'.
16. = *yuuyaha* 'dress, prepare for a ceremony, adorn selves'.

sakwa'o'omawutu.[17]
Oohowa elohaa'ay.
Oohowa elohaa'ay.
Oowa eelo.
Aw yuuyaha.
aw yuuyahay,
paasami paavönmanatuy aw[18] *yuuyaha'ay,*
qöya'o'omawutu.[19]
Oohowa elohaa'ay.
Oohowa elohaa'ay.
Oowa eelo.

Throughout, along your fields here, the young corn plants are fluttering
    their pollen-laden wings.
They will make themselves grow upward here.
They adorn themselves to go there,
they adorn themselves to go there,
the blue/green clouds adorn themselves
to go to the fields, to the young corn plants.
(Vocables.)
They adorn themselves to go there,
they adorn themselves to go there,
the white clouds adorn themselves
to go to the fields to the young corn plants.
(Vocables.)

This song describes how clouds from the southwest and northeast are
adorning themselves with rain so that they can come to the fields to water
the young corn plants. The blue/green clouds (*sakwa'omawt*) from the
southwest and the white clouds (*qöya'omawt*) from the northeast are
coming from ritually opposite directions. In this song, since only two
directions are named, the southwest is named first and northeast second,
in counterclockwise fashion.

    The corn plants, *paavönmamant,* are described as fluttering their
pollen-laden wings, *talasimasay puyayatota,* indicating their growing

---

17. = *sakwa'o'omawt* 'blue/green clouds'.
18. *aw* here would be *amumi* 'to them' in normal speech.
19. = *qöya'o'omawt* 'white clouds'.

vitality. The image created by this phrase is one of corn leaves covered with pollen that has fallen from the tassels. The corn plants are said to be growing themselves up, *naawungwina*. The allusion to flapping wings and growing up recalls the wing flapping of fledgling birds as they exercise their wings before they flutter out of the nest. Initiates to religious societies are also described as fledglings—individuals who are growing in knowledge. The image of pollen-laden wings of the young corn plants flapping in the breeze thus invokes the idea that the young corn plants are fledglings that are growing in maturity with the nurturing blue/green and white rain from the southwest and northeast.

71. *Angaktsìntawi*[1]
(Black Song 81)

Hahay'imanatu,[2]
Hahay'imanatu,
Hahay'imanatu.
Haa hawyona hay'iye, hawyo.
Hahay'imanatu'u kuyapkuyiy[3] *angqw*[4] *wuutayani,*[5]
umumi'i,[6]
péwi'i.[7]
Aa'angwusnasomtaqa[8] *yep*[9] *su'its*[10] *talavay*[11] *yep taatawiyu'u,*[12]
tawlawmumuyngwu,[13]
yep su'an[14] *qaatsitniqö'ö.*[15]

1. *angaktsìntawi* 'Long-Hair katsina song'.
2. = *Hahay'imanat* '(two) Hahay'i maidens'.
3. *kuyapkuyiy*, object form of *kuyapkuyi'am* 'their dippers of water'.
4. *angqw* 'from it, from there'.
5. *wuutayani*, future plural of *wuuta* 'pour'.
6. *umumi'i*, pausal form of *umumi* 'to you (plural), on you'.
7. = *pew'i*, pausal form of *pew* 'toward here, coming this way'.
8. = *Angwusnasomtaqa* 'Crow Mother katsina'.
9. *yep* 'here'.
10. *su'its* 'early in the day'.
11. *talavay* 'in the morning'.
12. = *taatawiy*, object form of *taatawi'at* 'her songs'.
13. = *tawlawmumuyangwu*, habitual tense form of *tawlawmumuya* 'keep singing extensively'.
14. *su'an* 'in just the right way'.
15. = *qátsitniqw* 'when life will/should be, so that life will be'.

Hee'e'eehee hee'e'eehee,
hee hee'e'eehee.
Tawmumuyngwuy.[16]
Ooho woohowaay eehee eeheloo.
Aaha aa'aahaahaa, ii'ihii hii.
Hapi me.[17]
Oo'ohoowa ehee'eeheelo.

Hahay'i maidens,
Hahay'i maidens,
Hahay'i maidens.
(Vocables.)
The Hahay'i maidens will pour their dipper of water
on you
coming this way.
The Crow Mother katsina here early in the morning
keeps singing her songs
so that life will go on in the right way.
(Vocables.)
She keeps singing and singing.
(Vocables.)
Listen, there is more.
(Vocables.)

This song is about events at *Powamuya,* the Bean dance, although it is not a song sung at *Powamuya.* The Long-Hair katsinas are singing about a pair of Hahay'i maidens who appear at the ceremony. Hahay'imana carries a gourd of water and walks around the village offering to give people a drink. When she puts the dipper up to their lips she over-pours it so that the water spills over the edge of the dipper down the shirt of the person. This water pouring is symbolic of hopes for abundant rain in the coming growing season.

The Crow Mother katsina appears very early in the morning on the day of the *Powamuya* ceremony. She stands at the hatchway of the *Powamuya* kiva and, holding a plaque (*poota*) of cornmeal and prayer feathers, sings a long song in a low tone that is hardly audible. Her song is about

16. = *tawmumuyngwu,* habitual tense form of *tawmumuya* 'be singing intensively'.
17. *hapi me,* formulaic expression introducing the song's second part, *oomi* 'upward'.

life as it should be lived. All around her katsinas are busy delivering dolls (*tithu*) to girls and bows and arrows to boys throughout the village. At intervals in her song the *Powamuya* ritual leader (*powamuymongwi*) comes out of the kiva and sprinkles cornmeal on her. When she finishes her song, this leader gives her prayer feathers and sends her home. Her purpose has been to inspire people to renew their efforts to follow the communal lifeway based on corn.

72. Angaktsìntawi$_1$
(Black Song 85)

Hii'iiyay'elooya yee.
Tsukumongwit$_2$ itanamu$_3$ tsukutiyotu$_4$ yep$_5$ ikwatsimu$_6$ pay$_7$ itam$_8$ hàalay-
      'unangway$_9$ itàakwatsmuy aw$_{10}$ tiitii'i'ökiwa,$_{11}$
umumi$_{12}$ péwi'i.$_{13}$
Ayahi'aa aa'ayahii'aay.
[Keresan *Kaatsina yoo$_{14}$ shiiwaynayo, oosaara,$_{15}$*
Payaakyaamo$_{16}$ o'eewo'ee wo'ehee. Keresan]

(Vocables of the Long-Hair katsinas.)

1. *angaktsìntawi* 'Long-Hair katsina song'.
2. = *tsukumomngwit* 'clown leaders'.
3. = *itanam* 'our fathers'.
4. = *tsukutotim* 'clown boys'.
5. *yep* 'here'.
6. = *ikwatsim* 'my friends'.
7. *pay,* expressive particle.
8. *itam* 'we'.
9. *hàalay'unangway* 'with happy hearts, with beneficent intentions'.
10. *aw* 'for it'. Here this means 'for them' and would be *amumi* in non-song usage.
11. = *tiiti'ökiwa* 'have come in dance (and thereby to soothe)'.
12. = *umumi* 'to you (plural)'.
13. = *pew'i,* pausal form of *pew* 'toward here, coming this way'.
14. *yoo* seems to represent the Keresan word for 'yonder'; cf. Santa Ana *yu?* (Davis 1964: 168).
15. *oosaara* represents 'sun' in Keresan; cf. Santa Ana *?úṣâ·çA* (Davis 1964: 165).
16. *Payaakyaamo* is believed to mean 'clown', cf. *Payatamu,* a katsina representing the clown as a totem of the Eagle clan (*Kwaangyam*). The Keresan source has not been identified.

Clown leaders, our fathers, and clown boys here, my friends, we have
 come in dance with happy hearts for our friends,
to you here.
(Vocables of the sound of singing.)
(Two lines in Keresan with references to the sun and to clowns.)

In this short song, the katsinas address the clowns who are apparently in
the plaza saying that they have come to dance for the people. The clowns
represent the people who are always falling short in their efforts to live
the Hopi way. Since the clown groups are often made up of men of
different ages, the katsinas address the married men as "our fathers," and
the unmarried boys as "my friends."

73. *Angaktsìntawi$_1$*
(Black Song 89)

Haw$_2$ uma$_3$ ínamu.$_4$
Uma hapi$_5$ itamuy$_6$ yuuyahinaya,$_7$
taatö$_8$ Weenimay$_9$ áwi'i.$_{10}$
Ep$_{11}$ itam$_{12}$ wuupat$_{13}$ qatsi'nangwat$_{14}$ pitsangwayat$_{15}$ umungem$_{16}$ yuuya-
hiwa,$_{17}$
haa'oo$_{18}$ ínamu.
Lee lehe.

1. *angaktsìntawi* 'Long-Hair katsina song'.
2. *haw,* vocative particle.
3. *uma* 'you (plural)'.
4. = *inam* 'my fathers'.
5. *hapi* 'truly, surely, certainly'.
6. *itamuy* 'us', object form of *itam* 'we'.
7. *yuuyahinaya* 'dress (them) as for a ceremony, adorn (plural)'.
8. *taatö* 'to the southeast'.
9. *Weenimay,* object form of *Weenima,* the southeast katsina home.
10. = *aw'i,* pausal form of *aw* 'to it, to there'.
11. *ep* 'there, at it'.
12. *itam* 'we'.
13. *wuupat,* object form of *wuupa* 'long'.
14. *qatsi'nangwat,* object form of *qatsi'nangwa* 'will to live'.
15. *pitsangwayat,* object form of *pitsangwa'at* 'its countenance'.
16. *umungem* 'for you (plural), for your benefit'.
17. *yuuyahiwa* 'have been dressed as for a ceremony, be adorned (plural)'.
18. *haa'oo,* vocative particle.

Oove'e,[19]
taawa[20] *ína'a,*[21]
yoytuveniy[22] *ang*[23] *tuu'awinmakyangw*[24] *hoyoyotimani.*[25]
Oo'hohoo,
oo'oho'oo.

Hark, you, my fathers.
You have adorned us
to the southeast, to *Weenima.*
There we have been adorned with the countenance of a long life with the
    will to live for you,
o my fathers.
(Vocables.)
Up above,
my father the sun
will be moving along [with] his rain marks informing people.
(Vocables.)

The katsinas are acknowledging that they have been adorned with the
fathers' prayers at their homes at *Weenima* in the southeast cardinal
direction. In turn, accepting the heartfelt nature of these prayers, the
katsinas have prepared themselves with the countenance (*pitsangwa*) of
the will to live a long life, meaning that the katsinas have adorned themselves with all of the determination and striving to live the perfect life.
They are going to show the people what it takes to live a long life. As
perfect beings, katsinas try to encourage the people to accept the
hardships and sacrifices that one has to make in order to continue to live
by the practices that define the Hopi lifeway. After vocables, the katsinas
observe that their father, the sun, is going along informing people about
the coming rain by means of his rain marks. Hopis say that a ring around
the sun is an omen that rain will come.

19. *oove'e,* pausal form of *oove* 'up above, at the place above'.
20. *taawa* 'sun'.
21. *ína'a,* pausal form of *ina* 'my father'.
22. = *yòytutuveniy,* object form of *yòytutuveni'at* 'his rain marks'.
23. *ang* 'along it, along there, in that area, in several places'.
24. *tuu'awinmakyangw* 'while going along informing'.
25. *hoyoyotimani* 'will move along'.

74. *Angaktsìntawi*₁
(Black Song 98)

*Hin pa*₂ *hìngqawni,*₃
*tatkya*₄ *Weenimay*₅ *épe'e,*₆
*Kooyemsimongwitu.*₇
*Puma*₈ *itamuy*₉ *itàatitwiyu*₁₀ *akwa*₁₁ *peevewna,*₁₂
*yépe'e.*₁₃
*Qa*₁₄ *paas*₁₅ *pi*₁₆ *pas*₁₇ *Kooyemsi*₁₈ *hiihìita*₁₉ *titwi'ta.*₂₀
*Pi pay*₂₁ *panis*₂₂ *hìita'a,*₂₃
*wutsilawe'sa*₂₄ *putakw*₂₅ *umumi*₂₆ *pávantingwu,*₂₇
yépe'e.
Lee lehee la.

1. *angaktsìntawi* 'Long-Hair katsina song'.
2. *hin pa* '(I) wonder if'.
3. *hìngqawni* 'will say something, say what'.
4. *tatkya* 'in the southeast'.
5. *Weenimay,* object form of *Weenima,* the southeast katsina home.
6. = *ep'e,* pausal form of *ep* 'there, at it'.
7. = *Koyemsimongwit* '(pair of) Mudhead katsina leaders'.
8. *puma* 'they'.
9. *itamuy* 'us', object form of *itam* 'we'.
10. = *itàatitwiy,* object form of *itàatitwi* 'our customary way of dancing'.
11. = *akw* 'with, using'.
12. *peevewna* 'doubt, cast doubt on'.
13. = *yep'e,* pausal form of *yep* 'here'.
14. *qa* 'not'.
15. = *pas* 'very'.
16. *pi* 'truly'.
17. *pas* 'very'.
18. *Kooyemsi* 'Mudhead katsina'.
19. *hiihìita,* object form of *hiihimu* 'some things'.
20. = *titwi'yta* 'be adept or skilled at several things'.
21. *pay,* expressive particle.
22. *panis* 'constantly'.
23. *hìita'a,* pausal form of *hìita,* the object form of *himu* 'something, what'.
24. *wutsilawe'sa* 'only if (they) do things by sleight of hand, doing magic tricks', adverbial (*-sa* 'only') subordinate clause (*-e'* 'if') form based on *wutsilawu* 'be doing something by artifice, sleight of hand'.
25. *putakw* 'with that, by means of that, using that'.
26. *umumi* 'to you (plural)'.
27. *pávantingwu,* habitual tense form of *pávanti* 'get better, improve'.

Oovi[28] *púma'a,*[29]
umumi péwi'i,[30]
yooyanaanakwusaqw'ö,[31]
Kooyemsim[32] *ikwil'a'yat*[33] *kuywikiy*[34] *iikwìltotaqw'ö,*[35]
pu'[36] *ítamu*[37] *talwiptoyakyangw*[38] *ùmtoyakyangw*[39] *yookinayangwu.*[40]
Oo'ho ooho wa ee'he eehe lo.

We wonder what they will say,
in the southeast at *Weenima*,
the Mudhead katsina leaders.
They cast doubt on us by [their] use of our customary way of dancing,
here.
It is not really the Mudhead katsinas who know how to dance all kinds of dances.
Only if they keep doing things
by sleight of hand, by the use of that do they make it look better to you.
here.
(Vocables.)
That's why when they (the clouds, the Long-Hair katsinas)
start off on their journey as rain
toward you here,
the Mudhead katsinas, as (our) hired carriers, put containers of water on their backs to carry,

28. *oovi* 'that's why'.
29. *púma'a,* pausal form of *puma* 'they'.
30. = *pew'i,* pausal form of *pew* 'toward here, coming this way'.
31. = *yoynànkwusaqw'ö,* subordinate clause pausal form of *yoynànkwusa* 'start on a journey as rain'.
32. = *Kookoyemsim* 'Mudhead katsinas'.
33. *ikwil'a'yat* 'hired carriers', plural of *ikwil'aya.*
34. *kuywikiy,* object form of *kuywiki'am* 'their container(s) of water carried by a string or bail'.
35. *iikwìltotaqw'ö,* subordinate clause pausal form of *iikwìltota* 'put on the back to carry (plural)'.
36. *pu'* 'now, then'.
37. = *itam* 'we' (referring to the same non-Mudhead katsinas as *púma'a* in the first clause of this sentence).
38. = *talwiptoynakyangw* 'while making lightning'.
39. = *ùmtoynakyangw* 'while making slow booming sounds'.
40. = *yoknayangwu,* habitual tense form of *yoknaya* 'make it rain (plural)'.

and then we, while making lightning and slow booming sounds, produce
the rain.
(Vocables.)

The Long-Hair katsinas, who are singing this song, are talking behind the
backs of the Mudhead leaders (*Koyemsimongwit*), who are also apparently
present at this dance. The role of the Mudheads in the katsina world is
that of a maternal uncle who gives advice and teaches appropriate daily
roles and cultural knowledge. In this song, the Mudheads are testing the
Long-Hair katsinas, doubting that they can perform an efficacious ceremony, here translated as a doubt about their "customary way of dancing."
However, say the Long-Hair katsinas, the Mudheads only appear to know
how to perform a ceremony. They disparagingly accuse the Mudheads of
using magic tricks (*wutsilawu* 'be doing things by sleight of hand') to
impress people. But, the Long-Hair katsinas say, when the rain comes,
they are the ones making the lightning and thunder while the Mudheads
are only their hired water carriers! The implication is that if the Mudheads
knew more ceremonies they wouldn't have to be water boys. Instead, they
would be like the Long-Hair katsinas, who are actually the ones who are
making the lightning, thunder and rain.

75. *Angaktsìntawi$_1$*
(Black Song 104)

Hii'i yay'aawe.
Umùu'uuyiyu$_2$ ánga'a,$_3$
oo'omàwtu$_4$ paatuwataviyani.$_5$
Putakw$_6$ púma'a,$_7$
oomi$_8$ naawungwinayani.$_9$

1. *angaktsìntawi* 'Long-Hair katsina song'.
2. = *umùu'uyiy,* object form of *umùu'uyi* 'your planted field(s)'.
3. = *ang'a,* pausal form of *ang* 'along, at several places, in an area'.
4. = *oo'omawt* 'clouds'.
5. = *paatuwatapyani* 'will lay water on the land (plural)'.
6. *putakw* 'with that, by means of that, using that'.
7. *púma'a,* pausal form of *puma* 'they'.
8. *oomi* 'upward'.
9. = *naawungwnayani* 'will make selves grow'.

Le lehe la.
Hii'i yay'aawe.
Umùu'uuyiyu aanga'a,{10}
oo'omawtu paatuwataviyani.
Putakw púma'a,
oomi naawungwinayani.
Lee lehe laa.
Yaahi yaahiy hiiya.
Hapi me.{11}
Humi'uuyimanatu{12} síqölöva{13} taayiimuyiwni.{14}
Humi'uuyimanatu síqölöva taayiimuyiwni.
Humi'uuyimanatu síqölöva taayiimuyiwni.
Lee lehe laa.
Ayahii aaha iihii.

(Vocables.)
Along your planted fields,
the clouds will lay water on the land.
Using that, they will make themselves grow upward.
(Vocables.)
Along your planted fields,
the clouds will lay water on the land.
Using that, they will make themselves grow upward.
(Vocables.)
Listen, there is more.
The corn plant maidens will look in awe along the flowery expanses.
The corn plant maidens will look in awe along the flowery expanses.
The corn plant maidens will look in awe along the flowery expanses.
(Vocables.)

The katsinas, speaking indirectly, describe how they as clouds will water
the people's planted fields, here expressed as "will lay water on the land"
(*paatuwatapyani*). With this water the plants will make themselves grow
up, *naawungwnayani*. It is important to understand why this word is a

10. = *ang'a,* pausal form of *ang* 'along it, along there, in that area, in several places'.
11. *hapi me,* formulaic expression introducing the song's second part, *oomi* 'upward'.
12. = *humi'uyimamant* 'corn plant maidens'.
13. = *sìiqòlpa* 'in, along the flowery expanse(s)'.
14. = *taayimuyiwni* 'will look in awe'.

reflexive form, with the reflexive prefix *naa-* and the causative suffix *-na*. In contrast to those who think that people make plants grow by watering them, in Hopi belief, the plants do not grow in this passive way. Rather, plants, being animate beings, actively raise themselves up (*naawungwnaya*) by means of the rainwater. In the second part of the song, the katsinas describe how the corn plant maidens, who are the corn plants, and, by metaphorical implication, the people, will look with grateful hearts at the fields of flowering plants that were nurtured by their rain.

76. Angaktsìntawi *~1~*
(Black Song 108)

Uma ~2~ yep ~3~ yuuyahiwa, ~4~
naanan'ivo'o. ~5~
Oomawkiikinawita, ~6~
angqw ~7~ pew ~8~ oo'omawutu ~9~ kuukuyivani. ~10~
Lee lehe la.
Ayàngqö ~11~ tatkyaqw ~12~ Weenimayu ~13~ ángaqö, ~14~
oo'omawutu kuukuyvata'a, ~15~
angqw pew yooya'öki, ~16~
péwi'i. ~17~

1. *angaktsìntawi* 'Long-Hair katsina song'.
2. *uma* 'you (plural)'.
3. *yep* 'here'.
4. *yuuyahiwa* 'have prepared as for a ceremony, have been adorned (plural)'. In this context, *yuuyahiwa* refers to the preparation of the prayer feathers.
5. *naanan'ivo'o*, pausal form of *naanan'ivo* 'to the different directions around'.
6. = *oomàwkiikinawit* 'along the dwelling places of the clouds'.
7. *angqw* 'from it, from there'.
8. *pew* 'toward here, coming this way'.
9. = *oo'omawt* 'clouds'.
10. = *kuukuyvani* 'will appear, will make their appearance, will come into view'.
11. = *ayàngqw* 'from over there'.
12. *tatkyaqw* 'from the southeast'.
13. = *Weenimay*, object form of *Weenima*, the southeast katsina home.
14. = *angqw* 'from it'.
15. = *kuukuyvat'a*, pausal form of *kuukuyvat* 'after (they) come into view, make their appearance'.
16. = *yoy'ökini* 'will arrive, come as rain'.
17. = *pew'i*, pausal form of *pew* 'toward here, coming this way'.

Umùu'uyiy[18] *ang*[19] *paatalawintani.*[20]
Yan[21] *uma naawakinaya.*[22]
Lolmani.[23]
Hiy'ayahiy'a hiy'ayahiy'a.
Hapi me.[24]
Hapi me.
Ahaha ha ay.

You have prepared (the prayer feathers) here,
to the different directions around.
Along the cloud houses,
coming from there, the clouds will make their appearance.
(Vocable.)
From over there, from the southeast, from *Weenima*,
after the clouds make their appearance,
coming from there, they arrive as rain,
coming this way.
They will be making it glisten with water along your planted fields.
You pray for it to be this way.
It will be beautiful.
(Vocables.)
Listen, there is more.
Listen, there is more.
(Vocables.)

The katsinas observe that the people have prepared their prayer feathers, that is, their prayers, and sent them to the four cardinal directions, the "different directions around." From all four directions, the clouds, responding to these prayers, will make their appearance. Then the katsinas, focusing on the clouds from the southeast direction, from *Weenima*, say that after the clouds make their appearance from their cloud houses, that is, after they rise up over the horizon in the southeast direction and build

18. *umùu'uyiy,* object form of *umùu'uyi* 'your (plural) planted plant(s)'.
19. *ang* 'along it, along there, in that area, in several places'.
20. *paatalawintani* 'will be making it glisten with water'.
21. *yan* 'like this, in this way, thus'.
22. = *naanawakna* 'pray (plural)'.
23. *lolmani* 'will be beautiful, good, proper'.
24. *hapi me,* formulaic expression introducing the song's second part, *oomi* 'upward'.

into rain clouds, they will come to the people as rain. They will make the fields glisten with water. The word *paatalawinta* 'be making it glisten with water' is derived from *paahu* 'water' and *taalawinta* 'be making it light, illuminated'. It embodies the idea that the new life that will grow in the fields is metaphorically equivalent to the light of a new day. The katsinas say that this beautiful spectacle of pools of water is what the people have been praying for.

77. Hehey'a paslawu*₁*
(Black Song 119)

Hehey'a.
Hehey'a.
Paslawu,₂
ayamo.₃
Paslawu,
ayamo.
Mowàape₄ isòòqölöt₅ paslawkyangw₆ momoymuy₇ ang₈ wahima.₉
Wahima.

Hehey'a.
Hehey'a.
He is hoeing a field
over there.
He is hoeing a field
over there.
While hoeing a patch of mustard plants at Mowàapi, he goes along throw-
    ing them to the women.
He goes along throwing them.

1. *Hehey'a paslawu* 'Hehey'a hoes a field'.
2. *paslawu* 'be hoeing a field'.
3. = *ayám* 'over there'.
4. *Mowàape* 'at Mowàapi'. Mowàapi is also known as "Mount Beautiful." It is a butte about two miles southwest of the southwesternmost tip of Third Mesa.
5. *isòòqölöt*, object form of *isòòqölö* 'patch of mustard plants'.
6. *paslawkyangw* 'while hoeing a field'.
7. *momoymuy*, object form of *momoyam* 'women'.
8. *ang* 'along it, along there, in that area, in several places'.
9. *wahima* 'go along throwing'.

The katsinas are commenting on the traditional activity of cultivating and gathering mustard greens, perhaps as a way of reminding people not only about the traditional tasks of hoeing and food preparation, but also about what those tasks represent. The katsinas describe an activity done in the spring by groups of girls and boys. As the boys gather the greens, they throw bunches to the girls who collect them and take them home. The gathering of wild greens traditionally played a part in the socialization of yong people, teaching them the appropriate moral behvior and social relationships that sustain Hopi communities. The song describes this activity as being performed by the Hehey'a katsina but it is not clear just which katsinas sing this song.

78. *Hehey'akatsìntawi₁*
(Black Song 53)

Haw'o₂ ínamu.₃
Uma₄ hapi₅ yep₆ móngwiyesvat'a,₇
uma hàalaytsootsong.yata'a,₈
umùupahoveniy₉ yuuwasinat'a,₁₀
aw₁₁ uma sustalyokvaniqata₁₂ naawakina.₁₃
Pútakwa',₁₄

1. *hehey'akatsìntawi* 'Hehey'a katsina song'.
2. *haw'o,* vocative particle.
3. = *inam* 'my fathers'.
4. *uma* 'you (plural)'.
5. *hapi* 'truly, surely, certainly'.
6. *yep* 'here'.
7. = *mong.yesvat'a,* pausal form of *mong.yesvat* 'after (they) sit as leaders'.
8. = *hàalaytsotsong.yat'a,* pausal form of *hàalaytsotsong.yat* 'after smoking the pipe with untroubled minds'.
9. *umùupahoveniy,* object form of *umùupahoveni* 'your (plural) marked prayer feathers, prayer feathers with ritual markings'.
10. = *yuwsinat'a,* pausal form of *yuwsinat* 'after dressing (them)'.
11. *aw* 'to it, to there'.
12. = *sustalyokvaniqat,* object form of *sustalyokvaniqa* 'an all-day rain', literally, 'that which will rain all day'.
13. = *naawakna* 'pray'. In normal speech in this context, this would be in the plural, *naanawakna*.
14. *pútakwa',* pausal form of *putakw* 'with that, by means of that, using that'.

naanan 'ivaqö₁₅ tálawiptimakyangw₁₆ yoy 'ùmtimakyangw₁₇ uysonaq₁₈ paa-vataalawinani.₁₉

O, my fathers.
After you sit down here as (ritual) leaders,
and after you smoke the pipe with untroubled minds,
and after you clothe your prayer feathers with markings,
you pray for an all-day rain.
By means of that,
from the different directions around, while going along with lightning
   flashing and going along thundering, the rain will make it glisten with
   puddles of water throughout the planted fields.

The katsinas are addressing the ritual leaders, the men who are preparing
for the katsinas' performance. They describe the ritual activities that take
place in the kiva as a series of conditions that should take place in order
for the katsinas to hear their prayers and come as rain. The process begins
when the ritual leaders assume leadership of the village for the duration
of the ceremonial day by sitting in a circle in the kiva. At this time they
make their ritual prayers to the katsinas by smoking their pipes. The
smoke is symbolic of the clouds, and by implication, of the rain that is the
object of their prayers. The katsinas emphasize that they must smoke with
untroubled minds, meaning that the prayers must be uttered with the
utmost sincerity, unblemished with thoughts of self-aggrandizement or
other personal goals that are counter to the harmony and well-being of the
community. The katsinas observe that after the men clothe their prayer
feathers with "markings," they should pray for an all-day rain. The
"markings" may refer to the symbolic marks made on the strings to which
the feathers are tied, although it may be another way of talking about
imbuing the prayer feathers with prayers.

   The expression "by means of that" is a standard song way of saying
"as a result of your prayers." Then the katsinas describe the flashing
lightning, rumbling thunder, and such quantities of rain that the people's

---

15. = *naanan 'ivaqw* 'from the different directions around'.
16. = *talwiptimakyangw* 'while going along with lightning flashing'.
17. *yoy 'ùmtimakyangw* 'while going along thundering (slowly)'.
18. *uysonaq* 'throughout the midst of the planted area(s)'.
19. = *paavatalawnani* 'will make it glisten with puddles of water'.

planted fields will glisten with puddles of water that come with summer thunderstorms.

79. Hehey'akatsìntawi$_1$
(Black Song 54)

Hoohopaqö$_2$ oo'omàwtu,$_3$
puma$_4$ pew$_5$ tùutukwiwmakyango$_6$ umùu'uyiy$_7$ ang$_8$ paatalawinani.$_9$
Yang$_{10}$ uma$_{11}$ uuyisonaq,$_{12}$
yang taatawyuuyuwintani.$_{13}$
Hapi me.$_{14}$
Naalönaanan'ivaqö$_{15}$ oo'omàwtu kuukuyivani.$_{16}$

From places in the northeast, the clouds,
while coming along stacked up, they will make it glisten with water along
    your planted fields.
Along here in the planted area,
you will be dancing and singing songs along here.
Listen, there is more.
From each of the four directions the clouds will come into view.

In this song the katsinas are creating a mental image of how the clouds in the northeast are moving and building into thunderheads by describing them as *pew tuutukwiwma,* coming along stacked up, as they move toward

---

1. *hehey'akatsìntawi* 'Hehey'a katsina song'.
2. = *hoohopaqw* 'from places in the northeast'.
3. = *oo'omawt* 'clouds'.
4. *puma* 'they'.
5. *pew* 'toward here, coming this way'.
6. = *tùutukwiwmakyangw* 'while going along stacked up in several stacks'.
7. *umùu'uyiy,* object form of *umùu'uyi* 'your (plural) plants'.
8. *ang* 'along it, along there, in that area, in several places'.
9. = *paatalawnani* 'will make it glisten with water'.
10. *yang* 'along here, in this area'.
11. *uma* 'you (plural)'.
12. = *uysonaq* 'throughout the midst of the planted area(s)'.
13. = *taatawyuyuwintani* 'will be dancing and singing songs'.
14. *hapi me,* formulaic expression introducing the song's second part, *oomi* 'upward'.
15. = *nalönanan'ivaqw* 'from each of the four directions'.
16. = *kuukuyvani* 'will appear, come into sight (plural)'.

the planted fields. In Hopi belief, the clouds are animate beings. Their coming as rain is an intentional result of their determination that the people deserve their gift of rain. Always implied in the purposeful activity of their "coming" is the idea that the clouds are looking toward the Hopi lands to see if the people are deserving of their gift of rain. Are they working hard? Are they taking care of their fields? Are they following traditional practices and the moral imperatives that facilitate communal life? If the katsinas deem that the people are living properly and thus are deserving, then they will arrive as rain and make the planted fields glisten with water. This is the reciprocal relationship between the katsinas and the people—they will come as clouds and rain if the people live right. When they come, the people will sing and dance gratefully. In the second section, after formulaic *hapi me,* the katsinas describe how the clouds will "come into view," that is, they will peek above the horizon and begin building into thunderheads, from all four directions.

80. Hehey'akatsìntawi$_1$
(Black Song 63)

Hinii'i niyaa niyaay aa.
Yooyokni.$_2$
Yooyokni'i.$_3$
It'a,$_4$
uma$_5$ nawakinaya,$_6$
ìnamu.$_7$
Yep$_8$ uma umuu'unangwvaasiy$_9$ sunsayaqö'ö,$_{10}$

1. *hehey'akatsìntawi* 'Hehey'a katsina song'.
2. = *yooyokni* 'it will be raining'.
3. = *yooyokni'i,* pausalized form of *yooyokni* 'it will be raining'.
4. *it'a,* pausal form of *it,* the object form of *i'* 'this'.
5. *uma* 'you (plural)'.
6. = *naanawakna* 'pray for (plural)'.
7. = *inam* 'my fathers'.
8. *yep* 'here', meaning where the people are.
9. = *umùu'unangwvàasiy,* object form of *umùu'unangwvàasi* 'your heartfelt wish, hope, prayer'.
10. = *sunsayaqw'ö,* subordinate clause pausal form of *sunsaya* 'be together as one (plural)'.

yangqw₁₁ pew₁₂ yooyangw₁₃ haahawiwmani,₁₄
uuyisonaqa₁₅ umumi.₁₆
Umumi yoyhoyoyotani.₁₇
Uysonaqa₁₈ paavataalawinani'i,₁₉
yánga'a.₂₀
Umumi,
umumi yoyhoyoyotani.
Uysonaqa paavataalawinani'i,
yánga'a.

(Vocables.)
It will be raining.
It will be raining.
This,
you are praying for,
my fathers.
If you are united as one in your heartfelt prayers here₍ₐ₎,
from here₍ᵦ₎, the rain will come along descending,
throughout the midst of the planted areas to you.
To you it will be moving as rain.
Throughout the midst of the planted areas, it will make it glisten with
     puddles of water
along here₍ₐ₎.
To you,
the rain will be moving to you.
Throughout the midst of the planted areas, it will make it glisten with
     puddles of water
along here₍ₐ₎.

11. *yangqw* 'from here', meaning from where the katsinas are.
12. *pew* 'toward here, coming this way'.
13. *yooyangw* 'rain'.
14. = *haahawiwmani* 'will go/come along descending'; *pew haahawiwmani* 'will come along descending'.
15. = *uysonaq* 'throughout the midst of the planted area(s)'.
16. *umumi* 'to you (plural)'.
17. *yoyhoyoyotani* 'will be moving as rain'.
18. = *uysonaq* 'throughout the midst of the planted area(s)'.
19. = *paavatalawnani'i,* pausalized form of *paavatalawnani* 'will make it glisten with puddles of water'.
20. = *yang'a,* pausal form of *yang* 'here, along here, in these places, in this area', referring to where the people are.

The katsinas are assuring the people that it will rain if their hearts are united in sincere prayer. Because this is a communal society, everyone must work in concert for the good of the community, rising above their self-interests and problems, to help and share with others. When everyone prays with the same goals and lives in harmony, the rain will descend and spread throughout the fields among the plants, resulting in a land glistening with puddles of water. Because rain is animate, it is more appropriate to say that it climbs down, comes down, or descends rather than it falls. The fields covered with glistening puddles of water are described by *paavatalawna*, a compound that includes *taalawva*, which means to become light or bright. Sometimes *taalawva* refers to the light of a new day, but here it has to do with the way plants, and by implication people, are revitalized. The coming of rain, just as the dawning of a new day, is seen as the rebirth of life.

Finally it should be noted that, while attempting to adhere closely to a literal translation of the words of the song, some confusion may arise when the same word in the translation refers to different things. In this song the words for "here" are marked differently: here$_{(a)}$ and here$_{(b)}$. "Here$_{(a)}$" refers to where the people and their fields are in this the present Fourth World (*yep, yang*) and "here$_{(b)}$" refers to the cloud homes in the Fifth World the katsinas are coming from (*yangqw* 'from here').

81. *Hehey'aktsìntawi*$_1$
(Black Song 88)

Hii niyay aa.
Ítamu$_2$ taalawsiwawayina.$_3$
Itam$_4$ yep$_5$ taalawsiwawayina.
Itam yep umumi'i,$_6$
tiitiwunima,$_7$

1. *hehey'aktsìntawi* 'Hehey'a katsina song'.
2. = *itam* 'we'.
3. *taalawsiwawayna* 'be making delighted at the beginning of the day'.
4. *itam* 'we'.
5. *yep* 'here'.
6. *umumi'i*, pausal form of *umumi* 'for you (plural)'.
7. *tiitiwunima* 'be dancing in performance'.

taawanawita.[8]
Yahinay oo oo.
Hapi me.[9]
—*(inaudible)*—
Sikyavoliwmanatu,[10]
puma[11] *yang*[12] *sìiqölönawita,*[13]
puma yang kuwan'ew'unangway[14] *tàataviyani,*[15]
taawanawita.
Sakwavoliwmanatu,[16]
puma yang sìiqölönawita,
puma yang kuwan'ew'unangway tàataviyani,
taawanawita.

(Vocables.)
We are making [you] delighted at the beginning of the day.
We are making [you] delighted at the beginning of the day here.
We, for you here,
are dancing in performance,
all day long.
(Vocables.)
Listen, there is more.
—*(inaudible)*—
The yellow butterfly maidens,
they, along the flowery expanses here,
they will be placing deposits along here with beautiful hearts
all day long.
The blue/green butterfly maidens,
they, along the flowery expanses here,
they will be placing deposits along here with beautiful hearts
all day long.

8. = *taawanawit* 'all day long'.
9. *hapi me,* formulaic expression introducing the song's second part, *oomi* 'upward'.
10. = *sikyavolmamant* 'yellow butterfly maidens'.
11. *puma* 'they'.
12. *yang* 'along here, in this area'.
13. = *sìiqölönawit* 'along the flowery expanse(s)'.
14. *kuwan'ew'unangway* 'with beautiful hearts, with beneficent intentions'.
15. = *tàatapyani* 'will be placing deposits (plural)'.
16. = *sakwavolmamant* 'blue/green butterfly maidens'.

The Hehey'a katsinas announce that they have come to delight the people at the beginning of the day with their performance. After some vocables, the katsinas describe how the yellow butterfly maidens, that is, the yellow butterflies, are "placing deposits" throughout the field of flowers. This is a way to describe how the butterflies are transferring pollen from one flower to the next. In this process of pollinating the fields of flowers, they are taking the beautiful life essence from one flower and placing it on another flower so as to create another life. The compound word *kuwan-'ew'unangway* emphasizes the larger idea that the colorfully pleasing hearts of the butterflies embodies the purity and beauty of all new life that comes with fertilization. The sentiment is repeated for the blue/green butterflies.

82. *Hehey'aktsìntawi$_1$*
(Black Song 91)

Ha'óo$_2$ haw$_3$ íngumu.$_4$
Ha'óo haw ínamu.$_5$
Uma$_6$ yep$_7$ umùukivay$_8$ naasave'e,$_9$
tsootsong.yakyango$_{10}$ yoynaawakinayaqö'ö,$_{11}$
angqw$_{12}$ pew$_{13}$ naanan'ivaqö$_{14}$ oo'omawutu$_{15}$ yoynaanakwusani,$_{16}$
taawanawita.$_{17}$

1. *hehey'aktsìntawi* 'Hehey'a katsina song'.
2. *ha'óo,* vocative particle.
3. *haw,* vocative particle.
4. = *ingum* 'my mothers'.
5. = *inam* 'my fathers'.
6. *uma* 'you (plural)'.
7. *yep* 'here'.
8. *umùukivay,* object form of *umùukiva* 'your (plural) kiva'.
9. *naasave'e,* pausal form of *naasave* 'in the middle'.
10. = *tsootsong.yakyangw* 'while smoking (plural)'.
11. = *yoynanawaknaqw'ö,* subordinate clause pausal form of *yoynanawakna* 'pray for rain (plural)'.
12. *angqw* 'from it, from there'.
13. *pew* 'toward here, coming this way'.
14. = *naanan'ivaqw* 'from the different directions around'.
15. = *oo'omawt* 'clouds'.
16. = *yoynànkwusani* 'will start on a journey as rain'.
17. = *taawanawit* 'all day long'.

Yahinay'oo.
Me,$_{18}$
yang$_{19}$ haqami$_{20}$ uuyisonaqa$_{21}$ yoyngyàlpuva'a,$_{22}$
taatawyuuyuwinani,$_{23}$
yánga'a.$_{24}$
Yaa'a.
Yan$_{25}$ uma naawakinaya,$_{26}$
ínamu.
Ayahiy'a ayahiy'aa haay.

Hark, o my mothers.
Hark, o my fathers.
You here in the middle of your kiva
have been praying for rain while smoking,
and coming from there, from the different directions around, the clouds
    will start their journey as rain,
all day long.
(Vocable.)
Listen,
along here throughout, in the postlude of the rain in the midst of the
    planted areas,
[you] will be singing songs and dancing
along here.
(Vocable.)
You have been praying for it to be like this,
my fathers.
(Vocables of the sound of singing.)

The katsinas call for the attention of the people, addressing the women
first as their mothers and then the men as their fathers. Then they speak

18. *me,* an expression to direct another's attention: 'you see, listen, behold, look'.
19. *yang* 'along here, in this area'.
20. = *aqwhaqami* 'throughout'.
21. = *uysonaq* 'throughout the midst of the planted area(s)'.
22. = *yoyngyàlpuva* 'in the postlude of the rain, during the time after it has stopped raining'.
23. = *taatawyuyuwintani* 'will be dancing and singing songs'.
24. = *yang'a,* pausal form of *yang* 'here, along here, in these places, in this area'.
25. *yan* 'like this, in this way, thus'.
26. = *naanawakna* 'pray (plural)'.

to the men who are the ritual leaders for this ceremony, addressing them as "you." They note that they have been smoking and praying in the middle of the kiva. This does not refer to the physical center of the kiva, but rather, figuratively to its "heart" in the area where the hatchway ladder reaches the floor. In return, the katsinas, who have received these prayers, promise that the clouds will start on their journey as rain from all the directions. The katsinas predict that in the period just after the rain ends, here rendered as in the "postlude" of the rain, the people will be singing and dancing in happiness "along here," meaning throughout their planted fields. The katsinas remind the people, "this is what you have been praying for," that is, for a rain that will revitalize all living things.

83. *Hehey'akatsìntawi*₁
(Black Song 103)

*Qatsiyaahinawisa.*₂
*Ítamu*₃ *naanan'ivaqö*₄ *oo'omawutu*₅ *yooyanaanakwusani.*₆
Qatsiyaahinawisa.
Ítamu naanan'ivaqö oo'omawutu yooyanaanakwusani.
*Mee'e.*₇
*Umùupaasanawita,*₈
*humi'uuyimanatu*₉ *wúngwiwmakyango*₁₀ *yangsava*₁₁ *anìwtini.*₁₂
Umùupaasanawita,
*kaway'uuyinawita*₁₃ *wúngwiwmakyangw yangsava anìwtini.*
*Uma*₁₄ *amùunawit*₁₅ *hàalàytimani.*₁₆

1. *hehey'akatsìntawi* 'Hehey'a katsina song'.
2. = *qatsiyàynawisa* 'go to begin life (plural)'.
3. = *itam* 'we'.
4. = *naanan'ivaqw* 'from the different directions around'.
5. = *oo'omawt* 'clouds'.
6. = *yoynànkwusani* 'will start on a journey as rain'.
7. = *me* 'behold'.
8. = *umùupasanawit* 'along your fields'.
9. = *humi'uyimamant* 'corn plant maidens'.
10. = *wúngwiwmakyangw* 'while growing'.
11. *yangsava* 'this long'.
12. *anìwtini* 'will grow'.
13. = *kaway'uyinawit* 'along the watermelon plantings'.
14. *uma* 'you (plural)'.
15. = *amunawit* 'along their course'.
16. *hàalàytimani* 'will go along expressing gladness'.

Aaha ayahi'a aaha ayahi'a.

We are coming to begin life.
We, the clouds, will start on a journey as rain from the different directions
    around.
[repeat]
Behold.
Along your fields,
as the corn plant maidens are growing, they (their ears) will mature this
    long.
Along your fields,
along your watermelon plantings, as they are growing, they (the water-
    melons) will mature this long.
You will go along them expressing gladness.
(Vocables.)

The katsinas announce that they are coming to begin life, meaning that
they are coming to vitalize the corn plants with their rain so that the plants
will produce new lives, that is, ears of corn. They say that, as the clouds,
they will begin coming from all the cardinal directions. When this
happens the people should look at their fields. They will see that as the
corn plant maidens grow, that is, as the ears of the corn plants mature,
they will grow long. Likewise, they will see that as their watermelon vines
lengthen into mature plants, the watermelons will grow long. The katsinas
predict that when this happens, the people will go walking among their
planted fields expressing thankful gladness at the sight of these maturing
crops.

84. Hemiskatsìntawi₁

(Black Song 61)

TIITAWI₂

Aaha iihii.
Yokvaqö'ö,₃
paavönyeevewmaanatu,₄
hàalay'unangway₅ paasimasayu₆ púma'a,₇
puyayatani,₈
yánga'a.₉
Pu'₁₀ tuwaati'i,₁₁
paavopkomatu'u,₁₂
hàalay'unangway töökiyuuyuwinani.₁₃
Mee'ee aa'ahaa'ay.

RUKÙNTAWI₁₄

Yokvaqö'ö,
paavönyevewmanatu hàalay'unangway paasimasay puyayatimani,₁₅
yánga'a.
Ang₁₆ uma₁₇ hàalay'unangway taayimakyango₁₈ taatawyuuyuwinani,₁₉

1. *hemiskatsìntawi* 'Hemiskatsina song'.
2. *tiitawi* 'in-place song', the middle main song which is sung in place in the kiva or in the plaza.
3. = *yokvaqw'ö,* subordinate clause pausal form of *yokva* 'rain'.
4. = *paavönyevewmamant* 'young corn plant maidens'.
5. *hàalay'unangway* 'with happy hearts, with beneficent intentions'.
6. = *paasimasay,* object form of *paasimasa'am* 'their moisture-beaded wings'.
7. *púma'a,* pausal form of *puma* 'they'.
8. *puyayatani* 'will be flapping, fluttering'.
9. = *yang'a,* pausal form of *yang* 'here, along here, in these places, in this area'.
10. *pu'* 'now, then'.
11. *tuwaati'i,* pausal form of *tuwat* 'in turn, for (one's) part'.
12. *paavopkomatu'u,* pausal form of *paavopkomat* 'water creatures'.
13. = *töökiyuyuwintani* 'will be dancing while making characteristic calls'.
14. *rukùntawi* 'rasping song, song with rasper accompaniment'.
15. *puyayatimani* 'will go along flapping fluttering'.
16. *ang* 'along it, along there, in that area, in several places'.
17. *uma* 'you (plural)'.
18. = *taymakyangw* 'while going along looking'.
19. = *taatawyuyuwintani* 'will be dancing and singing songs'.

haw'óo[20] *ínamu.*[21]
Pu' túwati'i,
paavopkomatu[22] *hàalay'unangway töötöökimani.*[23]
Aa'aha'ay aahay'aa.

IN-PLACE SONG

(Vocables.)
When it rains,
the young corn plant maidens,
with happy hearts,
they will be flapping their moisture-beaded wings
along here.
Then, for their part,
the water creatures
will be dancing and making their calls with happy hearts.
(Vocables.)

RASPING SONG

When it rains,
the young corn plant maidens will go along flapping their moisture-bead-
    ed wings with happy hearts
along here.
As you go along there looking upon it with happy hearts you will be
    dancing and singing songs,
o my fathers.
Then for their part,
the water creatures will be making their calls with happy hearts.
(Vocables.)

This song was identified by the singer as a dressing-for-journey song for
the last dance of the day at *Nimàntikive,* the Home dance. As recorded, it
consists of an in-place song, the *tiitawi,* where the katsinas dance in a
straight line, one behind the other and a rasping song, *rukùntawi,* where

20. *haw'óo,* vocative particle.
21. *ínamu,* pausal form of *inam* 'my fathers'.
22. = *paavopkomat* 'water creatures'.
23. = *töötöqtimani* 'will go along shouting, calling'.

the katsinas face forward in a line with rasping katsinas kneeling in front of them.

In the in-place song, the katsinas use beautiful metaphorical imagery to recreate the pleasant sensation felt by the young corn plant maidens as the rain falls on their leaves, described as moisture-beaded wings, as they flap in the breeze. Indeed, the katsinas note that all living beings who depend on water for life, here described as water creatures (*paavopkomat*), experience this same sensation of joy with the coming of rain. Just as the young corn plant maiden's leaves flap in joy as it rains, so too do the water creatures dance and make their cries of happiness. In the rasping song the katsinas remark that the people ("you") will also be going along dancing and singing with happiness at the sight of the vitality in all living things brought by the rain.

85. Hemiskatsìntawi₁
(Black Song 82)

Oo'omawutu₂ kuukuyivani,₃
naalönanan'ivaqö.₄
Puma₅ umùu'uyiyu₆ ánga'a;₇
puma ang₈ yoo'oyhoyoyootimani,₉
taawanawita.₁₀
Me'ee'ee, ahaha'ay, ahaha'ay.
Hapi me.₁₁
Naalönanan'ivaqö
oo'omawutu pew₁₂ umumi₁₃ kuukuyivani,

1. *hemiskatsìntawi* 'Hemiskatsina song'.
2. = *oo'omawt* 'clouds'.
3. = *kuukuyvani* 'will appear, will make their appearance, will come into view'.
4. = *nalönanan'ivaqw* 'from each of the four directions'.
5. *puma* 'they'.
6. = *umùu'uyiy,* object form of *umùu'uyi* 'your (plural) planted field(s)'.
7. = *ang'a,* pausal form of *ang* 'along it, along there, in that area, in several places'.
8. *ang* 'along it, along there, in that area, in several places'.
9. = *yoyhoyoyotimani* 'will be moving along as rain'.
10. = *taawanawit* 'all day long'.
11. *hapi me,* formulaic expression introducing the song's second part, *oomi* 'upward'.
12. *pew* 'toward here, coming this way'.
13. *umumi* 'to you (plural)'.

taawanawita.
Me'ee'ee ahaha'ay.

The clouds will make their appearance
from each of the four directions.
They will go along your planted fields;
they will be moving along there as rain
all day long.
(Vocables.)
Listen, there is more.
From each of the four directions
the clouds will make their appearance to you here
all day long.
(Vocables.)

The katsinas are describing their planned appearance as clouds from all four cardinal directions. They promise to move in rain along the planted fields all day long.

86. *Honànkatsìntawi$_1$*
(Black Song 78)

Pahoyeesiwa.$_2$
Pahoyeesiwa,
ínamu.$_3$
Uma$_4$ taawanawita$_5$ umùupaho'iniy$_6$ aw$_7$ okiwlawu,$_8$
yépe'e.$_9$

1. *honànkatsìntawi* 'Badger katsina song'.
2. = *pahoyesiwa* 'be sitting and working on prayer feathers (plural)'.
3. = *inam* 'my fathers'.
4. *uma* 'you (plural)'.
5. = *taawanawit* 'all day long'.
6. *umùupaho'iniy,* object form of *umùupaho'ini* 'your (plural) tray of prayer feathers'.
7. *aw* 'to it, to there'.
8. *okiwlawu* 'be humbling oneself, as in prayer'.
9. = *yep'e,* pausal form of *yep* 'here'.

Oovi₁₀ itam₁₁ naanan'ivaqö₁₂ umumi₁₃ yooya'ökini.₁₄
Aha'aa'ihihi.
Yang₁₅ haqami₁₆ kitsokinawita,₁₇
itangum₁₈ itanam₁₉ tsoongoy₂₀ akw₂₁ itamuy₂₂ naanan'ivo'o,₂₃
naawakinaya.₂₄
Angqw₂₅ itam umumi yooya'öki.₂₆
Paavataalawinani.₂₇
Oohoway eeheloy aa'haa'a.

[You] are sitting making prayer feathers.
[You] are sitting making prayer feathers,
my fathers.
You are humbling yourselves before your trays of prayer feathers all day
    long,
here.
That's why we will come to you as rain from the different directions
    around.
(Vocable.)
Throughout the villages here,
our mothers and our fathers, with their smoking pipes, to the different
    directions around,
pray to us.
We (will) come to you as rain from there.
[We] will make it glisten with puddles of water.

10. *oovi* 'that's why'.
11. *itam* 'we'.
12. = *naanan'ivaqw* 'from the different directions around'.
13. *umumi* 'to you (plural)'.
14. = *yoy'ökini* 'will arrive, come as rain'.
15. *yang* 'along here, in this area'.
16. = *aqwhaqami* 'throughout'.
17. = *kitsokikinawit* 'throughout the villages'.
18. *itangum* 'our mothers'.
19. *itanam* 'our fathers'.
20. *tsoongoy,* object form of *tsoongo'am* 'their smoking pipes'.
21. *akw* 'with, using'.
22. *itamuy* 'us', object form of *itam* 'we'.
23. *naanan'ivo'o,* pausal form of *naanan'ivo* 'to the different directions around'.
24. = *naanawakna* 'pray (plural)'.
25. *angqw* 'from it, from there'.
26. = *yoy'öki* 'arrive, come as rain'.
27. = *paavatalawnani* 'will make it glisten with puddles of water'.

(Vocables.)

The Badger katsinas are addressing the ritual leaders who are sitting in the kiva preparing prayer feathers. They describe how these men humble themselves as they prepare the prayer feathers and pray over them all day long. As part of this ritual, the men pass the smoking pipe (*tsootsongo*) from one to another and each man fervently smokes and prays over the prayer feathers for rain and all good things of life for the people. In answer to these prayers, to the pleading "voice" of the prayer feathers, *okiwlawu,* the katsinas promise to come as rain from all directions. This sentiment is repeated after some vocables, with the added description that with their rain, the katsinas will make the land glisten with puddles of water.

87. *Hoolikatsìntawi,*
(Black Song 107)

Hiiy'aa yahiy aaha.
Pew$_2$ umumi$_3$ yoyhoy- hoyoyotani.$_4$
Pew umumi naanan'ivaqw$_5$ yoy'umumutani.$_6$
Umungem$_7$ umùu'uyinawita$_8$ paataalawnayaqw'ö,$_9$
"Pay$_{10}$ kwakwháta"$_{11}$ uma kitota;$_{12}$
"Pay hàalayi"$_{13}$ uma$_{14}$ kitota.

1. *hoolikatsìntawi* 'Hooli katsina song'.
2. *pew* 'toward here, coming this way'.
3. *umumi* 'to you (plural)'.
4. = *yoyhoyoyotani* 'will be moving as rain'.
5. *naanan'ivaqw* 'from the different directions around'.
6. *yoy'umumutani* 'will be thundering'.
7. *umungem* 'for you (plural), for your benefit'.
8. = *umùu'uynawit* 'along your (plural) planted fields'.
9. = *paatalawnayaqw,* subordinate clause form of *paatalawnaya* 'make it glisten with water (plural)'.
10. *pay,* expressive particle.
11. = *kwakwháta* 'express thanks'.
12. *kitota* 'say (plural)'.
13. *hàalayi* 'be happy'.
14. *uma* 'you (plural)'.

Paavönnawita₁₅ umungem yooki.₁₆
Yooya'ökiwni.₁₇
Aha aaha ha iihi ihi.
Haalawlolosi ya'ay hooliho.
Haalawlolosi ya'ay hooliho.
Aa ayahi'a aa'aha ii'ihi.

(Vocables.)
Toward you, [we] will come moving as rain.
Toward you, [we] will come thundering from the different directions around.
When [we] make it glisten with water for you along your planted fields, you say "We're thankful";
you say "There is happiness."
It is raining along the young corn plants for you.
[We] will have arrived as rain.
(Vocables.)

The katsinas are singing about how they will come moving as rain, thundering from all the directions to the people's planted fields. They promise to make the fields glisten with puddles of water. Then they speak for the people, saying "thank you" and "we are happy," at the coming of the rain. The katsinas close by assuring the people that it will be raining along their young corn plants.

88. *Hootetawi₁*
(Black Song 75)

Nu'₂ umumi₃ tayati.₄
Nu' umumi tayati.

15. = *paavönnawit* 'along the young corn plants'.
16. *yooki* 'rain' (verb). (This is reduplicated *yooyoki* in Third Mesa usage.)
17. *yoy'ökiwni* 'will have come, arrived as rain', future of *yoy'ökiwa*.

1. *hootetawi* 'Hoote (katsina) song'.
2. *nu'* 'I'.
3. *umumi* 'to you (plural)'.
4. *tayati* 'be amused'.

Ima₅ hapi₆ Sootukwinangwmongwitu₇ yòytalawiptoyakyangw₈ umu'ova₉
  yoy'umumutoyaqö'ö,₁₀
uma₁₁ tsaatsawna.₁₂
Nu' umumi tayati.
Áhoote.₁₃
Yang₁₄ yoyngyàlpuva'ay,₁₅
yang paatàlpuva'ay,₁₆
hàalay'unangway₁₇ taayimuyiwni.₁₈
Oo'howaa eeheloy.
Oo'oo'oo'ohowa eeheloy.

I am amused at you.
I am amused at you.
Truly when these Star-Cumulus Cloud katsina leaders make it be thunder-
  ing above you while making lightning in the rain,
you become afraid.
I am amused at you.
Áhoote.
In the postlude of the rain along here,
along an area glistening with water,
you will, with happy hearts, look upon it in awe.
(Vocables.)

5. *ima* 'these'.
6. *hapi* 'truly, surely, certainly'.
7. = *Sootukwnangwmomngwit* 'Star-Cumulus Cloud katsina leaders'.
8. = *yòytalwiptoynakyangw* 'while making lightning in the rain'.
9. *umu'ova* 'along above you'.
10. = *yoy'umumutoynaqw'ö*, subordinate clause pausal form of *yoy'umumutoyna* 'make it be thundering'.
11. *uma* 'you (plural)'.
12. *tsaatsawna* 'become afraid, frightened, scared (plural)'.
13. *Áhoote* is a form of the cry of the Hoote katsina in some villages. At Third Mesa the cry is *hoote*. The katsina is named after his cry.
14. *yang* 'along here, in this area'.
15. *yoyngyàlpuva'ay,* pausal, expressive form of *yoyngyàlpuva* 'in the postlude of the rain, during the time after it has stopped raining'.
16. *paatàlpuva'ay,* pausal, expressive form of *paatàlpuva* 'along a land glistening with water'.
17. *hàalay'unangway* 'with happy hearts, with beneficent intentions'.
18. *taayimuyiwni* 'will look in awe'.

The Hoote katsinas are amused at people who are afraid of thunder and lightning during a rainstorm. In performance at *Powamuya* (the Bean dance), the Sootukwnangmomngwit (the Star-Cumulus Cloud katsina leaders) appear carrying lightning frames and bullroarers. They are amused that people would be afraid, since lightning and thunder are part of the rainstorms that they so earnestly pray for. In addition, the katsinas remark that after the rain (*yoyngyàlpuva*), the people will happily look in awe along the land glistening with water (*paatàlpuva*).

89. *Hootetawi*₁
(Black Song 90)

Oo'omawutu₂ kuukuyivani.₃
Ánawit₄ tuveniy₅ hoohonginani.₆
Uuyisonaqa₇ yoyhoyoyotani.₈
Paatuwataviyani.₉
Aa'hootee.₁₀
Uuyisonaqa uma₁₁ taatawtimani'i.₁₂
Hiy'a hiy'aya hiy aa'aaha.

The clouds will make their appearance.
Along it (as they move along) [they] will be making their markings stand.
[They] will be moving as rain throughout the midst of the planted areas.
[They] will lay water on the land.
Áhoote.
You will go along singing throughout the midst of the planted areas.
(Vocables.)

1. *hootetawi* 'Hoote (katsina) song'.
2. = *oo'omawt* 'clouds'.
3. = *kuukuyvani* 'will appear, come into sight'.
4. *ánawit* 'along its course'.
5. = *tutuveni* 'markings, visual representation, writing'.
6. = *hoohongnani* 'will make (them) stand (intermittently)'.
7. = *uysonaq* 'throughout the midst of the planted area(s)'.
8. *yoyhoyoyotani* 'will be moving as rain'.
9. = *paatuwatapyani* 'will lay water on the land (plural)'.
10. = *áhoote,* characteristic cry of the Hoote katsina. At Third Mesa, his cry is *hoote.*
11. *uma* 'you (plural)'.
12. *taatawtimani'i* pausalized form of *taatawtimani* 'will go along singing songs'. In this context the plural, *taatawtiwisni,* would be exprected.

The Hoote katsinas are describing the sequence of events in a summer rainstorm as seen from a distance. First, clouds appear above the horizon. Then, as the clouds move along, their rain appears as vertical lines descending on the land. *Yoyleki* is the standard term for lines of falling rain but in this song, the Hoote katsinas specifically describe how they will make their rain stand as vertical markings, *tuveniy hoohongnani*. As these cells of rain lines move along the land, they will lay their water in the midst of the planted areas. The katsinas utter their signature vocable, *áhoote* and predict that as a result of this rain, the people will walk throughout their fields singing their happiness.

90. *Koyemsitawi*₁
(Black Song 76)

Itam₂ kawaayot₃ meloonit₄ anìwtotani'i.₅
Itam kawaayot meloonit anìwtotani'i.
Tuma₆ haani₇ hani.₈
Tuma haani.
Haani tuma haaniy.₉
Aha ihi aha ihi.

1. *koyemsitawi* 'Mudhead katsina song'.
2. *itam* 'we'.
3. *kawaayot*, object form of *kawaayo* 'watermelon'. *Kawaayo,* from Spanish *caballo* 'horse', here stands for the compound *kawayvatnga* 'watermelon' ("horse [*kaway-*] squash [*-vatnga*]"). Borrowings from Spanish strongly tend have a long vowel in Hopi corresponding to the stressed vowel in the Spanish original. *Kawaayo* here appears to be no exception, but in non-song Hopi, at least at Third Mesa, this word is always pronounced with an exceptional short second syllable: *kawayo.* Song language seems to have preserved a form closer to the Spanish original.
4. *meloonit*, object form of *melooni* 'muskmelon'. *Melooni,* shows, by contrast with *kawayo* 'horse' (see previous note), the regular retention of a long vowel corresponding to the stressed vowel of the Spanish original, *melón.*
5. *anìwtotani'i*, pausalized form of *anìwtotani* 'will make crop or plant grow (plural)'. This is a song form corresponding to secular *aniwnayani.* The song form has the causative ending *-ta* (plural *-tota*) instead of causative *-na* (plural *-naya*).
6. = *tum* 'let's', hortative particle.
7. *haani* 'descend (plural)'.
8. = *haani* 'descend (plural)'.
9. *haaniy,* expressive form of *haani* 'descend (plural)'.

Itam umumi$_{10}$ *pó'o'tota.*$_{11}$
Itam umumi pó'o'tota.
Qa$_{12}$ *pas*$_{13}$ *pi*$_{14}$ *pas antsa*$_{15}$ *itam umumi pó'o'tota,*
umùukaway'uyiy$_{16}$ *ánga'a.*$_{17}$
Kawayvatnga$_{18}$ *melooni yangsay*$_{19}$ *pó'okiwyungwa.*
Po'oo,$_{20}$ *po'oo,*
po'oo, po'oo,
kololololo.

We will make the watermelons and muskmelons grow.
We will make the watermelons and muskmelons grow.
Let us descend, descend.
Let us descend.
Descend, let us descend.
(Vocables.)
We are stooping over for you (here and there).
We are stooping over for you.
We are not really stooping over for you
along your watermelon plantings.
The watermelons and muskmelons are stooping over big like this.
Stooping over, stooping over,
stooping over, stooping over,
(vocable).

This is an example of a coming-into-the-kiva song that is sung during a night dance as the katsinas are climbing down the ladder and taking their places. During this activity, the katsinas use gestures and antics to entertain the audience while final preparations for the performance are being made. In this song the Mudhead katsinas (Kookoyemsim) are singing

10. *umumi* 'to you (plural)'.
11. *pó'o'tota* 'be bent over, stooped over in a C-shape (plural)'.
12. *qa* 'not'.
13. *pas* 'very'.
14. *pi* 'truly'.
15. *antsa* 'truly, really, indeed'.
16. *umùukaway'uyiy,* object form of *umùukaway'uyi* 'your watermelon plants, plantings'.
17. = *ang'a,* pausal form of *ang* 'along it, along there, in an area, in several places'.
18. *kawayvatnga* 'watermelon(s)'.
19. *yangsay* 'of this size, this big, big like this (plural)'.
20. *po'oo* 'bending over', the root of *pó'o'ta* 'be bent over, stooped over in a C-shape'.

about how they are going to make the watermelons and muskmelons grow. Indeed, being rain, they are the perfect farmers to raise fields of perfect melons to maturity. But since they arrive at the villages as clouds, they must descend to the human world to water the fields. So they say, *Tuma haani*, Let's climb down. That is, let us rain on the fields.

Then they use a play on words that emphasizes the rounded shapes of the fully grown melons as they lie in the fields just before harvest. By saying they are stooping over, the Mudheads are comparing their backsides in their bended-over position to the appearance of fully ripe melons. The implication is that with their rain, the melons will grow large. At this point the katsinas open their arms wide to show how large the melons have grown. Like this, *yangsay*, they say.

91. *Koyemsitawi*₁
(Black Song 86)

Maana₂ ikwatsi,₃
ya₄ um₅ hisat₆ lööqökni?₇
Ep₈ um sakwaput₉ qaa'öta,₁₀ qötsaqa'öta₁₁ ngúmantakyango,₁₂
noovataqw'ö,₁₃
noonove'₁₄
hàalayyani.₁₅
Ahaa ihii.
Hinay'anina yahiwayohona hinay'anina.₁₆

1. *koyemsitawi* 'Mudhead katsina song'.
2. *maana* 'girl, young unmarried woman, maiden'.
3. *ikwatsi* 'my friend'.
4. *ya,* question particle.
5. *um* 'you'.
6. *hisat* 'sometime, when'.
7. *lööqökni* 'will go to the groom's mother's house to begin the wedding ceremony'.
8. *ep* 'there, at it'.
9. *sakwaput,* object form of *sakwapu* 'blue corn'.
10. = *qaa'öt,* object form of *qaa'ö* 'corn, dry ears of corn'.
11. = *qötsaqa'öt,* object form of *qötsaqa'ö* 'white corn'.
12. = *ngúmantakyangw* 'while grinding cornmeal into flour'.
13. *noovataqw'ö,* subordinate clause pausal form of *noovata* 'prepare food'.
14. *noonove'* 'if (they) are eating'.
15. *hàalayyani* 'will be happy (plural)'.
16. This line of vocables and the following may represent words of some other language.

Yahiyayhonawey'aay'a.
Yongyaya,$_{17}$
yongyaya yangqw$_{18}$ tayta.$_{19}$
Yongyaya,
yongyaya yangqw tayta.
Yang$_{20}$ pam$_{21}$ waymakyango,$_{22}$
na'mangwuy$_{23}$ tuuhuyilawu.$_{24}$
Aha ihii, ahaa ihii.

Girl, my friend,
When will you go to the house of your boyfriend's mother to begin the
      wedding ceremony?
When you are grinding blue corn, white corn there,
and preparing them as a meal,
and if they are eating it
they will be happy.
(Vocables.)
The chipmunk,
the chipmunk is watching from here.
The chipmunk,
the chipmunk is watching from here.
While he walks along here,
he keeps giving people his gifts.
(Vocables.)

This song is sung as katsinas exit a kiva after a winter night dance. Here
the Mudhead katsinas are jesting with the girls in the audience, asking
them when they are going to start the marriage process. Traditionally the
marriage process begins when the girl lives for a time at the home of her
future husband, grinding corn and preparing meals for his family. In doing

---

17. *yongyaya* 'chipmunk, whitetail antelope squirrel, *Ammospermophilus leucurus*'.
18. *yangqw* 'from here'.
19. *tayta* 'be watching'.
20. *yang* 'along here, in this area'.
21. *pam* 'that, that one, he, she, it'.
22. = *waymakyangw* 'while walking along'.
23. *na'mangwuy,* object form of *na'mangwu'at* 'his gifts (re katsina)'. *Na'mangwu* means
      a gift brought by a katsina, such as food, produce, toys. It seems to have no internal
      analysis.
24. = *tuuhuylawu* 'be giving things away to people'.

so she demonstrates her willingness to perform the humble work that is necessary to care for a family and maintain a household. In this song the Mudheads predict that if the boy's family eats the food she has prepared and are happy, they will accept her as their son's future wife. The underlying message to this teasing is a serious one that urges girls who are of age to get married and accept their responsibilities as future mothers of the next generation.

After some vocables the Mudheads liken themselves to chipmunks and say they are watching the people, that is, looking for individuals with good hearts for they will be the recipients of their beneficence. With their sacks bursting with gifts, they compare themselves to chipmunks with cheeks full of food. The verb *tayta,* in its metaphorical meaning, connotes the sense of looking with the mind's eye to determine the sincerity of the heart of a person. The implication is that gifts of rain and other good things of life are due to people they see caring for others and fulfilling their obligations.

92. *Masawkatsìntawi₁*
(Black Song 84)

Hahayiye aahayiyee, aawhayiye.
Yan₂ ura₃ momoyam₄ lavayhurusukita₅ nöönöse'e,₆
a'ni₇ naanamiq₈ hìngqaqwangwu.₉
Úra'i,₁₀
antsa'a.₁₁

1. *masawkatsìntawi* 'Màasaw katsina song'.
2. *yan* 'like this, in this way, thus'.
3. *ura,* modal of recollection: 'as I recall, as you'll recall'.
4. *momoyam* 'women'.
5. =*lavayhurusukit,* object form of *lavayhurusuki* 'speech *hurusuki*'.
6. = *nöönöse'e,* pausal form of *nöönöse'* 'when they eat', from *nöönösa* 'eat (plural)'.
7. *a'ni* 'very (male speaker)'.
8. *naanamiq* 'behind each other's backs'.
9. *hìngqaqwangwu,* habitual tense form of *hìngqaqwa* 'say things (plural)'.
10. *úra'i,* pausal form of *ura,* modal of recollection: 'as I recall, as you'll recall'.
11. *antsa'a,* pausal form of *antsa* 'truly, really, indeed'.

Me₁₂ ura yongyaywùuti₁₃ koongyay₁₄ iingyàlte'e,₁₅
hiihin₁₆ lavaynumngwu.₁₇
Úra'i,
antsa'a.
Ura tumsi₁₈ tsooviwe'e,₁₉
nanaptiwqw₂₀ tsooviy₂₁ tuuvingtinumngwu;₂₂
màasawtiniqey₂₃ tavilawngwu,₂₄
ókiwa.₂₅
Haayay haayaa.
Ókiwa.
Haqami₂₆ yang₂₇ lavaymuyiwa.₂₈
Lavaymuyiwa.
Yan itam₂₉ umuy₃₀ öqalaya.₃₁
Hapi me.₃₂
Me ura tumsi koongyay iingyalte'e,

12. *me,* an expression to direct another's attention: 'you see, listen, behold, look'.
13. *yongyaywùuti* 'adulterous woman'.
14. *koongyay,* object form of *koongya'at* 'her husband'.
15. = *iingyàlte'e,* pausal form of *iingyàlte'* 'if (she) rejects'; cf. *iingyàlti* 'tire of, not want around'.
16. *hiihin* 'in various ways, in all kinds of ways'.
17. = *lalvaytinumngwu,* habitual tense form of *lalvaytinuma* 'go around talking about'.
18. *tumsi* 'clanswoman'.
19. *tsooviwa* 'have been taken in sexual intercourse (female)'; cf. *tsoova* 'have sexual intercourse (male subject)'.
20. *nanaptiwqw,* subordinate clause form of *nanaptiwa* 'for some fact(s) to become known'.
21. *tsooviy,* possessed object form of *tsooviw* 'act of sexual intercourse'.
22. *tuuvingtinumngwu,* habitual tense form of *tuuvingtinuma* 'go around asking'.
23. *màasawtiniqey* 'to become a death spirit'.
24. *tavilawngwu,* habitual-tense form of *tavilawu. Tavilawu* is not a recognized word; its use here could have been intended to mean either bury the dead or appoint or choose herself to die and be buried, i.e., wanting to die from shame.
25. = *okiw* 'humbly, pitifully'.
26. = *aqwhaqami* 'throughout'.
27. *yang* 'along here, in this area'.
28. *lavaymuyiwa* 'be talked about, be talking about, there is talk'.
29. *itam* 'we'.
30. *umuy,* object form of *uma* 'you (plural)'.
31. *öqalaya* 'annoy (plural)'. The verb *öqala* normally means 'encourage', but the katsinas are using it in a special way.
32. *hapi me,* formulaic expression introducing the song's second part, *oomi* 'upward'.

qa₃₃ hìita₃₄ tuwiyat₃₅ lavaynumngwu.
Noqw₃₆ nuy₃₇ umumi₃₈ tunatyawmaqö'ö,₃₉
pi₄₀ kur₄₁ ima₄₂ nalqatmomoyam₄₃ sòosok₄₄ hìita₄₅ akw₄₆ mongvasya.₄₇
Kiiyamuy₄₈ ang'a,₄₉
yuuyupkyaqe'e,₅₀
mötsikvu₅₁ kyevelvikyungwa.₅₂
Kwasit₅₃ mumuyi'yyungwa.₅₄
Löhavut₅₅ kawàytanga'yyungwa.₅₆
Pantaqat₅₇ ura ep₅₈ hàalayngwu,
yongyaywùuti,
kivung.wùuti,₅₉
tokotswùuti.₆₀
Yan itam umuy öqalaya.

33. *qa* 'not'.
34. *hìita*, object form of *himu* 'something, what'.
35. *tuwiyat*, object form of *tuwi'at* 'his practical knowledge, skill'.
36. *noqw* 'but, whereas, and so'.
37. *nuy*, object form of *nu'* 'I' (in object form because it is the subject of the adverbial clause).
38. *umumi* 'you, to you (plural)'.
39. = *tunatyawmaqw'ö*, subordinate clause pausal form of *tunatyawma* 'go along watching'.
40. *pi* 'truly'.
41. *kur*, modal of inference.
42. *ima* 'these'.
43. *nalqatmomoyam* 'single women, women who now live alone', as of widows, divorcees.
44. *sòosok*, object form of *sòosoy* 'all'.
45. *hìita*, object form of *himu* 'something, what'.
46. *akw* 'with, using'.
47. *mongvasya* 'be benefiting from (plural)'.
48. *kiiyamuy*, object form of *kii'am* 'their houses'.
49. *ang'a*, pausal form of *ang* 'along it, along there, in that area, in several places'.
50. *yuuyupkyaqe'e*, pausal form of *yuuyupkyaqe* 'in the innermost rooms'; cf. *yuupovi* 'innermost room'.
51. *mötsikvu* 'trash, garbage, refuse'.
52. *kyevelvikyungwa* 'be stacked right up to the ceiling (plural)'.
53. *kwasit*, object form of *kwasi* 'penis(es)'.
54. *mumuyi'yyungwa* 'have as a front tier of stacked ears of corn (plural)'.
55. *löhavut*, object form of *löhavu* 'testicle(s), scrotum(s)'.
56. *kawàytanga'yyungwa* 'have stored watermelons (plural)'.
57. *pantaqat*, object form of *pantaqa* 'one that is like that'.
58. *ep* 'there, at it'.
59. *kivung.wùuti* 'woman who habitually visits around'.
60. *tokotswùuti* 'mean, grouchy woman'.

(Vocables.)
Thus you'll recall that when women eat speech *hurusuki,*[61]
they criticize each other behind their backs.
You'll recall,
really.
See, you'll recall that when the adulteress gets tired of her husband,
she goes around talking about him in all kinds of ways.
You'll recall,
really.
You'll recall that if the clanswoman has sexual relations,
and if the facts become known, she goes around asking if others know she
    has had sexual relations;
and she keeps wanting to die of shame and become a death spirit,
poor thing.
(Vocables.)
Poor thing.
There is talk around here everywhere.
There is talk.
Thus we annoy you.
Listen, there is more.
See, you'll recall that when the clanswoman rejects her husband,
she goes around saying he doesn't know how to do anything.
But as I watch you (to see what you are doing),
it seems that these single women really benefit from everything.
In their houses,
in the back rooms,
the trash reaches the ceiling.
They have penises as the first tier of stacked ears of stored corn.
They have scrotums/testicles as stored watermelons.
In that kind of place she is happy,
the adulterous woman,
the habitually visiting woman,
the ill-tempered woman.
Thus we annoy you.

This song is an admonition about behavior—malicious gossip and extra-
marital affairs—that is counterproductive to community harmony. The

61. *hurusuki,* a thick blue cornmeal pudding.

katsinas begin with vocables that are intended to mimic the gibberish of gossip. Then they clearly voice their concern about women who visit the homes of other women claiming to be helping them make blue cornmeal pudding (*hurusuki*) but who are really there to gossip about others behind their backs. They are likening the making of pudding to feasting on juicy gossip. The song word *lavayhurusuki* is a metaphor for the way gossip is made. Just as vicious gossip is produced by mixing up words, *hurusuki* is made by stirring flour and other ingredients in a bowl. In this way the katsinas are admonishing women who are gossiping about others.

In this particular song the gossip concerns a woman who, tired of her husband, had been going around saying all kinds of presumably degrading things about him, and at the same time having sexual relations with other men. Her criticisms of her husband were a way to justify her adulterous behavior. But then, she begins to worry that the true facts about her behavior might become known, so she goes around gossiping, pretending that it was not her and trying to find out who it was, but really she is trying to find out if others know about her activities. When she finds out that others do know, she figuratively wants to die, so ashamed is she of what she has done. The katsinas are only partly sympathetic. Poor thing (*okiw*), they say, everyone is going about talking about her. They close the first section by implying that what they are saying is probably going to annoy people, particularly those who are engaging in that kind of behavior, but they feel they need to expose this kind of antisocial activity.

In the second part of the song the katsinas address single women who think they can have sexual relations with many men. The katsinas then describe the way such women engage in these activities in the back rooms of their houses, typically where food is stored. Except, instead of the precious food reserved for survival, the katsinas liken the penises and testicles that the women gain to trash, that over time with so many repeated sexual engagements, fills the rooms and reaches the ceiling. Penises are likened to ears of corn that the women become dependent on just as everyone else depends on corn. After repeated sexual encounters, a woman has so many that she can stack them like stored ears of corn. Testicles are likened to round melons that too can be stored. The katsinas end by commenting that while such women think they are fulfilling themselves and making themselves happy with such activities, ultimately they will be discovered. Thus, the katsinas say, while we may annoy you, we are actually warning you of the consequences of your actions.

93. Nukushehey'akatsìntawi₁
(Black Song 114)

Hinoq₂ uma₃ pöösöng'ang₄ momoyam₅ nalqatsiwuyu₆ kwangwa'iw-
yungwa.₇
Himu₈ pi₉ pay₁₀ hin'eway₁₁ taaqa₁₂ pasve₁₃ tumalay₁₄ tapkintangwu.₁₅
Taayungwa'.₁₆
Taayungwa'ay.₁₇
Túsanmaqtöyat₁₈ ánan'ivo₁₉ kawayho'i,₂₀ melonho'i₂₁ naa'awintiwa,₂₂
yánga'a.₂₃
Aahaw₂₄ yaniwa.₂₅
Aahaw yaniwa.
Àaha iihi.
Àaha iihi.
Qa₂₆ naala.₂₇

1. nukushehey'akatsìntawi 'Plain Hehey'a katsina song'.
2. = hintiqw 'why, what for, for what purpose'.
3. uma 'you (plural)'.
4. = pöpsöva 'in corners'.
5. momoyam 'women'.
6. = nalqatsiwuy, object form of nalqatsi 'life alone, without a partner'.
7. kwangwa'iwyungwa 'remain with something that is attractive'.
8. himu, indefinite pronoun: 'something, what, one, you'.
9. pi 'truly'.
10. pay, expressive particle.
11. hin'eway 'unattractive, plain-looking'.
12. taaqa 'man'.
13. pasve 'at/in the/his field'.
14. tumalay, object form of tumala'at 'his work'.
15. tapkintangwu, habitual tense form of tapkinta 'be doing something to the end of the day'.
16. = taayungwa'a, imperative form of taayungwa 'look (plural)'.
17. taayungwa'ay, expressive imperative form of taayungwa 'look (plural)'.
18. túsanmaqtöyat, object form of túsanmaqtö'at 'his dirty hands'.
19. ánan'ivo 'to each side of it'.
20. kawayho'i 'load of watermelons'.
21. melonho'i 'load of muskmelons'.
22. naa'awintiwa 'be known community-wide'.
23. = yang'a, pausal form of yang 'here, along here, in these places, in this area'.
24. = aw 'to it, to there'.
25. = yaniwma 'be happening this way'.
26. qa 'not'.
27. naala 'alone'.

*Qa naala waynuma.*₂₈
*Ihiwkatsina*₂₉ *ngasta*₃₀ *tootsi'ytakyango*₃₁
*mansonve*₃₂ *yortinumay.*₃₃
Aha iihi.
*Aw*₃₄ *naanawiniway.*₃₅
Aw naanawiniwa.
*Tookii'i,*₃₆
*maana*₃₇ *kiiyat*₃₈ *wuuvi.*₃₉
Àaha iihi.
Àaha iihi hii.

Why do you women sitting in corners remain attracted to living single?
It would be good to consider the plain-looking man who spends his days
    working in his field.
Look at him.
Look at him.
To one side and the other of his dirty hands, the loads of watermelons and
    loads of muskmelons are known community-wide
around here.
It happens this way.
It happens this way.
(Vocables.)
He is not alone.
He does not walk around by himself.
The Plain Hehey'a katsina, having no shoes,
is looking around among the girls.
(Vocables.)

28. *waynuma* 'be walking around'.
29. *Ihiwkatsina* 'Plain Hehey'a katsina'. (The element *ihiw-* is unidentified.) This is a synonym of *Nukushehey'a*.
30. *ngasta* 'lacking'.
31. = *tootsi'ykyangw* 'while having shoes'; *ngasta tootsi'ykyangw* 'while having no shoes'.
32. *mansonve* 'in the midst of girls, at the center of attention of girls, women'.
33. = *yortinuma* 'be looking about, turning the head so as to see'.
34. *aw* 'to it, to there'.
35. = *nanawinya* 'be plotting (plural)'.
36. = *tooki'i,* pausal form of *tooki* 'last night, last evening'.
37. *maana* 'girl, young unmarried woman, maiden'.
38. *kiiyat,* object form of *kii'at* 'his house'.
39. *wuuvi* 'climb up, ascend'; *kiiyat wuuvi* 'come to his house as a visitor'.

They (women) are planning secretly to go to him.
They are planning secretly to go to him.
Last night,
a girl came to his house as a visitor.
(Vocables.)

In this song the katsinas are addressing single women, chiding them that they should be looking to marry men who are plain and hardworking. They are implying that women should not stay single and be choosy, looking only for the good-looking men, but rather they should be looking for those who will provide for their families. A woman's role and obligation as a member of the Hopi community is not to remain single, but to marry and carry on the duties of wife and mother who, in these roles, contributes in many ways to the ongoing vitality of the community. The katsinas urge these women to consider humble unassuming men who work hard in their fields getting their hands dirty. Look, they say, at the man who is growing great loads of muskmelons and watermelons that are famous throughout the village—his loads of melons are proof that he is a successful farmer. The katsinas remark that such men are desirable and, in fact, are themselves looking around at the girls. After some vocables, perhaps that symbolically give the girls time to look at these humble men, as represented by the Plain Hehey'a katsina, who has no shoes, the katsinas observe that some women are planning to visit these men at their homes in the evening. The message of this song is that women should choose their husbands for their work ethic and commitment to the corn lifeway.

94. Palasowitsmi'ytawi₁
(Black Song 97)

Yaahiy yaahiiya yahi yahi ya'ay hooli.
Ayángqw₂ taavangqw₃ oo'oomawutu,₄
ang₅ puma₆ yang₇ umùu'uyinawit₈ yang haahaawiwmani.₉
Yan₁₀ uma₁₁ naawakinaya.₁₂
Lee lehe la.
Ay hooli ho'hooli, ayahi'a.

(Vocables.)
From over there, from the southwest, the clouds,
along there they, through your planted fields here, will go along descend-
  ing here.
You are praying that it should be like this.
(Vocables.)

This song by the Red-Whiskered Long-Hair katsinas (*Palamowitsmi'y-*
yùngqam 'the ones that have red whiskers') describes how the clouds will
come from the southwest with rain and descend on the planted fields. The
katsinas observe that the people have been praying that it will happen as
described.

1. *palasowitsmi'ytawi* 'Red-Whiskered Long-Hair katsina song'.
2. *ayángqw* 'from over there'.
3. *taavangqw* 'from the southwest'.
4. = *oo'omawt* 'clouds'.
5. *ang* 'along it, along there, in that area, in several places'.
6. *puma* 'they'.
7. *yang* 'along here, in this area'.
8. = *umùu'uynawit* 'along your planted fields'.
9. = *haahawiwmani* 'will go/come along descending'.
10. *yan* 'like this, in this way, thus'.
11. *uma* 'you (plural)'.
12. = *naanawakna* 'pray (plural)'.

95. Sa'lakwmanàwyatuy Amungem Yungtawi'am $_1$
(Black Song 112)

Hololo wiina.
Hololo wiina.
Hololo loolo winaye.
Paavönyevewmongwitu $_2$ Paamuyawuyu $_3$ nalönangwuyu $_4$ umùuvìikya $_5$
   yaala. $_6$
Yaalati. $_7$
Hee.
Angqw $_8$ pew $_9$ Neelaqö $_{10}$ kwiningyaqö $_{11}$ pamuyawumongwitu, $_{12}$
qöya'omawnakwa'amu $_{13}$ oove $_{14}$ tsómiwyungwa. $_{15}$
Waaya'ani, $_{16}$
Soongwuqa $_{17}$ tumasi. $_{18}$

(Vocables.)
The young corn plant leaders have put an end to Paamuya of the four
   directions in your area of use.
It has ceased.
(Vocable.)

1. *Sa'lakwmanàwyatuy,* object form of *Sa'lakwmanàwyat* '(two) little Sa'lako maidens';
   amungem 'for them'; *yungtawi'am* 'their entering song': 'their entering song for the little
   Sa'lako maidens', a song sung while the Sa'lako maidens come into the kiva as their
   "house" is being set up for their performance.
2. = *paavönyevewmomngwit* 'young corn plant leaders'.
3. = *Paamuyawuy,* object form of *Paamuya,* the lunar month that roughly corresponds to
   January.
4. = *nalönangwuy* 'of the four directions'.
5. = *umùuvìikyava* 'along your area of use'.
6. *yaala* 'make abate, put an end to (weather)'. *Yaala* in the song seems to be *yaal-a* [abate-
   -CAUSATIVE]; the simplex verb *yaala* 'abate, subside, pass' is intransitive.
7. = *yàlti* 'cease'.
8. *angqw* 'from it, from there'.
9. *pew* 'toward here, coming this way'.
10. = *Neelaqw* 'from Neela' (an unidentified place).
11. = *kwiningyaqw* 'from the northwest'.
12. = *pamuymomngwit* '*Paamuya* leaders'.
13. = *qöya'omawnakwa'am* 'their white down feather headdresses'.
14. *oove* 'up above, at a/the place above'.
15. = *tsómikiwyungwa* 'be in bunches'.
16. = *waayani* 'will move away'. (Emory thought this was simply a vocable.)
17. *Soongwuqa* 'the Milky Way'.
18. *tumasi* 'a female entity', cf. *tumsi* 'clanswoman'.

Coming from there, from Neela, from the northwest, the Paamuya leaders
and their white down feather headdresses, are coming in bunches up
above.
The Milky Way woman
will go away.

This song is sung as the props are being set up in a darkened kiva for the
Little Sa'lako maiden performance (Song 96). The song describes the
importance of the winter snows that cover the ground and regenerate the
water table, creating the necessary conditions for the germination of the
corn seeds that will be planted later in the spring. The lunar month of
Paamuya, which roughly corresponds to January, is the period of heavy
snow at Hopi. In this song the young corn plant leaders (*paavönyevew-
mongwit*) have put an end to the coming of snow, implying that the snowy
period is past.

The Sa'lako katsinas describe how the water moon month leaders
(*pamuymomngwit*), who are the clouds symbolized by the bunches of
down feathers on their headdresses, are appearing from the northeast,
from Neela. The last line, which personifies the Milky Way as a female
entity and describes her as going away, "The Milky Way woman will go
away," suggests that the seasons have changed and that the white clouds
of summer will now replace the snow clouds of winter.

96. Sa'lakwmanàwyatuy₁ Taawi'am₂
(Black Song 111)

Aaha iihi.
Yoysingölay₃ qalavala;₄
yoyqöqöngöy₅ qalavala;

---

1. *Sa'lakwmanàwyatuy,* object form of *Sa'lakwmanàwyat* '(two) little Sa'lako maidens'.
2. *taawi'am* 'their song'
3. *yoysingölay,* short for *umùuyoysingölay* object form of *umùuyoysingöla* 'your rain flower
   hoops', ritual objects symbolic of rain.
4. an unrecognized word; perhaps = *qa nàwvala* 'not be in vain, not waste one's time or
   effort on'.
5. *yòyqöqöngöy,* short for *umùuyòyqöqöngöy* object form of *umùuyòyqöqöngö* 'your rain
   racing stones', ritual objects symbolic of rain.

Kisiwvave'e,$_6$
suviptuyqave$_7$ pavönyeevewsonaqa$_8$ ítamuyu$_9$ nana'alöngöta$_{10}$ yooyale-
    kita,$_{11}$ taalawipita,$_{12}$
itam$_{13}$ naatuwanmani,$_{14}$
tivongyapami'i.$_{15}$
Mee'e aa'a mee'e aa'a.
Hay'a haaya.
Taalawvayi;$_{16}$
taalawvayi;
iy$_{17}$ taalawvayiy.$_{18}$
Aaha.
Hapi me.$_{19}$
Umùuvìikya'i,$_{20}$
umùuvìikya'i,
mongwiyamuyu$_{21}$ ánawita$_{22}$ móngwisonmiq$_{23}$ ayalawu.$_{24}$
Hiy'ay aa.
Yòytuveqöngöytsongoy$_{25}$ ayalawu,

6. = *Kisiwvangaqw* 'from Shadow Spring', the spring at *Kìisiw* (Shadow Springs), the northeast katsina home.
7. *suvituyqave* 'at the point with sumacs', a description of *Kìisiw*.
8. = *paavönyevewsonaq* 'throughout the midst of the young corn plant maidens'.
9. = *itam* 'we'.
10. = *nana'löngöt*, object form of *nana'löngö* 'different kinds of'.
11. = *yoylekit*, object form of *yoyleki* 'rain lines'.
12. = *talwìipikit*, object form of *talwìipiki* 'lightning'.
13. *itam* 'we'.
14. = *natwantimani* 'will go along practicing customs related to the rejuvenation of life, life-promoting practices'.
15. = *tivongyapami* 'to the dance-display place'.
16. = *taalawváy*, exclamatory form of *taalawva* 'dawn, become light, a new day'.
17. *iy*, an exclamatory element.
18. = *taalawváy*, exclamatory form of *taalawva* 'dawn, become light, a new day'.
19. *hapi me*, formulaic expression introducing the song's second part, *oomi* 'upward'.
20. *umùuvìikya'i*, pausal form of *umùuvìikya* 'your area set aside for a particular use'.
21. = *mongwiyamuy*, object form of *mongwi'am* 'their leader, leadership'.
22. = *ánawit* 'along its course'.
23. = *mongsonmiq* 'into leadership positions'.
24. *ayalawu* 'be asking someone to do something'.
25. = *yòytuveqöqöngtsongoy*, short for *umùuyòytuveqöqöngtsongoy*, object form of *umùuyòytuveqöqöngtsongo* 'your rain racing-stone smoking pipes', a kind of pipe used in ritual smoking as part of praying for rain.

*Paamuuyawnaalönangwmongwitu₂₆ pamösi'omaw₂₇ yooniwsonaqa.₂₈
Taalawvahayi.₂₉*

(Vocables.)
[Your efforts] with [your] rain flower-hoops are not in vain, (?)
with [your] rain racing stones [they] are not in vain, (?)
[because] at Shadow Spring,
at the point with sumacs, [we are making ourselves ready so that]
    throughout the midst of the young corn plant maidens, we will go
    along practicing the different kinds of rain lines and of lightning,
for the rejuvenation of life
[as we move] toward the dance-display place.
(Vocables.)
Let it become the day;
let it become the day;
oh, let it become the day!
(Vocable.)
Listen, there is more.
Along in your area of activity,
along in your area of activity,
[you] are asking, along their leadership, [others] into leadership positions.
(Vocables.)
[You] are asking your elaborate rain racing-stone smoking pipes to get
the Four-Directional Cloud Chiefs of Paamuya [to come] as [low-lying]
    fog clouds amidst their obligations.
Let it become the day!

The Sa'lako maidens sing this song at a nighttime kiva performance after
Powamuya, the Bean dance. They begin their song by commenting favor-
ably on the work of the people who have been throwing their "rain
flower-hoops" (*yoysingöla*) (corn husk rings) and their "rain racing-
stones" (*yòyqöqöngö*) (hardened ball-like items of clay used in springtime
races). The katsinas are saying that these ritual efforts to hurry the coming

---

26. = *Paamuynalönangwmomngwit* 'the Four-Directional Cloud Chiefs of the month of
    Paamuya'.
27. = *pamös'o'omawt* 'fog clouds'.
28. = *yoniwsonaq* 'in the midst of obligations'.
29. = *taalawváy* 'let it become the day!', exclamatory form of *taalawva* 'dawn, become
    light, a new day'.

of the rains have not been in vain (if the song word *qalavala* is correctly understood). In return for these ritual practices on the part of the people, the Sa'lako Maidens say they are preparing themselves at Shadow Spring (*Kisiwva*), their home in the northeast direction. *Kìisiw* is a shrine at a high elevation where sumac grows abundantly. They promise to practice making lightning and rain as they move toward the dance-display place, *tivongyapavi,* in the village plaza. By placing these gifts throughout the fields of young corn plant maidens they will rejuvenate life. The repeated expression "Let it become the day" is a metaphorical way of emphasizing how the repeated coming of rain will bring new life to the planted fields just as the dawn of every new day is understood to bring new life and new beginnings.

In the second section of the song, after *hapi me,* the katsinas observe that there are many different leaders in the community, each with different obligatory responsibilities to perform, here expressed succinctly as "along your area of activity." Some are asked to be in leadership positions where it is their duty to pray and smoke the pipes on behalf of all the people in order to get the Four-Directional Cloud Chiefs of the month of Paamuya to come as low lying clouds (fog clouds). The metaphorically depicted reciprocity here is between the leaders who have fervently smoked and prayed and the clouds who have come and spent their moisture as fog. The description of the smoking pipe (*yòytuveqöngöytsongo*) as a rain racing-stone pipe is a reference to the fact that these pipes are made of the same kind of clay as the racing stones (*qööqöngö*) which runners kick along with their feet in an effort to metaphorically hurry the coming of the rains.

97. Soyohìmkatsinmuy₁ Taawi'am₂
(Black Song 83)

Yoo'oynànkwusa,₃
péwi'i.₄
Yoo'oynànkwusa,
péwi'i.

---

1. *soyohìmkatsinmuy,* object form of *soyohìmkatsinam* 'all kinds of katsinas, mixed katsinas'.
2. *taawi'am* 'their song'.
3. = *yoynànkwusa* 'start on a journey as rain'.
4. = *pew'i,* pausal form of *pew* 'toward here, coming this way'.

Haqami$_5$ yang$_6$ paavönnawita$_7$ oo'oomawutu$_8$ yoynànkwusani.
Ayángqw$_9$ Öngtupqangaqö,$_{10}$
Kooyemsimongwitu$_{11}$ yoytatawiy$_{12}$ akw$_{13}$ umumi$_{14}$ naanakwusani.$_{15}$
[Keresan *Henat'isi$_{16}$ kaatsa'anomay.* Keresan]

[They] have started on a journey as rain,
coming this way.
[They] have started on a journey as rain,
coming this way.
All along the young corn plants here, the clouds will start their journey as
    rain.
From over there, from the Grand Canyon,
the Mudhead katsina leaders will start their journey toward you with their
    rain songs.
(Keresan words with a reference to clouds.)

The katsinas sing that they have begun their journey to the people moving
as rain, *yoynànkwusa.* Unsaid but understood is the fact that they have
received the prayerful requests of the people for them to come as well as
prepared themselves, that is, adorned themselves with rain. They say that
they will move as rain along the young corn plants, *paavönnawit,* on the
planted fields. In the last line of the song these mixed katsinas add that a
pair of Mudhead katsina leaders, *Koyemsimongwit,* will be coming from
their home in the Grand Canyon, *Öngtupqa,* the "Salt Canyon," in the
northwest direction with their "rain songs"—another way of referring to
their coming as rain.

5. = *aqwhaqami* 'throughout'.
6. *yang* 'along here, in this area'.
7. = *paavönnawit* 'along the young corn plants'.
8. = *oo'omawt* 'clouds'.
9. *ayángqw* 'from over there'.
10. = *Öngtupqangaqw* 'from the Grand Canyon'.
11. = *Koyemsimongwit* '(two) Mudhead katsina leaders'.
12. *yòytatawiy,* object form of *yòytatawi'am* 'their rain songs'.
13. *akw* 'with, using'.
14. *umumi* 'to you (plural)'.
15. = *nànkwusani,* future of *nànkwusa* 'start on a journey (plural)'.
16. *henat'isi* represents a Keresan word for 'clouds', cf. Santa Ana *hénaɥ* (Davis 1964: 166),
    -ši 'plural subject' (*id.*: 179).

98. *Soyohìmkatsinmuy₁ Taawi'am₂*

(Black Song 106)

Yoo'oo- yoynànkwusa,₃
péwi'i.₄
Yoo'oo'- yoynànkwusa,
péwi'i.
Haqami₅ yang₆ paavönnawita₇ oo'oomawutu₈ yoynànkwusani.₉
Aaha aha.
Ayángqw₁₀ Öngtupqangaqö,₁₁
Kooyemsimongwitu₁₂ yòytatawiy₁₃ akw₁₄ umumi₁₅ naanakwusani.₁₆
[Keresan *Heenat'isi₁₇ kaatsa'anoomay.* Keresan]

[They] have started off on their journey as rain,
coming this way.
[They] have started off on their journey as rain,
coming this way.
All along the young corn plants here, the clouds will start their journey as
  rain.
(Vocables.)
From over there, from the Grand Canyon,

1. *soyohìmkatsinmuy*, object form of *soyohìmkatsinam* 'all kinds of katsinas, mixed katsinas'.
2. *taawi'am* 'their song'.
3. = *yoynànkwusa* 'start on a journey as rain'.
4. = *pew'i*, pausal form of *pew* 'toward here, coming this way'.
5. = *aqwhaqami* 'throughout'.
6. *yang* 'along here, in this area'.
7. *paavönnawit* 'along the young corn plants'.
8. = *oo'omawt* 'clouds'.
9. = *yoynànkwusani* 'will start on a journey as rain'.
10. *ayángqw* 'from over there'.
11. = *Öngtupqangaqw* 'from the Grand Canyon'.
12. = *Koyemosmongwit* 'Mudhead katsina leaders'.
13. *yòytatawiy*, object form of *yòytatawi'am* 'their rain songs'.
14. *akw* 'with, using'.
15. *umumi* 'to you (plural)'.
16. = *nànkwusani* 'will start on a journey (plural)'.
17. *Heenat'isi* represents a Keresan word for 'clouds', cf. Santa Ana *hénaห'i* 'cloud' (Davis
    1964: 166), *-ši* 'plural subject' (*id.*: 179).

the Mudhead katsina leaders will start their journey toward you with their rain songs.
(Keresan words with a reference to clouds.)

This song is almost identical to Song 97.

99. Soyohìmkatsinmuy₁ Taawi'am₂
(Black Song 93)

Naanakwusiwa.₃
Ayangqö₄ Kisiwuvangaqö₅ wuuwukwmuyu₆ pöötapyamuy₇ ánawit₈ ítamu₉
   umumi₁₀ naanakwusa,₁₁
péwi'i.₁₂
Paatuwvotay₁₃ taalawinani.₁₄
Paamotoro₁₅ ang₁₆ hoohongivani.₁₇
Putakw₁₈ namur₁₉ umumi yooya'öki,₂₀
péwi'i.
Ahaa haa ii.

1. *soyohìmkatsinmuy,* object form of *soyohìmkatsinam* 'all kinds of katsinas, mixed katsinas'.
2. *taawi'am* 'their song'.
3. = *nànkwusiwa* 'for a journey by several to have begun'.
4. = *ayángqw* 'from over there'.
5. = *Kisiwvangaqw* 'from Shadow Spring'.
6. = *wuuwukwmuy,* object form of *wuuwuyom* 'old ones, elders'.
7. *pöötapyamuy,* object form of *pöötavi'am* 'their consecrated path'.
8. *ánawit* 'along its course'.
9. = *itam* 'we'.
10. *umumi* 'to you (plural)'.
11. = *nànkwusa* 'start on a journey (plural)'.
12. = *pew'i,* pausal form of *pew* 'toward here, coming this way'.
13. *paatuwvotay,* short for *itàapatuwvotay,* object form of *itàapatuwvota* 'our water shields, rings of ripples in water'.
14. = *taalawnani,* future of *taalawna* 'make bright'.
15. *paamotoro* 'water pillars, splashes of raindrops'.
16. *ang* 'along it, along there, in that area, in several places'.
17. = *hoohongvani* 'will stand up repeatedly'.
18. *putakw* 'with that, by means of that, using that/those'.
19. *namur* 'let it be so'.
20. = *yoy'öki* 'arrive, come as rain'.

Pew₂₁ pútakwa₂₂ námura₂₃ umùu'uyinawit₂₄ yang₂₅ paatu₂₆ hantani.₂₇
Pew pútakwa námura umùu'uyinawit yang naatukwsintani.₂₈
Oohoho oho owa ehe eelo.

The journey has begun.
From over at Shadow Spring, along the elders' consecrated path, we have
set out on our journey to you,
coming this way.
We will make our water shields glisten.
The water pillars will repeatedly stand up along there.
Let it be that [we] come to you as rain using those,
coming this way.
(Vocables.)
Let it be that, using those (the water pillars), the waters will be descend-
ing this way throughout your planted fields along here.
Let it be that, using those, they (the plants) will be making themselves
mature this way along here throughout your planted fields.
(Vocables.)

The katsinas are describing their journey moving in rain from their home
at Shadow Spring in the northeast direction. They are traveling along a
consecrated path, *pöötavi*. As they move from their homes in the four
directions, they travel along a virtual path formed by the prayers sent by
the people. But as they approach and enter the village, they travel on a
path of consecrated cornmeal and feathers that the elders have laid out for
them.

The katsinas promise to make the "water shields glisten" and they
describe how they will make the "water pillars repeatedly stand up." The

21. *pew* 'toward here, coming this way'.
22. = *putakw* 'with that, by means of that, using that/those'.
23. *námura* 'let it be so'.
24. = *umùu'uynawit* 'along your (plural) planted fields'.
25. *yang* 'along here, in this area'.
26. *paatu* 'waters'. This is an animate plural form which reflects the animate nature of
rainwater in the songs. Normally, the word for water, *paahu*, as a typical inanimate noun,
occurs in singular form only; its reduplicated distributive form, *paavahu*, refers to water
in different locations, as in various springs or ponds.
27. *hantani* 'will be descending (plural)'.
28. *naatukwsintani* 'will be making selves mature'. The song uses the singular form for a
plural meaning; the plural form is *naatukwsintotani*.

"water shields" (*paatuwvota*) refer to the concentric ripples formed in puddles of rainwater when raindrops strike the surface. The word also describes the concentric rings of coiled plaques that, in the distant past, were used as shields. The image of raindrops as "water pillars" (*paamotoro*) comes from the meaning of *motoro,* a stalactite. Here it is used to create the image of a raindrop striking the surface of a puddle with such force that it rebounds vertically.

The katsinas hope that by "using those," referring to the water pillars and water shields, their waters will flow throughout the planted fields. Because plants are animate, they will take this rainwater and raise themselves up, that is, mature and bear fruit.

This song is very similar to Song 47 and to Song 122.

100. *Tasapkatsìntawi$_1$*
(Black Song 115)

Ahay aa ahay'a.
Naanan'ivo'o$_2$
uu'unangwvasilawu,$_3$
qöya'omàwtuy.$_4$
Qöyahonawuy$_5$ aw$_6$ paatayayatoya.$_7$
Ímuyu$_8$ amungem$_9$ tsúyakiwta'a,$_{10}$
yépe'e.$_{11}$
Mee'e hooli hoo hooli hooli hoo.

(Vocables.)
To the different directions around

1. *tasapkatsìntawi* 'Navajo katsina song'.
2. = *naanan'ivo* 'to the different directions around'.
3. = *u'nangwvaslawu* 'keep praying repeatedly in a heartfelt manner for good results'.
4. = *qöya'o'omàwtuy,* object form of *qöya'o'omawt* 'white clouds'.
5. *Qöyahonawuy,* object form of *Qöyahonaw* 'White Bear'.
6. *aw* 'on it'.
7. = *paatayayatoyna* 'be pouring water while shaking things', a reference to rain with thunder.
8. = *imuy,* object form of *ima* 'these'.
9. *amungem* 'for them, for their benefit'.
10. *tsúyakiwta'a,* imperative form of *tsúyakiwta* 'be grateful for being able to enjoy'.
11. = *yep'e,* pausal form of *yep* 'here'.

you keep praying sincerely
for white clouds.
They are pouring water on the White Bear as they shake things.
Be grateful for them, for being able to enjoy it
here.
(Vocables.)

The katsinas are encouraging the people to keep praying to the different directions around, meaning to all four cardinal directions for white clouds, that is, for the cumulus clouds that are signs of rain. They remark that these clouds are pouring their water as they shake things, meaning that they are raining and thundering. They are coming with all this rain to the White Bear. This is a reference to the Bear clan, who were the first to settle the village of Orayvi. The clan is described as white to emphasize the spiritual purity of the prayers from this clan that rendered them deserving of this rain. The katsinas close their song by reminding the people to be grateful for this rain.

101. *Tsa'kwaynatawi*₁
(Black Song 79)

Ahay'a.
*Ayangqö,*₂
*taavangqw*₃ *yooyangw*₄ *haahawimani.*₅
*Umùutuwapongyava*₆ *paatuwataviyani.*₇
Liilay aa'i.
Ahay'a.
Ayangqö,
*hoopaqw*₈ *yooyangw haahawimani.*

1. *tsa'kwaynatawi* 'Tsa'kwayna katsina song'.
2. = *ayángqw* 'from over there'.
3. *taavangqw* 'from the southwest'.
4. *yooyangw* 'rain'.
5. = *haahawtimani* 'will come/go along descending at intervals'.
6. *umùutuwapongyava* 'along your land'.
7. = *paatuwatapyani* 'will lay water on the land (plural)'. The plural is used here because its subject is *yooyangw* 'rain', a liquid. In Hopi grammar liquids govern plural grammatical agreement.
8. *hoopaqw* 'from the northeast'.

Umùutuwapongyava paatuwataviyani.
Uni'i,$_9$
yang$_{10}$ paasanawita$_{11}$ sikyavavönmanatu$_{12}$ sakwayevewmanatu$_{13}$ nalönaa-
     tsiva'a,$_{14}$
tímokimuy$_{15}$ oomi$_{16}$ naawungwinaqw'ö.$_{17}$
Ohoo'o hoo hoo hoowa, ehee'e hee hee heeloy.
Aaha ee.
Aahaa ee.
Aaha hayi ee.
Uni'i,
yang paasanawita sikyavavönmanatu sakwayevewmanatu naatuksi-
     naqw'ö,$_{18}$
tímokimuy oomi$_{19}$ naawungwinaqw'ö.
Ohoo'o hoo hoo hoowa, ehee'e hee hee heeloy.
Aaha ee aha ehe aha a'e.
Aha heeye.
Hapi me.$_{20}$
Haw$_{21}$ uma$_{22}$ ínamu,$_{23}$
yoytaatawilawu.$_{24}$
Haa'aw haayiyee haa'aw hayiiyee.

(Vocable.)
From over there,
from the southwest, the rain will be coming along descending.

9. *uni'i* 'how delightful it is', pausal form of *uní* 'how delightful'.
10. *yang* 'along here, in this area'.
11. = *paasanawit* 'along the fields'.
12. = *sikyavavönmamant* 'yellow young corn plants'.
13. = *sakwayevewmamant* 'blue/green young corn plant maidens'.
14. = *nalönatsva'a*, pausal form of *nalönatsva* 'in four places one above the other'.
15. *tímokimuy* 'young corn ears on the stalk (object form)'. (The nominative, *tímoki*, is used only in the singular.)
16. *oomi* 'upward'.
17. = *naawungwnaqw'ö*, subordinate clause pausal form of *naawungwna* 'make self grow'.
18. = *naatukwsinaqw'ö*, subordinate clause pausal form of *naatukwsina* 'make self mature'.
19. *oomi* 'upward'.
20. *hapi me*, formulaic expression introducing the song's second part, *oomi* 'upward'.
21. *haw*, vocative particle.
22. *uma* 'you (plural)'.
23. = *inam* 'my fathers'.
24. = *yòytatawlawu* 'keep singing songs for rain'.

Along your land, it will lay down water.
(Vocables.)
From over there,
from the northeast the rain will be coming along descending.
Along your land, it will lay down water.
How delightful it is,
when along the fields here, the yellow young corn plants and the blue/
    green young corn plant maidens
make themselves grow with their corn ears in four places one above the
    other.
(Vocables.)
How delightful it is,
while along the fields here, the yellow young corn plants and the young
    blue/green corn plant maidens make themselves mature,
and make themselves grow with their young ears in four places one above
    the other.
(Vocables.)
Listen, there is more.
You, my fathers,
keep singing songs for rain.
(Vocables.)

The katsinas are promising that rain will be coming from the southwest
and northeast directions. The use of the expressions "descending" instead
of "falling," and "lay down the water," instead of "rain on," reflect the
animate nature of the rain. In like manner, the corn plants are referred to
as animate beings who raise themselves up.

The song contains a beautiful image metaphor of the corn plants
raising themselves with four ears, one above the other. Perfect cornstalks
have four corn ears on them, alternating up the stalk, that are symbolic of
the nourishing rains that come from each of the four cardinal directions.
The young corn ear on the stalk is a *tímoki,* which literally translates as
"child bundle." The mental image metaphor created is that each ear of
corn tightly enveloped in the green leaves of the husk is a baby swaddled
in blankets. The likening of the four corn ears on the stalk to wrapped
children is a particularly beautiful way to express the fundamental corn
metaphor pervading all Hopi thought that likens growing corn ears to
growing children.

The katsinas close by urging the people to continue singing their
songs for rain, that is, to continue praying sincerely and living a fulfilled

life by the tenets of the corn lifeway. The implication is that if they do, the rains will continue to come.

102. *Tsa'kwaynatawi$_1$*
(Black Song 92)

Haw$_2$ uma$_3$ ínamu,$_4$
uma yep$_5$ hiihìita$_6$ ang$_7$ naamongsungwam.$_8$
Ínamu,
uma yep hísatngaqw$_9$ yep wuyolvayit,$_{10}$ tutavot$_{11}$ uma sùutok.ya.$_{12}$
Yep uma inumi$_{13}$ as$_{14}$ hopiyungta.$_{15}$
Yep uma inumi as hopimatsiwta.$_{16}$
Naanan'ivo$_{17}$ uma leekya'yta;$_{18}$
nit$_{19}$ uma itamuyu$_{20}$ maqastiqe$_{21}$ kwèetsikma.$_{22}$
Haw uma ínamu,

1. *tsa'kwaynatawi* 'Tsa'kwayna katsina song'.
2. *haw*, vocative particle.
3. *uma* 'you (plural)'.
4. =*inam* 'my fathers'.
5. *yep* 'here'.
6. *hiihìita*, object form of *hiihimu* 'some things, many different things'.
7. *ang* 'along it, along there, in that area, in several places'.
8. *naamongsungwam* 'fellow leaders'.
9. *hísatngaqw* 'since an earlier time'.
10. *wuyolvayit*, object form of *wuyolvayi* 'recollections, remembrances, words from long ago'.
11. *tutavot*, object form of *tutavo* 'advice, instruction, council'.
12. *sùutok.ya* 'forget (plural)'.
13. *inumi* 'to me'.
14. *as* 'presumably': something is claimed to be so without full evidence. *Himu as* means something like "should, I wish you would."
15. *hopiyungta* 'be initiated as Hopis'.
16. *hopimatsiwta* 'have a Hopi identity'.
17. *naanan'ivo* 'to the different directions around'.
18. *leekya'yta* is an unknown word; it seems to mean 'be respected in what one says'.
19. *nit* 'and, after that'.
20. = *itamuy* 'us', object form of *itam* 'we'.
21. *maqastiqe*, subordinate clause form of *maqasti* 'become afraid'.
22. *kwèetsikma* 'scurry off in all directions'.

umùu'unangwvàasiy$_{23}$ umùulavayiy$_{24}$ namitngàltiqö'ö,$_{25}$
humi'uysonaqa,$_{26}$ mori'uysonaqa$_{27}$ yookinayani.$_{28}$
Hapi me.$_{29}$
Mùnqape$_{30}$ maana$_{31}$ naasomit$_{32}$ qa$_{33}$ navoti'yta.$_{34}$
Ura$_{35}$ piw$_{36}$ ii'its,$_{37}$
ura piw ngúmantaqe'e,$_{38}$
tawmumuyaqw'ö,$_{39}$
pas$_{40}$ pam$_{41}$ sonkiwngwu.$_{42}$
Ura piw qööyintaqö'ö,$_{43}$
pas pam lolmaningwu.$_{44}$
Mùnqape tootim$_{45}$ hömsomit$_{46}$ qa navoti'yta,
yépe'e.$_{47}$
Ura piw ii'its,

23. *umùu'unangwvàasiy,* object form of *umùu'unangwvàasi* 'your heartfelt wish'.
24. *umùulavayiy,* object form of *umùulavayi* 'your (plural) speech, words'.
25. = *namitngàltiqw'ö,* subordinate clause pausal form of *namitngàlti* 'get mixed, mix together'.
26. *humi'uysonaq* 'throughout the midst of the area(s) planted with corn'.
27. *mori'uysonaq* 'throughout the midst of the area(s) planted with beans'.
28. = *yoknayani* 'will make it rain (plural)'.
29. *hapi me,* formulaic expression introducing the song's second part, *oomi* 'upward'.
30. *Mùnqape* 'at Mùnqapi'.
31. *maana* 'girl, young unmarried woman, maiden'.
32. *naasomit,* object form of *naasomi* 'side hairdo'.
33. *qa* 'not'.
34. *navoti'yta* 'know'.
35. *ura,* modal of recollection: 'as I recall, as you'll recall'.
36. *piw* 'also, too, again'.
37. *ii'its* 'promptly, early, soon'.
38. *ngúmantaqe'e,* subordinate clause pausal form of *ngúmanta* 'be grinding cornmeal into flour'.
39. *tawmumuyaqw'ö,* subordinate clause pausal form of *tawmumuya* 'be singing intensively'.
40. *pas* 'very'.
41. *pam* 'that, that one, he, she, it'.
42. = *sosonkiwngwu,* habitual tense form of *sosonkiwa* 'be pleasing'.
43. = *qööyintaqw'ö,* subordinate clause pausal form of *qööyinta* 'be toasting cornmeal in a pot prior to grinding it into flour'.
44. *lolmaningwu,* habitual tense form of *lolma* 'good' (with linking *-ni-*).
45. *tootim* 'boys'.
46. *hömsomit,* object form of *hömsomi* 'hairknot'.
47. = *yep'e,* pausal form of *yep* 'here'. This seems to refer to Mùnqapi, where the song was sung.

piw ura kuyvatoqö'ö,[48]
haqami[49] *qalalàykinaqw'ö,*[50]
pas pam sonkiwngwu.
Ura piw talavàytötöqw'ö,[51]
pas pam lolmaningwu.

O you, my fathers,
you are fellow leaders here in many different things.
My fathers,
you here have forgotten the recollections and advice from long ago.
Here you come to me as though you have been initiated as Hopis.
Here you appear to me as though you have a Hopi identity.
You are respected in what you say to the different directions around,
yet you become afraid of us and scurry off in all directions.
O you, my fathers,
when your heartfelt wishes and your words unite together,
we will make it rain throughout the areas planted with corn and with
    beans.
Listen, there is more.
At Mùnqapi, a girl doesn't know the *naasomi* hairdo [any longer].
You'll recall also early in the morning,
when she used to be grinding cornmeal into flour,
and would be caught up in singing,
it sounded beautiful.
You'll recall also when she used to be toasting it,
that was good.
At Mùnqapi the young men don't know the hairknot (any longer),
here.
You'll recall also early in the morning,
when they used to get up to run somewhere (to greet the sun) and pray,
and would start clanking their bells throughout,
it sounded beautiful.
You'll recall also when they used to give their calls of the morning,
that was good.

---

48. = *kuyvatoqw'ö,* subordinate clause pausal form of *kuyvato* 'get up early to go run and
    pray'.
49. = *aqwhaqami* 'throughout'.
50. *qalalàykinaqw'ö,* subordinate clause pausal form of *qalalàykina* 'begin clanking'.
51. = *talavàytötöqqw,* subordinate clause form of *talavàytötöqa* 'be giving the calls of the
    morning'.

The katsinas are admonishing the people of Mùnqapi for forgetting past customs that represent the hard work and perseverance that is necessary to sustain the communal lifeway. They chastise the fathers who are described as leaders in "many different things," a reference to the fact that each person has many different leadership roles. The katsinas say that the fathers have forgotten the lessons of *wuyolvayi,* literally "old (*wuyo-*) speech (*-lvayi*)," words referring to the teachings and advice and words of wisdom from long ago that comprise the Hopi oral tradition. They challenge the trueness of heart of these leaders, accusing them of pretending to have made contact with the katsinas through their prayers. This is said indirectly by suggesting that they have not been initiated. Initiation into the katsina society brings with it increased knowledge of the beliefs and responsibilities of members of the society. By implying that they have not been initiated, the katsinas are saying that they do not have the knowledge or the power to make contact with the katsinas. They also suggest that these leaders are pretending to be Hopis, but, to the katsinas, appearances do not matter. What is important is the way they live their lives, *hopimatsiwta* 'have a Hopi identity'. This is not to be understood as referring to a Hopi ethnic identity, that is, being a member of the Hopi tribe, but rather as living according to Hopi principles and practices.

They observe that the prayers of the leaders are effective to the different directions around, meaning that when they pray for rain to the four cardinal directions, the katsinas *do* arrive as rain. However, the katsinas imply that these leaders are afraid of coming to them with their prayers and so shy away from them, hiding and avoiding the practicing of their responsibilities and obligations. The katsinas plead with them to renew their efforts to live right. They promise that when the people's practices of living match their words of prayer, they *will* come and rain on their planted fields.

In the second section of the song the katsinas describe traditional activities of the girls and boys that are no longer practiced. This is not a call to return to living as they did a century ago, but it is a call to maintain performance of certain symbolic practices that stand for that past perfect life. They lament that the unmarried girls (maidens) no longer wear their hair in side hairbuns, *naasomi,* the hairstyle of prepubescent girls. The suggestion is that by not adopting the traditional features of dress that indicate life stages and roles, the girls will not learn the traditional teachings that underlie these overt symbols. Likewise, they lament that the girls are not grinding corn and singing in the early morning, implying that they are not learning the ways of everyday food preparation and the practice of singing to relieve the tedium of hard work. They also imply that the girls are not learning how to toast the cornmeal. This refers to the process of grinding corn. It is first ground to a coarse state (*hakwurkwi*), then toasted in a kettle, and finally returned to the metate to be ground into fine flour (*ngumni*). Then the katsinas turn to the boys, lamenting that they no longer wear the traditional *hömsomi* hairstyle, where the long hair is tied in a knot at the nape of the neck. Nor do they rise early in the morning, pray and run to greet the sun. Traditionally, the boys used to wear bells around their waists and these would jingle with pleasing sounds as they ran. They would also "give their calls of the morning," a reference to the cheers that expressed their vitality as they ran.

103. *Tsa'kwaynatawi$_1$*
(Black Song 94)

Nuu'u,$_2$
Tsa'kwayna.
Okiw$_3$ nu'$_4$ yep$_5$ waynuma.$_6$
Pangso$_7$ nu' itanamuy$_8$ ayalawu.$_9$
Umùu'uyiy$_{10}$ nu' ang$_{11}$ taynuma.$_{12}$
Umùutuwaqatsi$_{13}$ tutuveniwyungwa.$_{14}$
Ta'a$_{15}$ pu'$_{16}$ hintani,$_{17}$
itanamuy lavay'ayamatu?$_{18}$

1. *tsa'kwaynatawi* 'Tsa'kwayna katsina song'.
2. *nuu'u*, pausal form of *nu'* 'I'.
3. *okiw* 'humble, pitiful'.
4. *nu'* 'I'.
5. *yep* 'here'.
6. *waynuma* 'be walking around'.
7. *pangso* 'to there'.
8. *itanamuy*, object form of *itanam* 'our fathers'.
9. *ayalawu* 'be asking someone to do something'.
10. *umùu'uyiy*, object form of *umùu'uyi* 'your (plural) plants, planted fields'.
11. *ang* 'along it, along there, in that area, in several places'.
12. *taynuma* 'be looking around'.
13. *umùutuwaqatsi* 'your (plural) land(s)'.
14. = *tutuven'iwyungwa* 'be marked with lines or notches (plural)'.
15. *ta'a* 'all right, I agree'.
16. *pu'* 'now, then'.
17. *hintani* 'will be some way'.
18. = *lavay'ayamat* 'their spokespeople'.

Pay$_{19}$ nam$_{20}$ yooyokpuva'a,$_{21}$
kawaayo'o,$_{22}$ melooni$_{23}$ anìwtini.$_{24}$
Umùutimuy$_{25}$ noonvaqw$_{26}$ lolmani.$_{27}$
Pi$_{28}$ paas$_{29}$ kur$_{30}$ antsa'a,$_{31}$
ura$_{32}$ yaniwmani.$_{33}$
Namunwanvöhu$_{34}$ tuuvoyni.$_{35}$
Maakiw$_{36}$ úra'i,$_{37}$
so'tini.$_{38}$
Mamanhoyam$_{39}$ ura it$_{40}$ óvekniwuy,$_{41}$
piw$_{42}$ poli'init$_{43}$ qa$_{44}$ navoti'ytani.$_{45}$
Yaayan$_{46}$ úra'a,$_{47}$
itàakwa'a,$_{48}$

19. *pay,* expressive particle.
20. *nam* 'may it be so'.
21. *yooyokpuva'a,* pausal form of *yooyokpuva* 'along the places it has rained'.
22. *kawaayo'o,* pausal form of *kawaayo* = *kawayo* 'watermelon'.
23. *melooni* 'muskmelon'.
24. *anìwtini* 'will develop, grow'.
25. *umùutimuy,* object form of *umùutim* 'your(plural) children'. Though in object form, this is the subject of the subordinated verb *noonova* (next note).
26. = *noonovaqw,* subordinate clause form of *noonova* 'be eating, eat repetitively (plural)'.
27. *lolmani* 'will be beautiful, good, proper'.
28. *pi* 'truly'.
29. = *pas* 'very'.
30. *kur,* modal of inference.
31. *antsa'a,* pausal form of *antsa* 'truly, really, indeed'.
32. *ura,* modal of recollection: 'as I recall, as you'll recall, remember'.
33. *yaniwmani,* future of *yaniwma* 'be happening in this way'.
34. = *namunwanvö* 'path for the running of the stone race'.
35. *tuuvoyni,* future of *tuuvoyi* 'vanish, get obliterated'.
36. *maakiw* 'hunting'.
37. *úra'i,* pausal form of *ura,* modal of recollection: 'as I recall, as you'll recall, remember'.
38. *so'tini* 'will end'.
39. = *mamanhòoyam* 'little girls'.
40. *it,* object form of *i'* 'this'.
41. = *óvekiniwuy,* object form of *óvekiniw* 'social outing for unmarried girls and boys after a summer katsina dance'.
42. *piw* 'also, too, again'.
43. *poli'init,* object form of *poli'ini* 'butterfly whorl hairdo'.
44. *qa* 'not'.
45. *navoti'ytani* 'will know'.
46. *yaayan* 'in these ways'.
47. *úra'a,* pausal form of *ura,* modal of recollection: 'as I recall, as you'll recall, remember'.
48. *itàakwa'a,* pausalized form of *itàakwa* 'our grandfather'.

Sikyakuku itàamumi₄₉ it tùutuwutsngwu.₅₀
I'wayo hoona aayaw loloosi.
Hapi me.₅₁
Sikyahoonawmongwit₅₂ ínamu,₅₃
sakwavahomongwi₅₄ ína'a,₅₅
hekpata₅₆ atpipo₅₇ pó'o'kyango₅₈
naanan'ivo'o,₅₉
púma'a,₆₀
oo'omawutuy₆₁ wángwaylawu.₆₂
Paypu₆₃ námusa₆₄ umùulavayiy₆₅ antani.₆₆

I am
Tsa'kwayna.
I am walking around here feeling dejected.
I am asking our fathers to go there.
I am looking around in your fields.
Your lands are marked [by erosion].
All right now, how will it be,
spokespeople of our fathers?
Well, let it be so, in places where it has rained,
that watermelons and muskmelons will grow.
When your children eat, it will be good.

49. = *itamumi* 'to us'.
50. *tùutuwutsngwu*, habitual tense form of *tùutuwutsi* 'tell about'.
51. *hapi me*, formulaic expression introducing the song's second part, *oomi* 'upward'.
52. = *Sikyahonawmomngwit* 'Yellow Bear leaders'.
53. = *inam* 'my fathers'.
54. *sakwavahomongwi* 'blue/green prayer feather leader'.
55. *ína'a*, pausalized form of *ina* 'my father'.
56. = *hekwpat*, object form of *hekwpa* 'white fir'. This is either an error for *salavi* 'Douglas fir' (object form *salavit*) or else in some non-Third Mesa usage, *hekpa* may refer to Douglas fir. The white fir is never used in ceremonies.
57. = *atpip* 'beneath'.
58. = *pó'o'kyangw* 'while bending over'.
59. *naanan'ivo'o*, pausal form of *naanan'ivo* 'to the different directions around'.
60. *púma'a*, pausalized form of *puma* 'they'.
61. = *oo'omàwtuy*, object form of *oo'omawt* 'clouds'.
62. *wángwaylawu* 'keep summoning, calling for'.
63. = *paapu* 'nowadays, anymore, now'.
64. *námusa* 'let it be so' (variant of *námura*).
65. *umùulavayiy*, object form of *umùulavayi* 'your (plural) speech, words'.
66. *antani* 'will be like that, be right'.

It seems true, you recall,
that things will be happening in this way.
The stone-racing path will vanish.
The hunting, you recall they say,
will end.
The little girls, remember, will have no knowledge of the social outing,
nor of the butterfly whorl hairdo.
In these ways, you'll recall,
our grandfather
Sikyakuku used to tell us about it.
(Vocables.)
Listen, there is more.
The Yellow Bear leaders, my fathers,
the blue/green prayer feather leader, my father,
while they bend the head down (to pray) beneath the Douglas fir
to the directions around
they [call],
[they] call to the clouds (to come).
May your words (of prayer) come true this time.

In this song, the Tsa'kwayna katsina is admonishing the people for the way they are living their lives. He is sad, *okiw,* discouraged with what he sees as he walks around and observes the activities, practices and ways of living of the people in the village. Katsinas do care about the well-being of the people—that is the whole idea of katsina. Tsa'kwayna asks the fathers to look at their fields. He observes that their land is marked with erosion, here likened to the incised lines of petroglyphs, *tutuveni,* implying that they have not been taking proper care of their fields and that this deterioration of the land is a metaphor for moral decay in the community.

Then Tsa'kwayna addresses those in leadership positions, here referred to as the people's spokespersons (*lavay'ayamat*), meaning those in the position of advisors who can influence others. The expression *ta'a pu' hintani* (all right now, how will it be?) expresses his frustration. He challenges them: What are you going to do about your lives? He hopes that if the people reassess the way they are living and turn their lives around, it will rain and the watermelons and muskmelons will grow to maturity, their children will eat, and life will be good once more. The implication is that with these changes in their behavior, the community will survive. This is the way life should be lived, *lolmani.* He reminds the people of these things, knowing that they know them, but simply that they need encouragement.

Then he reverts to his discouraged state of mind, saying that it has come to what was predicted long ago. The phrase *pi paas kur antsa'a,* this was bound to happen, is a reference to the dissolution of communities in the past when people failed to live right. He cites traditional practices that represent the heart of Hopi life that are no longer being followed. The racing path will disappear from disuse because the boys no longer run races to encourage the rains to come. The practice of hunting for sustenance will end and, by implication, this will create an imbalance in the natural world. He is concerned that the little girls no longer understand why they participate in appropriately sanctioned social outings (*óvekiniw*) on occasions and in places where they can properly meet boys. This is a reference to the custom where, after a summer dance, the girls used to go to the edge of the mesa on the pretense that they were looking at the scenery. The boys would follow to meet them, sometimes forming a group behind the girls to serenade them. He also predicts that the girls will not understand why they should wear the butterfly hairdo, *poli'ini,* that signifies their readiness for marriage. Tsa'kwayna recalls that the children's grandfather Sikyakuku, used to teach them about these important practices, implying that the children no longer have the proper respect for their elders and no longer listen to them for advice and knowledge.

Now Tsa'kwayna, by addressing those in leadership roles as Yellow Bear leaders, is putting them in the position of model Hopis in the hopes that they will assume their responsibilities. He advises the leaders to take their blue/green prayer feather leaders, that is, their prayer feathers, and humble themselves before the Douglas fir branches that have been planted in the plaza for the ceremony, and pray sincerely and fervently to the clouds to come. Tsa'kwayna hopes that their words will be sincere so that their prayers will come true, implying that in times past their prayers have not resulted in rain because they have not been heartfelt, free of ill-will and other thoughts that are counter to the well-being of the community. This song is almost the same as Song 123.

104. *Tukwunàngwkatsìntawi*₁

1. *tukwunàngwkatsìntawi* 'Cumulus Cloud katsina song'.

(Black Song 65)

Itam,$_2$
itam nanawinya,$_3$
tatkya$_4$ Weenimayuy$_5$ épe'e.$_6$
Angqw$_7$ itamuy'u,$_8$
sunsa'unangway$_9$ taayimakyango,$_{10}$
uuyisonaqa$_{11}$ naanakwusani.$_{12}$
Noqw$_{13}$ yang$_{14}$ ikukunawita$_{15}$ ivookom$_{16}$ patsqawuwutani,$_{17}$
yooyangyalapuva'a.$_{18}$
Yan$_{19}$ naanawakina,$_{20}$
pahowuuyomongwitu'uy.$_{21}$
Umuy$_{22}$ naanan'ivo$_{23}$ tuyqawvaqö'ö,$_{24}$
naanaqavo'o,$_{25}$
yooya'ökiwni.$_{26}$

2. *itam* 'we'.
3. *nanawinya* 'be planning, making plans (plural)'.
4. *tatkya* 'in the southeast'.
5. = *Weenimay,* object form of *Weenima,* the southeast katsina home.
6. = *ep'e,* pausal form of *ep* 'there, at it'.
7. *angqw* 'from it, from there'.
8. *itamuy'u,* pausal form of *itamuy* 'us', object form of *itam* 'we'.
9. *sunsa'unangway* 'with hearts together as one'.
10. = *taymakyangw* 'while going along looking, seeing, watching'.
11. = *uysonaq* 'throughout the midst of the planted area(s)'.
12. = *nànkwsani* 'will start on a journey (plural)'.
13. *noqw* 'but, whereas, and so'.
14. *yang* 'along here, in this area'.
15. = *ikukunawit* 'along my footprints, along my tracks'.
16. = *ivòokom* 'my creatures'.
17. *patsqawuwutani* 'will be getting spattered with muddy water'.
18. = *yoyngyàlpuva* 'in the postlude of the rain, during the time after it has stopped raining'.
19. *yan* 'like this, in this way, thus'.
20. = *naanawakna* 'want, pray for (plural)'.
21. = *pahowuyomomngwitu'uy,* pausal exclamatory form of *pahowuyomomngwit* 'elder prayer feather leaders'.
22. *umuy,* object form of *uma* 'you (plural)'. Even though 'you' is the subject of *tuyqawva* 'prevail', it is in the object form here because of the adverbial status of the subordinate clause.
23. *naanan'ivo* 'to the different directions around'.
24. = *tuyqawvaqw'ö,* subordinate clause pausal form of *tuyqawva* 'prevail (with your prayers)'.
25. *naanaqavo'o,* pausal form of *naanaqavo* 'day after day, every day'.
26. = *yoy'ökiwni* 'will have come, arrived as rain'.

Awhay'a awhay'aa ha.
Hapi me.$_{27}$
Ayamo$_{28}$ *kwiningya*$_{29}$ *Taatatsiwkivayuy*$_{30}$ *épe'e,*
soyohim'oomaw$_{31}$ *kuukuyvata'a,*$_{32}$
angqw pew$_{33}$ *kitsokiva*$_{34}$ *uuyiyamuyu*$_{35}$ *pava'o'oytimani.*$_{36}$

We,
we are making plans,
in the southeast, at *Weenima.*
From there while we
go along watching with our hearts together as one in intention,
we will set out on a journey through the midst of the planted fields.
And so, along my tracks here, my creatures will be getting spattered with
    muddy water,
in the postlude of the rain.
You pray (that it be) this way.
[You] elder prayer feather leaders,
when you prevail (with your prayers) to the different directions around,
day after day
they will have arrived as rain.
(Vocables.)
Listen, there is more.
Over in the northwest at Ball Game kiva,
after all kinds of clouds come into view,
coming from there, they will go along the villages placing water on their
    planted fields.

The Cumulus Cloud katsinas are making plans at their home in the southeast direction at *Weenima* to set out on their journey to come to the
planted fields as rain. After going along watching how the people are

---

27. *hapi me,* formulaic expression introducing the song's second part, *oomi* 'upward'.
28. = *ayám* 'over there'.
29. *kwiningya* 'in the northwest'.
30. = *Tatatsiwkivay,* object form of *Tatatsiwkiva* 'Ball Game kiva'.
31. = *soyohim'o'omawt* 'all kinds of clouds'.
32. = *kuukuyvat* 'after coming into sight (plural)'.
33. *pew* 'toward here, coming this way'.
34. *kitsokiva* 'in the villages'.
35. = *uuyiyamuy,* object form of *uuyi'am* 'their planted fields'.
36. *paa'o'oytimani* 'will go along placing water'.

living their lives, they comment that their hearts are united with the intention of coming to them as rain, that is, they are convinced of the sincerity of the people's prayers. Then they describe how they move throughout the fields, here described as "along my tracks," *ikukunawit,* with such great amounts of rain that mud splashes up on "my creatures," *ivòokom,* a reference to all living beings that are nurtured by the rainwater. Although it is not specified, the reference here may be to the leaves of the short Hopi corn plants that, when drenched with rain, bend over and touch the earth. In this way they gain support from Mother Earth. The katsinas say that the people have been praying for this to happen. They reiterate that when the elder leaders with their prayer feathers, here called elder prayer feather leaders, make prayers that are heard in all the four cardinal directions day after day, such prayers will prevail, meaning that the rains will come. This is the reciprocal drenching—the people metaphorically "drench" the katsinas with their prayers and the katsinas reciprocate by drenching their planted fields with rain.

The katsinas then observe that clouds are coming into view over in the northwest direction at the Ball Game kiva and that these clouds will be coming to place their water, that is, the rain, on the planted fields. The Ball Game kiva is possibly a reference to the home of *Pöqangwhoya* and *Palöngawhoya,* the "War Twins" or "Hero Twins," in the northwest direction. In their exploits these twins are always playing the ball game.

Songs Recorded by George List in 1960

105. *Angaktsìntawi*[1]
(List 11451, Track 1)

"Iyahayi[2] *möyhoyatu.*[3]
"Iyahay möömu.[4]
"Umuhkway[5] *uuyiyat*[6] *aw*[7] *yokva.*[8]
"Ang[9] *paatalawva.*[10]
"Aw uuma[11] *munlalaytoni,*[12]
"haw[13] *ímömu.*[14]
"Umuhkway uma[15] *amum*[16] *momortoni,*[17]
"taawanawita."[18]
"Itahso,[19]

1. *angaktsìntawi* 'Long-Hair katsina song'.
2. *iyahayi* and *iyahay* in the next line have not been identified. Initial *i-* is probably the possessive prefix 'my'. *-yahayi* is assumed to mean something like 'dear'.
3. = *möyhoyat* 'two little grandchildren'.
4. *möömu,* pausal form of *möm* 'grandchildren'.
5. = *umùukway* 'your (plural) grandfather's', object form of *umùukwa* 'your (plural) grandfather'.
6. *uuyiyat,* object form of *uuyi'at* 'his planted plant(s)'.
7. *aw* 'to it, to there'.
8. *yokva* 'rain' (verb).
9. *ang* 'along it, along there, in that area, in several places'.
10. *paatalawva* 'come to glisten with water'.
11. = *uma* 'you (plural)'.
12. *munlalaytoni* 'will/should go to channel runoff water'.
13. *haw,* vocative particle.
14. *imöm* 'my grandchildren'.
15. *uma* 'you (plural)'.
16. *amum* 'with, accompanying, together with'.
17. *momortoni* 'will/should go swimming'.
18. = *taawanawit* 'all day long'.
19. = *itàaso* 'our grandmother'.

"itahkway$_{20}$ uuyiyat itamuy$_{21}$ aw ökiq'ö,$_{22}$
"itahkway uuyi'at$_{23}$ kuwan'ewsoniwa.$_{24}$
"Itamuy ang uuyisonaq$_{25}$ waymakyang$_{26}$ tayma.$_{27}$
"Sihpepeytota.$_{28}$
"Pu'$_{29}$ ang peehu$_{30}$ siiviwiwuyungwa.$_{31}$
"Kaway'uyi'at$_{32}$ melon'uyi'at$_{33}$ pölöneyang$_{34}$ hotam'iwta.$_{35}$
"Ahaw$_{36}$ itupko?"$_{37}$
"Owí$_{38}$ oovi$_{39}$ itam$_{40}$ hahlayi,$_{41}$
"itahso'o."$_{42}$
"Is haw.$_{43}$
"Is uní.$_{44}$ Askwalí."
Ahaha.

"My dear(?) (two) little grandchildren.
"My dear(?) grandchildren.
"It has rained on your grandfather's plants.

20. = *itàakway* 'our grandfather's', object form (object of possession) of *itàakwa* 'our grandfather'.
21. *itamuy* 'us', object form of *itam* 'we'. This is in object form even though it is the subject of the verb (next note) because of the adverbial status of the clause.
22. = *ökiqw'ö*, subordinate clause pausal form of *öki* 'arrive, come (plural)'.
23. *uuyi'at* 'his planted plant(s)'.
24. *kuwan'ewsoniwa* 'look invigorated'.
25. = *uysonaq* 'throughout the midst of the planted area(s)'.
26. = *waymakyangw* 'while walking along'.
27. *tayma* 'go along looking, seeing, watching'.
28. *sihpepeytota* 'be forming buds all over (plural)', said to be the First Mesa equivalent of Third Mesa *sìipölölötota*.
29. *pu'* 'and, now, then'.
30. *peehu* 'some things, some of them'.
31. = *siwiswukiwyungwa* 'have tendrils cascading (plural)'.
32. *kaway'uyi'at* 'his watermelon plant(s)'.
33. *melon'uyi'at* 'his muskmelon plant(s)'.
34. *pölöneyang* 'mixed with or having ball-shaped things (like nubbins of fruit) all around'.
35. *hotam'iwta* 'be spread out, as of runners or vines'.
36. *ahaw* 'isn't it so?'.
37. *itupko* 'my younger brother'.
38. *owí* 'yes'.
39. *oovi* 'that's why'.
40. *itam* 'we'.
41. = *hàalayi* 'be happy'.
42. = *itàaso'o*, pausal form of *itàaso* 'our grandmother'.
43. *is haw*, an expression indicating admiration or that one is impressed.
44. *is uní* 'how nice, how delightful'.

"It has begun to shimmer with water along there.
"You should go channel the runoff water there,
"o my grandchildren.
"You should go swimming (play in the water) with your grandfather,
"all day long."
"Grandmother,
"when we came to grandfather's plants,
"our grandfather's plants looked invigorated.
"While walking along in the midst of the plants, we were going along
    looking.
"They were forming buds all over.
"And along there some of them had cascading tendrils.
"His watermelon and muskmelon plants were spread out with runners
    amidst all the nubbins.
"Isn't it so, my younger brother?"
"Yes, that's why we are happy,
"grandmother."
"I am impressed.
"How nice! Thank you."
(Vocable.)

This song is about how grandchildren should accompany their grandfather to his fields after a rain to appreciate how life gains vitality with rain. It is a homily on culturally defined roles—the teaching role of grandparents as well as the duty of children to respect their elders and learn from them. It is a reminder to the children of the activities that they should engage in to gain in knowledge about how to live the Hopi way as well as an introduction to some of the responsibilities and tasks they will have to engage in as adults. The young grandchildren are metaphorically likened to the nascent fruit on the growing plants—both represent the beginning stages of life and thus the promise of a continuing life for the people. In their complementary role as teachers, the grandparents represent the knowledge that comes with growth to maturity, just as the ripe melons represent fulfillment that comes with the rain. It is sung as a conversation, with the exchanges between the katsinas and people marked with quotes.

The katsinas, addressing the two grandchildren with a diminutive, observe that it has rained on the grandfather's plants, invigorating them. This rejuvenation of life is implied by the description of the plants as shimmering with water. The use of the word *kuwan'ewsoniwa* 'look invigorated', which is composed of *kuwan'ew* 'colorful' and *sóniwa* 'be pleasing', embodies the Hopi focus on color as a sign of life. The katsinas suggest that the children play in the rainwater all day long, specifically telling them to channel the runoff water, perhaps so that they learn how to direct the water to each plant, a task that they will have to perform as adults.

The katsinas then converse as if the children are back home telling their grandmother about the beauty of the plants they saw that were refreshed and renewed by the rain. They tell her that while they were walking among the plants, they noticed the many tendrils, spreading runners and buds forming on the melon plants. The older grandchild speaks to his brother asking him, rhetorically, to reconfirm that the melons have gained vitality with the rain. He tells his grandmother that this sight of thriving plants is why they are happy. The grandmother closes the song by responding to the children's obvious delight at their day, by exclaiming "How nice." She thanks them for recounting their observations, and implicitly, for the rain that has nourished the melons in the field so that they are prospering. The focus of this song is on the flowers and the developing melons as signs of life. They are metaphorically mirrored in the presence of the two grandchildren, who are signs of continuing generations of Hopis.

106. *Angaktsìntawi*$_1$
(List 11459, Track 17)

Iyahay$_2$ *möyhoyatu.*$_3$
Iyahay möömu.$_4$
Umuhkway$_5$ *uuyi'at*$_6$ *kuwan'ewsoniwa.*$_7$

My dear(?) (two) little grandchildren.
My dear(?) grandchildren.

1. *angaktsìntawi* 'Long-Hair katsina song'.
2. *iyahay,* said to be a First Mesa vocative form possibly meaning 'my dear'.
3. = *möyhoyat* '(two) little grandchildren.
4. *möömu,* pausal form of *möm* 'grandchildren'. Note that in ordinary usage 'grandchildren' is always a possessed form: *imöm* 'my grandchildren', *möm'at* 'his/her grandchildren'.
5. = *umùukway,* object form of *umùukwa* 'your (plural) grandfather'.
6. *uuyi'at* 'his planted plants'.
7. *kuwan'ewsoniwa* 'look invigorated'.

Your grandfather's planted field looks invigorated.

This song is a fragment of Song 105.

107. Angaktsìntawi₁
(List 11452, Tracks 6–7)

Itam₂ pew₃ yuuyahiwa.₄
Itam öki.₅
"Kwakwháy₆ uma₇ öki."
Uma yep,₈
kitotat'a.₉
itanamu,₁₀
hahlaytiq'ö,₁₁
itamuy₁₂ na'qalaq'ö,₁₃
oomaw₁₄ kuukuyivani,₁₅
taawanawita.₁₆
Lee lehe la.
Yuuyahiwa.
Tukwunangwmanatu₁₇ qöya'omawuy₁₈ naasomta.₁₉

1. *angaktsìntawi* 'Long-Hair katsina song'.
2. *itam* 'we'.
3. *pew* 'toward here, coming this way'.
4. *yuuyahiwa* 'have been dressed as for a ceremony, be adorned (plural)'.
5. *öki* 'arrive, come (plural)'.
6. *kwakwáy* 'thank you' (male speaker).
7. *uma* 'you (plural)'.
8. *yep* 'here'.
9. *kitotat'a*, pausal form of *kitotat* 'after saying [this] (plural)'.
10. = *itanam* 'our fathers'.
11. = *hàalàytiqw'ö*, subordinate clause pausal form of *hàalàyti* 'become happy'.
12. *itamuy* 'us', object form of *itam* 'we'.
13. = *na'qalaqw'ö*, subordinate clause pausal form of *na'qala* 'encourage, hearten each other'.
14. = *oo'omawt* 'clouds'. (*Oomaw*, as in the song, is the singular form but the plural verb *kuukuyvani* (next note) shows that the plural meaning is intended.)
15. = *kuukuyvani* 'will appear, will make their appearance, will come into view (plural)'.
16. = *taawanawit* 'all day long'.
17. = *tukwunangwmamant* 'cumulus cloud maidens'.
18. *qöya'omawuy*, object form of *qöya'omaw* 'white cloud'.
19. *naasomta* 'wear tied on the side of the head'.

I'omaw'inakwa,[20]
pew yooki'i.[21]
Oho oho wa aha ii aa'haa.

We have been adorned to come here.
We came.
"Thank you for coming."
You that are here,
after saying this,
our fathers,
you became happy,
and after we have heartened each other,
the clouds will make their appearance
all day long.
(Vocables.)
They are adorned.
The cumulus cloud maidens are wearing white clouds tied on the sides of
    their heads.
[You] down feathers worn on my head,
come and rain.
(Vocables.)

The katsinas describe how they have been adorned, implicitly with the people's prayers, although this is unsaid, and, in return for these prayers, they have come to the villages. The katsinas then speak as though they are the people: "Thank you for coming," say the people to the katsinas. The katsinas then revert back to speaking for themselves, observing that the fathers of the village are happy that they have come. The katsinas' remark that they and people "hearten each other" describes the reciprocal relationship between the katsinas and the people. The katsinas were heartened by the people's prayers and efforts to live right and, for their part, they have come as rain, for which the people have given their thanks. The katsinas promise to make their appearance as clouds all day long, implying that it will rain throughout the day.

   After some vocables, the katsinas comment in a third party way on how the cumulus clouds, referred to using the maiden metaphor, are wear-

20. *i'omaw'inakwa* 'the down feathers worn on my head'.
21. *yooki'i,* imperative of *yooki* 'rain'.

ing white clouds tied on the sides of their heads. This likens the hairbuns (*naasomi*) worn by prepubescent girls on the sides of their heads to the white clouds that make their appearance and build into the dark thunderheads. Both young girls and rain-bearing clouds are in the formative stages of producing life; metaphorically they are pregnant with the promise of future life. The katsinas close with a likening of themselves to the down feathers on the tops of their heads that are also signs of clouds moving and building in preparation for rain. The *naasomi* hairstyle and the down feather headdresses are both metaphorical clouds. The final line, rain here, *pew yooki'i,* is an imperative to the clouds to come as rain.

108. *Angaktsìntawi*$_1$
(List 11452, Track 13)

Uma$_2$ tsootsonglawkyang$_3$ uma naawakinaya.$_4$
Uma oo'omawutuy$_5$ uma wuuwankyang$_6$ uma tsootsong.ya,$_7$
ínamu.$_8$
Lee lehe la.
Itam$_9$ hapi$_{10}$ túwati$_{11}$ pew$_{12}$ umumi$_{13}$ yookinawisa.$_{14}$
Umu'uyiy$_{15}$ ang$_{16}$ paatalawvaqö'ö,$_{17}$

1. *angaktsìntawi* 'Long-Hair katsina song'.
2. *uma* 'you (plural)'.
3. = *tsootsonglawkyàakyangw* 'while keeping on smoking (tobacco) (plural)'.
4. = *naanawakna* 'pray, want (plural)'.
5. = *oo'omàwtuy,* object form of *oo'omawt* 'clouds'.
6. = *wuuwankyàakyangw* 'while thinking, focusing on (plural)'.
7. *tsootsong.ya* 'be smoking (tobacco) (plural)'.
8. = *inam* 'my fathers'.
9. *itam* 'we'.
10. *hapi* 'truly, surely, certainly'.
11. = *tuwat* 'in turn, for one's part'.
12. *pew* 'toward here, coming this way'.
13. *umumi* 'to you (plural)'.
14. = *yoknawisa* 'go/come to make it rain (plural)'.
15. = *umùu'uyiy,* object form of *umùu'uyi* 'your (plural) planted plants, planted fields'.
16. *ang* 'along it/them'.
17. = *paatalawvaqw'ö,* subordinate clause pausal form of *paatalawva* 'come to glisten with water'.

putakw[18] *puma*[19] *ang oomi*[20] *naawungwinani.*[21]
Wiiya ahiya hiina.

While you keep on smoking, you are praying.
While you are focusing your thoughts on the clouds, you are smoking,
my fathers.
(Vocables.)
Truly for our part we are coming to make it rain for you.
Along your planted fields when it begins to glisten with water,
using that, they will make themselves grow upward along there.
(Vocables.)

The katsinas observe that the fathers are praying while they are smoking; they are doing this continually, thinking of the clouds that they hope will come. The smoke from their pipes is likened to clouds, the object of their prayers. In return, in the basic reciprocal relationship between the katsinas and the people, the katsinas, for their part, *tuwat,* promise to come to make it rain, *yoknawisa.* They close by saying that after they make the planted fields glisten with water, that is, after a soaking rain makes puddles in the fields, the plants, as animate beings, will use this water to raise themselves up.

109. *Angaktsìntawi*[1]
(List 11457, Track 2)

Patangsimanatuy[2] *naawakinaya.*[3]
Ayo'o,[4]
hoopo[5] *kiinasami'i.*[6]

18. *putakw* 'with that, by means of that, using that'.
19. *puma* 'they'.
20. *oomi* 'upward'.
21. = *naawungwnayani* 'will make selves grow'.

1. *angaktsìntawi* 'Long-Hair katsina song'.
2. = *patangsimamàntuy,* object form of *patangsimamant* 'squash blossom maidens'.
3. = *naanawakna* 'pray, want (plural)'.
4. *ayo'o,* pausal form of *ayó'* 'toward over there'.
5. *hoopo* 'to the northeast'.
6. *kiinasami'i,* pausal form of *kiinasami* 'to the middle of where people live'.

tuvevakwamongwitu₇ itamuy₈ naawakinaq'ö,₉
angq₁₀ itam₁₁ hahlaykyang₁₂ umumi₁₃ pew₁₄ tiiti'ökiwa.₁₅
Lee lehe la.
Oovi₁₆ úma'a,₁₇
yephaqamo₁₈ umuu'unangvaasiy₁₉ sunsayaqö'ö,₂₀
taavangq₂₁ yooyang₂₂ hoyoyotani.₂₃
Umuu'uyinawit₂₄ yang₂₅ paatalawvaqö'ö,₂₆
ang₂₇ uma₂₈ hahlaykyang₂₉ taatawtimani.₃₀
Awiha hini ya'ahini ya in yoowina in yoowina.
In yoowina, in yaw yooy yoowina.
Hapi me.₃₁
Mookwa₃₂ qaa'ö₃₃ íngu'u.₃₄
Uma yep₃₅ umuu'unangvaasiy sunsayaqö'ö,

7. = *tuvevakwamomngwit* 'toad leaders of various colors'.
8. *itamuy* 'us', object form of *itam* 'we'.
9. = *naawaknaqw'ö*, subordinate clause pausal form of *naawakna* 'pray, want'.
10. = *angqw* 'from it, from there'.
11. *itam* 'we'.
12. = *hàalaykyangw* 'while being happy, happily'.
13. *umumi* 'to you (plural)'.
14. *pew* 'toward here, coming this way'.
15. *tiiti'ökiwa* 'have come in dance (and thereby to soothe)'.
16. *oovi* 'that's why'.
17. *úma'a*, pausal form of *uma* 'you (plural)'.
18. = *yephaqam* 'approximately here'.
19. = *umùu'unangwvàasiy*, object form of *umùu'unangwvàasi* 'your (plural) heartfelt hope, prayer'.
20. = *sunsayaqw'ö*, subordinate clause pausal form of *sunsaya*, 'be in harmony (plural)'.
21. = *taavangqw* 'from the southwest'.
22. = *yooyangw* 'rain'.
23. *hoyoyotani* 'will be moving'.
24. = *umùu'uynawit* 'along your (plural) planted fields'.
25. *yang* 'along here, in this area'.
26. = *paatalawvaqw'ö*, subordinate clause pausal form of *paatalawva* 'come to glisten with water'.
27. *ang* 'along it, along there, in that area, in several places'.
28. *uma* 'you (plural)'.
29. = *hàalaykyangw* 'while being happy, happily'.
30. *taatawtimani* 'will go along singing'.
31. *hapi me*, formulaic expression introducing the song's second part, *oomi* 'upward'.
32. *mookwa* 'double-headed ear of corn'.
33. *qaa'ö* 'corn, dry ear(s) of corn'.
34. *íngu'u*, pausal form of *íngu* 'my mother'.
35. *yep* 'here'.

taavangq yooyang hoyoyota,$_{36}$
péwi'i,$_{37}$
umuu'uyiy$_{38}$ *ang yookinayani.*$_{39}$
Lee lehe la.

[They] are praying for squash blossom maidens.
Over there,
to the northeast, to the middle of where the people live.
the toad leaders of various colors prayed for us [to come],
so we have come in dance from there happily for you.
(Vocables.)
That's why when you
bring your heartfelt prayers into harmony,
the rain will be moving from the southwest.
It will become glistening with water along your planted fields here
and along there you will go along singing happily.
(Vocables.)
Listen, there is more.
The double-headed ear of corn is my mother.
When you are in harmony here in your heartfelt prayers,
the rain will be moving from the southwest,
coming this way,
and will make it rain along your planted fields.
(Vocables.)

It appears that the opening vocables and lines of this song are missing. The extant segment begins with the katsinas' observation that the people are praying for the squash blossom maidens to come, meaning that they want the squash plants to blossom. The toad leaders of various colors, speaking for all the creatures of the earth, have also prayed for the squash blossom maidens to come. So, say the katsinas, in response to your (the people's) prayers, we have come happily in dance for you. They remind the people that when they unite their prayers in heartfelt harmony, the rains will come from the southwest, making the land and the plants glisten

36. *hoyoyota* 'be moving'.
37. = *pew'i,* pausal form of *pew* 'toward here, coming this way'.
38. = *umùu'uyiy,* object form of *umùu'uyi* 'your (plural) plants'.
39. = *yoknayani* 'will make it rain (plural)'.

so that the people will be prompted to walk about their fields singing happily.

Then, in the second section of the song, the katsinas refer to a double-headed ear of corn (*mookwa*), a reference to two ears of corn that develop from a single stem. The joined-at-the-base feature may be a metaphorical reference for the need for people to have their hearts joined together, that is, everyone must be united in purpose and activity in order to maintain communal harmony and to deserve the gifts of the katsinas. This communal lifeway requires everyone to accept the burden of participating in activities that contribute to the well-being of the community. The mention of the double-headed corn may also be a reference to twins and their special powers, making this a suggestion from the katsinas that special powers of this sort are needed to revitalize the people. Again the katsinas remind the people to pray in heartfelt togetherness and, when they do, the rain will move from the southwest along their planted fields.

110. *Angaktsìntawi₁*
(List 11457, Track 6)

Aahaha iihiihi aahaha iihiihi.₂
Haa'o₃ haaw₄ ínamu,₅
sakwavahomongwitu.₆
Tokilayu₇ ahsa'₈ taalawvaqö'ö,₉
sakwavahoy₁₀ yuwasinaq'ö,₁₁

1. *angaktsìntawi* 'Long-Hair katsina song'.
2. This string of vocables belongs to the Long-Hair katsinas.
3. *haa'o*, vocative particle.
4. *haaw*, vocative particle.
5. = *inam* 'my fathers'.
6. = *sakwavahomomngwit* 'blue/green prayer feather leaders' (pl. of *sakwavahomongwi*).
7. = *tokilay*, short for *umùutokilay*, object form of *umùutokila* 'your (plural) set date, the date that you set'.
8. = *àasa'* 'as much, many as, enough'.
9. = *taalawvaqw'ö*, subordinate clause pausal form of *taalawva* 'dawn, become light, a new day', here used in the sense of passing a day.
10. *sakwavahoy*, short for *umùusakwavahoy*, object form of *umùusakwavaho* 'your blue/green prayer feathers'.
11. = *yuwsinaqw'ö*, subordinate clause pausal form of *yuwsina* 'clothe, adorn'.

pu'$_{12}$ túwati,$_{13}$
taaha'am$_{14}$ paakwa$_{15}$ itamuy$_{16}$ paahovenaya.$_{17}$
Lee lehe la.

(Vocables.)
Hark, o my fathers,
[you] blue/green prayer feather leaders.
Enough days have dawned to reach the date you set,
you have adorned your blue/green prayer feathers,
now, for your part,
you and their maternal uncle, the toad, mark us with prayer feathers.
(Vocables.)

This song describes some of the traditional ritual activities that take place during a performance. The katsinas, addressing the fathers as blue/green prayer feather leaders, tell them that the time that has been set has arrived and describe how the leaders, as well as the toad, the maternal uncle of all natural creatures, mark them with the blue/green prayer feathers, that is, infuse them with the prayers of all.

111. *Hehey'akatsìntawi$_1$*
(List 11453, Track 8)

Hii niniyay'a.
Haw'o$_2$ haaw$_3$ haaw ínamu.$_4$
Haw'o haaw haaw íngumu.$_5$

12. *pu'* 'now, then'.
13. = *tuwat* 'in turn, for (one's) part'.
14. *taaha'am* 'their maternal uncle'.
15. *paakwa* 'toad'.
16. *itamuy* 'us', object form of *itam* 'we'.
17. = *pahovenaya* 'mark (as, with) prayer feathers (plural)'.
1. *hehey'akatsìntawi* 'Hehey'a katsina song'.
2. *haw'o,* vocative particle.
3. *haaw,* vocative particle.
4. = *inam* 'my fathers'.
5. = *ingum* 'my mothers'.

Paypi núwupi₆ umuhtuwaniy₇ aw₈ pitu.₉
Itam₁₀ naanakwusani,₁₁
umuhpahoyu₁₂ itamuyu₁₃ yuuwasinaq'ö.₁₄
Ítamu₁₅ pankyang₁₆ naanan'ivo'o,₁₇
umuulavayiy₁₈ tuu'awvaqö'ö,₁₉
puma₂₀ yang₂₁ uuyisonaq₂₂ yang yooyoktivakyang₂₃ paavataalawiyungni.₂₄
Yaahinay'o.₂₅
Pu'₂₆ uma₂₇ yephaqam₂₈ inumi₂₉ naawakinaq'ö,₃₀
wuyomihaqami₃₁ umuhqatsiyu₃₂ naavokyawintani,₃₃
yépe'e.₃₄
Pu' uma yephaqam inumi naawakinaq'ö,
wuyomihaqami umuhqatsiyu naavokyawintani,
yépe'e.
Anii ii hii'ii.
Aahaa iihii aa'aya hi'aa.

6. *paypi núwupi* 'of necessity, it can't be helped, it's inevitable'.
7. = *umùutuwaniy*, object form of *umùutuwani* 'your (plural) set time, the time that you set'.
8. *aw* 'to it, to there'.
9. *pitu* 'arrive, come, get there, reach a destination'.
10. *itam* 'we'.
11. = *nànkwusani* 'will start on a journey (plural)'.
12. = *umùupahoy*, object form of *umùupaho* 'your (plural) prayer feathers'.
13. = *itamuy* 'us', object form of *itam* 'we'.
14. = *yuwsinaqw'ö*, subordinate clause pausal form of *yuwsina* 'clothe'.
15. = *itam* 'we'.
16. = *pankyangw* 'while being that way'.
17. *naanan'ivo'o*, pausal form of *naanan'ivo* 'to the different directions around'.
18. = *umùulavayiy*, object form of *umùulavayi* 'your (plural) speech, words'.
19. = *tuu'awvaqw'ö*, subordinate clause pausal form of *tuu'awva* 'come with a message'.
20. *puma* 'they'.
21. *yang* 'along here, in this area'.
22. = *uysonaq* 'throughout the midst of the planted area(s)'.
23. = *yooyoktivakyangw* 'while beginning to rain repeatedly'.
24. = *paavatalawyungwni* 'will be glistening with puddles in several places'.
25. *yaahinay'o*, a vocable of the Hehey'a katsinas.
26. *pu'* 'now, then'.
27. *uma* 'you (plural)'.
28. *yephaqam* 'approximately here, around here somewhere'.
29. *inumi* 'to me'.
30. = *naawaknaqw*, subordinate clause form of *naawakna* 'pray, want'.
31. *wuyomihaqami* 'all the way towards old age'.
32. = *umùuqatsiy*, object form of *umùuqatsi* 'your lives'.
33. *naavokyawintani* 'there will be enjoyment to the fullest'.
34. = *ep'e*, pausal form of *ep* 'there, at it'.

Aahiiniya hiiniyaa.

(Vocables.)
Hark, hark, o my fathers.
Hark, hark, o my mothers.
As it had to be, it has come to the time you set.
We will set out on our journey,
when you have adorned us with your prayer feathers.
When we go to all the directions in that way,
and we bring messages of your words,
they will begin to rain in the midst of the planted fields along here, as
    they make it glisten with puddles of water all over.
(Vocable.)
Now when you pray to me here,
there will be enjoyment of your lives towards old age
here.
Now when you pray to me here,
there will be enjoyment of your lives towards old age
here.
(Vocables.)

This is the last song of the day. The katsinas, speaking to the fathers and
mothers, announce (*paypi núwupi*) that the time has come for them to
return to their katsina homes. As a practical matter the last dance and their
departure usually occurs when the sun starts to descend below the rooftops. The katsinas say they will start out on their journey back home after
they have been invested with the prayer feathers, that is, with the people's
final prayers. This occurs at the end of the last dance when the katsinas
form a line facing the plaza and receive prayer feathers and a pinch of
cornmeal from the katsina father. Then they turn and file out of the plaza
along the consecrated path. The katsinas promise that they will take the
people's messages, that is, their prayers, with them to all the directions,
that is, to their katsina homes in the four cardinal directions. Then, in
answer to the prayers, they will come and rain throughout the planted
fields, making them glisten with puddles of rainwater. The katsinas then
twice repeat the reciprocal relationship between themselves and the
people. Pray to us, and when you do, our gifts will help you live to an old
age fulfilled with health, happiness, and freedom from want and suffering.

112. Hemiskatsìntawi*1*
(List 11457, Track 8)

Aaha iihi, aaha iihi.
*Sonway*2 *taalawkuyiva,*3
*ayaaqö.*4
*Ayángq*5 *hoopaq*6 *síqöyavunit,*7 *sikyavunit*8 *taalawkuyiva.*
*Angq*9 *itam[ungem]*10 *tawamanat*11 *pöhtaviwaqö'ö,*12
*put*13 *itam ánawit*14 *ina'amangwuy*15 *uuyimanatuy*16 *pew*17 *umungem*18
    *wiikivaniwa,*19
*tivongyapami'i.*20
Aaha iihi.
Me aa ahay a. (repeat)
Ahaya'a.
Aaha iihiihi.
Aaha iihi hiya.

(Vocables of the sound of singing.)
The beautiful day made its appearance,
from over there.

1. *hemiskatsìntawi* 'Hemiskatsina song'.
2. *sonway* 'beautiful'.
3. = *taalawkuyva* 'for daylignt to make its appearance'.
4. = *ayángqw* 'from over there'.
5. = *ayángqw* 'from over there'.
6. = *hoopaqw* 'from the northeast'.
7. *síqöyavunit* 'in adorned white', adverbial form of *síqöyavuni* 'the adorned white one'.
8. *sikyavunit* 'in yellow', adverbial form of *sikyavuni* 'the yellow one'.
9. = *angqw* 'from it, from there'.
10. *itamungem* 'for us, for our benefit'.
11. = *tawamanawt*, object form of *tawamanaw* 'oriole'.
12. = *pöötaviwaqw'ö*, subordinate clause pausal form of *pöötaviwa* 'be laid out as a consecrated path'.
13. *put*, object form of *pam* 'that, that one, he, she, it'.
14. *ánawit* 'along its course'.
15. = *ina'mangwuy*, object form of *ina'mangwu* 'my katsina-brought gift(s)'.
16. = *uuyimamàntuy*, object form of *uuyimamant* 'plant maidens'.
17. *pew* 'toward here, coming this way'.
18. *umungem* 'for you (plural), for your benefit'.
19. = *wikvaniwa* 'have brought'.
20. *tivongyapami'i*, pausal form of *tivongyapami* 'to the dance-display place'.

From the northeast over there, the day made its appearance in adorned
    white and in yellow.
From there, when the consecrated oriole [feather] path was laid out for us,
along that we have brought here for you our gifts, the plant maidens,
to the dance-display place.
(Vocables of the sound of singing.)

This song describes events that take place in the early morning hours prior
to the first dance at *Nimàntikive,* the Home dance. The katsinas observe
that when they first arrived, a beautiful day had just made its appearance
from the northeast in white and yellow. These colors describe how the
light of dawn comes first in white and then in yellow, as the sky takes on
the color of a new day. The implication is that the new day brings new
life.

    In these early morning hours before anyone is stirring, the katsinas
have entered the plaza along a path made of consecrated cornmeal. Sometimes the path is also embellished with pollen or colorful feathers; the
yellow color of the oriole is mentioned here, perhaps to allude to the sun
and the coming of a new day. The katsinas bring armloads of green cornstalks with the ears still attached and they literally cover the plaza with
this largess. These corn plants, referred to here as their plant maidens,
uuyimamant, with their ears still attached (also referred to as 'wrapped
children' in Song 101) represent their gift burden which they bring in
return for the people's heartfelt prayers and right living. The green corn
harvested at this time is only a sign of the bountiful harvest to come, for
most of the corn is harvested in the fall when it is picked as dried ears that
are husked and stacked for storage.

113. *Hemiskatsìntawi$_1$*
(List 11460, Track 6)

*Hahlay'unangway$_2$ taalawkuyiva,$_3$
ayangqö.$_4$*

---

1. *hemiskatsìntawi* 'Hemiskatsina song'.
2. = *hàalay'unangway* 'with a happy heart, with beneficent intentions'.
3. = *taalawkuyva* 'for daylight to make its appearance'.
4. = *ayángqw* 'from over there'.

Ayángq₅ hoopaq₆ qöyawunuhqa₇ sikyangwuhntaalawkuyiva.₈
Angq₉ itangem₁₀ tawamanaw₁₁ pöhtaviwaqö'ö,₁₂
put₁₃ itam₁₄ ánawit₁₅ itana'mangwuy₁₆ uuyimanatuy₁₇ umungem₁₈ wiiki-
    vaniwa,₁₉
tivongyapami'i.₂₀
Aahaa iihii.
Pew₂₁ yoyhoyoyotani,₂₂
pew.
Aayahiy'a.
Ahaay aa.
Hiy'a aa iihi iihi.

With a happy heart, the day has made its appearance,
from over there.
From over in the northeast the white dawn has made its appearance as
    yellow dawn.
From over there the consecrated path has been laid out with the oriole
    [feathers] for us,
and along that we have brought along our gifts for you, the plant maidens,
to the dance-display place.
(Vocables of the sound of singing.)
Rain will be moving this way,
coming this way.

5. = *ayángqw* 'from over there'.
6. = *hoopaqw* 'from the northeast'.
7. = *qöyawunùuqa* 'one that stands as white, white dawn'.
8. = *sikyangwùntalawkuyva* 'for daylight to make its appearance as yellow dawn'.
9. = *angqw* 'from it, from there'.
10. = *itamungem* 'for us, for our benefit'.
11. *tawamanaw* 'oriole'.
12. = *pöötaviwaqw'ö*, subordinate clause pausal form of *pöötaviwa* 'be laid out as a conse-
    crated path'.
13. *put,* object form of *pam* 'that, that one, he, she, it'.
14. *itam* 'we'.
15. *ánawit* 'along its course'.
16. = *itàana'mangwuy*, object form of *itàana'mangwu* 'our gifts brought by the katsinas'.
17. *uuyimamàntuy*, object form of *uuyimamant* 'plant maidens'.
18. *umungem* 'for you (plural), for your benefit'.
19. = *wikvaniwa* 'have brought'.
20. *tivongyapami'i,* pausal form of *tivongyapami* 'to the dance-display place'.
21. *pew* 'toward here, coming this way'.
22. *yoyhoyoyotani* 'will be moving as rain'.

(Vocables of the sound of singing.)

This is a variant of Song 112, with differences in the opening lines. In this version the katsinas sing that the day has dawned with a happy heart, again making the day animate with life. At the end of the song the katsinas assure the people that rain will be moving this way for you, that is, to the people's fields.

114. *Hemiskatsìntawi₁*
(List 11465, Track 9)

Haaya₂ ínamu.₃
"Hoopaq₄ oomakingaqö,₅
"okiw₆ pew₇ yokva,₈
"námura."₉
Yan₁₀ uma₁₁ naawakinaya.₁₂
Hoopaq oongaq₁₃ muunang₁₄ hoyoyotimani,₁₅
yánga'a.₁₆
Paavataalawinani.₁₇
Ahaa iihiiy.
Pew yoyhoyoyotimani,₁₈
yánga'a.

1. *hemiskatsìntawi* 'Hemiskatsina song'.
2. *haaya,* vocative particle.
3. = *inam* 'my fathers'.
4. = *hoopaqw* 'from the northeast'.
5. = *oomàwkingaqw* 'from the dwelling place of the clouds'.
6. *okiw* 'humbly, pitifully'.
7. *pew* 'toward here, coming this way'.
8. *yokva* 'rain' (verb).
9. *námura* 'let it be so'.
10. *yan* 'like this, in this way, thus'.
11. *uma* 'you (plural)'.
12. = *naanawakna* 'pray (plural)'.
13. = *oongaqw* 'from above'.
14. = *muunangw* 'flowing water, runoff water'.
15. *hoyoyotima* 'be moving along'.
16. = *yang'a,* pausal form of *yang* 'here, along here, in these places, in this area'.
17. = *paavatalawnani* 'will make it glisten with puddles of water'.
18. *yoyhoyoyotimani* 'will be moving along as rain'.

*Uuyisonaq*₁₉ *yang*₂₀ *paatalawiyungni.*₂₁
Aaha haa.

Hark my fathers.
"From the northeast cloud dwelling place,
"humbly may it
"come and rain."
So you pray.
From up in the northeast the runoff water will be moving along,
along here.
It will make it glisten with puddles of water.
(Vocables.)
There will be rain moving along,
along here.
In the planted fields along here, it will glisten with water.
(Vocables.)

The katsinas observe that the fathers are praying humbly to the clouds in
their northeast home to come and rain. In response, the katsinas say that
the runoff water will move along, making the land glisten with puddles of
water and the plants in the planted fields glisten with the rainwater.

115. *Hemiskatsìntawi*₁
(List 11451, Tracks 5, 6, 7)

*Haw*₂ *ínamu.*₃
*Paahoy*₄ *tuutuvenaya.*₅
"*Okiw*₆ *pew*₇ *yookva,*₈

---

19. = *uysonaq* 'throughout the midst of the planted area(s)'.
20. *yang* 'along here, in this area'.
21. = *paatalawyungwni* 'will glisten with water in several places'.
1. *hemiskatsìntawi* 'Hemiskatsina song'.
2. *haw,* vocative particle.
3. = *inam* 'my fathers'.
4. *paahoy,* short for *umùupahoy,* object form of *umùupaho* 'your prayer feathers'.
5. = *tutuvèntota* 'make many marks (plural)'.
6. *okiw* 'humbly, pitifully'.
7. *pew* 'toward here, coming this way'.
8. = *yokva* 'rain' (verb).

"námusa."$_9$
Yan$_{10}$ uma$_{11}$ naawakinaya.$_{12}$
Hoopaq$_{13}$ oongaq$_{14}$ muunang$_{15}$ hoyoyotimani,$_{16}$
yánga'a.$_{17}$
Paavataalawinani.$_{18}$
Mee, aha, haa.
Pew yoyhoyoyotimani,$_{19}$
yánga'a.
Uuyisonaq$_{20}$ yang$_{21}$ paavataalawiyungni.$_{22}$

Hark my fathers.
You have marked your prayer feathers.
"Humbly may it come and rain,
"let it be so."
So you pray.
From up in the northeast the runoff water will be moving along,
along here.
It will make it glisten with puddles of water.
(Vocables.)
There will be rain moving along,
along here.
In the planted fields along here, it will glisten with puddles of water.

This song differs only slightly from Song 114. Here, instead of quoting the father's prayers asking for rain from the northeast, the katsinas observe that the fathers have marked their prayer feathers, meaning that they have infused them with their prayers for rain.

9. *námusa* 'let it be so'.
10. *yan* 'like this, in this way, thus'.
11. *uma* 'you (plural)'.
12. = *naanawakna* 'pray (plural)'.
13. = *hoopaqw* 'from the northeast'.
14. = *oongaqw* 'from above'.
15. = *muunangw* 'flowing water, runoff water'.
16. *hoyoyotimani* 'will be moving along'.
17. = *yang'a*, pausal form of *yang* 'here, along here, in these places, in this area'.
18. = *paavatalawinani* 'will make it glisten with puddles of water'.
19. *yoyhoyoyotimani* 'will be moving along as rain'.
20. = *uysonaq* 'throughout the midst of the planted area(s)'.
21. *yang* 'along here, in this area'.
22. = *paavatalawyungwni* 'will glisten with puddles of water in several places'.

116. Honànkatsìntawi$_1$
(List 11462, Track 8)

Ha'o$_2$ ínamu,$_3$ íngumu.$_4$
Ha'o ha'o ínamu, íngumu.
Ayám$_5$ tatkya'a,$_6$
Honanpave'e,$_7$
Honanwuhtaqa,$_8$
tiw'aymuyu$_9$ yuuwasinat'a,$_{10}$
angq$_{11}$ pew$_{12}$ umumi$_{13}$ tiiti'ayalawu,$_{14}$
péwi'i.$_{15}$
Aha haa.
Haa'aahay'aa ooway ee'elo, aaha.
Hay'i yayo.
Hay'i yayo.

Hark my fathers, my mothers.
Hark, o my fathers, my mothers.
Over there in the southeast,
at Badger Spring,
Old Man Badger,
after having clothed his nephews,
is bidding them (to come) from there to do a ritual performance for you,
coming this way.
(Vocables.)

1. honànkatsìntawi 'Badger katsina song'.
2. ha'o, vocative particle.
3. =inam 'my fathers'.
4. = ingum 'my mothers'.
5. ayám 'over there'.
6. tatkya'a, pausal form of tatkya 'in the southeast'.
7. = Honànpave'e, pausal form of Honànpave 'at Badger Spring'.
8. = Honanwùutaqa 'Old Man Badger'.
9. = tiw'aymuy, object form of tiw'aymat 'his nephews, nieces'. A tiw'aya is a man's
   sister's child or a person of his clan or phratry one generation younger.
10. = yuwsinat'a, pausal form of yuwsinat 'after dressing, clothing'.
11. = angqw 'from it, from there'.
12. pew 'toward here, coming this way'.
13. umumi 'to you (plural)'.
14. tiiti'ayalawu 'be bidding others to perform'.
15. = pew'i, pausal form of pew 'toward here, coming this way'.

The katsinas are calling the attention of the fathers and mothers of the village to Old Man Badger who is at his home at Badger Spring in the southeast direction (*tatkya*). As maternal uncle, Old Man Badger is advising his nephews of their obligations, one of which, since they are katsinas, is to take gifts to the people in return for their right living. This song describes how Old Man Badger adorns these katsinas with the good things of life and then sends them off to perform at the village.

117. *Koyemsiyungtawi*$_1$
(List 11462, Track 13)

Aha ihíi.
Itam,$_2$
itam yuuyahiwa,$_3$
ayamo.$_4$
Itam,
itam yuuyahiwa,
ayamo.
Ayám$_5$ *atkya*$_6$ *Palatkwape*$_7$ *itangum*$_8$ *itamuy*$_9$ *yuuwasina.*$_{10}$
Aha ihii.
Pew$_{11}$ *umumi*$_{12}$ *yoyhani;*$_{13}$
hani.$_{14}$
Pew umumi yoyhani;
hani.

1. *koyemsiyungtawi* 'Mudhead katsina entering song'.
2. *itam* 'we'.
3. *yuuyahiwa* 'have been dressed as for a ceremony, adorned (plural)'.
4. = *ayám* 'over there'.
5. *ayám* 'over there'.
6. *atkya* 'down, down there, down below'.
7. *Palatkwape* 'at *Palatkwapi*, the Red-Walled City'.
8. *itangum* 'our mothers'.
9. *itamuy* 'us', object form of *itam* 'we'.
10. = *yuwsina* 'dress, clothe, adorn'.
11. *pew* 'toward here, coming this way'.
12. *umumi* 'to you (plural)'.
13. *yoyhani* 'descend as rain'.
14. = *haani* 'descend (plural)'.

Haqami₁₅ yang₁₆ uysonaq₁₇ paatotiq₁₈ paavakt₁₉ töökiyuuyuwintani.₂₀
Aha iihi.
Pew umumi yoyhani,
hani,
pew umumi yoyhani,
hani.
Haqami yang uysonaq paatotiq paavakt töökiyuuyuwintani
"Waaq waaq,"
kitotani.₂₁
Uma'ay aha ihii.

(Vocables.)
We,
we have been adorned,
over there.
We,
we have been adorned,
over there.
Over there down at Palatkwapi our mothers adorned us.
(Vocables.)
Coming this way, we descend as rain for you;
we descend.
Coming this way, we descend as rain for you;
we descend.
Throughout the midst of the planted fields when puddles form, the toads
   will be dancing as they make their cries.
(Vocables.)
Coming thisway, we descend as rain for you;
we descend.
Coming this way, we descend as rain for you;
we descend.

15. = *aqwhaqami* 'throughout'.
16. *yang* 'along here, in this area'.
17. *uysonaq* 'throughout the midst of the planted area(s)'.
18. = *paatotiqw*, subordinate clause form of *paatoti* 'for puddles to form, as from the rain'.
19. = *paavakwt* 'toads'.
20. = *töökiyuyuwintani* 'will be dancing while making characteristic calls'.
21. *kitotani* 'will say (plural)'.

Throughout the midst of the planted fields when puddles form, the toads
will be dancing as they make their cries.
"*Waaq, waaq,*"
they will say.
(Vocables.)

The Mudhead katsinas, the *Kookoyemsim,* sing this song as they are
coming down the ladder into the kiva and taking their places in the dance
line during a winter night dance. They describe how their mothers, that is,
their people mothers, adorned them with prayers over there (*ayám*) down
(*atkya*) at *Palatkwapi*, the "Red-Walled City." *Palatkwapi* is not an actual
site, but refers to the many places to the southwest of the Hopi mesas
where peoples who were to become the Hopis lived before they arrived
at their current homes. In return for the people's prayers, the Mudheads
say they are descending as rain throughout the planted fields. They remark
that when the puddles are formed by the rain, the toads will be making
their cries of happiness. The toads here stand for all creatures that depend
on water for life. In their emergence from the ground after a rain, they are
metaphors for the appearance of all new life that blooms and gains vitality
after a rain. The song ends with vocables that mimic the cries of the toads.

118. *Palhikwmanàwyat₁ Taawi'am₂*
(List 11467, Track 17)

Ókiwa,₃ ókiwa, hákimu.₄
Ókiwa, ókiwa, nuu'u.₅
Pay₆ nu'₇ okiw₈ yan'eway₉ Kohkyahngtiyoniikyango,₁₀

1. *Palhikwmanàwyat* 'two little Moisture Drinking Maidens'.
2. *taawi'am* 'their song'.
3. = *okiw* 'humbly, pitifully'.
4. = *hakim* 'some people, who (plural)'.
5. *nuu'u,* pausal form of *nu'* 'I'.
6. *pay,* expressive particle.
7. *nu'* 'I'.
8. *okiw* 'humbly, pitifully'.
9. *yan'eway* 'such as this, like this, being this homely looking'.
10. = *Kòokyàngwtiyoniikyangw* 'while being a Spider Boy'. (The pronunciation of 'Spider
    Boy' as *Kohkyahngtiyo* in the song corresponds to that of the Second Mesa village
    Musangnuvi.)

itahtimuy$_{11}$ *amungem*$_{12}$ *qatsi'nangwat*$_{13}$ *tuyqawvani,*$_{14}$
yépe'e.$_{15}$
Ohoo.
Pu'$_{16}$ *naanan'ivaq*$_{17}$ *pew'i,*$_{18}$
yooyang$_{19}$ *ökini.*$_{20}$
Yang$_{21}$ *haqami*$_{22}$ *tuwapongnawit*$_{23}$ *yang paavönmanatu*$_{24}$ *oomi*$_{25}$ *paatsina-*
   wiyungni.$_{26}$

Poor things, poor things [you] people.
Poor thing, poor thing me.
Though I'm just homely-looking like this, a Spider Boy,
I will attain the will to live for our children,
here.
Then coming from the different directions around,
rain will come.
Along here throughout, along the land, along here the young corn plants
   will be sprouting upward with moisture.

This song is sung while the stage is being set in the kiva for the performance of the two Moisture Drinking Maiden katsinas. Such songs are meant
to entertain the audience. In this song Spider Boy is giving a lesson about
humility. Humility is a necessary element of sincere prayer. If people are
humble and persist in practicing the hard work and reciprocities required
by the corn lifeway, then the rains will come that support growth in both
plants and people. Spider Boy is known to be simple and homely in
person, but strong and determined in living the perfect life toward which

11. = *itàatimuy,* object form of *itàatim* 'our children'.
12. *amungem* 'for them, for their benefit'.
13. *qatsi'nangwat,* object form of *qatsi'nangwa* 'will to live'.
14. *tuyqawvani* 'will attain'.
15. = *ep'e,* pausal form of *ep* 'there, at it'.
16. *pu'* 'now, then'.
17. = *naanan'ivaqw* 'from the different directions around'.
18. *pew'i,* pausal form of *pew* 'toward here, coming this way'.
19. = *yooyangw* 'rain'.
20. *ökini* 'will arrive, come (plural)'.
21. *yang* 'along here, in this area'.
22. = *aqwhaqami* 'throughout'.
23. = *tuuwapongyanawit* 'along the land'.
24. = *paavönmamant* 'young corn plants'.
25. *oomi* 'upward'.
26. *paatsinawyungwni* 'will be sprouting with moisture (plural)'.

all Hopis strive. His actions model the kind of person who works hard and dedicates himself to the well-being of the community.

In this song, Spider Boy speaks to the people, asserting that even though he is plain in appearance, he is strong of character and determined to attain the will to live (*qatsi'nangwat*) for the benefit of the people, here said to be "our children." Here he intends to show people how to live by the moral imperatives that will bring fulfillment to everyone. Implied, but not stated, is the cascade of practices that characterize Hopi life and their relationship with the katsinas—if people live right, work hard and care for others, then the rains will come from all the directions. The rainwater will spread throughout the young corn plants, giving them the vitality so they will sprout upward (*oomi*) with moisture (*paatsinawyungwni*) from the rain.

119. *Qa'ötotimuy₁ (or Ngayayatotaqamuy₂) Taawi'am₃*
(List 11462, Track 5)

Okiwqawilawu,₄
ínamu₅ ayo'o.₆
Aya ha yaa aa hiyay'ami.
Okiwqawilawu,
ínamu ayo'o,
hoopo₇ ikituwunimi'i.₈
Nana'löngöt₉ oomawnaawakinaya.₁₀
Nit aahaaha.

My fathers
are humbly pleading toward over there.

1. *Qa'ötotimuy*, object form of *Qa'ötotim* 'Corn Boys'.
2. *Ngayayatotaqamuy*, object form of *Ngayayatotaqam* 'Those that Sway', a katsina type. This song is appropriate to either katsina type.
3. *taawi'am* 'their song'.
4. = *okiwqawlawu* 'be humbly pleading'.
5. = *inam* 'my fathers'.
6. *ayo'o,* pausal form of *ayó'* 'toward over there'.
7. *hoopo* 'to the northeast'.
8. = *ikituwungwnimi'i,* pausal form of *ikituwungwnimi* 'to my spiritual homeland'.
9. *nana'löngöt,* object form of *nana'löngö* 'of different kinds'.
10. = *oomawnanawakna* 'pray for clouds (plural)'.

(Vocables.)
My fathers
are humbly pleading toward over there,
to the northeast, to my spiritual homeland.
They are praying for clouds of the different kinds.
(Vocables.)

The katsinas observe that the people are persistently and insistently begging, that is, humbly pleading, *okiwqawilawu,* for their prayers to be heard by the clouds in the northeast, here described as "my spiritual homeland" (*ikituwungwni*). The people are praying for clouds of the different kinds, meaning clouds from the different directions.

120. *Qa'ötotimuy₁ Taawi'am₂*
(List 11463, Track 6)

Taalawva.₃
Ítimu₄ havivokyalyat'a,₅
taalawsonmi'i,₆
naawakinaya.₇
Ayaha yaa hi.
Taalawva.
Ítimu havivokyalyat'a,
taalawsonmi'i,
qatsi'nangwat₈ naawakinaya.
Sonway₉ ngumanvöhtaviwaqö'ö,₁₀

1. *Qa'ötotimuy,* object form of *Qa'ötotim* 'Corn Boys'.
2. *taawi'am* 'their song'.
3. *taalawva* 'dawn, become light, a new day'.
4. = *itim* 'my children'.
5. *havivokyalyat'a,* pausal form of *havivokyalyat* 'after (you) become wide awake (plural)'.
6. *taalawsonmi'i,* pausal form of *taalawsonmi* 'toward the center of daylight, of the light of sunrise'.
7. = *naanawakna* 'pray (plural)'.
8. *qatsi'nangwat,* object form of *qatsi'nangwa* 'will to live'.
9. *sonway* 'beautiful'.
10. = *ngumanvöötaviwaqw'ö,* subordinate clause pausal form of *ngumanvöötaviwa* 'be laid out as a path of consecrated cornmeal'.

ánawit₁₁ qaa'ömanatuy₁₂ wiikivaniwa.₁₃
Aa'aha ii'ihii.
[The *töqngwa'at₁₄* is all vocables or in some other language.]
Ayaa hewma . . . .

It has dawned as a new day.
My children, after waking,
go toward the center of the light of sunrise,
[and] pray.
(Vocables.)
It has become a new day.
My children, after waking,
go toward the center of the light of sunrise,
[and] pray for the will to live.
When the beautiful cornmeal path has been laid out [for us],
then along it [we] bring the corn maidens.
(Vocables.)

The Corn Boy katsinas are describing how people, after waking, should face the light of dawn and pray for the will to live (*qatsi'nangwa*), that is, for the determination to live a communal life of sharing and caring. Each new day brings the promise of new life. Morning prayers to the east are a way that Hopis renew their resolve to live right. Although it is not stated in the song, it is traditional practice for boys to run at sunrise. There the Corn Boys may be encouraging the boys to continue this practice. Then they say that when the cornmeal path is laid out for them, that is, when they are invited into the village, they will come bringing the corn maidens. The katsinas are not literally bringing corn but rather are implying that, as a result of their gift of rain, the corn plants will grow and produce the corn that will be sustenance for the people.

11. *ánawit* 'along its course'.
12. = *qa'ömamàntuy,* object form of *qa'ömamant* 'corn maidens'.
13. = *wikvaniwa* 'have brought'.
14. *töqngwa'at* 'its (the song's) "chorus" '.

121. Qa'ötotimuy₁ Taawi'am₂
(List 11463, Track 11)

Aaha.
Ayám₃ hoopaq₄ kiinasave'e,₅
ayám hoopaq kiinasave'e,
nayangvu₆ qa'ömana₇ itamuy,₈
itamuyu₉ naawakinaya.₁₀
Aa hawi'aa aayay.

(Vocable.)
Over there in the northeast, in the middle of where the people live,
over there in the northeast, in the middle of where the people live,
the *nayangvu* corn maidens [pray] to us,
pray to us.
(Vocables.)

The Corn Boy katsinas are saying that over there, in the northeast, corn
maidens are praying to them. The corn maidens who are praying are the
corn plants. Metaphorically they are young girls. They are praying from
a position in the middle of where the people live, a reference to the heart
of the village which is the village plaza when it is consecrated for a
performance.

1. *Qa'ötotimuy,* object form of *Qa'ötotim* 'Corn Boys'.
2. *taawi'am* 'their song'.
3. *ayám* 'over there'.
4. *hoopaq* 'in the northeast'.
5. *kiinasave'e,* pausal form of *kiinasave* 'in the middle of where people live'. This refers to the village and its related farmlands.
6. *nayangvu* is not a recognized word.
7. *qa'ömana* 'corn maiden'. The context would have this be understood as the plural, *qa'ömamant*.
8. *itamuy* 'us', object form of *itam* 'we'.
9. = *itamuy* 'us', object form of *itam* 'we'.
10. = *naanawakna* 'pray (plural)'.

122. Soyohìmkatsinmuy$_1$ Taawi'am$_2$
(List 11451, Track 3)

Naanakwusiwa.$_3$
Ayaqö$_4$ hoopaqö$_5$ Kisiwuvangaqö$_6$ wuuwukmuy$_7$ pöhtapyamuy$_8$ ánawit$_9$
ítamu$_{10}$ umumi$_{11}$ naanakwusa,$_{12}$
péwi'i.$_{13}$
Paatuwvootay$_{14}$ taalawinaya.$_{15}$
Paamotoro$_{16}$ ang$_{17}$ hoohoongivani.$_{18}$
Putak$_{19}$ itam$_{20}$ umumi naanakwusa,
péwi'i.
Yang$_{21}$ pútakwa$_{22}$ námusa$_{23}$ umu'uyi$_{24}$ naawungnayani.$_{25}$
Hay'a.
Yang pútakwa námusa umuu'uymanatu$_{26}$ naatuuksintani.$_{27}$

1. soyohìmkatsinmuy, object form of soyohìmkatsinam 'all kinds of katsinas, mixed katsinas'.
2. taawi'am 'their song'.
3. = nànkwusiwa 'for a journey by several to have begun'.
4. = ayángqw 'from over there'.
5. = hoopaqw 'from the northeast'.
6. = Kisiwvangaqw 'from Shadow Spring'.
7. = wuuwukmuy, object form of wuuwuyom 'elders, old ones'.
8. = pòötaviyamuy, object form of pòötavi'am 'their consecrated path'.
9. ánawit 'along its course'.
10. = itam 'we'.
11. umumi 'to you (plural)'.
12. = nànkwusa 'start out on a journey (plural)'.
13. = pew'i, pausal form of pew 'toward here, coming this way'.
14. paatuwvotay, short for itàapatuwvotay, object form of itàapatuwvota 'our water shields, rings of ripples in water'.
15. = taalawnaya 'make glisten (plural)'.
16. paamotoro 'water pillars, splashes of raindrops'.
17. ang 'along it, along there, in that area, in several places'.
18. = hoohongvani 'will stand up (in several places)'.
19. = putakw 'with that, by means of that, using that'.
20. itam 'we'.
21. yang 'along here, in this area'.
22. = putakw 'with that, by means of that, using that'.
23. námusa 'let it be so' (variant of námura).
24. = umìu'uyi 'your (plural) plants'.
25. = naawungwnayani 'will make selves grow'.
26. = umìu'uyimamant 'your plant maidens'.
27. = naatukwsintani 'will be making selves mature'.

The journey has begun.
From over at Shadow Spring in the northeast, along the elders' conse-
crated path, we have set out on our journey to you,
coming this way.
We make it glisten with our water shields.
The water pillars will repeatedly stand up along there.
With that, we start on our journey to you,
coming this way.
With that, may your plants here make themselves grow.
(Vocable.)
With that, may your plant maidens here be making themselves mature.

The katsinas are making a journey from their home in the northeast at
Shadow Spring. They are along a consecrated path laid by the elders, that
is, a path of prayers from the people. They describe how they are coming
as rain with two vivid images, *paatuwvota*, "water shields," which are the
concentric ripples that result when raindrops hit puddles of water, and
paamotoro, "water pillars," which are the splashes that rebound when
raindrops strike the surface of the puddles. We note here that however
poetic and creative the words *paatuwvota* and *paamotoro* may seem, these
are words of everyday usage. They illustrate the rich metaphoric nature
of everyday speech.

The katsinas say that by means of this rain, the plant maidens will
raise themselves up. The plant maidens are the corn plants; metaphorically
they are the young girls. This song is very similar to Songs 47 and 99.

123. *Tsa'kwaynakatsìntawi*[1]
(List 11452, Track 15)

Nu'[2] *Tsa'kwayna.*
Okiw[3] *nu' yep*[4] *waynuma.*[5]

1. *tsa'kwaynakatsìntawi* 'Tsa'kwayna katsina song'.
2. *nu'* 'I'.
3. *okiw* 'humble, pitiful'.
4. *yep* 'here'.
5. *waynuma* 'be walking around'.

Talsohu$_6$ itana$_7$ nuy$_8$ ayalawu.$_9$
Umuhtuwaqatsiy$_{10}$ nu' ang$_{11}$ taynuma.$_{12}$
Umuhtuwaqatsi$_{13}$ tutuveniwyungwa.$_{14}$
Ta'a$_{15}$ pu$_{16}$ hintani,$_{17}$
itanamuy$_{18}$ lavay'ayamatu?$_{19}$
Pay$_{20}$ nam$_{21}$ yooyokpuva'a,$_{22}$
kawayo,$_{23}$ melooni$_{24}$ aniwitini.$_{25}$
Umuhtimu$_{26}$ nonvaq'ö,$_{27}$
lolmani.$_{28}$
Lii la.
Pi$_{29}$ kur$_{30}$ pas$_{31}$ antsa$_{32}$ ura$_{33}$ yaniwmani.$_{34}$

6. = *Taalawsohu* 'Morning Star'.
7. *itana* 'our father'.
8. *nuy* 'me', object form of *nu'* 'I'.
9. *ayalawu* 'be asking someone to do something'.
10. = *umùutuwaqatsiy,* object form of *umùutuwaqatsi* 'your (plural) land(s)'.
11. *ang* 'along it, along there, in that area, in several places'.
12. *taynuma* 'be looking around'.
13. = *umùutuwaqatsi* 'your (plural) land(s)'.
14. = *tutuven'iwyungwa* 'be marked with lines or notches (plural)'.
15. *ta'a* 'all right'.
16. = *pu'* 'now'.
17. *hintani* 'will be in some way, how will (it) be'.
18. *itanamuy,* object form of *itanam* 'our fathers'.
19. = *lavay'ayamat* 'their spokespeople'.
20. *pay,* expressive particle.
21. *nam,* impersonal hortative particle: 'may it, let it be so'.
22. *yooyokpuva'a,* pausal form of *yooyokpuva* 'along the places where it rains, has rained'.
23. *kawayo* 'watermelon(s)', said to be a First Mesa usage. At Third Mesa, the stand-alone form *kawayo* means 'horse' (from Spanish *caballo*), but in compounds, the combining form *kaway-* stands for *kawayvatnga* 'watermelon' by ellipsis of *-vatnga* (from *patnga* 'squash').
24. *melooni* 'muskmelon(s)'.
25. = *anìwtini* 'will develop, grow'.
26. = *umùutim* 'your (plural) children'.
27. = *noonovaqw'ö,* subordinate clause pausal form of *noonova* 'be eating (plural)'.
28. *lolmani* 'will be beautiful, good, proper'.
29. *pi* 'truly, indeed, as a matter of fact'.
30. *kur,* modal of inference.
31. *pas* 'very'.
32. *antsa* 'truly, really, indeed'.
33. *ura,* modal of recollection: 'as I recall, as you'll recall'.
34. *yaniwmani* 'will be happening this way'.

Namunwanvöhu₃₅ tuuvoyni.₃₆
Maakiw₃₇ úra'i,₃₈
so'tini.₃₉
Mamanhooyamu₄₀ óvekniwuy'u,₄₁
polii'init₄₂ qa₄₃ navoti'ymani.₄₄
Yantaniqat₄₅ itamumi'i,₄₆
itahkwa'a,₄₇
ura tuhtuwutsngwu.₄₈
Ii way hoona.

I am Tsa'kwayna.
I am walking around here feeling humbled.
Our father the Morning Star is asking me to do something.
I am looking around your lands.
Your lands are marked [by erosion].
All right, now, how is it to be,
spokesmen for our fathers?
May it be that in places where it rains,
the watermelon and muskmelon may grow.
When your children eat [them],
it will be good.
(Vocables.)
[But] indeed it must be quite true, as you recall, that things will be happening in this way:

35. = *namunwanvö* 'path for the running of the stone race'.
36. *tuuvoyni* 'will vanish, disappear, get obliterated'.
37. *maakiw* 'the hunt, hunting'.
38. *úra'i,* pausal form of *ura,* modal of recollection.
39. *so'tini* 'will end, will come to an end, will die out'.
40. = *mamanhòoyam* 'little girls'.
41. = *óvekiniwuy'u,* pausal, object form of *óvekniw* 'social outing for unmarried girls and boys after a summer katsina dance'.
42. = *poli'init,* object form of *poli'ini* 'butterfly whorl hairdo'.
43. *qa* 'not'.
44. *navoti'ymani* 'will go along knowing'.
45. *yantaniqat* 'that it would be like this', object form of *yantaniqa* 'one that will/would be this way'.
46. *itamumi'i,* pausal form of *itamumi* 'to us'.
47. = *itàakwa'a,* pausalized form of *itàakwa* 'our grandfather'.
48. = *tùutuwutsngwu,* habitual tense form of *tùutuwutsi* 'tell a story, narrate historical facts, reporting on factual events and experiences'.

The stone-racing path will vanish.
Hunting, as you recall,
will be no more.
The little girls will no longer know
their social outing
or the butterfly whorl hairdo.
That it would be like this for us,
our grandfather,
you'll recall, used to tell in stories.
(Vocables.)

This song of admonition is similar to Song 103 that was recorded by Robert Black, except the last section of the Black song is missing in this version. The Tsa'kwayna katsina is walking about saddened by his observations that the people are no longer practicing traditional activities that insure communal harmony and community survival. He looks at the bare furrows in their lands, comparing these lines of erosion to the grooves of petroglyphs (*tutuveni*) that scar rocks. His description of the land is a metaphor about the moral decay observed within the community.

Tsa'kwayna says that the katsinas' father, Morning Star, has asked him to walk about and observe how the people are departing from the Hopi lifeway. It is probable that Morning Star was chosen to make these observations since this body (the planet Venus) moves through a clearly visible path throughout the year. In Hopi belief, this presence makes Venus one of the celestial bodies that are out and about and able to see how the people are living their lives.

Tsa'kwayna asks the spokesmen for the people what they intend to do about this situation, this abuse of the natural world. At Emergence the people who were to become the Hopis agreed to be stewards of the land. The implication in this song is that this neglect is symbolic of many departures from the traditional lifeway. He engages in wishful thinking, hoping that if the people return to right living, the melons will grow and their children will eat. This is the way life should be. But, discouraged, he describes how people are no longer following traditional practices. The boys are no longer running races to hurry the coming of rain and for this reason the racing path will disappear from non-use. People will no longer hunt. The girls will no longer know how to properly meet boys, because they are no longer participating in culturally sanctioned social outings. They will no longer wear their hair in traditional butterfly whorl style that indicates their readiness for marriage. The katsina closes by warning the people that their grandfather keeps telling stories to them (the katsinas) about how the people's life is going to deteriorate in these ways.

124. Wùutaqkatsìntawi $_1$
(List 11451, Track 9)

Wuhtaqharurutiwa. $_2$
Wuhtiharurutiwa. $_3$
Yanhaqamo $_4$ wuktuvoyla $_5$ ngölökpiy $_6$ ang $_7$ nasiyamuy $_8$ yuuyahiwva, $_9$
umungemi. $_{10}$
Antsa $_{11}$ tuvevolvitsangwa $_{12}$ qa $_{13}$ pam $_{14}$ naavokyawniwa. $_{15}$
Uma $_{16}$ wutimiqsa $_{17}$ nanamunwa, $_{18}$
ókiwa, $_{19}$
tuvevoliwmanatu. $_{20}$
Aw hayna we.
Is $_{21}$ tumso, $_{22}$
is tumso um $_{23}$ nuy $_{24}$ siivutoyayanata 'a, $_{25}$

1. *wùutaqkatsìntawi* 'Old Man katsina song'.
2. = *wùutaqharurutiwa* 'for men to be getting older and older toward ripe old age'.
3. = *wùutiharurutiwa* 'for women to be getting older and older toward ripe old age'.
4. = *yanhaqam* 'in approximately this way'.
5. = *wukwtuvoyla* 'mark of old age'.
6. = *ngölöshoyay,* object form of *ngölöshoya 'am* 'their wooden crook, mark of old age'.
7. *ang* 'along it, along there, in that area, in several places'.
8. *nasiyamuy,* object form of *nasi 'am* 'their adornment'.
9. *yuuyahiwva* 'come dressed, adorned, clothed in (plural)'.
10. = *umungem* 'for you (plural), for your benefit'.
11. *antsa* 'truly, really, indeed'.
12. *tuvevolvitsangwa* 'countenance of butterflies of various colors'.
13. *qa* 'not'.
14. *pam* 'that, that one, he, she, it'.
15. = *naavokyawintiwa* 'for fulfillment to be being enjoyed by all'.
16. *uma* 'you (plural)'.
17. = *wùutimiqsa* 'toward married womanhood only'.
18. *nanamunwa* 'be hurrying as though racing (plural)'.
19. = *okiw* 'humbly, pitifully'.
20. = *tuvevolmamant* 'butterfly maidens of various colors'.
21. *is,* intensifying particle.
22. = *tumsi* 'clanswoman'.
23. *um* 'you'.
24. *nuy* 'me', object form of *nu' * 'I'.
25. = *siivutoynat 'a,* pausal form of *siivutoynat* 'after providing with pottery containers'.

piw₂₆ nuy kuysiptoyanani.₂₇

Men are getting older and older toward ripe old age.
Women are getting older and older toward ripe old age.
In this way the marks of old age have come dressed with their adornment
    on their crook,
for you.
Truly the countenance of butterflies of various colors is not the aim of
    fulfillment.
You are just racing toward becoming married women,
[you] poor things,
[you] butterfly maidens of various colors.
(Vocables.)
Indeed, clanswoman,
indeed, clanswoman, after you provide me with a bowl,
then you will also provide me with a water jar.

This song by Old Man katsina (*Wùutaqkatsina*) addresses the concept of
fulfillment in life and the responsibilities that individuals have along the
way toward old age. For Hopis, fulfillment is to be found throughout
one's life so that one can move toward old age and pass on having
enjoyed health, happiness, and freedom from want and suffering during
all the stages of one's life. He makes reference to the crook, a symbol of
old age. He reminds the people that, in a figurative sense, the crook is
adorned with all the things that bring fulfillment in old age—health,
happiness, freedom from want and strife.

    The katsina reminds the young girls of marriageable age that they are
rushing toward womanhood, flitting about like beautiful colorful butterflies in an effort to find a husband. But, he admonishes, this will not bring
fulfillment. He likens their rush toward marriage to hurrying along as if
in a stone race. In their hurry they will not enjoy their youth, meaning that
they will not enjoy the fulfillment that comes with that stage of their lives.
He reminds them that marriage brings a lifetime of service to family and
clan relatives. As clanswomen (*tumsi*) they will have many responsibilities
that come with their kin, clan, and religious society memberships. These
obligations are symbolized by mention of cooking pots (*siivu*) and storage
containers (*kuysivu*), two basic items in every woman's home that

26. *piw* 'also, too, again'.
27. = *kuysiptoynani* 'will provide with water storage vessels'.

represent some of the specific tasks of cooking for others and putting away food for future use that she must perform daily for her family and others in her community.

125. *Kur Himuwa Katsìntawi₁*
(List 11451, Track 12)

Oheew.
Haw'o₂ sínomu.₃
Haw'o haw₄ sínomu.
Ura₅ hísato,₆
qatsinahuyvaniwq'ö,₇
mongwinahuyvaniwq'ö,₈
ayám₉ atkya₁₀ Palatkwape'e,₁₁
sínomuyu₁₂ Nöngakiwqat₁₃ épe'e,₁₄
humivota₁₅ pasiwtiqö'ö,₁₆
humi'uyit₁₇ unisavat₁₈ pasiwtiqö'ö,

1. *kur himuwa katsìntawi* 'don't-know-which-one katsina song'. The katsina who performed this song has not been identified.
2. *haw'o*, vocative particle.
3. = *sinom* 'people'.
4. *haw*, vocative particle.
5. *ura*, modal of recollection: 'as I recall, as you'll recall'.
6. = *hisat* 'sometime, when, long ago'.
7. = *qatsinahuyvaniwqw'ö*, subordinate clause pausal form of *qatsinahuyvaniwa* 'be choices made in ways of life'.
8. = *mongwinahuyvaniwqw'ö*, subordinate clause pausal form of *mongwinahuyvaniwa* 'be choices made in ways of leadership'.
9. *ayám* 'over there'.
10. *atkya* 'down, down there, down below'.
11. *Palatkwape'e*, pausal form of *Palatkwape* 'at Palatkwapi, the Red-Walled City'.
12. = *sinomuy*, object form of *sinom* 'people'.
13. *Nöngakiwqat*, object form of *Nöngakiwqa* 'the Emergence'.
14. = *ep'e*, pausal form of *ep* 'there, at it'.
15. *humivota* 'coiled plaque for shelled corn'.
16. = *pasìwtiqw'ö*, subordinate clause pausal form of *pasìwti* 'get planned'.
17. *humi'uyit*, object form of *humi'uyi* 'corn plant(s)'.
18. *unisavat*, object form of *unisava* 'of an ideal short length, height'.

i'$_{19}$ hapi$_{20}$ yantaqat$_{21}$ aa'ayawat$_{22}$ mamkiway$_{23}$ ahoy$_{24}$ kuk.wuwayaqö'ö,$_{25}$
i' hapi yantaqat umungem$_{26}$ qatsi'nangwa$_{27}$ pöhtavi$_{28}$ puuhutiwa.$_{29}$
Yan'i.$_{30}$
Yan$_{31}$ hísato umungem qatsi'nangwa pöhtavi puuhutiwa.

(Vocable.)
Hark people.
Hark, hark people.
You'll recall long ago,
when there were choices made in the ways of life,
and there were choices made in the ways of leadership,
over there down at the Red-Walled City,
where there was the Emergence of the people,
the (life of) shelled corn on a coiled plaque was planned,
the short corn plant was planned,
when you think back to these purposes and to your duties,
truly in this way the will to live and the consecrated path are renewed for
   you,
So it is.
[And] so it was when the will to live and the consecrated path were
   renewed for you long ago.

In this song the katsinas are reminiscing about the Emergence and the
choice of the humble short ear of corn as a way of life, described here as
"choices made in the ways of life and ways of leadership." In Hopi belief,
when all people emerged into this Fourth World, they were given a choice

19. *i'* 'these', referring to the previous lines.
20. *hapi* 'truly, surely, certainly'.
21. *yantaqat* 'like this, in this way, thus'.
22. = *ayawat,* object form of *ayawa* 'purpose, reason for being'.
23. *mamkiway,* possessed object form of *mamkiwa* 'things received, allotments, birthrights, duties'.
24. *ahoy* 'back to'.
25. = *kuk.wuwayaqw'ö,* subordinate clause pausal form of *kuk.wuwaya* 'retrace steps', *ahoy kuk.wuwaya* 'reflect or think back on the past (plural)'.
26. *umungem* 'for you (plural), for your benefit'.
27. *qatsi'nangwa* 'will to live'.
28. = *pöötavi* 'consecrated path'.
29. = *puuhutiwa* 'be renewed'.
30. *yan'i* 'thus it is, so it is', pausal form of *yan* 'like this, in this way, thus, so'.
31. *yan* 'like this, in this way, thus, so'.

of lifeways by Màasaw. Some chose hunting, some chose gathering, and some chose farming as a way of life. Each way of life would require different kinds of leadership roles.

The reference here to Palatkwapi, the "Red-Walled City," is not to a particular place, but generally to the idea that the people "emerged" from somewhere in the south where they settled at different times in different pueblos built with reddish colored sandstone. Every time they moved it was as if they emerged and renewed their efforts to live the life of corn in another settlement as they migrated northward toward their present home on the mesas.

The choice of the short ear of corn by the people destined to become the Hopis is here expressed as a "life of shelled corn on a coiled plaque." This is a life of communal caring and sharing and humble hard work. It requires that each person attend to obligations and responsibilities that place the well-being and survival of the entire community above individual desires. In Hopi belief no one individual is any more important than another. Leaders, for example those of ritual societies, are expected to lead exemplary lives, showing others how to follow a path of life that will enable the Hopis to realize their destiny as a people. The reference to life of corn on a coiled plaque may also be a way of likening the ever-expanding concentric rings on the plaques to the expansion of corn as it became the dominant lifeway.

The katsinas implore the people to "retrace their footsteps," that is, to think back to the life of corn they chose. They remind the people that when they accepted this life path and the will to live, that is, the determination to live by the practices that are required to live this life, then the consecrated path will be renewed for their benefit. In this song the consecrated path does not refer to the cornmeal path along which the katsinas enter the village, but rather to the way of life that the katsinas, in their concern for the people, help to sustain through their advice and admonitions.

Songs Contributed by
Emory Sekaquaptewa

126. Angaktsìntawi[1]

Kwakwhá.[2]
Umùutuwaniyuy[3] àasatti.[4]
Oovi[5] yangqaqw[6] qöya'omawmamàntu,[7]
qaa'öyu,[8] yoylekiy[9] naayuwasinat'a,[10]
yangqaqw itamumi[11] nánakwusa.[12]
Oovi uma[13] túwati,[14]
umùu'unangwvàasiy,[15]
itamuy[16] sínevelantoyaqw'ö,[17]
itam[18] tuwat[19] tuu'awvaqö'ö,[20]
sìitàlpuva'a,[21]
taayimuyiwni.[22]
Yowiina yowiina yowiina, yowiina hii.

1. *angaktsìntawi* 'Long-Hair katsina song'.
2. *kwakwhá* 'thank you (male speaker)'.
3. = *umùutuwaniy,* object form of *umùutuwani* 'your (plural) set time, the time that you set'.
4. *àasatti* 'become the appointed time for it'.
5. *oovi* 'that's why'.
6. *yangqaqw* 'from here somewhere' (including a sense of being unexpected).
7. = *qöya'omawmamant* 'white cloud maidens'.
8. = *qaa'öy,* object form of *qaa'ö'am* 'their corn, dry ears of corn'.
9. *yoylekiy,* object form of *yoyleki'am* 'their rain lines'.
10. = *naayuwsinat'a,* pausal form of *naayuwsinat* 'after adorning selves'.
11. *itamumi* 'to us'.
12. = *nànkwusa* 'start on a journey (plural)'.
13. *uma* 'you (plural)'.
14. = *tuwat* 'in turn, for (one's) part'.
15. *umùu'unangwvàasiy,* object form of *umùu'unangwvàasi* 'your (plural) heartfelt wish(es), hope(s), prayer(s)'.
16. *itamuy* 'us', object form of *itam* 'we'.
17. *sínevelantoyaqw'ö,* subordinate clause pausal form of *sínevelantoya* 'provide with the perfection of something that is owed, due to another'.
18. *itam* 'we'.
19. *tuwat* 'in turn, for (one's) part'.
20. = *tuu'awvaqw'ö,* subordinate clause pausal form of *tuu'awva* 'come with a message'.
21. *sìitàlpuva'a,* pausal form of *sìitàlpuva* 'along a land brightened with flowers'.
22. = *taayimuyiwni* 'will look in awe'.

Aahaa aaha haa haa.
Ii'ihii hii hii.

Let's be thankful.
It has become the time that you set.
That's why the white cloud maidens from around here,
after having adorned themselves with their corn and with their rain lines,
have begun their journey to us from around here.
That's why, when you, for your part,
provide us with your heartfelt prayers
as the perfection of sincerity that we are due,
and we, for our part, come with the message,
you will look in awe
along a land brightened with flowers.
(Vocables.)

This is the final song of the day at *Nimàntikive,* the Home dance, which
is the final katsina appearance of the year. With thankfulness the katsinas
acknowledge that the time that was "set," that is, predetermined, for the
end of their presence in the villages for the season has arrived. This is
referred to as *tiingavi,* the preordination that a performance will take place
at a certain time. This date and the planning for this last dance occurred
in ritual session sometime during the winter months. With their thanks
(*kwakwhá*), the katsinas are acknowledging all the hard physical, mental
and spiritual work by the people that was involved in preparing for and
hosting the katsinas throughout the spring and summer months. All of this
work—the weeks of smoking and praying in the kiva, the food preparation
in the homes throughout the village—must be undertaken by every member of the community with a spirit of dedication to live by the tenets of
the corn lifeway.

The katsinas then turn to address the central theme of the song, the
promise of new generations, by sanctifying the new powers of procreation
possessed by the women who have become brides during the past year. At
the end of the day at the last dance these brides make an appearance
dressed in their white bridal robes (*oova*). By their appearance before the
katsinas who are perfect beings, they have become spiritually sanctified
and thus fully fledged in their new stage of motherhood. Just as the
katsinas are not seen as physical beings, but as rain and flowers, likewise
the brides are not seen as specific individuals, but as symbolic of the
renewal of life and new generations of people. They are metaphorically

referred to in the song as white cloud maidens (*qöya'omawmamant*), because like clouds with rain, they now have the power to create new life. With this appearance they have completed their journey, that is, the process of getting married.

Just as the katsinas are adorned with all things that stand for life, many of which appear as symbols on their clothing, so too do the brides wear signs of new life on their clothing. They appear enveloped in a robe as if they are ears of corn in their husk, the wrapping being symbolic of their procreative potential since both women and ears of corn are filled with seeds for the next generation. The white color of the robe is symbolic of the purity of their countenance. The checkerboard patterned tassels hanging from the corners of the robes represents the corn, *qaa'ö*, and the white cotton strings hanging from the robe and the bridal sash symbolize the rain lines, *yoyleki*, that will nourish all new life.

The katsinas then, as white cloud maidens, promise that after they adorn themselves with all these signs of life, and after the people proffer their most heartfelt prayers, they will begin their journey to the people as rain. This is the reciprocal agreement between the katsinas and the people. That is, after the katsinas promise to come as rain, they lay out what the people must do to deserve their beneficence. It is often expressed in song with the phrase *uma tuwat,* you, for your part. Since this is the last dance of the katsina season, this is the final opportunity for the people to send their prayers with the katsinas. *Sínevelanatoya,* 'provide with the perfection that is our due' begins with *sihu* 'flower' (*sí-*), and in this way makes reference to the beautifully perfect nature of such prayers. Katsinas, being perfect beings, are due nothing less than the most heartfelt prayers.

The katsinas promise that, for their part, they will in turn "come with the message," the people's prayers, that is, they will take these prayers home with them to their leaders at the katsina dwelling places. Although it is not stated explicitly, it is implied that the people have been judged deserving and thus the katsinas have arrived as rain. The people will then look upon their land that has been brightened with flowers as a result of their rain. The reference to the land as having flowers, not simply as having growing plants, uses the flower stage as the harbinger of the food that is to come, and by implication of the lives that will be nourished by this food. Flowers are the universal Uto-Aztecan symbol of the fulfilled life—that pristine state where there is food and happiness and freedom from strife.

127. Angaktsìntawi$_1$

Haw,$_2$ haw.
Tuqayvastota'a.$_3$
Hak$_4$ waynuma.$_5$
Atkya$_6$ tsootsonglalwa.$_7$
Tsoongoy$_8$ naa'itnalalwa.$_9$
Noqw$_{10}$ nu'$_{11}$ Pavawkyàytiyo$_{12}$ tunatyayamuy$_{13}$ ömàataqe'e,$_{14}$
nu' umuy$_{15}$ aa'awna,$_{16}$
yépe'e.$_{17}$
Owí$_{18}$ uma$_{19}$ ii'itsyani.$_{20}$
Itangumuy,$_{21}$ itanamuy$_{22}$ aw$_{23}$ yooya'ökini.$_{24}$
Ep$_{25}$ puma$_{26}$ úmuyu$_{27}$ nùutayta,$_{28}$

1. angaktsìntawi 'Long-Hair katsina song'.
2. haw, vocative particle.
3. tuqayvastota'a, imperative form of tuqayvastota 'pay attention, listen attentively (plural)'.
4. hak 'someone'.
5. waynuma 'be walking around'.
6. atkya 'down, down there, down below'.
7. tsootsonglalwa 'keep on smoking (tobacco) (plural)'.
8. tsoongoy, object form of tsoongo'am 'their smoking pipe(s)'.
9. naa'itnalalwa 'keep on passing (a pipe) along from one to another (plural)'.
10. noqw 'but, whereas, and so'.
11. nu' 'I'.
12. Pavawkyàytiyo 'Swallow Boy'.
13. tunatyayamuy, object form of tunatya'am 'their religious intentions'.
14. ömàataqe'e, subordinate clause pausal form of ömàata 'understand, take in'.
15. umuy, object form of uma 'you (plural)'.
16. aa'awna 'inform'.
17. = yep'e, pausal form of yep 'here'.
18. owí 'yes'.
19. uma 'you (plural)'.
20. ii'itsyani 'should be prompt (plural)'.
21. itangumuy, object form of itangum 'our mothers'.
22. itanamuy, object form of itanam 'our fathers'.
23. = amumi 'to them'.
24. = yoy'ökini 'will arrive, come as rain'.
25. ep 'there, at it'.
26. puma 'they'.
27. = umuy, object form of uma 'you (plural)'.
28. = nùutayyungwa 'be awaiting (plural)'.

lolmat$_{29}$ pöötaviy$_{30}$ ánga'a.$_{31}$
Yaa hiya haahi yaahi yaaw.
Yaahi yaahiya aaw yahi yahi.
Aahaa aa'aa'aha ha.
Hapi me.$_{32}$
Hisnentiqw$_{33}$ tunatyayamuy suvo'oyiwqw'ö,$_{34}$
naanan'ivaqw$_{35}$ pew$_{36}$ yooya'ökini.
Hisnentiqw tunatyayamuy suvo'oyiwqw'ö,
paatàlpuva'a,$_{37}$
taayimuyiwni.$_{38}$

Hark, hark.
Pay attention.
Someone is traveling about.
Down below, they keep on smoking.
They keep passing the pipe along.
And I, Swallow Boy, understand their religious intentions,
and I am informing you of them,
here.
Yes, you should be prompt.
You should arrive as rain to my mothers and my fathers.
There they are awaiting you,
along their beautiful consecrated path.
(Vocables.)
Listen, there is more.
Hopefully, if their religious intentions have been united as one,
you will come here as rain from all the directions.
Hopefully, if their religious intentions have been united as one,
along a land glistening with water,
it will be looked on in awe.

29. *lolmat,* object form of *lolma* 'beautiful, good, proper'.
30. *pöötaviy,* object form of *pöötavi'am* 'their consecrated path'.
31. = *ang'a,* pausal form of *ang* 'along it, along there, in an area, in several places'.
32. *hapi me,* formulaic expression introducing the song's second part, *oomi* 'upward'.
33. *hisnentiqw* 'hopefully'.
34. *suvo'oyiwqw'ö,* subordinate clause pausal form of *suvo'oyiwa* 'have been united as one'.
35. *naanan'ivaqw* 'from the different directions around'.
36. *pew* 'toward here, coming this way'.
37. *paatàlpuva'a,* pausal form of *paatàlpuva* 'along a land glistening with water'.
38. *taayimuyiwni* 'will look in awe'.

The katsinas are singing as if they are Swallow Boy, a spiritual being who is acting as a messenger to the katsinas. Here he is reporting about the activities of the men in the kiva as they are making preparations for a performance. His observation that the men are smoking and passing the pipe refers to the way they are sitting in a circle and praying by taking a puff on the smoking pipe and then passing the pipe to the next man. Forming the clouds by smoking and passing the pipe is part of the process of laying down the path for the katsinas to come. Swallow Boy says that he understands the religious intentions of the men, meaning that he has heard and appreciated the sincerity of their prayers.

The choice of Swallow Boy as the messenger carries a number of symbolic referents. Swallows are not only swift in flight but also frequent puddles and pools of water that form after a hard rain. In this capacity, they are harbingers of the rain that will come with the katsinas. The way they characteristically swoop down to catch the insects that hover above bodies of water is mimicked by Swallow Boy's activities of flying down to hear the prayers of the people and then swiftly rising to take these prayers to the katsinas.

After hearing the sincere intentions of the people, Swallow Boy exhorts the katsinas to be prompt in their response to the sincere prayers of the people. He tells them to arrive as rain to the people, who are referred to as mothers and fathers, because they are anxiously awaiting them and, in anticipation, have laid out a path of consecrated cornmeal, *hooma,* for them to travel along into the village.

In the second verse, Swallow Boy then reiterates the reciprocal nature of the relationship between the katsinas and the people. If the people's prayers have been made in united sincerity "as one," then you, the katsinas, will arrive in rain from all four directions. The word *paatàlpuva* 'along a land glistening with water' describes the nature and quantity of rain that arrives in return for heartfelt prayers. Summer thunderstorms drench the land quickly with so much water that it stands in temporary pools and puddles on the land. These shallow sheets of water glisten in the sun, giving the land a brightness that has the countenance of new life. The katsinas predict that the people will look upon this scene with appreciative awe. Use of the verb *tayma* here implies much more than just looking and seeing water. It also encompasses the expectation and knowledge of all the good things that will be nourished by the rain.

128. *Angaktsìntawi*$_1$

Hinoqw$_2$ *uma*$_3$ *nánàatsovi.*$_4$
Núwupi$_5$ *úma'a,*$_6$
qatsivaptsiwta,$_7$
ínamu.$_8$
Paysoq$_9$ *úma'a,*
umùu'unangwvasiy$_{10}$ *suukye'*$_{11}$ *taviyata'a,*$_{12}$
umùupahoyu,$_{13}$ *umùuhom'oyiy*$_{14}$ *aw*$_{15}$ *naawakinaqw'ö,*$_{16}$
yokvani,$_{17}$
umùu'uyiy$_{18}$ *ánga'a.*$_{19}$
Paatalawinani.$_{20}$
Lee lehee la.$_{21}$
Pantaqat$_{22}$ *ánga'a,*
ang$_{23}$ *uma hàalàytimani,*$_{24}$

1. *angaktsìntawi* 'Long-Hair katsina song'.
2. = *hintiqw* 'why, what for, for what purpose'.
3. *uma* 'you (plural)'.
4. *nánàatsovi* 'be reluctant because of a feeling of inadequacy for the task, lack self-assurance to act'.
5. *núwupi* 'it's inevitable, unavoidable'.
6. *úma'a,* pausal form of *uma* 'you (plural)'.
7. *qatsivaptsiwta* 'have one's turn at life'.
8. = *inam* 'my fathers'.
9. *paysoq* 'just, only, simply'.
10. *umùu'unangwvasiy,* object form of *umùu'unangwvasi* 'your (plural) heartfelt prayers'.
11. *suukye'* 'along one line, in harmony'.
12. *taviyata'a,* pausal form of *taviyat* 'after putting, placing (plural)'.
13. = *umùupahoy,* object form of *umùupaho* 'your (plural) prayer feathers'.
14. *umùuhom'oyiy,* object form of *umùuhom'oyi* 'your prayer (plural) offering'.
15. *aw* 'to it, to there'.
16. = *naawaknaqw'ö,* subordinate clause pausal form of *naawakna* 'pray, want'.
17. *yokvani* 'will rain'.
18. *umùu'uyiy,* object form of *umùu'uyi* 'your (plural) plants'.
19. = *ang'a,* pausal form of *ang* 'along it, along there, in an area, in several places'.
20. = *paatalawnani* 'will make it glisten with water'.
21. vocables characteristic of the Long-Hair katsinas.
22. *pantaqat* 'in that way, in that circumstance'.
23. *ang* 'along it, along there, in that area, in several places'.
24. *hàalàytimani* 'will go along expressing gladness'.

ang uma nàasaptimakyangw.[25]
Yan[26] *uma tawma,*[27]
tawma,
túwati.[28]
Oh'oho hoo'oo oo'o'o'oo hoowa.
Ee' ehe hee'ee ee'e'ee heelo.
Ayahiy aahaa.

Why do you doubt yourselves?
It is unavoidable that you
are to assume the responsibilities of your generation,
my fathers.
It is only that you,
after putting your heartfelt wishes in harmony,
you pray on your prayer feathers and offerings,
and it will rain,
along your planted fields.
It will make the land glistening with water.
(Vocables of the Long-Hair katsinas.)
In that way along there,
along there, you will go expressing gladness,
while you go along there meeting each other coming and going.
In this way you go along singing,
for your part,
you go along singing.
(Vocables of the sound of singing.)

This song is an admonition from the katsinas. They are chastising the
people for their lack of resolve in accepting the responsibilities of their
generation. It is addressed to everyone in the community who has failed
to assume the obligations they have to those to whom they are related
through kin, clan and religious society membership. The institutionaliza-
tion of obligations and responsibilities is designed to insure the integrity

25. *nàasaptimakyangw* is literally 'while going along making (it) the same length, height',
   but in the song it is a substitution for *nàasawvantimakyangw* 'while going along meeting
   one another coming and going'.
26. *yan* 'like this, in this way, thus'.
27. *tawma* 'go along singing'.
28. = *tuwat* 'in turn, for (one's) part'.

and prosperity of the community. Hopi villages survive as self-sufficient entities to the extent that all members place community survival above personal gain. The responsibility of each individual is not simply to make new life, but "to see that life goes on." The katsinas are urging the people to remember this communal ethic to which they agreed when they were accepted in the villages.

The katsinas use the term *qatsivaptsiwta* 'have one's turn at life' to refer to those in the community who have reached that stage of their lives when they need to fully assume these responsibilities and obligations to the community but for some reason feel inadequate and are hesitating to shoulder those roles. The katsinas remind these individuals that only after they accept their responsibilities and make efforts to live in harmony with each other, will it rain on their planted fields—again restating the reciprocal relationship between the katsinas, in their role as the conscience of the community, and the people.

The phrase *umùu'unangwvasiy suukye' taviyata'a* (after putting your heartfelt wishes in harmony), more literally "after placing your prayers along one line," embodies the idea that the people's prayers go together along a linear path that is aimed and, metaphorically, shot as an arrow from the people to the katsinas. Prayers are infused in prayer feathers, the word for which, *paaho*, is derived from *paa* (water) and *hoohu* (arrow). In this song this process is described as "putting your prayers on the feathers and offerings," *umùupahoyu, umùuhom'oyiy aw naawakinaqw'ö* (you pray on your prayer feathers and offerings).

While the song begins as an admonition, it closes on a positive, encouraging note. The katsinas reassure the people that if they direct their prayers properly, the land will glisten with water and they will be able to go along expressing their gladness as they walk throughout their fields, meeting others, who are also singing their happiness over the coming of rain.

129. *Angaktsìntawi₁*

Ura₂ sé'elhaqamo,₃
itamuy₄ yep₅ tiitiiwunimaqw'ö,₆
i'₇ yep Oomawwùutaqa₈ itana,₉
itamumi₁₀ nakwsuqe'e,₁₁
"Yee hehe.
"Yee hehe.
"Ya₁₂ uma₁₃ yephaqam₁₄ hàalayya?"₁₅
Yan₁₆ ura itamumi lavàytita'a,₁₇
itamuy yep öqaalata'a,₁₈
itamuy yep taawanawita₁₉ hàalayyaniqat,₂₀
naawaakinaqw'ö,₂₁
pu'₂₂ itam₂₃ hàalay'unangway₂₄ tiiti'ökiwa.₂₅
Lee lehee la.

1. *angaktsìntawi* 'Long-Hair katsina song'.
2. *ura,* modal of recollection: 'as I recall, as you'll recall'.
3. = *sé'elhaqam* 'sometime this morning'.
4. *itamuy* 'us', object form of *itam* 'we'.
5. *yep* 'here'.
6. = *tiitiwunimaqw'ö,* subordinate clause pausal form of *tiitiwunima* 'be dancing in perform-ance'.
7. *i'* 'this'.
8. *Oomawwùutaqa* 'Old Man Cloud'.
9. *itana* 'our father'.
10. *itamumi* 'to us'.
11. *nakwsuqe'e,* subordinate clause pausal form of *nakwsu* 'start on a journey'.
12. *ya,* question particle.
13. *uma* 'you (plural)'.
14. *yephaqam* 'here, around here, approximately here'.
15. *hàalayya* 'be happy (plural)'.
16. *yan* 'like this, in this way, thus'.
17. *lavàytita'a,* pausal form of *lavàytit* 'after speaking'.
18. = *öqalata'a,* pausal form of *öqalat* 'after encouraging'.
19. = *taawanawit* 'all day long'.
20. = *hàalayyaniqat* 'that should be happy'.
21. = *naanawaknaqw'ö,* subordinate clause pausal form of *naanawakna* 'pray, want (plural)'.
22. *pu'* 'now, then'.
23. *itam* 'we'.
24. *hàalay'unangway* 'with happy hearts, with beneficent intentions'.
25. *tiiti'ökiwa* 'have come in dance (and thereby to soothe)'.

Oovi$_{26}$ *ítamu,*$_{27}$
hàalaykyangw$_{28}$ *tiitiwunima;*$_{29}$
hàalaykyangw taatawyuuyuwinaya,$_{30}$
yépe'e.$_{31}$
Hapii mee.$_{32}$
Uma yépe'e,
lolmat$_{33}$ *qatsit*$_{34}$ *wuuwanmaqam,*$_{35}$
ínamu.$_{36}$
Uma$_{37}$ *yépe'e,*
nanava'ngwaqw'ö,$_{38}$
naanan'ivaqw$_{39}$ *pew*$_{40}$ *yooya'ökini.*$_{41}$
Yan uma naawakinaya.$_{42}$
Lee lehe laa.
Oovi ítamu,
hàalaykyangw tiitiwunima;
hàalaykyangw taatawyuuyuwinaya,
yépe'e.
Oho ohooway oowa eelo aaha'hay'a aaha'ahay'a.

We recall that sometime this morning,
when we were dancing here,
this Old Man Cloud, our father here,
approached us [and said],
"(Vocables of delight upon finding something.)

26. *oovi* 'that's why'.
27. = *itam* 'we'.
28. *hàalaykyangw* 'while being happy, happily'.
29. *tiitiwunima* 'be dancing in performance'
30. *taatawyuuyuwinaya* 'be dancing and singing songs (plural)'.
31. = *yep'e*, pausal form of *yep* 'here'.
32. = *hapi me*, formulaic expression introducing the song's second part, *oomi* 'upward'.
33. *lolmat*, object form of *lolma* 'beautiful, good, proper'.
34. *qatsit*, object form of *qatsi* 'life'.
35. = *wuuwanmaqam* 'those that go along thinking, worrying'.
36. = *inam* 'my fathers'.
37. *uma* 'you (plural)'.
38. = *nanava'ngwaqw'ö*, subordinate clause pausal form of *nanava'ngwa* 'be helping each other'.
39. *naanan'ivaqw* 'from the different directions around'.
40. *pew* 'toward here, coming this way'.
41. = *yoy'ökini* 'will arrive, come as rain'.
42. = *naanawakna* 'pray (plural)'.

"I see that you are happy to be here."
We recall that after he spoke to us in this way,
and after he encouraged us (to be) here,
he prayed
that we should (all) be happy here all day long,
so now we have come dancing with happy hearts.
(Vocables.)
That's why we
are happily dancing
[and] are happily dancing and singing songs
here.
Listen, there is more.
You here,
who go along thinking about the good life,
my fathers,
you here,
when you help each other,
the rain will come here from the different directions around.
In this way you pray.
(Vocables.)
That's why we
are happily dancing
[and] are happily dancing and singing songs
here.
(Vocables.)

This song was sung at the first performance of the day. Typically, during
the summer months, there are four dances in the morning and four dances
after the noon meal. Each dance consists of three songs, each of which is
sung facing a different direction. Normally the first dance of the day is
performed after dawn when everyone is gathered around the edge of the
plaza. However, here the katsinas arrived in the plaza and began dancing
and singing about 3 or 4 in the morning. The only individual up to greet
them was the katsina father, here described as Old Man Cloud, *Oomawwùutaqa*. He expresses his surprise at discovering them there, but
encourages them to return later in the morning to hearten the people. The
katsina father observes that the katsinas are happy to be in the village.
They promise to perform all day long with happy hearts. These performances, described as *tiitiwunima* (dancing in performance), are meant to
encourage the people by easing their hearts and minds from the daily

travails and problems that challenge them in their efforts to live according to the tenets of the corn lifeway.

The likening of the katsina father to Old Man Cloud implies that he, like a cloud, has attained a spiritual purity that enables his prayers to persuade the clouds to come with their gift of rain. It is also a reference to the katsina father who is sitting in the kiva making clouds with his smoking pipe. Metaphorically, Old Man Cloud is bent over from carrying his gift burden of rain. All of the katsinas' gifts are considered as gift burdens since the katsinas, like the people, have obligations that are sometimes onerous. Their burden is to come as rain if the people, in turn, perform their life burdens of working hard and living by the moral imperatives of the corn lifeway. In many images Old Man Cloud is depicted as a man bent over from a lifetime of performing the many burdens of sharing, caring and cooperating.

In the second section of the song the katsinas remind the people that their thoughts about the "good life," *lolmat qatsit*, that is, a life of plenty that is free from suffering, will be rewarded with rain only if they help each other. The beauty of a humble life lived according to the moral imperatives of the Hopi lifeway forms the basis of the communal ethic that is at the heart of all katsina songs.

130. *Angaktsìntawi,*

Haa'o₂ íngumu,₃
haa'o ínamu,₄
uma₅ naawuwayani.₆
Ura₇ hísato₈ atkyaqw₉ suvuyoyangw₁₀ tokyephoyoyotangwu.₁₁

1. *angaktsìntawi* 'Long-Hair katsina song'.
2. *haa'o,* vocative particle.
3. = *ingum* 'my mothers'.
4. = *inam* 'my fathers'.
5. *uma* 'you (plural)'.
6. *naawuwayani* 'should reflect, think back'.
7. *ura,* modal of recollection: 'as I recall, as you'll recall'.
8. = *hisat* 'sometime, when, long ago'.
9. *atkyaqw* 'from below, from down there', a reference to the southwest direction, downslope from the Hopi villages.
10. *suvuyoyangw* 'long and steady drizzle, gentle rain'.
11. *tokyephoyoyotangwu,* habitual tense form of *tokyephoyoyota* 'be moving all night'.

Tuuwapongyava$_{12}$ sòosoy$_{13}$ hímu'u,$_{14}$
sìitalngwu.$_{15}$
Pu'$_{16}$ tuwat$_{17}$ paavopkomatu,$_{18}$
yoyngyàlpuva'a,$_{19}$
töötökiy$_{20}$ ákwa'a,$_{21}$
soosonkiwlawngwu.$_{22}$
Oo oho hoo hoo, hoo ohowa.
Ee ehe ee hee, hee ehelo.

O my mothers,
o my fathers,
you should think back.
Remember when a steady drizzle used to be moving all night from down
    below.
Along the land, everything
would be bright with flowers.
Then, for their part, the water creatures,
in the postlude of the rain,
with their calls,
would keep making it pleasing.
(Vocables.)

This song is in the form of an imperative, requesting the people to reflect
back to the time when the rains came regularly from down below
(*atkyaqw*), that is, from the southwest direction, and all the land was in
bloom. This is a description of the perfect life when people lived by the
moral imperatives of the corn lifeway. Apparently the people are not
living according to these principles and so the katsinas are appealing to
their moral conscience, admonishing them to mend their ways so that the
rains will come and their lives will be fulfilled.

12. *tuuwapongyava* 'along the land'.
13. *sòosoy* 'all'.
14. *hímu'u*, pausal form of *himu*, indefinite pronoun: 'something, what, one, you'.
15. *sìitalngwu*, habitual tense form of *sìitala* 'be bright with flowers'.
16. *pu'* 'now, then'.
17. *tuwat* 'in turn, for (one's) part'.
18. = *paavopkomat* 'water creatures'.
19. *yoyngyàlpuva'a*, pausal form of *yoyngyàlpuva* 'in the postlude of the rain, during the
    time after it has stopped raining'.
20. *töötökiy*, object form of *töötöki'am* 'their calls, cries'.
21. *ákwa'a*, pausal form of *akw* 'using, by means of, with'.
22. = *sosonkiwlawngwu*, habitual tense form of *sosonkiwlawu* 'keep making it pleasing'.

Suvuyoyangw, a long and steady drizzle that moves along soaking the land and deeply watering the plants is the most desirable kind of rain. The song phrase *tuuwapongyava soosoy himu'u siitalngwu,* literally "all things bright with flowers along the land," conveys the idea that everything on the land, including animals and plants as well as people, will have been refreshed by this rain and thus will be "blooming," that is, showing renewed vitality. The blooming nature of life connotes the promise of new life. Describing the land as a "sand altar," *tuuwapongya,* is a way of referencing the special reverence that the people have for it. In the Hopi mind their land is a spiritually invested place that embodies all things that insure their survival.

The katsinas remind the people that when it rains, the *paavopkomat* (water creatures), meaning all living creatures who depend on water, come to life and sing in happiness at the coming of the rain. Emory poetically described the period after a rain as "in the postlude of the rain," when all the land and all the life on it are pleasing to see. The message of this song is that right living brings plentiful rain, blooming fields and, by implication, a fulfilled life.

131. *Angaktsìntawi$_1$*

Ahaay ahaa'ay.
Aahaa wiy'aa.
Pas$_2$ hapi$_3$ uma$_4$ nuy$_5$ no'aya,$_6$
paavönmanatu.$_7$
Kur$_8$ uma yeephaqam$_9$ umùumasay$_{10}$ kuwantimakyangw$_{11}$ puyayato[ta,]$_{12}$

1. *angaktsìntawi* 'Long-Hair katsina song'.
2. *pas* 'very'.
3. *hapi* 'truly, surely, certainly'.
4. *uma* 'you (plural)'.
5. *nuy* 'me', object form of *nu'* 'I'.
6. *no'aya* 'amuse, entertain, please (plural)'.
7. = *paavönmamant* 'young corn plants'.
8. *kur,* modal of inference.
9. = *yephaqam* 'here, approximately here'.
10. *umùumasay,* object form of *umùumasa* 'your (plural) wings'.
11. *kuwantimakyangw* 'while going along putting color on'.
12. *puyayatota* 'be flapping, fluttering (plural)' (the last syllable is lost in the song by haplology with the following syllable *ta-* which begins *tal'angwnawit* 'all summer long' in the next line).

tal'angwnawita.[13]
Lee lehe laa.
Ayángqw[14] *taavangqö*[15] *yooyangw'u,*[16]
ùmtimakyangw[17] *uuyisonaqa,*[18]
ang[19] *puma*[20] *paatalawnayaqw'ö,*[21]
ang uma tawma.[22]
Taatawtimani:[23]
"Siyaahay'eloya, asii'iiyaay'elo ya.
Ohayo ohayo ohayo ohayo yaahay eeloya."

(Vocables of the happy sound of laughter.)
Truly you please me very much,
you young corn plants.
It seems that while putting color on your wings here, you are fluttering
    them
all summer long.
(Vocables.)
The rain from over there in the southwest,
when it goes along booming through the midst of the planted fields,
it will make the land glisten with water
and you will go along singing.
You will go along singing songs:
"—(a song consisting of vocables)—."

This is an uplifting song that celebrates the vigor and beauty of growing
corn plants, here described as young corn plants, *paavönmamant,* who are,
by metaphorical implication, young Hopi girls. This song opens with
vocables of happiness and laughter. The katsinas, speaking to the corn
plants, observe that they are putting on color and fluttering their wings,

13. = *tal'angwnawit* 'all summer long'.
14. = *ayángqw* 'from over there'.
15. = *taavangqw* 'from the southwest'.
16. *yooyangw'u,* pausal form of *yooyangw* 'rain'.
17. *ùmtimakyangw* 'while going along booming (slowly)'.
18. = *uysonaq* 'throughout the midst of the planted area(s)'.
19. *ang* 'along it, along there, in that area, in several places'.
20. *puma* 'they'.
21. = *paatalawnayaqw'ö,* subordinate clause pausal form of *paatalawnaya* 'make it glisten
    with water (plural)'.
22. *tawma* 'go along singing'.
23. *taatawtimani* 'will go along singing songs'.

that is, their leaves, using two figurative ways to describe the process of growing and flourishing. The idea that healthy, growing things have color is a way of referencing the health and perfection of the katsina world. In addition, it is a description of the way corn kernels that are translucent when immature take on yellow, red, blue colors as they mature. Also implied in this song is the likening of the growing corn plants to young people who still need the help of the community in order to "bloom" and become productive adults. In this sense the rain is a metaphor for the nourishment that all children need in order to raise themselves up.

The katsinas say the rain from the southwest will come along thundering, placing its water throughout the fields and making everything on the land glisten. The katsinas predict that their gift of rain will cause the people to walk among their planted fields singing in happiness.

132. *Angaktsìntawi*₁

Qöyangwun-,₂ sikyangwùntaalawkuyiva.₃
Qöyangwun-, sikyangwùntaalawkuyiva,
ayám₄ oove₅ taawa₆ itana₇ lolmat₈ pitsangwa'ikyangw₉ kuyvaqö'ö.₁₀
Aw₁₁ uma₁₂ wuupat₁₃ qatsi'unangwata,₁₄
siwi'ytaniqata,₁₅
naawakinaya.₁₆

1. *angaktsìntawi* 'Long-Hair katsina song'.
2. *qöyangwun-* 'white dawn . . .', the first part of the compound *qöyangwùntalawkuyva* 'for daylight to make its appearance as white dawn'.
3. = *sikyangwùntalawkuyva* 'for daylight to make its appearance as yellow dawn'.
4. *ayám* 'over there'.
5. *oove* 'above, up above, at a place above'.
6. *taawa* 'sun'.
7. *itana* 'our father'.
8. *lolmat,* object form of *lolma* 'beautiful, good, proper'.
9. = *pitsangwa'ykyangw* 'while having a countenance'.
10. = *kuyvaqw'ö,* subordinate clause pausal form of *kuyva* 'appear, come into sight'.
11. *aw* 'to him'.
12. *uma* 'you (plural)'.
13. *wuupat,* object form of *wuupa* 'long, tall'.
14. = *qatsi'nangwat,* object form of *qatsi'nangwa* 'will to live'.
15. = *siwi'ytaniqat,* object form of *siwi'ytaniqa* 'that which will have vitality'. This word for having vitality is related to *siwi'at* 'tendrils', a sign of vitality in plants.
16. = *naanawakna* 'pray (plural)'.

Lee.
Puu'u, [17]
ítamu [18] *umungemi* [19] *nana'alöngöta* [20] *qaa'ömanatuy* [21] *wiikimuyiwaqw'ö,* [22]
yépe'e. [23]
Put [24] *uma ömàatotat'a,* [25]
yumaki'ikyangw [26] *wuyomiq* [27] *qatsi'unangwata* [28] *naavokyawintani,* [29]
yépe'e. [30]
Yowi'aa.

Daylight makes its appearance as white dawn, yellow dawn.
Daylight makes its appearance as white dawn, yellow dawn,
and up there our father the sun makes his appearance with a beautiful
    countenance.
You pray to him
for the will to live a long life
and for things that will have vitality.
(Vocable.)
Then,
when we have brought the different kinds of corn maidens for you,
here,
and once you receive them,
while having them as mothers, you will enjoy the will to live toward old
    age,
here.
(Vocable.)

17. *puu'u,* pausal form of *pu'* 'now, then'.
18. = *itam* 'we'.
19. = *umungem* 'for you (plural), for your benefit'.
20. *nana'löngöt,* object form of *nana'löngö* 'different kinds of'.
21. = *qa'ömamàntuy,* object form of *qa'ömamant* 'corn maidens'.
22. *wikmuyiwaqw'ö,* pausalized subordinate clause form of *wikmuyiwa* 'have brought'.
23. = *yep'e,* pausal form of *yep* 'here'.
24. *put,* object form of *pam* 'that, that one, he, she, it'.
25. = *ömàatotat'a,* pausal form of *ömàatotat* 'after receiving'.
26. = *yumaki'ykyangw* 'while having as a ceremonial mother'.
27. *wuyomiq* 'toward old age'.
28. = *qatsi'nangwat,* object form of *qatsi'nangwa* 'will to live'.
29. *naavokyawintani* 'there will be enjoyment to the fullest'.
30. = *yep'e,* pausal form of *yep* 'here'.

The katsinas are singing metaphorically about the stages of life by describing the coming of the white dawn and then the yellow dawn of a new day. Full daylight comes when the sun (*taawa*), in beautiful countenance, *lolmat pitsangwa,* makes its appearance over the horizon and the rebirth of a new day has fully occurred. At dawn people step outside their homes and offer prayers to the east. In this way Hopis see the dawn of a new day as an opportunity for them to renew their determination to live according to the moral imperatives of the corn lifeway. This idea is expressed by the word *qatsi'nangwa* (the will to live), a compound composed of *qatsi* (life) and *unangwa* (heart). In this song it is combined with *siwi'ytaniqa,* that which has the promise of vitality. Tendrils, *siwi'at,* are willful signs of growth and thus vitality on the part of plants. The implication here is that just as plants, nourished by the rain, put out tendrils, so too should people persist with the determination to live right.

The katsinas encourage the people to pray for this will to live, and when they do, they, the katsinas, will bring the different kinds of corn maidens, meaning corn of different colors, to them. In this case these corn maidens are to be understood as perfect ears of corn with full kernels to the tip. These ears symbolically represent nurturing mothers. The metaphor is that these corn maidens, like human mothers, provide nurture and nourishment to the people so that they will live into old age. Just as mothers feed their families every day, so too will the corn feed the people every day. This is the reason that people are said to nurse from Mother Earth, that is, take life from the things of the earth. The use of corn maidens in the sense of mothers in this song can also be understood as a metaphorical reference to the idea of rebirth. Just as dawn brings a rebirth of a new day, an idea that was alluded to at the opening of the song, so too does giving perfect ears of corn, *totsmingwu,* called "corn mothers," to infants, allude to the hopes that they will have a perfect life.

133. *Angaktsìntawi*[1]

Ayangqöö'ö,[2]
taavangqö,[3]
sakwa'oomaw[4] *tùutukwiwmakyango,*[5]
umu'uyiy[6] *aw*[7] *yookiinayani.*[8]
Ayangqöö'ö,
hoopaqö,[9]
qöya'oomaw[10] *tùutukwiwmakyango,*
talaawiptimakyangw[11] *yoy'ùmtimaani.*[12]
Oo'ohoo ohoo ohoowa.
Yaahiina, yaahii yaahii ya.
Hiy'aa aha aha yaaheloo.

From over there,
from the southwest,
the blue/green clouds, while going along stacked up,
will make it rain on your planted fields.
From over there,
from the northeast,
the white clouds, while going along stacked up,
and while going along with lightning flashing, will go along thundering.
(Vocables.)

1. *angaktsìntawi* 'Long-Hair katsina song'.
2. = *ayangqw'ö,* pausal form of *ayángqw* 'from over there'.
3. = *taavangqw* 'from the southwest'.
4. = *sakwa'omaw* 'blue/green cloud'.
5. = *tùutukwiwmakyangw* 'while going along stacked up in several stacks', a reference to thunderheads. This is a stative (*-iw-*) progressive (*-ma*) verb based on *tùutukwi* 'peaks, buttes, mountains', the plural of *tuukwi* 'promontory, peak, butte'.
6. = *umùu'uyiy,* object form of *umùu'uyi* 'your (plural) planted fields'.
7. *aw* 'to it, to there'.
8. = *yoknayani* 'will make it rain (plural)'. (In this song, the inflected forms are in the singular except for this one, *yoknayani*. This one form is the key to the understanding that all are plural in intent despite the exercise of poetic licence in leaving the rest of them in singular form.)
9. = *hoopaqw* 'from the northeast'.
10. = *qöya'omaw* 'white cloud'.
11. = *talwiptimakyangw* 'while going along with lightning flashing'.
12. = *yoy'ùmtimani* 'will go along thundering (slowly)'.

The katsinas sing about how they are stacking themselves up as clouds preparatory to raining on the people's fields. They will be coming from two directions, first the southwest and then the northeast. The two directions are opposite pairs that are arranged in counterclockwise order. Each direction is associated with a different color; the clouds from the southwest are blue/green and those from the northeast are white.

The description of the clouds as stacked brings to mind vivid images of thunderheads piling up prior to a summer rainstorm. Jagged flashes of lightning and great peals of rumbling thunder always accompany these summer storms and these very real events are noted by the katsinas. However, because the clouds, in the Hopi universe, are animate, the lightning and thunder are said to be purposely moving across the land, leaving rain in their wake.

134. *Avatshoyat$_1$ Taawi'at$_2$*

Ayamo$_3$ kivanasave,$_4$
tookilat$_5$ naasami$_6$ pítuqw'ö,$_7$
itanam$_8$ paho'iniy$_9$ naa'itnakyango,$_{10}$
umungem$_{11}$ péwi'i,$_{12}$
wuupat$_{13}$ qatsi'nangwat,$_{14}$
nátuwanmumuya.$_{15}$

1. *Avatshoyat,* object form of *Avatshoya* 'Corn Dancer'.
2. *taawi'at* 'his song' (*Avatshoyat taawi'at* 'Corn Dancer's song').
3. = *ayám* 'over there'.
4. *kivanasave* 'in the middle of the kiva'.
5. *tookilat,* object form of *tookila* 'night'. *Tookila* is the subject of its clause but the object form is used because of the adverbial status of the subordinate clause.
6. *naasami* 'to the middle, halfway'.
7. *pítuqw'ö,* subordinate clause pausal form of *pitu* 'arrive, come, get there, reach a destination'.
8. *itanam* 'our fathers'.
9. *paho'iniy,* object form of *paho'ini'am* 'their tray of prayer feathers'.
10. = *naa'itnakyàakyangw* 'while passing around among selves'.
11. *umungem* 'for you (plural), for your benefit'.
12. = *pew'i,* pausal form of *pew* 'toward here, coming this way'.
13. *wuupat,* object form of *wuupa* 'long, tall'.
14. *qatsi'nangwat,* object form of *qatsi'nangwa* 'will to live'.
15. = *natwanmumuya* 'be repeatedly making efforts in support of life-promoting practices', a reference to the successive offering of prayers by those preparing prayer feathers.

Pu'$_{16}$ tuwat$_{17}$ ayangqö,$_{18}$
naanan'ivaqw$_{19}$ pew$_{20}$ oo'omawutu,$_{21}$
kuukuyvakyango,$_{22}$
umungem péwi'i,
naanatuwanit$_{23}$ paa'o'oyimani.$_{24}$

Over there in the middle of the kiva.
when it reaches midnight,
while our fathers pass their tray of prayer feathers around,
they repeatedly offer prayers,
for your benefit here,
for the will to live a long life,
Now for our part, from over there,
coming from the different directions around, [we] clouds,
when [we] make [our] appearance,
for your benefit,
[we] will come placing water on the different practices for the renewal of
    life.

This song describes some of the preparations that take place in the kiva
prior to the arrival of the katsinas. Because the center of the kiva metaphorically represents the place where all life emerged, prayers for the
renewal of life take place here. Just after midnight on the day of the performance, the fathers sit in a circle in the middle of the kiva and pass the
tray of prayer feathers from man to man. The prayer feathers are carefully
arranged in a circle with their breath ends at the edge of the tray so that,
as each man accepts the tray, he breathes his prayer over their breath. This
prayerful activity is centered on expressing the collective dedication of all
the people of the village to renew their efforts to engage in practices that

16. *pu'* 'now, then'.
17. *tuwat* 'in turn, for (one's) part'.
18. = *ayángqw* 'from over there'.
19. *naanan'ivaqw* 'from the different directions around'.
20. *pew* 'toward here, coming this way'.
21. = *oo'omawt* 'clouds'.
22. = *kuukuyvakyangw* 'while making their appearance'.
23. = *naanatwanit,* object form of *naanatwani* 'different sorts of life-promoting practices,
    practices for the renewal of life'.
24. = *paa'o'oytimani* 'will go along placing water'. (In a plural context like that of the
    song, this would be *paa'o'oytiwisni* in normal speech.)

support the renewal of life, here expressed as the will to live a long healthful and happy life.

The katsinas then say that they will, for the benefit of the people, come as clouds from the different directions and place their water on the different life-promoting practices (*natwani*), a reference to all the ritual practices as well as daily activities that promote the renewal of life. Typically in songs the katsinas say they will place their water on the planted fields, that is, they will nurture the plants with their rain, but here they are, metaphorically, nurturing the practices that promote the maintenance and rejuvenation of life with their rainwater. Indeed, planting corn is a practice that promotes the renewal of life and so in this indirect way, the katsinas are saying that their rainwater is nurturing this practice.

135. *Avatshoyat Taawi'at$_1$*

Yuuyahiwa,$_2$
ayamo$_3$ Nuvatukya'ove'e.$_4$
Oo'omawutu,$_5$
angqw$_6$ puma$_7$ naayuwasinaya,$_8$
péwi'i.$_9$
Yahii àahaay.
Pu'$_{10}$ tuwat$_{11}$ aye'e,$_{12}$
paavasnawita$_{13}$

1. *Avatshoyat taawi'at* 'Corn Dancer's song'.
2. *yuuyahiwa* 'have been dressed or prepared as for a ceremony, have become adorned (plural)'.
3. = *ayám* 'over there, at that place over there'.
4. *Nuvatukya'ove'e,* pausal form of *Nuvatukya'ove* 'at the San Francisco Peaks', punctive form of *Nuvatukya'ovi.*
5. = *oo'omawt* 'clouds'.
6. *angqw* 'from there'.
7. *puma* 'they'.
8. = *naayuwsinaya* 'dress or clothe selves, adorn selves'.
9. = *pew'i,* pausal form of *pew* 'toward here, coming this way'.
10. *pu'* 'now, then'.
11. *tuwat* 'in turn, for (one's) part'.
12. *aye'e,* pausal form of *ayé'* 'along over there, in that area over there'.
13. = *paavasnawit* 'along the fields'.

uuyimanatu₁₄ naawungwinani,₁₅
pu' tuwat aye'e,
tuuwapongyava₁₆ sìitalawvaqö'ö.₁₇
Taayungwa'áy.₁₈
Àahaay, aa'ììhi.

They have been adorned
over there at the San Francisco Peaks.
The clouds
from there, they adorned themselves,
to come here.
(Vocables of Corn Dancer)
Then, for their part, over there,
along the fields,
the plant maidens will make themselves grow,
while then, in turn, over there,
it becomes bright with flowers along the land.
Look upon it.
(Corn Dancer's closing vocables)

The song describes the preparations that the clouds are making at their home at *Nuvatukya'ovi*, the San Francisco Peaks. They have been adorning themselves with rain and other good things of life which they will bring to the people for their benefit. *Yuuyahiwa* refers to the many kinds of dressing preparations necessary to get ready for a ceremonial performance.

Then the katsinas remark on how the corn plants, the [corn] plant maidens, are making themselves grow, implicitly from their rain, although this is not articulated. The Hopi belief that all living things are in charge of their own destiny is embodied in the reflexive expression *naawungwnayani* 'will make selves grow'. Likewise the fields will become bright with flowers, again implicitly from the katsinas' rain. Life is a process of active engagement with the resources that Sand Altar Woman has provided. In

14. = *uuyimamant* 'plant maidens'.
15. = *naawungwnayani* 'will make selves grow'.
16. *tuuwapongyava* 'along the land'.
17. = *sìitalawvaqw'ö*, subordinate clause pausal form of *sìitalawva* 'become bright with flowers'.
18. = *taayungwa'áy*, expressive imperative form of *taayungwa* 'look (plural)'.

Hopi belief, a fulfilled life will not come from sitting back and taking what comes your way, but only from working hard and following the practices that preserve the life of the community. At the end of the song the katsinas encourage the people to look upon the gift of the katsinas—a land bright with the signs of growing life.

136. *Avatshoyat Taawi'at*[1]

Ha'o[2] *haw*[3] *íngumu.*[4]
Ha'o haa'o[5] *haw ínamu.*[6]
Itam[7] *umumi*[8] *tiiti'ökiwa.*[9]
Itam hàalayyani.[10]
Oovi[11] *uma*[12] *itamumi*[13] *qatsi'unangwata*[14] *naawakinaqw'ö,*[15]
umungem[16] *tuu'awimani.*[17]
Aa haa ay.

Hark, o my mothers.
Hark, o my fathers.
We have come in dance for you.
Let us (all) be happy.
That's why you (should) pray to us for the will to live,
and for your benefit we will take the message.
(Vocables.)

1. *Avatshoyat tawi'at* 'Corn Dancer's song'.
2. *ha'o,* vocative particle.
3. *haw,* vocative particle.
4. = *ingum* 'my mothers'.
5. *haa'o,* vocative particle.
6. = *inam* 'my fathers'.
7. *itam* 'we'.
8. *umumi* 'to you (plural)'.
9. *tiiti'ökiwa* 'have come in dance (and thereby to soothe)'.
10. *hàalayyani* 'will be happy (plural)'.
11. *oovi* 'that's why'.
12. *uma* 'you (plural)'.
13. *itamumi* 'to us'.
14. = *qatsi'nangwat,* object form of *qatsi'nangwa* 'will to live'.
15. = *naanawaknaqw'ö,* subordinate clause object form of *naanawakna* 'pray, want (plural)'.
16. *umungem* 'for you (plural), for your benefit'.
17. = *tuu'awmani* 'will go to announce, take a message'.

The Corn Dancer katsinas announce to the people, their mothers and fathers, that they have come to perform for them. They urge everyone, people and katsinas, to be happy. The katsinas remind of the reciprocal relationship that exists between them. If the people pray for the will to live, that is, for the strength to continue to strive to live the life of corn, then the katsinas promise to take these prayers back with them when they return to their homes. Unsaid but implied is that if their prayers are deemed sincere, the katsinas will come as rain.

137. *Avatshoyat Taawi'at*[1]

Kwiyavasnawita,[2]
kaway'uu'uuyit[3] *anga,*[4]
ang[5] *soosonway.*[6]
Ang kwangwahimu'yta.[7]
Anga,
anga himu'yta.[8]
Aahaa.
Wiya'ii, yo'a, yo'a, yo'a, yo'a, haa.

  Along the fields with windbreaks,
along the watermelon plants,
along there things are beautiful.
Along there they have pleasing things.
Along there,
along there they have things.
(Vocables.)

This song is sung by a chorus of Mudhead katsinas (*Kookoyemsim*) during a Corn Dancer performance. The katsinas are describing a watermelon field that has brush windbreaks designed to keep the sandy soil from

---

1. *Avatshoyat taawi'at* 'Corn Dancer's song'.
2. = *kwiyavasnawit* 'along the fields with windbreaks constructed on them'.
3. = *kaway'u'uyit*, object form of *kaway'u'uyi* 'multiple watermelon plants'.
4. = *ang* 'along it, along there, in that area, in several places'.
5. *ang* 'along it, along there, in that area, in several places'.
6. *soosonway* 'beautiful (plural)'.
7. *kwangwahimu'yta* 'have something pleasing, useful, convenient, readily accessible'.
8. *himu'yta* 'have something, have things'.

covering the plants. The "pleasing things" the katsinas refer to on the watermelon plants are the developing fruits. They are seen as beautiful because they hold the promise of nourishment that will sustain life.

138. *Hewtokatsìntawi$_1$*

Túwati,$_2$
túwati,
omàwkiikiinawita,$_3$
tukwunangwmamàntu,$_4$
paayoynguman'iniy$_5$ angqw$_6$ pew$_7$ na'sasa'yyungwa,$_8$
yang$_9$ puma$_{10}$ umùu'uyiy$_{11}$ put$_{12}$ ang$_{13}$ yoknayaniqe'e.$_{14}$
Yan'i,$_{15}$
yani$_{16}$ úma'a,$_{17}$
naawakinaya.$_{18}$
Hiy aa ii'ii.
Oovi,$_{19}$
umùu'uyiy ánga'a,$_{20}$

1. *hewtokatsìntawi* 'Hewto katsina song'. This song could also be danced and sung by the Tsa'kwayna katsina; their styles of dancing and singing are interchangeable.
2. = *tuwat* 'in turn, for (one's) part'.
3. = *oomàwkiikinawit* 'along the dwelling places of the clouds'.
4. = *tukwunangwmamant* 'cumulus cloud maidens'.
5. *paayoynguman'iniy,* object form of *paayoynguman'ini'am* 'their trays of rainwater cornmeal'.
6. *angqw* 'from it, from there'.
7. *pew* 'toward here, coming this way'.
8. *na'sasa'yyungwa* 'be prepared, have things ready (plural)'.
9. *yang* 'along here, in this area'.
10. *puma* 'they'.
11. *umùu'uyiy,* object form of *umùu'uyi* 'your (plural) plants'.
12. *put,* object form of *pam* 'that/those'. Here *put* means 'those' because it is in construction with *umùu'uyiy* 'your (plural) plants'.
13. *ang* 'along it, along there, in that area, in or to several places'.
14. *yoknayaniqe'e,* subordinate clause pausal form of *yoknayani* 'will make it rain (plural)'.
15. *yan'i,* pausal form of *yan* 'in this way, like this, thus'.
16. = *yan* 'like this, in this way, thus'.
17. *úma'a,* pausal form of *uma* 'you (plural)'.
18. = *naanawakna* 'pray (plural)'.
19. *oovi* 'that's why'.
20. = *ang'a,* pausal form of *ang* 'along it, along there, in an area, in several places'.

yoo- yokvaqö'ö,[21]
ang paatalawvaqö'ö,[22]
tuvevakwatu,[23] mösivakwatu,[24]
ang púma'a,[25]
töötökimakyangw[26] sosonkiwyani.[27]
Wii yaa wii yaa yaaw.
Wii yaa yaa'inyo.
Hiy'aa hiy'aa aayahiy aa aayahiy'aa.

For their part,
for their part,
along the cloud dwelling places,
the cumulus cloud maidens,
have prepared their rainwater as cornmeal on a tray coming from there,
and along here, they will make it rain on those plants of yours.
Like this,
you are praying for it to be
like this.
(Vocables.)
That's why,
when it rains
along your plants,
and the land begins to glisten with water along there,
the toads of various colors and the food-packet toads,
along there, they
will be pleasing while going along making their calls.
(Vocables.)

The Hewto katsinas are describing how they, as cumulus cloud maidens
(*tukwunangwmamant*), are preparing themselves at their cloud dwelling
houses to arrive as rain to the planted fields. In Hopi belief everything in
the universe has a purpose. Here they are talking about the role of the

---

21. = *yokvaqw'ö*, subordinate clause pausal form of *yokva* 'rain'.
22. = *paatalawvaqw'ö*, subordinate clause pausal form of *paatalawva* 'come to glisten with water'.
23. = *tuvevakwam* 'toads of various colors'.
24. = *mösivakwam* 'food-packet toads'.
25. *púma'a*, pausal form of *puma* 'they'.
26. = *töötöqtimakyangw* 'while going along making characteristic calls, sounds'.
27. *sosonkiwyani* 'will be pleasing (plural)'.

clouds who are preparing their rain as raindrops. Gathered in the clouds, these raindrops are in a state of readiness to descend. This state of rain is metaphorically likened to cornmeal that women grind and pile on trays preparatory to making various corn-based foods for their families. A particularly creative compound word, *paayoynguman'ini,* their trays of rainwater cornmeal, combines *paayoyangw,* rainwater, with *ngumni,* finely ground cornmeal, to emphasize the particulate state of both. This idea is then joined with *na'sasa'yungwa* to connote that this rain is in a state of readiness. In this way both rain and the cornmeal that results from the rain are being prepared to nourish the people.

The katsinas say they will "make it rain" on the people's plants. In Hopi belief, rain does not descend on its own. It has to be caused to rain, and prayer is the causal agent. Thus, just as the cloud maidens condense the moisture into raindrops in the clouds before they descend as rain, so must the young women grind the corn kernels into meal before it can be prepared as food. The katsinas remark that this bounty of the rain is what the people have been praying for.

This beautiful metaphor likening rain to cornmeal—the two essential sources of Hopi nourishment—is apparently very old. In cultures that pass their traditions along orally, the same ideas are transmitted in many formats, some of which can be recovered from prehistoric materials. The Hopis visually depict their ideas about the cosmos on katsina clothing, petroglyphs, as well as on pottery, textile and basketry design. One of the most poignant images that directly visualizes the metaphorical message in this song can be found on a fifteenth century mural from a kiva at Awat'ovi, a former Hopi community on Antelope Mesa. Two pairs of figures are seated on the ground, the "sand altar." Two of the figures are clearly seated on ears of corn. Each pair holds a tray into which descends a stream of particulate matter, representing both cornmeal and rain. Two of the figures are breathing in the goodness of this nourishing food as indicated by the arrow-shaped objects pointing into their mouths (Smith 1952: Fig. 80b).

In the second section of the song the katsinas remark metaphorically how the rains bring a rebirth of life to the land in terms of toads "of many colors," *tuvevakwam,* who make their cries of pleasure, *töötöki,* at the coming of rain. In their emergence from the ground after a rain, they are metaphors for the rebirth of life that comes with rain. The katsinas also describe the presence of spiritually food-laden toads, *mösivakwa,* who carry packets of food, *mösi'at,* that serve to nurture the prayers as they journey from the people to the katsinas.

139. Hewtokatsìntawi[1]

Ha'o[2] ha'o íngumu.[3]
Ha'o ha'o ínamu.[4]
Me[5] ura[6] kyaahisathaqamo,[7]
Qatsiyamakiwqat[8] pasìwtiqö'ö'ö,[9]
ura soyohìmqaaqa'öt[10] soona'ytaqata,[11]
angqw[12] pew[13] qatsituvinglawu.[14]
Ta'a,[15]
pu'[16] hintani?[17]
Ókiwa,[18]
kur[19] antsa[20] yanìwtini.[21]
Uma[22] peevewìntiqe'e'e,[23]
koliyawsi'uyit[24] momitaviya,[25]
yépe'e.[26]

1. hewtokatsìntawi 'Hewto katsina song'.
2. ha'o, vocative particle.
3. = ingum 'my mothers'.
4. = inam 'my fathers'.
5. me, a particle to direct another's attention.
6. ura, modal of recollection: 'as I recall, as you'll recall'.
7. = kyaahisathaqam 'sometime very long ago'.
8. Qatsiyamakiwqat, object form of Qatsiyamakiwqa 'the Emergence, that which emerges as life'.
9. = pasìwtiqw'ö, pausal form of pasìwtiqw 'when (it) was planned', subordinated form of pasìwti 'get planned'.
10. = soyohìmqaqa'öt, object form of soyohìmqaqa'ö 'all different kinds of corn'.
11. = soona'ytaqat, object form of soona'ytaqa 'that which has nutriment'.
12. angqw 'from it, from there'.
13. pew 'toward here, coming this way'.
14. qatsituvinglawu 'be petitioning for acceptance to join the life of a village'.
15. ta'a 'all right, I agree'.
16. pu' 'now, then'.
17. hintani 'will be some way, how will (it) be'.
18. = okiw 'humbly, pitifully'.
19. kur, modal of inference.
20. antsa 'truly, really, indeed'.
21. yanìwtini 'will happen this way'.
22. uma 'you (plural)'.
23. peevewìntiqe'e, pausal form of peevewìntiqe 'since (you) have come to doubt', subordinate clause form of peevewìnti 'become doubtful, come to disbelieve, lose faith'.
24. koliyawsi'uyit, object form of koliyawsi'uyi 'pretentious, flashy talk'.
25. momitaviya 'prefer, give preference to, favor (plural)'.
26. = yep'e, pausal form of yep 'here'.

Hìita$_{27}$ túwati$_{28}$ umùutimu$_{29}$ soona 'ykyangw$_{30}$ qaavomi 'i,$_{31}$
taymani?$_{32}$
Hìita púma 'a,$_{33}$
toko 'ykyango$_{34}$ wuyomiq 'a,$_{35}$
qatsita$_{36}$ naavokyawnani?$_{37}$
Aya wina hay 'iiye.
Aya wina wina wina, wina, ahay 'iiye.

Hark o my mothers.
Hark o my fathers.
Look, remember a long time ago
when the Emergence was planned,
remember all the different kinds of corn that had the nutriment,
and that coming from there, you were petitioning for acceptance to live
    here.
All right,
now how will it be?
It is pitiful
that this will really come true (as was predicted).
Since you have come to doubt,
you have given favor to pretentious talk
here.
What will your children have as sustenance
while they look toward the future?
What will they
have as substance,
[so as to] experience life to the fullest toward old age?
(Vocables)

27. *hìita*, object form of *himu* 'something, what'.
28. = *tuwat* 'in turn, for (one's) part'.
29. = *umùutim* 'your (plural) children'.
30. *soona 'ykyangw* 'while having nutriment'.
31. *qaavomi 'i*, pausal form of *qaavomi* 'toward tomorrow, toward the future'.
32. *taymani* 'will go along looking, watching for'.
33. *púma 'a*, pausal form of *puma* 'they'.
34. = *toko 'ykyangw* 'while having flesh'.
35. *wuyomiq 'a*, pausal form of *wuyomiq* 'toward old age'.
36. = *qatsit*, object form of *qatsi* 'life'.
37. *naavokyawnani* 'will experience to the fullest'.

This song is an admonition that addresses the people's faltering belief in the core precepts of the corn lifeway. The katsinas begin by asking their mothers and fathers to remember when life was planned at Emergence. At this time Màasaw offered everyone their choice of corn and the lifeway that each entailed. The katsinas remind them that they chose the small ear of corn that "had the nutriment." Nutriment (*soona'at*) here has two meanings. The corn's *soona'at,* its germ, is the literal nutriment. *Soona'at* also refers metaphorically to the belief that the core precepts of the communal lifeway are the figurative sustenance that sustains Hopi life. Then the katsinas remind people that when they petitioned for acceptance to the village, they agreed to live by the corn lifeway and to give up all other separate and independent ways of living. They lament that the people apparently doubt (*peevewìnti*) that the core beliefs and principles of the Hopi lifeway will sustain them because they are no longer living by them.

The katsinas then attempt, rhetorically, to stimulate the people to think about the consequences of their failure to adhere to the corn lifeway they originally chose. Essentially, the katsinas are asking, what are you going to do now? They comment that it is pitiful that it has come to this, to a state where gossip and self-aggrandizement run the village. The song word *koliyawsi'uyi* (pretentious, flashy talk) combines the words *koliyaw* (gossip), *sihu* (flower), and *uuyi* (plant), comparing gossip to a showy flowering plant, to convey the idea that gossip often initially attracts attention but in the end has no substance. The implied concern is that flowery language may impress others, but it can also be used to embellish information that leads to rumors that create divisions in the community.

The katsinas rhetorically ask, if you pursue this course, what will your children have to live by? This query implies that if they do not continue to live by corn and all the communal practices necessary for this life, then their children not only, literally, will not have enough to eat because their parents have been preoccupied with activities other than providing for their families, but also, figuratively, they will not have learned the social practices of living in a communal society and will not have learned how to perform all the religious and social obligations and practices that such a life entails. In order to "experience life to the fullest toward old age," that is, to live a life of health, happiness, and freedom from want, it is necessary to adhere to the moral imperatives of the Hopi lifeway. In essence, the katsinas are telling the people that if they reject this life, they will have no future, and, ultimately, by implication, the future of the community is at risk.

140. *Honànkatsìntawi$_1$*

Ha'óo$_2$ ha'óo haw$_3$ íngumu.$_4$
Ha'óo ha'oo haw ínamu.$_5$
Ayám$_6$ hapi$_7$ Kisiwvave'e,$_8$
Honanwùutaqa,$_9$
powatawiyu,$_{10}$ yòytatawiyu$_{11}$ taatawlawu,$_{12}$
pépe'e.$_{13}$
Piw$_{14}$ hapi ayamo$_{15}$ Kiqötsmoviyuy$_{16}$ épe'e,$_{17}$
itam$_{18}$ hapi umuy$_{19}$ powatawisa.$_{20}$
Umùu'unangw$_{21}$ hapi$_{22}$ qöninita,$_{23}$
yépe'e.$_{24}$
Oovi$_{25}$ úma'a,$_{26}$
qa$_{27}$ ansa$_{28}$ naanami$_{29}$ talöngwintota,$_{30}$

1. *honànkatsìntawi* 'Badger katsina song'.
2. *ha'óo*, vocative particle.
3. *haw*, vocative particle.
4. = *ingum* 'my mothers'.
5. = *inam* 'my fathers'.
6. *ayám* 'over there'.
7. *hapi* 'truly, surely, certainly'.
8. *Kisiwvave'e*, pausal form of *Kisiwvave* 'at Shadow Spring'.
9. *Honanwùutaqa* 'Old Man Badger'.
10. = *powatawiy*, object form of *powatawi'at* 'his curing song'.
11. = *yòytatawiy*, object form of *yòytatawi'at* 'his rain songs'.
12. *taatawlawu* 'keep singing songs'.
13. = *pep'e*, pausal form of *pep* 'at that place, there'.
14. *piw* 'also, too, again'.
15. = *ayám* 'over there'.
16. = *Kiqötsmoviyuy*, object form of *Kiqötsmovi* (Kykotsmovi), a Third Mesa village.
17. = *ep'e*, pausal form of *ep* 'there, at it'.
18. *itam* 'we'.
19. *umuy*, object form of *uma* 'you (plural)'.
20. *powatawisa* 'come to purify (plural)'.
21. = *umùu'unangwa* 'your (plural) hearts'.
22. *hapi* 'truly, surely, certainly'.
23. *qöninita* 'be whirling, turning around and around in place'.
24. = *yep'e*, pausal form of *yep* 'here'.
25. *oovi* 'that's why'.
26. *úma'a*, pausal form of *uma* 'you (plural)'.
27. *qa* 'not'.
28. *ansa* 'constant'.
29. *naanami* 'to one another'.
30. *talöngwintota* 'be going from day to day (plural)'.

yépe'e.
"Elo elo, elo elo.
[Keresan *"Ya'ay titiya,$_{31}$ vuniya$_{32}$ ma.*
"Ya'ay kowiya,$_{33}$ haniya$_{34}$ maatsiw. "$_{Keresan]}$
Yanhaqamo,$_{35}$
Honanwùutaqa,
powatawiyu, yòytatawiyu taatawlawu,
pépe'e.
Aaya'me aaya'me.
Polaynay$_{36}$ aa ii.

Hark, hark, o my mothers.
Hark, hark, o my fathers.
Over there, truly, at Shadow Spring,
Old Man Badger
keeps singing his purifying song and his rain songs
there.
Also, truly, over at Kiqötsmovi,
we are truly coming to purify you.
Your hearts are truly whirling
here.
That's why you
are not constant to one another as you go from day to day
here.
"(Vocables)
"(Keresan words)"

31. *Titiya* represents Keresan 'north', cf. Santa Ana *d^{y}íd^{y}A* (Davis 1964: 166). The cardinal directions in the other Pueblo languages, unlike the northwest, southwest, southeast, northeast directions of Hopi, are north, west, south, east, at least as translated by the sources available. The Keresan cardinal directions are from Davis (1964), Miller (1965), and Miller and Davis (1963); the Zuni directions are listed in Eriacho (1998: 33); and the Tewa directions are described in Harrington (1907–1908: 41–42).
32. *Vuniya* represents Keresan 'west', cf. Santa Ana *bə* 'west', *bánámí* 'westward' (Davis 1964: 165).
33. *Kowiya* represents Keresan 'south', cf. Santa Ana *ku* 'south', *kúwámí* 'southward' (Davis 1964: 167).
34. *Haniya* represents Keresan 'east', cf. Santa Ana *ha·* 'east', *há·námí* 'eastward' (Davis 1964: 166).
35. = *yanhaqam* 'in approximately this way'.
36. *polaynay,* expressive form of *polayna,* a vocable used to save one from the consequences of singing or saying something that is taboo.

Thus
Old Man Badger
keeps singing his curing song and his rain songs
here.
Polaynay (vocables).

This is a song of admonition from Old Man Badger who is singing a purifying and healing song for the community of Kiqötsmovi. The Badger clan (*Honanngyam*), known for their healing powers, previously lived at Shadow Spring, in the northeast cardinal direction. The Badger katsinas who are singing this song are not necessarily members of the Badger clan. They are simply bringing the curing message of Old Man Badger to restore the village to a state of spiritual health.

The verb *powata* means to cure someone of a physical ill or to change a behavioral problem such as drinking or smoking. Here the problem is that the people of the village are morally disoriented, described here as "their hearts are whirling" (*qöninita*), as manifest by their inconsistent treatment of each other from day to day. Communal societies survive when every member performs his or her respective responsibilities as determined by their stage of life and roles related to these stages. In this sense, the community, not separate families or clans in Hopi society, literally and figuratively support and nurture every member into fulfillment and old age. For this reason, when people abandon these moral imperatives that underpin the communal good, the integrity of the community is in jeopardy.

The katsinas are bringing this healing song from Old Man Badger in an effort to reinspire the people to return to a life in which everyone adheres to the practices that support the corn lifeway. This song is also a rain song (*yòytatawi*), because indirectly the katsinas are implying that until the people resolve to change their behavior and live with united hearts for the welfare of the community, they will not arrive as rain.

The use of Keresan words that enumerate the four directions may be a way for Old Man Badger to bring his healing powers into the village. Emory suggested that *maatsiw* may be a Keresan word describing the brushlike motion with a bird wing that is intended to symbolically sweep away the divisive activities that have been going on in the village. The word *polaynay* at the end of the song is a vocable used to save oneself from the consequences of singing about something taboo. In this context it may refer to the kind of protection that the Badger katsinas feel they need because they have been singing about a subject so fraught with potential destructive consequences that they do not want to be tainted by it.

141. *Koyemsitawi*$_1$

Weenimay$_2$ *ep*$_3$ *itam*$_4$ *Kooyemsim*$_5$ *naayuwasinat'a,*$_6$
angqw$_7$ *itam umumi*$_8$ *péwi'i,*$_9$
tiiti'ökiwa.$_{10}$
Taayiyungwa'a.$_{11}$

We Mudhead katsinas, after having adorned ourselves at *Weenima*,
from there we have come to you
in dance.
Watch [us].

The Mudhead katsinas (*Kookoyemsim*) sing that they have first adorned themselves with the people's prayers at their home at *Weenima* in the southeast cardinal direction and now they are coming to the village to dance for the people. Their directive, "Watch us," *Taayungwa'a*, is intended, literally, to invite the people to watch them dance as well as, figuratively, to watch them arrive as rain.

1. *koyemsitawi* 'Mudhead katsina song'.
2. *Weenimay*, object form of *Weenima*, the southeast katsina home.
3. *ep* 'there, at it'.
4. *itam* 'we'.
5. = *Kookoyemsim* 'Mudhead katsinas'.
6. = *naayuwsinat'a*, pausal form of *naayuwsinat* 'after clothing, adorning selves'.
7. *angqw* 'from it, from there'.
8. *umumi* 'to you (plural)'.
9. = *pew'i*, pausal form of *pew* 'toward here, coming this way'.
10. *tiiti'ökiwa* 'have come in dance (and thereby to soothe)'.
11. = *taayungwa'a*, imperative form of *taayungwa* 'look at, watch (plural)'.

142. *Qa'ötotimuy₁ Taawi'am₂*

Pay₃ ura₄ hísato.₅
Pay ura hísathaqam₆ tuuwapongyava₇ sìitalawvaqö'ö,₈
ang₉ ima₁₀ paavopkomatu₁₁ hàalay'unangway₁₂ naangöyimangwu.₁₃
Ayahayaa aahiyay'amii.
Naavaastoti'i,₁₄
íngumu,₁₅ ínamu.₁₆
Uma₁₇ yep₁₈ lolmat₁₉ qatsi'nangwat₂₀ yeesiwvaqö'ö,₂₁
naanan'ivaqw₂₂ pew₂₃ yooyaa'ökini.₂₄
Sìitàlpuva₂₅ uma taayimuyiwni.₂₆
Mee, aahaa aaha ahahaahaa. iihi ihihii.

Remember how it was long ago.
Remember how it used to become bright with flowers along the land,

1. *Qa'ötotimuy,* object form of *Qa'ötotim* 'Corn Boys'.
2. *taawi'am* 'their song'.
3. *pay,* expressive particle.
4. *ura,* modal of recollection: 'as I recall, as you'll recall'.
5. *hísato,* pausal of *hisat* 'sometime, when, long ago'.
6. *hísathaqam* 'sometime long ago'.
7. *tuuwapongyava* 'along the land'.
8. = *sìitalawvaqw'ö,* subordinate clause pausal form of *sìitalawva* 'become bright with flowers'.
9. *ang* 'along it, along there, in that area, in several places'.
10. *ima* 'these'.
11. = *paavopkomat* 'water creatures, the creatures of the natural world who are dependent on water for life'.
12. = *hàalay'unangway* 'with happy hearts, with beneficent intentions'.
13. = *naangöymangwu,* habitual tense form of *naangöyma* 'go along chasing one another'.
14. *naavaastoti'i,* imperative form of *naavaastoti* 'become caring of one another (plural)'.
15. = *ingum* 'my mothers'.
16. = *inam* 'my fathers'.
17. *uma* 'you (plural)'.
18. *yep* 'here'.
19. *lolmat,* object form of *lolma* 'beautiful, good, proper'.
20. *qatsi'nangwat,* object form of *qatsi'nangwa* 'will to live'.
21. = *yeesiwvaqw'ö,* subordinate clause pausal form of *yeesiwva* 'begin living (plural)'.
22. *naanan'ivaqw* 'from the different directions around'.
23. *pew* 'toward here, coming this way'.
24. = *yoy'ökini* 'will arrive, come as rain'.
25. *sìitàlpuva* 'along a land brightened with flowers'.
26. *taayimuyiwni* 'will look in awe'.

and how these, the water creatures, used to go along there chasing one
   another with happy hearts.
(Vocables.)
Become caring of one another,
my mothers and my fathers.
When you begin living with the will to live the beautiful life here,
[we] will come as rain from the different directions around.
You will look in awe along a land brightened with flowers.
(Vocables.)

This song of admonition is a plea in the form of a sermon to the people
from the Corn Boy katsinas. They urge the people to think back to the
past time when the land was beautiful with blooming flowers and the
water creatures (*paavopkomat*) were going along chasing each other (*naangöyma*) with happy hearts (*hàalay'unangway*). The intent is to create a
picture of a land where all creatures living on it are flourishing and
fulfilled. The implication is that this utopia is only attained when everyone
works together in harmony for the well-being of the community.

   The katsinas give their advice: *naavaastoti'i,* become caring of one
another. *Naavaasqatsi,* a life of mutual respect and caring, describes the
way individuals must put the good of the community above their self
interests. The katsinas set up a condition: if the people reform their ways
and begin living the humble life of corn, then they will come as rain from
all directions. When this happens, the people will be able to look with
grateful pleasure "along a land brightened with flowers," *sìitàlpuva.*

143. Qa'ötotimuy$_1$ (or Ngayayatotaqamuy$_2$) Taawi'am$_3$

Pay$_4$ ókiwa,$_5$
pay ókiwa nuu'u.$_6$
Pay nu'$_7$ yan'eway$_8$ Qa'ötiyoniikyango,$_9$
umungem$_{10}$ lolmat$_{11}$ qatsi'unangwata,$_{12}$
siwi'ytaniqat$_{13}$ wuuwantaqe'e,$_{14}$
umumi$_{15}$ tiitiwunuto.$_{16}$
Aya hayaa aa hiyay'amii.
Oovi$_{17}$ paasanawita$_{18}$ sòosoy$_{19}$ himu,$_{20}$
su'an$_{21}$ naatukwsinaqw'ö,$_{22}$
ang$_{23}$ uma$_{24}$ hàalay'unangway,$_{25}$
tal'angwnawita$_{26}$ taayimuyiwni.$_{27}$

1. *Qa'ötotimuy,* object form of *Qa'ötotim* 'Corn Boys'.
2. *Ngayayatotaqamuy,* object form of *Ngayayatotaqam* 'Those that Sway', a katsina type.
3. *taawi'am* 'their song'.
4. *pay,* expressive particle.
5. = *okiw* 'humbly, pitifully'.
6. *nuu'u,* pausal form of *nu'* 'I'.
7. *nu'* 'I'.
8. *yan'eway* 'such as this, like this, homely'.
9. = *Qa'ötiyoniikyangw* 'while being a Corn Boy'.
10. *umungem* 'for you (plural), for your benefit'.
11. *lolmat,* object form of *lolma* 'beautiful, good, proper'.
12. = *qatsi'nangwat,* object form of *qatsi'nangwa* 'will to live'.
13. *siwi'ytaniqat,* object form of *siwi'ytaniqa* 'that which will have vitality', literally, '... have tendrils'.
14. *wuuwantaqe'e,* subordinate clause pausal form of *wuuwanta* 'be thinking, worrying, wondering'.
15. *umumi* 'to you (plural)'.
16. *tiitiwunuto* 'go/come to stand dancing'.
17. *oovi* 'that's why'.
18. = *paasanawit* 'along the field'.
19. *sòosoy* 'all'.
20. *himu,* indefinite pronoun: 'something, what, one, you'.
21. *su'an* 'in just the right way, correctly'.
22. *naatukwsinaqw'ö,* subordinate clause pausal form of *naatukwsina* 'make self mature'.
23. *ang* 'along it, along there, in that area, in several places'.
24. *uma* 'you (plural)'.
25. *hàalay'unangway* 'with happy hearts, with beneficent intentions'.
26. = *tal'angwnawit* 'all summer long'.
27. *taayimuyiwni* 'will look in awe'.

Humble,
humble am I.
While being a Corn Boy such as this,
I have been thinking, for your benefit, about the will to live a good life
that will have vitality,
and I have come to be dancing dances for you.
(Vocables.)
That's why when everything along the fields,
makes itself mature as it should,
along there, you, with happy hearts,
will look upon it all summer long.

The Corn Boy katsina symbolizes the Hopi virtues of humility and selfless hard work that is necessary for the well-being of the community. His humble being is a metaphoric reference to the plain short ear of corn that the Hopi people chose at Emergence that defined their lifeway. Corn Boy represents the ideal of what every Hopi person should strive to be. His homely appearance stands for the modest, unselfish, unassuming demeanor that is the hallmark of individuals who care and share with others in the community however much self-sacrifice and hardship is required. Thus, in the song where he is thinking about "the will to live a good life that will have vitality," he is referring to the resolve one needs to have to live life for the continued well-being of the whole community. The embedded reference to tendrils in the phrase *siwi 'ytaniqa,* metaphorically likens the vitality in plant tendrils to people who are practicing practices devoted to the well-being and survival of their community. The implication is that if the people adhere to the tenets of humility and hard work they will be rewarded with a fulfilled life. Their plants, just as their children, will grow themselves up, here expressed by the phrase "mature as it should." Corn Boy comes to dance for the people in order to encourage and inspire them to rededicate themselves to strive to work selflessly for the well-being of the community. Although unsaid, it is clearly implied that when the people live this humble life of caring for and helping others, the katsinas will come as rain. As a consequence, Corn Boy says to the people, everything in your fields will flourish and mature, and you will go about looking upon all this plenty with happy hearts.

144. Qa'ötotimuy₁ (or Ngayayatotaqamuy₂) Taawi'am₃

Aa haa iihii.
I'omaw'inakwa₄ umumi₅ péwi'i,₆
sosonkiwyani.₇
Ayahaya aa hiyay'ami.
Uma₈ túwati,₉
umùu'uyiy₁₀ ang₁₁ paatalawvaqö'ö,₁₂
ang uma₁₃ taatawtimani;₁₄
ang uma hàalàytimani.₁₅
Haapi me.₁₆
Piw₁₇ tuuwat₁₈ aaye'e,₁₉
Naalönangwmongwitu,₂₀
talawipiy₂₁ hoohonginaya.₂₂
Aya haya aa hiyayami.
Uma túwati,
umùu'uyiy ang paatalawvaqö'ö,
ang uma taatawtimani;
ang uma hàalàytimani.

1. *Qa'ötotimuy*, object form of *Qa'ötotim* 'Corn Boys'.
2. *Ngayayatotaqamuy*, object form of *Ngayayatotaqam* 'Those that Sway', a katsina type.
3. *taawi'am* 'their song'.
4. *i'omaw'inakwa* 'the down feathers worn on my head'.
5. *umumi* 'to you (plural)'.
6. = *pew'i*, pausal form of *pew* 'toward here, coming this way'.
7. *sosonkiwyani* 'will be pleasing (plural)'.
8. *uma* 'you (plural)'.
9. = *tuwat* 'in turn, for (one's) part'.
10. *umùu'uyiy*, object form of *umùu'uyi* 'your (plural) plants'.
11. *ang* 'along it, along there, in that area, in several places'.
12. = *paatalawvaqw'ö*, subordinate clause pausal form of *paatalawva* 'come to glisten with water'.
13. *uma* 'you (plural)'.
14. *taatawtimani* 'will go along singing songs'.
15. *hàalàytimani* 'will go along expressing gladness'.
16. = *hapi me*, formulaic expression introducing the song's second part, *oomi* 'upward'.
17. *piw* 'also, too, again'.
18. = *tuwat* 'for your part'.
19. = *ayé'* 'along over there'.
20. = *Nalönangwmomngwit* 'Four-Directional Cloud Chiefs'.
21. = *talwipiy*, object form of *talwipi'am* 'their lightning'.
22. = *hoohongnaya* 'keep making (them) stand (plural)'.

(Vocables.)
The down feathers worn on my head
will be pleasing to you here.
(Vocables.)
You, for your part,
when it begins to glisten with water along your planted fields,
along there you will go singing;
along there you will go expressing gladness.
Listen, there is more.
Also for their part along over there,
the Four-Directional Cloud Chiefs
are making their lightning flashes stand.
(Vocables.)
You, for your part,
when it begins to glisten with water along your planted fields,
along there you will go singing;
along there you will go expressing gladness.

The Corn Boy katsinas are describing the swaying of the down feathers tied at the end of a string to the tops of their heads as they dance. The movement of these down feathers (*i'omaw'inakwa*) bouncing up and down is metaphorically equated with the building and movement of clouds before a storm, a pleasing and welcome image for the people, who have been praying to the katsinas to arrive as rain.

Then the katsinas, addressing the people, "you, for your part," describe how the people will go among their glistening planted fields singing in happiness over the coming of the rain. They describe how the Four-Directional Cloud Chiefs, who are the clouds from the four cardinal directions, will make flashes of lighting that appear to strike the land vertically. Lightning and thunder usually accompany the summer rainstorms that move across the high deserts in the southwest. In Hopi belief, lightning fertilizes the earth and everything on it. This concept is imaged in the fifteenth century kiva murals at Kawàyka'a and Awat'ovi. In these images vertical zigzags of lightning pierce the land, the "sand altar," represented as a horizontal line along the bottom of the mural, as well as enter the tops of ears of corn (Smith 1952: Figs. 76a and 81b respectively). The katsinas close by observing that when the rain makes the lands glisten, the people will go about their planted fields singing in happiness.

145. *Qa'ötotimuy₁ (or Ngayayatotaqamuy₂) Taawi'am₃*

Kwakwhá,₄
Qa'ömana₅ umungem₆ lolmat₇ wuuwantaqe'e,₈
itamuy₉ mongkimi₁₀ waawayilawu,₁₁
péwi'i.₁₂
Aya hayaa aahiyay'ami.
[Keresan *Titiya.₁₃ Vuniya.₁₄ Kowiya.₁₅ Haniya.₁₆* Keresan]
Oomaw'inakwa,₁₇
umungem paatayayatani.₁₈
Uuyisonaqa,₁₉
uuyimanatu₂₀ umungem,
naawungwintani.₂₁
Yahiy ooho oho hoo hoo iihi ihi hii hii.
[Keresan *Titiya. Vuniya. Kowiya. Haniya.* Keresan]
Oomaw'inakwa,
umungem paatayayatani.
Uuyisonaqa,
uuyimanatu umungem,

1. *Qa'ötotimuy*, object form of *Qa'ötotim* 'Corn Boys'.
2. *Ngayayatotaqamuy*, object form of *Ngayayatotaqam* 'Those that Sway', a katsina type.
3. *taawi'am* 'their song'.
4. *kwakwhá* 'thank you (male speaker)'.
5. *qa'ömana* 'corn maiden'.
6. *umungem* 'for you (plural), for your benefit'.
7. *lolmat,* object form of *lolma* 'beautiful, good, proper'.
8. *wuuwantaqe'e,* subordinate clause pausal form of *wuuwanta* 'be thinking, wondering'.
9. *itamuy* 'us', object form of *itam* 'we'.
10. *mongkimi* 'to the leadership place'.
11. = *wángwaylawu* 'keep summoning'.
12. = *pew'i,* pausal form of *pew* 'toward here, coming this way'.
13. *Titiya* represents Keresan 'north', cf. Santa Ana *dʸídʸA* (Davis 1964: 166).
14. *Vuniya* represents Keresan 'west', cf. Santa Ana *bə* 'west', *bánámí* 'westward' (Davis 1964: 165).
15. *Kowiya* represents Keresan 'south', cf. Santa Ana *ku* 'south', *kúwámí* 'southward' (Davis 1964: 167).
16. *Haniya* represents Keresan 'east' cf. Santa Ana *ha·* 'east', *hánámí* 'eastward' (Davis 1964: 166).
17. *oomaw'inakwa* 'the down feathers worn on my head'.
18. *paatayayatani* 'will be trembling with water'.
19. = *uysonaq* 'throughout the midst of the planted area(s)'.
20. = *uuyimamant* '(corn) plant maidens'.
21. *naawungwintani* 'will be making selves grow'.

naatukwsintani.[22]
Yahiy ooho oho hoo hoo, iihi ihi hii hii.

Thankfully,
The corn maiden has been thinking beautiful thoughts for your benefit
and keeps summoning us from the leadership place,
to come here.
(Vocables.)
(Keresan words for north, west, south, east.)
The down feathers worn on my head
will be trembling with water for your benefit.
In the midst of the planted fields,
the plant maidens
will be making themselves grow for you.
(Vocables.)
(Keresan words for north, west, south, east.)
The down feathers worn on my head,
will be trembling with water for your benefit.
In the midst of the planted fields,
the plant maidens
will be making themselves mature for you.
(Vocables.)

The Corn Boy katsinas are expressing their thanks that the corn maiden
(*qa'ömana*), who represents the corn plants, is thinking about the people.
The plants understand that the people need the rain. For this reason they
are repeatedly summoning the clouds to come from their homes in the
four cardinal directions. In this song the katsinas' cloud homes are
referred to as *mongki*, a word composed of *mongwi* 'leader' (*mong-*) and
kiihu 'house' (*-ki*) and translated here as the "leadership place." The four
directions are expressed here by Keresan rather than Hopi directional
words.

Then the katsinas say the down feathers worn on their heads (*oomaw-
'inakwa*) will be trembling with water (*paatayayata*) for the people's
benefit. This uses the extremely loud thundering sounds that seem to
cause the earth to shake to create an image of clouds shaking as the
thunder rolls along. This same idea is represented in a visual metaphor by

---

22. *naatukwsintani* 'will be making selves mature'.

the bouncing of the down feathers tied to the katsinas' heads as they dance. With the coming of the rain, the corn plants, here personified metaphorically as plant maidens (*uuyimamant*), will grow themselves for the people. Because every living thing in the Hopi universe is volitional, with the ability to control its fate, the plants are seen as willfully taking in the rain to make themselves grow to maturity.

146. *Qa'ötotimuy₁ (or Ngayayatotaqamuy₂) Taawi'am₃*

Heesita,₄ tsorosita₅ síqölönawita,₆
ang₇ ima₈ tátangayatu,₉
hàalay'unangway₁₀ naangöyimani.₁₁
Aye haya aahiyay'ami.
Pu'₁₂ tuwat₁₃ ayangqö,₁₄
naanan'ivaqö,₁₅
yooya'ökini.₁₆

Along the flowery expanses of mariposa lilies and blue asters,
there these yellowjackets
will go along, with happy hearts, chasing one another.
(Vocables.)
Then [we], for [our] part, from over there,
from the different directions around,
will arrive as rain.

1. *Qa'ötotimuy,* object form of *Qa'ötotim* 'Corn Boys'.
2. *Ngayayatotaqamuy,* object form of *Ngayayatotaqam* 'Those that Sway', a katsina type.
3. *taawi'am* 'their song'.
4. = *heesit,* object form of *heesi* 'mariposa lily/lilies'.
5. = *tsorosit,* object form of *tsorosi* 'blue aster(s)'.
6. = *sìiqölnawit* 'along the flowery expanse(s)'.
7. *ang* 'along it, along there, in that area, in several places'.
8. *ima* 'these'.
9. = *taatangayt* 'yellowjackets'.
10. = *hàalay'unangway* 'with happy hearts, with beneficent intentions'.
11. = *naangöymani* 'will go along chasing one another'.
12. *pu'* 'now, then'.
13. *tuwat* 'in turn, for (one's) part'.
14. = *ayángqw* 'from over there'.
15. = *naanan'ivaqw* 'from the different directions around'.
16. = *yoy'ökini* 'will arrive, come as rain'.

The katsinas are recalling the beautiful sight of yellowjackets chasing one other happily among the fields of mariposa lilies and blue asters. Although these flowers are not cultivated, it is a gratifying sight to see such an expanse of flourishing life in bloom that has the promise of life. The colorful flowers and yellowjackets bring to mind an image of the ideal world of the past where everything was full of life—a state of nature that every Hopi prays for. The katsinas close with the promise that they, for their part, will arrive as rain from the different cardinal directions to sustain this life.

147. Sivu'ikwiwtaqat Taawi'at$_1$

Sivu'ikwiwtaqa$_2$ qa$_3$ hìita$_4$ as$_5$ ápi'ewayniikyango,$_6$
ii- iikwilniyata$_7$ tulakinsivuta$_8$ akw$_9$ ima$_{10}$ siwamatu$_{11}$ tulakintota;$_{12}$
mamàntuy$_{13}$ púma'a,$_{14}$
tutuwnayakyangw$_{15}$ yang$_{16}$ tiitiwunima.$_{17}$
Le le he la.
Oovi$_{18}$ púma'a,
tuwi'yvayaqe'e,$_{19}$

1. Sivu'ikwiwtaqat taawi'at 'song of the Pot Carrier katsina'.
2. = Sivu'ikwiwtaqa 'Pot Carrier katsina, [the katsina] that carries a vessel on the back'.
3. qa 'not'.
4. hìita, object form of himu 'something, what'; qa hìita 'nothing'.
5. as 'presumably': something is claimed to be so without full evidence; himu as means something like 'should, I wish you would'.
6. = ápi'ewayniikyangw 'while seemingly useful'.
7. = iikwilniyat, object form of iikwilni'at 'his load on the back'.
8. = tulakinsivut, object form of tulakinsivu 'vessel for toasting cornmeal over fire'.
9. akw 'using, by means of, with'.
10. ima 'these'.
11. = siwamat 'their (males') younger sisters'.
12. tulakintota 'be toasting coarsely ground cornmeal (plural)'.
13. mamàntuy, object form of mamant 'girls'.
14. púma'a, pausal form of puma 'they'.
15. tutuwnayakyangw 'while showing how to do something (plural)'.
16. yang 'along here, in this area'.
17. = tiitiwunima 'be dancing in performance'
18. oovi 'that's why'.
19. tuwi'yvayaqe'e, subordinate clause pausal form of tuwi'yvaya 'learn (plural)'.

löqòmtiqe'e,$_{20}$
yang puma$_{21}$ *hàalaykyango*$_{22}$ *ngungumyakyangw*$_{23}$ *haahaninya.*$_{24}$

While the Pot Carrier katsina is seemingly a useless one,
these little sisters of his are using the load on his back, the toasting pot,
    to toast cornmeal,
and while they are showing the girls how to do it,
they are dancing along here.
(Vocables.)
That's why they,
when they learn,
when they go to begin their weddings,
they happily push and push down (the manos on the grinding stones)
    along here while they grind flour.

The Pot Carrier katsina (*Sivu'ikwiwtaqa*, "the one who carries a vessel on his back") is addressing one of the traditional tasks of women, that of preparing corn flour from shelled corn by grinding it on a metate. The parching pot that this katsina carries on his back is used to toast the coarsely ground cornmeal (*hakwurkwi*) before it is further processed into the fine corn flour (*ngumni*). Every woman has the daily responsibility of grinding sufficient quantities of corn into flour for her family. While it is a backbreaking, repetitive task, the proper processing of corn is something that every girl is expected to learn how to do before she is married.

Metaphorically, grinding corn is symbolic of the hard work and humility associated with work that sustains Hopi life. Performing humble work is one of the cornerstone moral imperatives of the Hopi ethic. No one is exempt from their obligations to perform such tasks. In this way everyone contributes equally to the maintenance of the community. The humble demeanor of this katsina is thus symbolic of Hopis who live this lifeway.

In this song the katsinas are describing how the younger sisters of this pot carrying katsina are toasting cornmeal to show the girls how it is done. They are also dancing as they are demonstrating. The katsinas'

---

20. *löqòmtiqe'e*, subordinate clause pausal form of *löqòmti* 'go to begin the weddings'.
21. *puma* 'they'.
22. = *hàalaykyangw* 'while being happy, happily'.
23. = *ngúmantotakyangw* 'while grinding into flour (plural)'.
24. = *haahannaya* 'be moving things down (plural)'.

sisters are not literally in the plaza performing this demonstration. Rather the katsinas are using this reference to remind the girls who are coming of age to pay attention and watch their mothers so that they will learn how to grind and toast corn. When the girls learn how to properly toast corn, they will have learned one more task that prepares them for their future role as a wife and mother. The word *löqòmtiqe* 'when they go to begin their weddings' refers to the period of time each of the girls spends in the house of her intended husband grinding corn and preparing meals for his family to demonstrate her skills and worth as a future wife.

The last line describes the process of grinding with the verb *haahanna* 'be moving things down'. This refers to the repeated and continuous pushing the corn under the mano down the slanted metate stone and then scooping that corn back up to the top of the metate with the hand to be repushed down again under the mano. This repeated motion is a metaphor for the lives of women who are literally and figuratively constantly in motion as they care for others. In addition, the repeated pushing down of the mano is understood to mean that the woman is causing the mano and thus the corn to climb down, the metaphoric equivalent to the way rain descends on the planted fields.

148. *Yöngöson'angaktsìntawi₁*

Aaha aa'aa'ayaamo.
Ayám₂ Kisiwu'oomàwkive'e,₃
ep₄ íma'a,₅
mongmatsiwtaqam,₆
ínamu.₇

1. *yöngöson'angaktsìntawi* 'Tortoise Long-Hair katsina song'.
2. *ayám* 'over there'.
3. = *Kisiw'omàwkive'e*, pausal form of *Kisiw'omàwkive* 'at the Shadow Springs dwelling place of the clouds'. *Kìisiw* 'Shadow Springs' is the northeast katsina home.
4. *ep* 'there, at it'.
5. *íma'a*, pausal form of *ima* 'these'.
6. *mongmatsiwtaqam* 'those who are known as leaders'.
7. = *inam* 'my fathers'.

Umùu'unangwvàasiyu,₈ umùutunatyayu₉ angqw₁₀ pew₁₁ taayimuyiwa.₁₂
Lee lehe la.
Owi'ii'ii₁₃ yesqamu,₁₄
uma₁₅ as₁₆ iitsyani.₁₇
Umùu'unangwvàasiy, umùutunatyayu sunsayaqö'ö,₁₈
pamniikyango₁₉ yooyangw₂₀ haahawiwmani.₂₁
Yana'o yana'o hiina ooyana'o hiina.
Yana'o yana'o yana'o aahaa ii'iihi'iihi hiihihihi.

(Vocables.)
Over at the Shadow Springs dwelling place of clouds,
there these are,
the ones who are known as leaders,
my fathers.
Coming from there, they look in expectation for your fervent hopes and
   religious intentions.
(Vocables.)
Yes, [you] who are living here
you should be prompt.
Your fervent hopes and religious intentions, when they are together as
   one,
that itself is the essence of the rain that will be coming down.
(Vocables.)

8. = *umùu'unangwvàasiy,* object form of *umùu'unangwvàasi* 'your (plural) heartfelt prayers'.
9. = *umùutunatyay,* object form of *umùutunatya* 'your (plural) religious intentions'.
10. *angqw* 'from it, from there'.
11. *pew* 'toward here, coming this way'.
12. *taayimuyiwa* 'look in awe'; *pew taayimuyiwa* 'look here in expectation'.
13. = *owí* 'yes'.
14. = *yesqam* 'those who are sitting, residing, living'.
15. *uma* 'you (plural)'.
16. *as* 'presumably': something is claimed to be so without full evidence. *Himu as* means something like "should, I wish you would."
17. *iitsyani* 'will/should be soon, early (plural)'.
18. = *sunsayaqw'ö,* subordinate clause pausal form of *sunsaya* 'be together as one, in harmony (plural)'.
19. = *pamniikyangw* 'while being that in itself'.
20. *yooyangw* 'rain'.
21. = *haahawiwmani* 'will go/come along descending, will be coming down'.

These Tortoise Long-Hair katsinas are at their cloud dwelling place in the northeast at Shadow Springs. They are observing that their fathers, that is, the katsinas' fathers, who are often called leaders, are waiting with expectation, looking to see the religious intention, *tunatya,* of the people. When the ritual leaders of the people sit down in ritual session in the kiva for the purpose of doing *tunatya,* they are defining the purpose of the ritual. The purpose is to set one's mind and heart on the things hoped for—rain, corn, a fulfilled life. *Tunatya* thus references the hoping—this is what the katsinas at their home are waiting to hear.

The katsinas tell the people—be prompt, be united in your hopes and commitment to the Hopi lifeway. They advise the people that when their prayers are united in heartfelt purpose, then they will come down as rain, *yooyangw haahawiwmani.* This idea that the prayers become rain is expressed by *pamniikyangw* (while being that in itself). In this sense the heartfelt prayers that the people "shower" on the katsinas will metaphorically return as rain.

149. *Yöngöson 'angaktsìntawi₁*

Ayám₂ hoop₃ tewakive,₄
Sakwavayuyamuy₅ épe'e.₆
Ep₇ itam₈ Yöngösòntiyotu₉ itàahikwsiy₁₀ oomàwtaqe'e,₁₁
angqw₁₂ pew₁₃ Hopìikimi,₁₄

1. *yöngöson 'angaktsìntawi* 'Tortoise Long-Hair katsina song'.
2. *ayám* 'over there'.
3. *hoop* 'in the northeast'.
4. *tewakive* 'in Tanoan country'.
5. *Sakwavayuyamuy,* object form of *Sakwavayu 'am* 'Blue Lake', literally 'their Blue/Green River'.
6. = *ep 'e* 'be there, be at', pausal (predicate) form of *ep* 'there, at it'.
7. *ep* 'there, at it'.
8. *itam* 'we'.
9. = *Yöngösòntotim* 'Turtle Boys'.
10. *itàahikwsiy,* object form of *itàahikwsi* 'our breath'.
11. *oomàwtaqe'e,* subordinate clause pausal form of *oomàwta* 'produce a cloud'.
12. *angqw* 'from it, from there'.
13. *pew* 'toward here, coming this way'.
14. *Hopìikimi* 'to Hopi land, to where the Hopis live'.

kiimatsqamuyu[15] *amumi*[16] *yòytiitiiwunuuto.*[17]
Lee lehe laa.
Eloo eelo eelo ya.
Yang[18] *umùutuwapongyava'a,*[19]
piw[20] *yang umùu'uyiy*[21] *ánga'a,*[22]
yooki- yooki- yo'o'okinayani.[23]
Yo'o yaahiy yahiy'oo, yo'o yaahiy yahiy.
Ooho'owa ehee'elo ahaa aa'aha iihii.
Hapi me.[24]
Töötöökilawu,[25]
péwi'ii'i.[26]
Töötöökilawu,
péwi'ii'i.
Yaan[27] *ima*[28] *Paakyeletiyootu*[29] *yooyokvaniqaat*[30] *töötöökilaw'u.*[31]
Leehe laa.
Eloo eelo eelo ya.
Yang umùutuwapongyava'a,
piw yang umùu'uyiy[32] *ánga'a,*
yooki- yooki- yo'o'okinayani.[33]
Yo'o yaahiy yahiy'oo, yo'o yaahiy yahiy.
Ooho'owa ehee'elo ahaa aa'aha iihii.

15. = *kiimatsiwtaqamuy,* object form of *kiimatsiwtaqam* 'residents, known residents'.
16. *amumi* 'to them'.
17. *yòytitiwunuto* 'go/come to stand dancing as rain'.
18. *yang* 'along here, in this area'.
19. = *umùutuwapongyava'a,* pausal form of *umùutuwapongyava* 'on your (plural) land, along your land'.
20. *piw* 'also, too, again'.
21. *umùu'uyiy,* object form of *umùu'uyi* 'your (plural) plants, planted fields'.
22. = *ang'a,* pausal form of *ang* 'along it, along there, in that area, in several places'.
23. = *yoknayani* 'will make it rain (plural)'.
24. *hapi me,* formulaic expression introducing the song's second part, *oomi* 'upward'.
25. = *töötöqlawu* 'keep making characteristic calls, sounds'.
26. = *pew'i,* pausal form of *pew* 'toward here, coming this way'.
27. = *yan* 'like this, in this way, thus'.
28. *ima* 'these'.
29. = *Paakyeletotim* 'Killdeer Boys'.
30. = *yooyokvaniqat,* object form of *yooyokvaniqa* 'that it will rain repeatedly'.
31. = *töötöqlawu'u,* pausalized form of *töötöqlawu* 'keep making characteristic calls, sounds'.
32. *umùu'uyiy,* object form of *umùu'uyi* 'your (plural) plants, planted fields'.
33. = *yoknayani* 'will make it rain (plural)'.

[We] are over in the northeast in Tanoan country,
at Blue Lake.
There we Turtle Boys have made our breath into clouds,
and from there to Hopi country here,
to the residents, we are coming dancing as rain.
(Vocables.)
Along your land here,
and along your planted fields here,
[we] will make it rain.
(Vocables.)
Listen, there is more.
They keep up their calls,
coming this way.
They keep up their calls,
coming this way.
In this way these Killdeer Boys keep up their calls that it will rain repeat-
edly.
(Vocables.)
Along your land here,
and along your planted fields here,
[we] will make it rain.
(Vocables.)

The Tortoise Long-Hair katsinas are singing about themselves as "Turtle Boys" who are living at Blue Lake, a place in the northeast sacred to the people of Taos Pueblo. In a beautiful metaphor, the Turtle Boys describe the process of cloud formation as "making their breath into clouds." In this way the moisture in the clouds is likened to the breath of the katsinas that they will then gather into clouds and cause to condense as rain.

They have made these preparations at their home and from there they will travel to Hopi country "dancing as rain," *yòytitiwunuto,* meaning that they are coming to rain on the planted fields. Here the katsinas' dance performance is a metaphor for the descent of rain. The katsinas specify that they are coming to rain along the people's sacred landscape, *umùu-tuwapongyava,* a way of expressing the deep respect that the Hopis have for their land. The description of the Hopi lands as a "sand altar," *tuwa-pongyava,* conveys the reverence that they have for the vast spaces from which they take their sustenance.

In the second part of the song, the Turtle Boys observe that the Kill-deer Boys are continuing to make their calls. Killdeer (*paakyele*) have a strong association with water and their continual screeching calls are reminders that it will rain. The katsinas then promise to make it rain along the planted fields.

150. *Yöngöson 'angaktsìntawi*₁

Haw₂ íngumu,₃ ínamu,₄
paypi 'i,₅
núwupi 'i,₆
umùutuwaniyuy₇ àasattiqö 'ö,₈
paahomanatuy₉ itamuy₁₀ yuuwasinat 'a,₁₁
itamumi₁₂ hoomat₁₃ óyaq 'ö,₁₄
umungem₁₅ yòytu 'awimani.₁₆
Owíi₁₇ aya 'amoo 'o.₁₈
Ayám₁₉ kwiningya₂₀ Talasivave 'e,₂₁

1. *yöngöson 'angaktsìntawi* 'Tortoise Long-Hair katsina song'.
2. *haw,* vocative particle.
3. = *ingum* 'my mothers'.
4. = *inam* 'my fathers'.
5. *paypi 'i,* pausal form of *paypi,* particle indicating resignation: 'let it be, might as well'.
6. *núwupi 'i,* pausal form of *núwupi* 'it can't be helped, it's inevitable'.
7. = *umùutuwaniyuy,* object form of *umùutuwani* 'your (plural) set time, the time that you set'.
8. = *àasattiqw 'ö,* subordinate clause pausal form of *àasatti* 'become the appointed time for it'.
9. = *pahomamàntuy,* object form of *pahomamant* 'prayer feather maidens'.
10. *itamuy* 'us', object form of *itam* 'we'.
11. = *yuwsinat 'a,* pausal form of *yuwsinat* 'after adorning (with prayers)', a subordinate clause form of *yuwsina* 'clothe'.
12. *itamumi* 'to us'.
13. *hoomat,* object form of *hooma* 'consecrated cornmeal'.
14. = *óyaqw 'ö,* subordinate clause pausal form of *oya* 'hand (to), hand out, deposit, place, put, set (several) in a particular position'.
15. *umungem* 'for you (plural), for your benefit'.
16. *yòytu 'awmani* 'will deliver a rain message'.
17. = *owí* 'yes'.
18. = *ayamo,* pausal (predicate) form of *ayám* 'over there'.
19. *ayám* 'over there'.
20. *kwiningya* 'in the northwest direction'.
21. *Talasivave 'e,* pausal (predicate) form of *Talasivave* 'at Pollen Spring'.

Momngwit,$_{22}$ mongsungwamuy$_{23}$ amumumyakyango'o,$_{24}$
itamuyu$_{25}$ nùutayilawuu.$_{26}$
Umùulavayiy$_{27}$ nùutayilawuu.
Ohaayona haayona hii, oha oha oha oha hii.
Aaha aahaa iihii hii'i.
Hapi me.$_{28}$
Ítamu$_{29}$ naanakwusaqw'ö,$_{30}$
uma$_{31}$ yep$_{32}$ itangum,$_{33}$ itanamu,$_{34}$ piw$_{35}$ uma ikwatsim$_{36}$ umùuqatsiy
    ö'qalyani,$_{37}$
ókiwa.$_{38}$
Yaahi, yahi, yahii yowiinaa.

O my mothers and my fathers,
so it is,
inevitably,
the time you set has come,
and after you adorn us with the prayer feather maidens,
and place the consecrated cornmeal on us,
we will deliver the rain message for you.
Yes, [they are] over there.
[They are] over in the northwest at Pollen Spring.
The leaders, with their fellow leaders,
keep waiting for us.

22. *momngwit* 'leaders'.
23. *mongsungwamuy*, object form of *mongsungwamat* 'their fellow leaders', a reference to leaders in a lesser role.
24. = *amumumyakyangw'o*, pausal form of *amumumyakyangw* 'while with them (plural)'.
25. = *itamuy* 'us', object form of *itam* 'we'.
26. = *nùutaylawu* 'keep waiting for'.
27. = *umùulavayiy*, object form of *umùulavayi* 'your (plural) words'.
28. *hapi me*, formulaic expression introducing the song's second part, *oomi* 'upward'.
29. = *itam* 'we'.
30. = *nànkwusaqw'ö*, subordinate clause pausal form of *nànkwusa* 'start on a journey (plural)'.
31. *uma* 'you (plural)'.
32. *yep* 'here'.
33. *itangum* 'our mothers'.
34. = *itanam* 'our fathers'.
35. *piw* 'also, too, again'.
36. *ikwatsim* 'my friends'.
37. *ö'qalyani* 'will be persistent, persevere, keep striving (plural)'.
38. = *okiw* 'humbly, pitifully'.

They keep waiting for your words.
(Vocables.)
Listen, there is more.
As we set out on our journey,
you here, our mothers, our fathers, and my friends should keep striving in
    your lives,
humbly.
(Vocables.)

This is the last song of the day. The katsinas have entertained the people all day with their beautiful rejuvenating and inspiring performances. There is a sense of sadness that this inevitable time has come for these wonderfully helpful spirit beings to depart. At this time the katsina father clothes the katsinas with the people's prayers so as to prepare them for their journey back home. To do this, the katsinas line up and the katsina father walks down the line placing a prayer feather in the left hand of each katsina and giving each a pinch of consecrated cornmeal (*hooma*) as food for their journey. The katsinas then turn and leave the plaza in single file traveling along the consecrated cornmeal path laid down by the elders.

In this song the katsinas describe how the people have adorned them with the prayer feather maidens (*pahomamant*) meaning that they have infused the prayers feathers with their prayers. It is these prayer feathers that the katsinas take them with them to their homes. The word *yuwsina* means 'clothe' in everyday speech, but here in the song it suggests the idea of fervently adorning, imbuing or infusing the prayer feathers with ones most heartfelt hopes.

In this song the katsina home is said to be at Pollen Spring (*Talasiva*). Although *talasi* is translated as "pollen," it almost always refers to corn pollen in ritual contexts. In this sense, the prayers of the people metaphorically act as pollen, fertilizing the katsinas so that they will become the rain, just as the pollen of the corn tassels falls on the silk, fertilizing the developing ears of corn.

As they depart and begin their journey back home with the people's prayers, the katsinas remind the people that they should continue to strive to live their lives humbly so as to be deserving of the katsinas' gifts. Notably, they address this hope not only to the mothers and fathers, but also to their friends, making it clear that the katsinas act on behalf of everyone, not just the Hopi people.

Appendix 1: Linguistic Comments

The Hopi Language

Hopi is the heritage language of the people who are identified as Hopis. Unfortunately it is not the mother tongue of too many younger Hopis and the present volume is part of Emory Sekaquaptewa's lifelong effort to provide tools for the revitalization of the language.

Hopi is a member of the large Uto-Aztecan language family. Uto-Aztecan languages are distributed from Idaho (Shoshone) in the north to Central America (Pipil) in the south. In the United States, Uto-Aztecan languages are found between the California coast (Luiseño and Gabrielino) and the Great Plains (Comanche). The largest language of this family in terms of population is Nahuatl or Mexicano, the language associated with the Aztec empire. The spread of the Uto-Aztecan languages seems to be archaeologically associated with the early spread of the cultivation of corn and the cultivation of corn continues to be a central part of Hopi culture.

It is also worth bearing in mind that Hopi is one of the several languages spoken among the Pueblo peoples of Arizona and New Mexico. The Zunis speak a language which is an isolate in the sense that it has no known linguistic relative. The other Puebloan peoples speak Tanoan and Keresan languages. There are three Tanoan languages: Tewa (Arizona Tewa at the First Mesa village of Hano, Ohkay Owingeh, San Ildefonso, Santa Clara, Nambe, Pojoaque, Tesuque), Tiwa (Taos, Picuris, Sandia, Isleta), and Towa (Jemez). Keresan is a group of closely related languages or dialects spoken in seven Pueblos in New Mexico (Acoma, Cochiti, Laguna, San Felipe, Santa Ana, Santo Domingo, Zia) (Miller and Davis 1963: 310). Traditionally there was widespread multilingualism among the Pueblos. This is reflected in the Hopi katsina songs, many of which have passages in the other languages.

A fuller sketch of the structure of Hopi is to be found in the Hopi Dictionary (1998: 861–900). What follows are a few notes to help understanding the use of the language in the songs and how it is translated.

Hopi grammar

Syntactically, Hopi is a "head-final" language. The verb, as the head word of the predicate, is in predicate-final position, as in the following example.

Ep   puma   úmuyu   nùutayta.
there   they   you   be awaiting

There they are awaiting you. (Song 127)

Similarly, the head of a prepositional phrase, such as "at the field," is the preposition ("at" in this English example). Since the head is final in the Hopi construction, Hopi has "postpositions" rather than "prepositions." In the following example, *ep* functions as the postposition and the noun *paasa* 'field', being the object of the postposition, is in its object form, *paasat*.

paasat   ep
field   at it/there

at the field

Postpositions are often incorporated as suffixes. *Ep* appears as the suffix -*ve* in *pasve,* which, equally with *paasat ep,* means 'at the field'. The difference between *paasat ep* and *pasve* is entirely stylistic. (*Pas-* is a combining form of *paasa.*)

The language has a rich system of suffixation both to derive and inflect words. Prefixes are relatively few, mainly of a pronominal nature. Major examples of this are possessive prefixes on nouns (*itàaki* 'our house', *umùuki* 'your house' — -*ki* is 'house') and the reflexive prefix *naa-* on verbs (e.g., *naayuwsina* 'dress oneself', the reflexive of *yuwsina* 'dress, clothe another').

Hopi tenses and verb aspects

Every Hopi verb stem is of either perfective or imperfective aspect and there are two major "tense" markers, -*ni* 'future' and -*ngwu* 'habitual'.[39]

---

39. Though we call the Hopi future and habitual "tenses" this is somewhat controversial. Benjamin Lee Whorf calls these "assertions," and says, "These resemble tenses but refer to realms of validity rather than of time" (1946: 176). Bernard Comrie, in the context of

A perfective verb describes an action that is viewed as completed while an imperfective verb describes an action viewed as on-going. The future tense marks an event as yet to happen and the habitual tense marks an event as distributed through time. The habitual tense corresponds to the English present tense when it is used in a sense of generalization, as in "He teaches chemistry." The unmarked tense with perfective verbs corresponds to the English past tense and with imperfective verbs to either past or present, depending on context. The following examples illustrate the interplay between tense and aspect.

perfective

pasta	(he) hoed weeds
pastani	(he) will hoe weeds
pastangwu	(he) hoes/used to hoe weeds (each time)

imperfective

paslawu	(he) is/was hoeing weeds
paslawni	(he) will be hoeing weeds
paslawngwu	(he) is/was hoeing weeds (regularly)

The difference between the perfective and imperfective in the habitual tense is hard to capture in a simple translation.

Alphabet

The sound system of Hopi is not very complicated by the standards of North American languages. This has allowed the development of an orthography that uses only a few markers that go beyond the letters of the conventional Roman alphabet: the vowel *ö,* the apostrophe (') for the glottal stop, and the accents ´ (acute) for exceptions to the general rules of word stress, ` (grave) for falling tone, and ^ (circumflex), for the combination of exceptional stress and falling tone (= grave + acute). The

---

trying to develop a formal theory of tense, says that "habitual meaning lies on the boundary of the three systems of tense, aspect, and mood" (1985: 40). David Crystal , in his discussion of the category "tense," observes that "the relationship between tense and time has been the subject of much study, and it is now plain that there is no easily stateable relationship between the two" (2003: 459). Willem de Reuse asserts that the Hopi habitual is semantically not a tense but rather an aspect (2005: 357).

Hopi alphabet is: *' a e g h i k l m n o ö p q r s t u v w y.* These letters are used in pretty much their international values with the following exceptions:

    ' represents the glottal stop [ʔ] (as in *na'am* 'their father'). The symbol *'* is not written at the beginning of a word. Thus a word such as *oomaw* 'cloud' begins in a phonetic glottal stop which is not written. However, the glottal stop that begins *oomaw* does appear in written form in its combining form - *'omaw,* as in *qötsa'omaw* 'white cloud'.

    g is used only in the combinations *ng* [ŋ], *ngw* [ŋʷ], *ngy* [ŋʲ] (as in *ngahu* 'medicine', *mongwi* 'leader', *yungyapu* 'wicker plaque').

    ö represents a low front rounded vowel [œ], (as in *pöhö* 'fur, wool').

    r represents an apicoalveolar sibilant, voiced before a vowel (as in *yori* 'look at') and voiceless at the end of the syllable (as in *yorta* 'keep looking at').

    u represents a high back unrounded vowel (phonetic [ɯ], as in *yu'at* ['jɯʔat] 'his/her mother').

    v represents a sound made with the upper and lower lips, voiced before a vowel (as in *tuva* 'pinyon nut') and voiceless at the end of the syllable (only in Second Mesa speech, as in *ev* 'there', which corresponds to Third Mesa *ep*).

    y represents the palatal glide (phonetic [j], as in *yep* 'here').

In addition to *ng ngw ngy,* the following letter combinations represent sounds which are functionally unitary: *kw* [kʷ], *ky* [kʲ], *qw* [qʷ], *ts* [tˢ], *'y* [ʔj] (as in *kwaahu* 'golden eagle', *atkya* 'down', *haqaqw* 'from somewhere', *u'utspi* 'door', *wi'yta* 'be fat').

Syllables

Hopi syllable structure is quite straightfoward: Every syllable begins with a single consonant onset. (Vowel-initial syllables at the beginning of a word seem to be an exception, but they begin with a phonetic glottal stop as an onset: *owa* 'stone' is phonetic [ʔowa]). An example like *angaktsìn-tawi* 'Long-Hair katsina song' divides *a-ngak-tsìn-ta-wi.* Syllables that end in more than one consonant are rare and always represent derived forms, that is, any second consonant at the end of a syllable is always a separate morpheme. An example is *nàlt* 'the two of them alone'. *Nàlt* is the dual of *naala* 'alone', the final -*t* of *nàlt* is the marker of the dual. *Nàlt,* in turn, can take the suffix -*ti,* which means roughly 'become', to produce the form *nàltti,* an example of a word with an uncommon three-consonant sequence. The syllables here divide, in accordance with the stated rule, *nàlt-ti.*

Stress

Stress on a Hopi word, unless marked to the contrary with the acute accent (´), falls on the non-final syllable containing the second mora. (A mora is a unit of phonological timing: a syllable ending in a short vowel contains one more; a syllable longer than that contains two moras.) This means that two-syllable forms are normally stressed on the first syllable, as in *sino* 'person', *taawi* 'song', *patnga* 'squash', with exceptions being marked: *ayám* 'over there', *kwakwhá* 'thank you [man speaking]'. Words of more than two syllables are stressed on the first syllable if that syllable contains a long vowel (*paaheva* 'search for water') or if it ends in a consonant (*atkyami* 'downwards'); otherwise, if the first syllable is short, the stress falls on the second syllable (*katsina, sosonkiwa* 'it looks or sounds beautiful'). The acute accent marks exceptions: *wárikiwta* 'be running', *ayám* 'that one over there', *mansáana* 'apple', *askwalí* 'thank you (woman speaking)', *kwakwhá* 'thank you (man speaking)'.

Some local differences

The grave accent (`) of Third Mesa spelling marks a syllable ending with a feature that is variable among the regional varieties of Hopi. In Third Mesa Hopi (3M), the grave accent marks falling tone, phonetically a syllable-final breathy voice or "murmur." In the Hopi of the Second Mesa village of Musangnuvi (2MM; Whorf 1946), these syllables end in an *h* sound, and in the Second Mesa village Songòopavi (2MS; Kalectaca 1978), the grave accent feature does not occur.[40]

---

40. There is insufficient information on First Mesa pronunciation or on that of the Second Mesa village of Supawlavi to include them in this discussion. The only published information available on First Mesa and Supawlavi pronunciation is a comment by Whorf (1946: 161, note 5): "The preaspirates do not occur in Sipaulovi [Supawlavi] or Polacca [= 1M], being replaced by plain stops, preceded by long vowels." According to Emory, Supawlavi pronunciation is the same as that of Songòopavi and First Mesa pronunciation is distinct.

3M	2MM	2MS	
wùuti	*wuhti*	*wuuti*	woman
itàaki	*itahki*	*itaaki*	our house
hööta	*höhta*	*hööta*	be opening
ongòmti	*ongohmti*	*ongomti*	collide
ùytima	*uhytima*	*uytima*	go along planting

The relationship among the different local varieties is not always entirely straightforward. Sometimes 3M grave accent occurs in an environment where *h* is excluded in 2MM, as before *s*:

3M	2MM	2MS	
kìisa	*kisa*	*kiisa*	chicken hawk
kiikìisam	*kiikisam*	*kiikiisam*	chicken hawks
pàasa'ti	*pása'ti*	*paasa'ti*	become that many

Sometimes 2MM has *h* where 3M grave accent does not occur, as before certain suffixes where 3M grave accent shows contextual variability while 2MM -*h*- is constant:

3M	2MM	2MS	
mamant$_{41}$	*mamahnt*	*mamant*	girls
mámàntuy	*mámahntuy*	*mámantuy*	girls (object form)
aamiwpu	*aamihwpu*	*aamiwpu*	buried
lewìwpu$_{42}$	*lewihwpu*	*lewiwpu*	painted

Another difference is in the treatment of syllable-final consonants. 2M has syllable-final *v* rather than 3M *p,* and vice versa. (2M syllable-final *v* is voiceless [ɸ] and is sometimes, because of influence from English spelling, written with the letter *f.*)

3M	2M	
ep	*ev*	there
paqlap	*paqlav*	next to the spring
nepni	*nevni*	wild greens

---

41. Grave accent is excluded from a final unstressed syllable with the "non-singular" suffix -*t(u-).*
42. Grave accent is heard before the resultative suffix -*pu* only on a stressed syllable.

The labialized consonants *kw, ngw,* and *qw* of 3M correspond to simple *k, ng, q* in syllable-final position in 2M.

3M	2M	
akw	*ak*	using it
hekwpa	*hekpa*	white fir
yooyangw	*yooyang*	rain
wungwna	*wungna*	cause to grow
suqwhikna	*suqhikna*	break it quickly
paniqw	*paniq*	for that reason, therefore

2MS lacks the complex syllable-final consonant - *'y-* of 3M and 2MM. In 2MS this corresponds to a simple glottal stop.

3M/2MM	2MS	
ki'yta	*ki'ta*	have (as) a house
pikya'yngwa	*pikya'ngwa*	axe
si'yva	*si'va*	begin to blossom

2MS shows a treatment of the "roundedness" feature that is different from 3M in some forms. In the word for 'wood', theoretical *ko-hu,* 3M shows an assimilation of the suffix vowel to the rounded stem vowel (*-hu* being replaced by *-ho*); 2M shows the addimilation of the stem vowel to that of the suffix, with the roundedness feature manifested only on the initial consonant (*ko* being replaced by *kwu*).

3M	2MS	
koho	*kwuhu*	wood

In similar fashion, the root *-hoy* 'back to' shows an unrounding of the vowel as it assimilates to the unrounded nature of the syllable-final glide *y* (*o* being replaced by *i*) with the roundedness feature manifested only on the initial consonant (*h* being replaced by *hw*).

3M	2MS	
ahoy	*ahwiy*	back to it
naahoy	*naahwiy*	apart, away from each other

This has provided 2M with a phoneme *hw* which is not found in 3M. (At this writing it is not known how items such as these are pronounced in 2MM.)

When a number of different correspondences apply in a given word, the words can look remarkably different from each other.

3M	2MM	2MS	
amupqòlpe	*amuvqöhlpe*	*amuvqölpe*	among them
owapkya'yngwa	*owavkya'yngwa*	*owavkya'ngwa*	stone axe
sùusungwni'yta	*sùsungni'yta*	*suusungni'ta*	have cooling
akwsingwpu	*aksihngpu*	*aksingpu*	remainder

There are also many local vocabulary differences that are at present undocumented. It should also be emphasized that the local differences are important and treasured and that any effort to establish one pronunciation—or spelling—over another would be quite unacceptable.

Vowel reduction

To a great extent, derivational processes in Hopi involve processes of vowel deletion, both of final vowels (apocope) and of word-internal vowels (syncope). In everyday language, final vowel loss may be suspended in "pausal" forms, which are elongated forms of words that appear as predicates, among other usages. Examples are *oomaw* 'cloud', pausal *oomawu*; *hikiy* 'a few', pausal *híkiyo*. The term "pausal" was introduced by Benjamin Lee Whorf in the earliest published grammatical sketch of Hopi.

> Many words have an elongated form called the pausal form when they end free sentences (not nonfinal clauses). The full pausal ends in a glottally reduplicated vowel -CVʔV, while the sentence-medial form abbreviates this to either -CV or -C. (Whorf 1946: 165)

Final vowel loss is commonly suspended in song forms regardless of syntactic context. In everyday usage, the process of vowel loss in non-final position (syncope) is an abstract principle of word formation, but in songs vowels that are normally lost in speech occur quite commonly (*oo'omawt* 'clouds', pausal *oo'omàwtu*; song form *oo'omawutu*). Sometimes, because of the retention of vowels, the song forms can be remarkably different from their ordinary equivalents. An example is the noun *yoyleki* 'rain lines'. In this word, *yoy-* is a reduced form of *yooya-,* the root of *yooyangw* 'rain' (*-ngw* is a noun suffix). The song form *yooyaleki,* however, shows the full form of the root *yooya-*. Because the vowel *-a-* has not been dropped, the vowel *oo* of the first syllable remains in an open syllable (syllable ending in a vowel) and so it remains long; long vowels shorten in derived closed syllables (syllables ending in a consonant); compare the syllabification: *yoy.le.ki, yoo.ya.le.ki.* (In the notes, the symbol " = " relates the occurring song forms to their equivalent everyday forms; thus the note from the song form *yooyaleki* will say " = *yoyleki* 'rain lines'.") The suspension of processes of vowel loss (apocope and syncope) gives song Hopi an "archaic" sound.

An otherwise unexplained class of exceptions to vowel shortening is to be found among roots which designate items regarded with reverence. Three conspicuous examples in everyday vocabulary are the roots for sun (*taawa*), cloud (*oomaw*), and the land (*tuuwa-*). These roots when in initial position in compounds exceptionally do not undergo shortening. Typical examples are: *taawakoyongo* 'peacock' (a "sun turkey"; 'turkey' is *koyongo*), *oomawyungyapu* 'wicker plaque with a cloud design' (*yungyapu* 'wicker plaque'), and *tuuwaqalalni* 'edge of the land: horizon, seashore' (*qalalni* 'boundary, edge'). Some words, such as *tawasipmasmi* 'wristwatch', *tawamansi* 'bright red kind of Indian paintbrush, *Castilleja linariifolia*', *tawamanaw* 'oriole' (but also *taawamanaw*), show shortened *tawa-,* which seems to indicate that in such words this element has lost its close connection with the meaning 'sun'. *Tuuwa* by itself, as mentioned above, means 'sand' and when it is used in compounds in the sense of 'sand' rather than 'land', it undergoes regular shortening: *tuwamöyikinta* 'be spreading out sand' (*möyikinta* 'be spreading it out to dry'). Also, when a compound containing one of these items that is "reverentially" protected from shortening occurs itself as a constituent of a compound, then regular shortening occurs: *Tuuwapongya* 'land' (the "sand altar") undergoes regular shortening and apocope to *tuwapong-* in *Tuwapongtumsi,* a female entity who is the personification of the land, sometimes rendered in English as the "Sand Altar Woman" or "Mother Earth."

It is possible that the song form *yooya'öki* 'arrive, come as rain' also fits this pattern, with the root *yooya-* remaining unreduced because of the reverential regard for the katsinas, who are the ones who come "as rain." In the songs, the root *yooya-* reduces quite regularly in compounds having to do with lightning and thunder, which happen "in the rain," but never in *yooya'öki,* where *yooya-* refers directly to the subject of the verb. We have presumed throughout this study that the everyday form would be *yoy'öki,* but since *yoy'öki* is not used in everyday language, this presumed everyday language form would be entirely conjectural except that Emory had no problem using *yoy'öki* in his explanatory sentence for the word in the appendix of compounds.

Archaism in song grammar

Everyday Hopi distinguishes singular, dual and plural. These categories are marked in nouns (cf. *maana* 'girl', *maanat* or *mànt* '(two) girls', *mamant* '(several) girls') and figure in the agreement between subject and predicate (singular and dual subjects take "singular" predicates and plural subjects take plural predicates). The suspicion is that the systematic distinction between dual and plural is historically fairly recent in Hopi. This suspicion is reinforced by the fact that some song nouns with plural meaning are used in what is the equivalent of their dual form in everyday present-day Hopi.[43] The most common examples of this are compounds with the root *maana.* They appear in a form that in everyday Hopi would be dual. An example is *sakwa'omawmanatu* 'blue/green cloud maidens' (as in Song 6). In everyday Hopi this would be *sakwa'omawmamant.* The equivalence between the song form and the expected everyday form is noted whenever there is a difference.

Not all nouns follow this pattern. *Oomaw* 'cloud', for example, whose plural is *oo'omawt,* usually occurs in the songs as *oo'omawutu,* grammatically the same as *oo'omawt* but with weak vowels retained (see above).

There is a similar phenomenon to be found among the verbs. In everyday Hopi, the agreement between the subject number of subject and the number of the predicate is quite regular. It is used in the calculus of singular/dual/plural, as mentioned above. But in the songs, quite frequently, "singular" forms of predicates cooccur with plural subjects. The suspicion is that this reflects an earlier stage of the language in which number marking on predicates was rather optional, much less rigid than is the case today in the conversational form of the language. A rather extreme example of reduced plural marking is to be found in Song 306,

---

43. Another indication that dual is a relatively recent addition to Hopi grammar is that the pattern for forming the dual differs from dialect to dialect of Hopi. Unlike the Third Mesa pattern, the simple addition of -*t,* cited above, the Hopi of Songòopavi adds -*vit: maana* 'girl', *maanavit* '(two) girls' (Kalectaca 1978: 49).

where there is but one plural marking, a -*ya* plural suffix on one verb, although the whole song refers to plurals.

Transcription Practices

The songs are divided into lines according to two principles: (1) while Emory was transcribing the songs he divided many lines intuitively; (2) pausal forms of words are taken as indicators of line breaks; and (3) main clause verbs are understood as being line-final. All questionable examples of line division were verified with Emory.

Hopi vowels are distinctively long (written double) and short. In songs vowels are often artificially lengthened to fit words to the timing of the lines of the song. We are somewhat inconsistent in representing such lengthening in the transcription.

It also needs to be noted that Emory, as a literate Third Mesa Hopi speaker, tended to transcribe the songs in terms of Third Mesa spellings. He would recognize a word and write it in terms of how he knew it. Only sometimes did it come to his attention that the song was sung in a specific, recognizable other dialect, and then he made the effort to represent the pronunciation of that dialect as well as he could. This means that the spellings presented in the song transcriptions, particularly the use of the grave accent, which is unique to Third Mesa (see previous section), are often misleading as to the dialect of the singer.

Some Translation Issues

Since a primary objective of this study has been to reveal the meanings and metaphors used in the songs, the translations offered are fairly literal, using commentaries after the songs, in the notes, and in the appendix of compounds to explicate subtleties where we have deemed it appropriate.

Most words in the songs are the same as their everyday counterparts, others differ from their everyday counterparts in fairly straightforward ways, and some are special to song usage. The latter have been termed "song words" (Sekaquaptewa and Washburn 2004: 465) and the ones that appear in the Hopi Dictionary (1998) are labeled "(in song)". Most of the song words are composed of everyday elements but in combinations that are restricted to song usage. Sometimes a song usage corresponds to an everyday usage in one variety of Hopi but not in another. An example is the imperfective verb meaning 'rain, be raining'. In song it is *yooki*. In Third Mesa Hopi it is always reduplicated as *yooyoki,* though it is reported to be *yooki* in everyday usage at First Mesa. A couple of elements used in song words are restricted to the song register and a few words remain unidentified.

Sometimes we depart from literal translation by translating a word differently from its everyday sense in some song contexts. The most conspicuous example of this is *maana* (combining form *-mana,* plural combining form *-mamant*). *Maana* normally means 'girl, unmarried young woman', but when this word is used (in compounds) in reference to pure, spiritual beings, it is rendered as "maiden," as in "corn maidens" or "butterfly maidens." In the compound *paavönmamant,* the element *-mamant* 'maidens' (*-manatu* in song form) is not translated at all since *paavönmamant* is simply the everyday word for young corn plants and shows how deeply embedded the maiden metaphor is in the language.

Another example of interest is the expression *naawungwnaya* 'make selves grow' (*naawungwinaya* or *naawungwina* in song language), the reflexive (*naa-*) plural (*-ya*) form of *wungwna* 'make grow, raise'. We translate this quite literally in an attempt to capture the Hopi concept of the volitional nature of plant growth, as in the following (Song 14):

paavönmanatu	*oomi*	*naawungwina*
young corn plants	upward	make selves grow

the young corn plants are making themselves grow upward

Many departures from strictly literal translation arise from differences in linguistic structure between Hopi and English. In the following (Song 29), the translation reverses the order of the Hopi words.

Paavönmanaatuy	*síqölööva'a*
young corn plants (object form)	along the flowery expanses

Along the flowery expanses of young corn plants

Another example (from Song 43) shows the difference between the Hopi clause-final verb and the English clause-medial verb. This example also illustrates the fact that pronouns are often added to the English translation; they are required in English but Hopi often omits them, leaving them to be understood from context.

paahoy   *tuutuvenaya.*
prayer feathers (possessed object form)   be marking (plural)
you are marking your prayer feathers.

In both of the examples above the noun is in an "object form." This means that it is in construction with another component of the phrase. It may be an object of a verb (as in the second example), an object of possession (as in the first example), or an object of some other part of speech, such as of a postposition (the Hopi language equivalent of the English preposition). Many of these object constructions require a translation that cannot be rigidly literal because of the wide range of ways required to express the Hopi "object" relationship in English.

Another difference between English and Hopi to be noted has to do with expressions of motion. In English there are many verbs, such as *bring, take; come, go,* where directionality is built into the verb root. In Hopi, the directionality is provided by an adverbial particle. Phrases with *pew* 'toward here, coming this way' provide a useful example: *Pew paki,* though it can be understood literally as 'toward.here enter', is the Hopi equivalent of "come in"; *pew yama,* literally 'toward.here exit', translates as "come out."

There is an overall exuberance of locative anchoring in Hopi expression. (This is typical of Uto-Aztecan languages.) The following passage from Song 94 illustrates this.

Ayángqw   *taavangqw*   *oo'oomawutu,*
from over there   from the southwest clouds

ang   *puma*   *yang*   *umùu'uyinawit*   *yang*
along there   they   along here   along your planted fields   along here

haahaawiwmani.
will go along descending

This is translated as

From over there, from the southwest, the clouds,
along there they, through your planted fields here, will go along
    descending here.

But in recognition of the fact that English and Hopi seriously differ regarding the expression of location and motion, both adverbially and within the verb, and the different normal order of elements in the two languages, a better English rendition would probably be

The clouds from over in the southwest
will be descending along your planted fields here.

Many of the translation details are identified and, we hope, clarified
in the notes throughout.

Appendix 2: Compounds in the Songs

*Himu lavayi qa suukw lavayit angqw tutkivut akw namikwap'iwte'
pahaanatniqw "compound word."*

Listed below, with analysis and comments in Hopi here and there for the
Hopi reader, are the compounds found in the songs. Also included are the
compounds used in naming the songs and those appearing in the commentaries on the songs. This list has its origin in the idea that there existed a
set of "song compounds," reflecting the creative genius and poetic licence
of the composers. Since it turned out not to be possible to differentiate
song compounds from everyday compounds in any principled way, it was
decided to include all the compounds encountered as a demonstration of
the creative genius of the language.

"Compounds" are all words that contain more than one lexical root.
This includes compound nouns and verbs with incorporated nouns as well
as complex adverbials. The length of a word or the intricacy of its internal
structure does not figure in determining whether a word is a "compound."
Ànki 'anthill(s)' is a compound and *wukukutivayani* 'will begin stepping
(plural)' is not. *Ànki* is the combination of two roots, *aanu* 'ant' (*àn-*) and
kiihu 'house' (*-ki*). *Wukukutivayani* contains but one root, *wuku-* 'move',
whose second syllable is reduplicated, *-ku,* to form the repetitive stem
wukuku-; after this appears the derivational suffix complex *-tiva,* a combination of the repetitive suffix *-ta* and the ingressive suffix *-iva.* The verb
wukukutiva is then inflected with the plural suffix *-ya* and the future suffix
-ni. The derivational and inflectional elements are not regarded as lexical
roots.

Compounds are often found in derivationally complex combinations
and are inflected according to the rules of Hopi grammar. An example of
a verb derived from the compound *ànki* is *ànkita* 'make an anthill', with
the "causative" suffix *-ta.* In the plural *ànkita* becomes *ànkitota,* as in
itam ànkitota 'we made an anthill'. Both *ànkita* and *ànkitota* can be
inflected for tense: *nu' ànkitani* 'I will make an anthill' (future), *itam
ànkitotangwu* 'we make anthills' (habitual). Another example of inflection
is that of possession; Hopi nouns can be inflected for possessor: *i'ànki*
'my anthill', *itàa'ànki* 'our anthill', *ànki'at* 'its anthill'. Another possible
inflection is that of case. Subjects of sentences are in the nominative case,
which is unmarked, i.e., *ànki* is a nominative-case form. The other noun

case in Hopi is the accusative case, which marks the object of a verb, object of possession, or object of a postposition. The accusative form of *ànki* is *ànkit*. In construction with the postposition *ep* 'at', *ànki* is in the accusative form: *ànkit ep* 'at the anthill'.

Other examples of compound nouns of various sorts are: *paqaplena* 'reed flute', from *paaqavi* 'reed' plus *leena* 'flute'; *hopoqmosayurmana* 'Northeastern Pueblo-style Buffalo dance girl', from the adverb *hoopoq* 'to the (distant) northeast' plus *mosayru* 'buffalo, bison' plus *maana* 'girl'; *lelen'aya* 'member of a musical band', from the verb *leelena* 'play a musical instrument' plus *aya('at)* 'helper'; *soyohìmqa'ö* 'corn with different kinds of kernels', from the expression *sòosoy himu* 'all kinds' plus *qaa'ö* 'dry ear(s) of corn'.

Verbs also show compounding. Examples of noun + verb compounds are: *huklaki* 'get dried out by the wind', with *huk-* from *huukyangw* 'wind' and *-laki* from *laaki* 'become dry'; *wakasheva* 'look for free-ranging cattle', from *waakasi* 'cow' and *heeva* 'seek, look for'. Some verb + verb compounds are: *qatuptu* 'get into a sitting position', from *qatu* 'sit' plus *pitu* 'arrive, come, get there, reach a destination'; *tsotsongvevèlti* 'cut down on smoking', from *tsootsongo* 'smoke (tobacco)' and *pevèlti* 'abate, subside, diminish in intensity'.

Many compounds can alternatively be expressed using syntactic constructions. An expression that means the same thing as *ànki* is *aanut kii'at,* literally 'ant's house', with the accusative case form of *aanu* 'ant' as possessor and the possessed form of *kiihu* 'house'.

Compounds may be used in the building of still larger compounds. *Ànki* 'anthill' combines with *namuru* 'ridge' to form *ànkinamuru* 'cluster of anthills' or the placename *Ànkinamuru,* which is a place on Third Mesa west of *Söhòötuyqa* 'Blue Point'. The compound *uyyuku* 'finish planting', from the verb *uuya* 'plant' plus the verb *yuku* 'finish', can combine with *mori* 'beans' to form *mori'uyyuku* 'finish planting beans'.

The internal structure of compounds is not overtly marked grammatically; one needs to understand the meanings involved to determine the hierarchical structure. The compound *ànkinamuru* 'cluster of anthills' has the structure < *àn-ki* > *namuru.* For many compounds it makes little difference as to the hierarchical structure. *Mori'uyyuku* may be understood as having the structure *mori* < *'uy-yuku* > ' < finish planting > beans' (if it is derived from *mori* plus *uyyuku* 'finish planting') or < *mori- 'uy* > *yuku* 'finish < bean-planting >' (if it is derived from *mori'uya* 'plant beans' plus *yuku*). *Hopoqmosayurmana* 'Northeastern Pueblo-style Buffalo dance girl' is possibly best regarded as simply *hopoq-mosayur-mana,* with neither *hopoqmosayru* 'Northeastern Pueblo-type of Buffalo dancer' nor *mosayurmana* 'Buffalo dance girl' as having priority.

Each Hopi root appears in a "combining form" when used in a compound. Combining forms and free forms are related in principled ways, but understanding the relationships in detail would require a highly technical account of the principles of Hopi pronunciation, including the phonetics of the sounds, the constraints on their occurrence, and the sound processes that affect combinations of sounds occasioned by putting elements together to form words. In the list below, both the base forms and their combining forms that appear in the specific compounds are presented.

alòngki 'a house belonging to someone other than a relative': *alöngö* 'different' (*alòng-*), *kiihu* 'house' (*-ki*).

angaktsìntawi 'Long-Hair katsina song', *anga'at* 'the long hair that falls to the back of his head', as in the traditional three-tiered Hopi men's hairstyle (*anga-*), *katsina* (*-ktsìn-*), *taawi* 'song' (*-tawi*).

Angwusnasomtaqa 'Crow Mother katsina': *angwusi* 'raven' (*angwus-*); *naasomta* 'wear something tied to the side(s) of the head' (*-nasomta*); *-qa*, relative suffix: 'the one that'; "the one that wears the raven (wings) on the sides of the head."

Avatshoya 'Corn Dancer': *avatsa* 'speckled corn' (*avats-*), *-hoya*, diminutive.

hàalay'unangway 'with happy hearts, beneficent intentions': *hàalayi* 'happy' (*hàalay-*); *unangwa* 'heart' (*-'unangwa*); *-y*, adverbializing suffix.

hàalaytsotsong.ya 'smoke the pipe with untroubled minds': *hàalayi* 'happy' (*hàalay-*), *tsootsong.ya* 'be smoking (tobacco) (plural)' (*-tsotsong.ya*).

Hahay'imanat '(two) Hahay'i maidens': *Hahay'i*, a female katsina who represents the ideal characteristics of womanhood; *maana* 'girl, young woman, maiden' (*-mana*); *-t*, non-singular.

haw'okatsìntawi 'Haw'o katsina song': *Haw'o*, *katsina* (*katsìn-*), *taawi* 'song' (*-tawi*). The Haw'o katsina is unknown at Third Mesa, at least by that name.

heesi 'mariposa lily/lilies, *Calochortus aureus*': *heeki('at)* 'its flare', a reference to something that flares out, as the lip of a bowl, a pig's snout (*hee-*), *sihu* 'flower' (*-si*).

hehey'akatsìntawi 'Hehey'a katsina song': *Hehey'a, katsina (katsìn-), taawi* 'song' (*-tawi*).

hemiskatsìntawi 'Hemiskatsina song': *hemis-, katsina (katsìn-), taawi* 'song' (*-tawi*). The *Hemiskatsinam* appear only as Home dance katsinas and only at certain villages. (*Hemis-* seems clearly related to *Heemis* 'Jemez Pueblo' [cf. Towa *Hį́įmį́š*], but the katsina has no recognized connection with Jemez Pueblo.)

hewtokatsìntawi 'Hewto katsina song': *Hewto,* a katsina; *katsina (katsìn-); taawi* 'song' (*-tawi*).

hom'oya 'hand out consecrated cornmeal': *hooma* 'consecrated cornmeal' (*hom-*), *oya* 'put, place, deposit'.

hom'oyi 'offering': *hooma* 'consecrated cornmeal' (*hom-*), *oyi* 'things placed' (*-'oyi*). *Hopi naawakne' pahotumalay na'saste' pu' put haqami tuutuskyat ang óyangwu, pam hapi hom'oyi.*

honànkatsìntawi 'Badger katsina song': *honani* 'badger' (*honàn-*), *katsina (katsìn-), taawi* 'song' (*-tawi*).

Honànpa 'Badger Spring': *honani* 'badger' (*honàn-*), *paahu* 'water' (*-pa*).

Honanwùutaqa 'Old Man Badger': *honani* 'badger' (*honan-*), *wùutaqa* 'old man'. *Honanwùutaqa hapi Honanngyamuy wu'ya'am. Pam hak kyapi Kìisiwuy ep qatukyangw it ngahuy pu' powatatawiy natwanlawu. Pay ephaqam oovi hopi it powamuymongwit pan piw piptsanangwu, tis pam Honanwungwaniqö.*

hòo'ekatsìntawi 'Hòo'e katsina song': *Hòo'e,* a katsina; *katsina (katsìn-); taawi* 'song' (*-tawi*).

hoolikatsìntawi 'Hooli katsina song': *Hooli,* a katsina; *katsina (katsìn-); taawi* 'song' (*-tawi*). *Hooli* refers also to the dragonfly and to a bow-tie- or dragonfly-shaped feather adornment on the back of the head of the Hooli katsina. It is unclear which sense is prior, the katsina, the insect, or the adornment.

Hopìiki 'Hopi land, where the Hopis live': *hopi (hopìi-), kiihu* 'house, dwelling place' (*-ki*).

hopimatsiwta 'have a Hopi identity': *hopi, maatsiwa* 'be known as' (*-matsiwa*).

hopivötskwani 'Hopi life plan': *hopi, pötskwani* 'life plan, plan of life' (*-vötskwani*) (see below).

hopiyungta 'be initiated as Hopis': *hopi, yungta* 'be entering'.

hömsomi 'hairknot at the nape of a man's neck': *höömi* 'hair' (*höm-*), *somi* 'something tied up or bound, knot'.

humi'uyisìiqölnawit 'along the flowery expanse(s) of corn plants': *humi-* 'corn', *uuyi* 'planted plant(s)' (-*'uyi*); *sihu* 'flower' (-*sìi-*); -*qölö* 'area, expanse' (-*qöl-*); -*nawit* 'along'.

humi'uyimamant 'corn plant maidens': *humi-* 'corn', *uuyi* 'planted plant(s)' (-*'uyi*), *mamant* 'maidens'.

humi'uysonaq 'throughout the midst the area(s) planted with corn': *humi-* 'corn'; *uuyi* 'planted plant(s)', prototypically a refernce to corn plants (-*'uy-*); -*sona-* 'center'; -*q*, diffusive suffix.

humisi'uyi 'blossoming corn plant(s)': *humi-* 'corn', *sihu* 'flower' (-*si-*), and *uuyi* 'planted plant(s)' (-*'uyi*).

humisimamant 'corn blossoms' ('corn blossom maidens'): *humi-* 'corn', *sihu* 'flower' (-*si-*), *mamant* 'maidens'.

humivota 'coiled plaque for shelled corn': *humita* 'shelled corn' (*humi-*), *poota* 'flat coiled plaque' (-*vota*).

i'omaw'inakwa 'the down feathers worn on my head': *i-* 'my', *oomaw* 'cloud' (-*'omaw*), *i-* 'my' (-*'i-*), *nakwa* 'feather(s) worn as a headdress'. A song variant, *oomaw'inakwa*, has only the medial possessive prefix 'my' (-*'i-*). The secular form is *i'omawnakwa*, with the prefix in initial position as is usual in Hopi grammar. *Katsina hapi i'omaw'inakwa, sen i'omawnakwa kite' pay kwavòöönakway pan ayàwtoynangwu.*

Ihiwkatsina 'Plain Hehey'a katsina': *ihiw-*, *katsina*. The unidentified element *ihiw-* also occurs (with *qatsi* 'life') in *ihiwqatsi* 'unprofaned life'. *Ihiwkatsina* is a synonym of *Nukushehey'a*.

ikituwungwnimi 'to my spiritual homeland': *i-* 'my', *kiihu* 'house, home' (-*ki-*); *tuu-*, indefinite object prefix (-*tu-*); *wungwni* 'something raised'; -*mi* 'to'. *Haqam hak tìitiwe', pep yumuy amumum ki'ykyangw qatsiy navote', pep hapi hak hopivewat nuumi'yvangwu; noqw pam hapi oovi hakiy kiituwungwni'atningwu.*

ikukunawit 'along my tracks, along the course of my footprints': *ikuku* 'my footprints, tracks', *ánawit* 'along its course' (-*nawit*).

ikwil'aya 'hired carrier, one who is hired to carry something on the back': *iikwìlta* 'put on one's (own) back to carry' (*ikwil-*), *aya'at* 'his helper, employee' (-*'aya*).

itàatitwi 'our customary way of dancing': *itàa-* 'our', *tiihu* 'dance' (-*ti-*), *tuwi* 'practical knowledge' (-*twi*).

kaway'u'uyi 'watermelon plants, plantings': *kawayvatnga* 'watermelon' (*kaway-*), *uu'uyi* 'planted plants' (-*'u'uyi*). Note that the combining form *kaway-* can mean 'horse', representing the root noun *kawayo*, or 'watermelon', representing the compound *kawayvatnga,* literally "horse squash" (see below). Once in a while there is potential ambiguity. The verb *kaway'u'uyi,* homophonous with 'watermelon plants' but based on the verb *u'uyi* 'steal' rather than on the noun *uu'uyi* 'plants', can mean either 'steal horses' or 'steal watermelons'.

kaway'uyi 'watermelon plant(s)': *kawayvatnga* 'watermelon' (*kaway-*); *uuyi* 'planted plant(s)' (-*'uyi*).

kaway'uynawit 'along the course of the watermelon plants or plantings': *kawayvatnga* 'watermelon' (*kaway-*), *uuyi* 'planted plant(s)' (-*'uy-*), -*nawit* 'along'.

kawayho'i 'load of watermelons': *kawayvatnga* 'watermelon' (*kaway-*), *ho'i* 'a load of several objects'.

kawàytanga'yta 'have stored watermelons': *kawayvatnga* 'watermelon' (*kawày-*), *tanga'yta* 'have contained in a closed container or structure'.

kawayvatnga 'watermelon': *kawayo* 'horse' (*kaway-*), *patnga* 'squash' (-*vatnga*).

kaway'uysonaq 'throughout the midst of the area(s) planted with watermelons': *kaway-* 'watermelon'; *uuyi* 'planted plant(s)'; -*sona-* 'center'; -*q,* diffusive suffix.

kiimatsiwtaqam 'those that are known to be residents, recognized as residents': *kiihu* 'house, village' (*kii-*); *maatsiwta* 'be known, recognized' (-*matsiwta*); -*qa,* relative suffix; -*m,* plural. *Hak hapi haqam kitsokive ki'yte' pan pep nùutum sino'iwtangwu, nìiqe oovi panwat ìipongaqw taytaqat aw maatsiwtangwu. Pep oovi hak ki'ykyangw put akw pep qeniptsiwte' pan hak kiimatsiwtangwu. Kiimatsiwtaqam hapi oovi sòosoyam haqam kitsokive kiiyese' pan puma kiimatsiwtaqamningwu.*

kiinasami 'to the middle of where the people live': *kiihu* 'house, dwelling place' (*kii-*), *naasami* 'to the middle' (-*nasami*).

kiinasave 'in the middle of where the people live': *kiihu* 'house, dwelling place' (*kii-*), *naasave* 'in the middle, at the center' (-*nasave*). *Songyawnen kiisonvit pàngqàwqe kiinasave. Niikyangw yep hapi Hopisinom hopivewat qatsit tunatyat naa'u'nantoynataqw oovi pangqw pan unangwa'am yayma.*

Kiqötsmovi (Kykotsmovi), a village at Third Mesa: *kiiqö* 'ruin' (*kiqö-*), *tsomo* 'hill' (-*tsmo*), -*vi* 'place'. Kiqötsmovi is the Hopi administrative center. It was also known as "New Oraibi" until it became a separate political entity.

Kisiw'omàwki 'the Shadow Springs dwelling place of the clouds', the katsina home of the northeast direction: *Kìisiw* 'Shadow Springs' (*Kisiw-*), *oomàwki* 'dwelling place of the clouds' (-*'omàwki*). *Kìisiw*

hapi hópitniqw hoopaq oo'ovaqe'ytaqat epeq paahu. Pam paahu ooveq angqw tùupelat atpipaqw paa'iwtaqat tùukwat akw aqw ùutsi'yta. Pangsoq pay taavi qa pákingwuniqw.

Kisiwva 'Shadow Spring': *Kìisiw* 'Shadow Springs' (*Kisiw-*), *paahu* 'water' (*-va).* *Kisiwva* is the spring at *Kìisiw*, the northeast katsina home. The name *Kìisiw* is based on *kìisi* 'shaded place'. The spring there never receives direct sunlight.

kitsokikinawit 'throughout the villages; along the course of the villages, going from village to village': *kitsokiki* 'villages', *amunawit* 'along their course' (*-nawit).*

kivanasave 'in the middle of the kiva': *kiva* 'ceremonial chamber', *naasave* 'in the middle' (*-nasave). Hakim kivàapeq pahotumalay aw yesve', akw pavasiwye' qa pas pas haqam kivat súnasave put aw yesngwu; niikyangw hakim suuvo unangway tavi'ykyàakyangw put hintsatskyangwuniqw oovi pam hakimuy sumi'nangwa'am songyawnen kivat àasonngaqw, naasaviyat angqw pasiwni yámakngwu.*

kivung.wùuti 'woman who habitually visits around': *kipngya* 'habitual visitor' (*kivung-*), *wùuti* 'woman'. *Kipngya* is a compound of *kiihu* 'house' (*ki-*) and *-pungya* 'associated with' (*-pngya*). *-pungya* appears only in combination, as in *amùupungyala* 'hang around with them', *nöömavungya* 'man who hangs around with his wife all the time' (*-vungya*).

kokom'uyi 'dark red corn plant(s)': *kokoma* 'dark red corn' (*kokom-*), *uuyi* 'planted plant(s)' (*-'uyi*).

koliyawsi'uyi 'pretentious, flashy talk': *koliyaw* 'gossip', *sihu* 'flower' (*si-*), *uuyi* 'planted plant(s)' (*-'uyi). Koliyawuy aw kwangw'o'oye' koliyawsi'uyit yukuyangwu. Sihut akw hopi hìita kwangwa'ewpiyat aw hóyoknaqw pu' sino put kwangwa'ingwu. Pu' sino put.sa aw kwangwtuwe' pu' hìita mongvaswat tatamtangwu, noqw oovi it aw katsinam taawiy akw itamuy meewantota.*

kookopòltawi 'song of the Kookopölö katsina(s)': *Kookopölö* (*kookopòl-*), *taawi* 'song' (*-tawi).* Kookopölö is a katsina with a hunchback. Women pray to him to have a child. The element *kooko-* may be based on the Zuni word for katsina, *kokko* (Newman 1958; 25) *-pölö* is probably from *pölö'at* 'ball- or lump-shaped thing'.

Kòokyàngwtiyo 'Spider Boy': *kòokyangw* 'spider' (*kòokyàngw-*); *tiyo* 'boy'.

korowistakatsìntawi 'Korowista katsina song': *Korowista*, *katsina* (*katsìn-*), *taawi* 'song' (*-tawi*). The name *Korowista* is said to be from Zuni. At Third Mesa, *Korowista* is also known as *Kwasa'ytaqa* 'the one that wears a manta', from *kwasa'yta* 'be wearing a manta' plus the relativizer *-qa* 'one that'.

Kowawayva, a spring in the southeast direction: *Kowaway-, paahu* 'water' (*-va*). *Kowaway-* is probably the same as Zuni *Kolhuwala:wa*, the home of the Zuni katsinas, located about seventy-five miles southwest of Zuni Pueblo. *Kolhuwala:wa* is referred to as "Kachina Village" in English.

koyaanisqatsi 'life of moral corruption': *koyaanis-* 'corrupted, chaotic', *qatsi* 'life'. The element *koyaanis-* is unknown origin; the long vowel in its second syllable is an indicator that it is not part of the inherited Uto-Aztecan vocabulary of Hopi.

Koyemosmongwit '(two) Mudhead katsina leaders': *Kooyemsi* 'Mudhead katsina' (*Koyemos-*); *mongwi* 'leader'; *-t,* non-singular. *Koyemsimongwit* (below) is a variant pronunciation. *Kooyemsi, koyemsi-,* and *koyemos-* all derive from a phonetically abstract form *Kooyeemosi.*

Koyemsimongwit '(two) Mudhead katsina leaders': *Kooyemsi* 'Mudhead katsina' (*Koyemsi-*); *mongwi* 'leader'; *-t,* non-singular.

koyemsiyungtawi 'Mudhead katsina entering song': *Kooyemsi* 'Mudhead katsina' (*Koyemsi-*), *yungtawi* 'entering song'.

kuk.wuwa (with *ahoy*) 'retrace steps (plural)': *kùuku'at* 'his footprints' (*kuk-*), *wuuwa* 'think' (*-wuwa*); *ahoy kuk.wuwa* 'reflect or think back on the past'.

kuwan'ew'unangway 'with beautiful hearts, with beneficent intentions': *kuwan'ew* 'colorfully, good, clear, pleasing'; *unangwa* 'heart' (*-'unangwa*); *-y*, adverb-forming suffix.

kuwan'ewsoniwa 'look invigorated': *kuwan'ew* 'colorfully, good, pleasing', *sóniwa* 'be beautiful, pleasing' (*-soniwa*).

kuwantalawvangaqw 'from the colorful beginning of the day (dawn)': *kuwana* 'color' (*kuwan-*); *taalawva* 'dawn, get light, become a new day' (*-talawva*); *angqw* 'from it' (*-ngaqw*).

kuwanvuyayata 'be fluttering in colorful liveliness': *kuwana* 'color' (*kuwan-*), *puyayata* 'be flapping, fluttering' (*-vuyayata*). *Puyayata* is based on *puya* 'open out, unfold' and literally means 'be repeatedly opening out', referring in *kuwanvuyayata* to the action of the butterflies' wings.

kuwan'èwqatsi 'life of happiness and plenty': *kuwan'ew* 'colorfully good or pleasing in the sense of beautiful liveliness' (*kuwan'èw-*); *qatsi* 'life'.

kuyapkuyi 'dipper of water': *kuyapi* 'ladle, dipper' (*kuyap-*); *kuuyi* 'drawn water' (*-kuyi*). *Hopit piptsani'atniqw katsinam yòypalat kuuyi'yvaya-ngwunìiqe oovi yoknaye' songyawnen kuyapkuyiy wuutayangwu.*

kuysiptoyna 'provide with water storage vessels': *kuuyi* 'contained liquid' (*kuy-*); *siivu* 'vessel' (*-sip-*); *-toyna* 'provide with'.

kuywiki 'container of water carried by a string or bail': *kuuyi* 'drawn water'; *wiki* 'item on a string for hand-carrying'.

Kwaangyam 'Eagle clan, members of the Eagle clan': *kwaahu* 'eagle' (*kwaa-*), *ngyam* 'clan members'. The corresponding singular is *Kwaawungwa* 'member of the Eagle clan'.

kwakwha'unangway or *kwakwha'unangwat* 'with tranquil hearts, with beneficent intentions': *kwakwha* 'peaceful, tranquil, gentle'; *unangwa* 'heart' (*-'unangwa*); *-y* or *-t,* adverb-forming suffix (same as accusative case suffix).

kwangwahimu'yta 'have something pleasing, useful, convenient, readily accessible': *kwangwa-* 'pleasant', *himu'yta* 'have something'.

kwangwatu'awva 'come with a pleasant message, pleasant news': *kwangwa-* 'pleasant', *tuu'awva* 'come with a message' (*-tu'awva*).

Kwikwilyaqa 'Striped Nose katsina, Stripe Nose': *kwikwilvu* 'striped (with several stripes)' (*kwikwil-*); *yaqa'at* 'his nose' (*-yaqa*). Kwikwilyaqa has horizontal stripes where the nose otherwise would be. His role is that of an imitator.

kwivikatsìntawi 'Vain katsina song': *kwiivi* 'proud, fastidious, vain, pretentious' (*kwivi-*), *katsina* (*katsìn-*), *taawi* 'song' (*-tawi*).

kwiyavasnawit 'along the course of the fields with windbreaks constructed on them': *kwiya* 'elongated windbreak made from brush', *paasa* 'field' (*-vas-*), *ánawit* 'along its course' (*-nawit*).

lavay'ayamat 'their spokespeople': *lavayi* 'speech, words', *ayamat* 'their helpers' (*-'ayamat*).

lavay'aysakwi 'gossip': *lavay'aya* 'spokesperson' (*lavay'ay-*), *sakwi* 'no longer effective'.

lavayhurusuki 'speech *hurusuki*': *lavayi* 'speech' (*lavay-*), *hurusuki,* a kind of blue cornmeal pudding or mush.

lavaymuyiwa 'be talked about, be talking about, there is talk': *lalvaya* 'talk about' (*lavay-*); *-muy-* 'intensively(?)'; *-iwa,* stative. Since *-muy-* is an element found exclusively in ritual vocabulary, its precise meaning is elusive.

lavaysakwiqatsilvayi'at 'the worn-out words of the language of her way of life': *lavayi* 'speech, words', *sakwi* 'worn out', *qatsi* 'life', *lavayi* 'speech, words', *-'at,* third person singular possessive suffix.

löwawaqaqa 'squishy sounds of sexual activity': *löwa* 'female genitals', *waqaqata* 'be making sloshing, splashing, squishy sounds' (*-waqaqa*).

ma'lokatsìntawi 'Ma'lo katsina song': *Ma'lo, katsina* (*katsìn-*), *taawi* 'song' (*-tawi*).

mansonve 'in the midst of girls, at the center of attention of girls, women': *maana* 'girl' (*man-*), *àasonve* 'inside of it'.

maphenlawu 'will be doing domestic chores': *maa'at* 'her hand' (*ma-*); *-phen-* '(?)'; *-lawu*, continuative.

masawkatsìntawi 'Màasaw katsina song': *Màasaw*, a spirit being (*masaw-*), *katsina* (*katsìn-*), *taawi* 'song' (*-tawi*).

mataqlö 'grinding bin': *mata* 'grinding slab, grinding stone, metate'; *-qölö* 'area, expanse' (*-qlö*).

melon'uyi 'muskmelon plant(s)': *melooni* 'muskmelon' (*melon-*), *uuyi* 'planted plant(s)' (*-'uyi*).

melonho'i 'load of muskmelons': *melooni* 'muskmelon' (*melon-*), *ho'i* 'a load of several objects'.

melon'uysonaq 'throughout the midst of the area(s) planted with muskmelons': *melooni* 'muskmelon' (*melon-*); *uuyi* 'planted plant(s)'; *-sona-* 'center'; *-q*, diffusive suffix.

mongkimi 'to the place of leadership': *mongwi* 'leader' (*mong-*), *kiihu* 'house, home' (*-ki*), *aw* 'to it' (*-mi*).

mongmatsiwtaqam 'those that are known as leaders': *mongwi* 'leader' (*mong-*); *maatsiwta* 'be known, recognized' (*-matsiwta*); *-qa*, relative suffix; *-m* 'plural'. *Mongwi hìita qeniy ep hintsakye' pan pam hakiy taytaqat aw maatsiwtangwu. "Kur i' hak it ep mong'iwtaqe oovi yantsaki," hak yan aw wuuwangwu. Ima hapi oovi mongmatsiwtaqam.*

mongsungwam 'fellow leaders': *mongwi* 'leader' (*mong-*), *sungwam* 'partners'. *Hopit wimhintsakpiyat ep pay sutsep qa suukw atsviy himu pasiwta. Hintsakpit ep haqawat hìita ang oyiwte' puma nanap put pan qeniy aw tunatyàltote' pan hìita hintsakpit aw nùutum antsatsnangwu; nìiqe oovi pas mong'iwtaqat panwat sungwamatningwu.*

Mongva 'Leadership Spring': *mongwi* 'leader' (*mong-*), *paahu* 'water' (*-va*). This is a place in the world of the katsinas.

mongwinahuyvaniwa 'be choices made in ways of leadership': *mongwi* 'leader', *naahuyvaniwa* 'be apportioned' (*-nahuyvaniwa*). *Hìita ang mongqeni'yvayaniqat put sinmuy namortiwyaqamuy ang oyìltiqw pu' pangqw qatsiyàyngwangaqw put puma nakpetiwisniqat oovi mongwinahuyvaniwa.*

mong.yesva 'sit as leaders, sit down in order to do tasks as leaders (i.e., smoke, pray, prepare prayer feathers)': *mongwi* 'leader' (*mong-*), *yesva* 'sit (plural)'.

mori'uysonaq 'throughout fields planted with beans': *mori* 'bean(s)'; *uuyi* 'planted plant(s)' (-*'uy*-); -*sona*- 'center'; -*q*, diffusive suffix.

morisi'uyi 'blossoming bean plant(s)'. *mori* 'bean(s)', *sihu* 'flower' (-*si*-), *uuyi* 'planted plant(s)' (-*'uyi*).

morisimamant 'bean blossom maidens': *mori* 'bean(s)', *sihu* 'flower' (-*si*-), *mamant* 'maidens'.

mösivakwam 'food-packet toads': *mösi'at* 'food packet for a prayer feather' (*mösi*-); *paakwa* 'toad' (-*vakwa*); -*m*, plural. The toads of various colors (*tuvevakwam*) and the food-packet toads are a ritual pair.

　　Mösivakwa taawit ep pakiwte' pay tuvevakwat angk tungwaniwtangwu. Hópitniqw pi ima paavakwt, songyawnen paahot an yooyangwuy wángwaylalwaqw oovi yokvaqw puma put akw qatsiy puuhutongwunìiqe hàalay'unangway nùutum töötökiy akw sosonkiwyangwu.

　　Pu' paahot piw engem tunös'oyni'at enang yukìlte' pam hapi put piw mösi'atningwu.

　　Ephaqam sami piw taqala'ytangwu. Pam samit tsukuyat epeq silaqvuyat angqw naap kuykyangw piw naap taytangwu; noqw pam hapi piw mösi'atningwu. Put mösiyat hakim enang mömtsayat put tùupepkoysimiq pavoyayangwu, tùupeplalwe'.

munlalayto 'go to channel runoff water': *muunangw* 'flowing water, runoff water' (*mun*-), *laalayto* 'go to herd' (-*lalayto*). *Tutskwava hövalankyangw put akw ang munyaqat naanahoy laalaylawngwunìiqe oovi munlalayngwu.*

muumunangwsonaq 'in the midst of streams of runoff water': *muumunangw* 'streams of runoff water' (cf. *muunangw* 'runoff water'); -*sona*- 'center'; -*q*, diffusive suffix. -*sona*- may be from the same origin as *soona'at* 'nutriment, the germ of the corn kernel'.

naakyasoniwa 'look reticent, reserved': *naakya* 'reticent, reserved', *sóniwa* 'look like' (-*soniwa*).

naamongsungwam 'fellow leaders': *naa*- 'to each other' (reflexive prefix), *mongwi* 'leader' (*mong*-), *sungwam* 'partners'.

naavaasqatsi 'life of mutual caring': *naavaasi* 'care for oneself or one another, be good to each other' (*naavaas*-), *qatsi* 'life'.

nalönanan'ivaqw 'from the four directions': *naalöyöm* 'four of them' (*nalö*-), *naanan'ivaqw* 'from different directions around' (-*nanan'ivaqw*).

nalönanan'ivo 'to the four directions': *naalöyöm* 'four of them' (*nalö*-), *naanan'ivo* 'to the different directions around' (-*nanan'ivo*).

Nalönangwmomngwit 'Four-Directional Cloud Chiefs', literally "Leaders of the Four Different Directions": *naalöyöm* 'four of them' (*nalö-*), *naangwuy* 'different from each other' (*-nangw-*), *momngwit* 'leaders' (the plural of *mongwi*). *Hópitniqw ima oo'omawt nalönangwkiva yeese, kwiningyaqnit, taavangnit, tatkyaqnit pu' hoopaq. Pay puma piw pang mongwimu'yyungqw puma momngwit hapi oovi Nalönangwmomngwit.*

nalönangwuy 'of the four directions': *naalöyöm* 'four of them' (*nalö-*); *naangwuy* 'different from each other' (*-nangwuy*).

nalönatsva 'in four places one above the other', a reference to an ideal development of ears of corn on the stalk: *naalöyöm* 'four (of them)' (*nalö-*), *natsva* 'above each other'.

nalqatmomoyam 'single women, women who now live alone', a reference to women who were once married but now are not, i.e., widows, divorcees: *nalqatu* 'live alone' (*nalqat-*), *momoyam* 'women'.

nalqatsi 'life alone, without a partner': *naala* 'alone', *qatsi* 'life'.

namitngàlti 'get mixed, mix together' (as of two or more different herds of livestock): *naami* 'to each other' (*nami-*), *tangàlti* 'go inside, enter' (*-tngàlti*).

namunwanvö 'path for the running of the stone race': *namunwa* 'be hurrying as though racing', *pöhu* 'road, path' (*-vö*). *Pay hisat kitsokivit nanap haqe' nanamuniwuy engem pö'yyungngwu, piw pàykye'haqe nangwtsatsavo pam pö'iwtangwu, namunwanvö.*

ngumanvòötaviwa 'be laid out as a path of consecrated cornmeal': *ngumni* 'finely ground cornmeal, corn flour' (*nguman-*), *pöhu* 'road, path' (*-vòö-*), *tavi* 'put, place, deposit' (*tav-*), *-iwa* 'stative'. *Pay ngumanvöötaviwa as homvöötaviniqw pay taawit ep panwat ephaqam ayàwtoynangwu.*

Nimànkatsìntawi 'Home dance katsina song': *nima* 'go home' (*nimàn-*), *katsina* (*katsìn-*), *taawi* 'song' (*-tawi*).

nukushehey'akatsìntawi 'Plain Hehey'a katsina song': *Nukushehey'a* 'Plain Hehey'a' (as opposed to *Kuwanhehey'a* 'Colorful Hehey'a'), *katsina* (*katsìn-*), *taawi* 'song' (*-tawi*).

Nuvatukya'ove 'at the San Francisco Peaks' and the name of the katsina home and its corresponding shrine there: *nuva* 'snow'; *-tukya-* an irregular combining form of *tuukwi* 'promontory, mesa, butte, peak'; *oove* 'above, up high' (*-'ove*). The noun form, *Nuvatukya'ovi*, shows the modification of the punctive suffix *-ve* with the noun-forming suffix *-i* into the "place" suffix *-vi*: the "place of the high snowy peaks." *Nuvatukya'ovi* is the Third Mesa form; a Second Mesa form of the word, *Nuvatukwi'ovi*, uses *-tukwi-* the regular combining form of *tuukwi*.

nuvawvaqölti 'become an area of mature corn': *nuvawva* 'ripen, come to fruition (re corn)', *-qölö* 'area, expanse' (*-qöl-*), *-ti* 'become'.

okiwqawlawu 'be humbly pleading': *okiw* 'humbly, pitifully', *-qawlawu* 'be saying it'. *-qawlawu* is found only in combination, e.g., *pàngqawlawu* 'be saying that', literally, 'be saying it that way': *pan* (*pàng-*), *-qawlawu*.

oo'omàwki 'dwelling places of clouds in different directions': *oo-*, reduplication marking the distributive; *oomaw* 'cloud' (*-'omàw-*); *kiihu* 'house, dwelling place' (*-ki*).

oomaw'inakwa 'the down feathers worn on my head': *oomaw* 'cloud', *i-* 'my' (*-'i-*), *nakwa* 'feather(s) worn as a headdress'. A variant, *i'omaw-'inakwa*, has two possessive prefixes 'my'. The secular form is *i'omawnakwa*, with the prefix in initial position as is usual in Hopi grammar.

oomaw'oya 'place as clouds': *oomaw* 'cloud', *oya* 'put, place' (*-'oya*).

oomàwki 'dwelling place of the clouds': *oomaw* 'cloud' (*oomàw-*), *kiihu* 'house, dwelling place'. *Oomàwki* is also the name of Humphreys Peak, in the San Francisco Peaks.

oomàwkiikinawit 'along the dwelling places of the clouds': *oomaw* 'cloud' (*oomàw-*); *kii-*, reduplication; *kiihu* 'house, dwelling place' (*ki-*); *ánawit* 'along its course'. *Oo'omawt haqe' tuwat ki'yyungqw pang pumuy amùupa maamase' pu' pàngqawngwu, "oomàwkiikinawit."*

oomawnanawakna 'be praying for clouds (plural)': *oomaw* 'cloud', *naanawakna* 'be praying, want' (*-nanawakna*), the plural of *naawakna*.

oomawvawikyam 'cloud ducks, clouds as though they were ducks': *oomaw* 'cloud'; *paawikya* 'duck or other waterfowl' (*-vawikya*); *-m*, plural. (The plural of *paawikya* is *paavawikt*.)

Oomawwùutaqa 'Old Man Cloud': *oomaw* 'cloud', *wùutaqa* 'old man'. *Pay suukwhaqam taawiy akw katsinam nana'amqat tawsomyaqe put pan pitsangwtoynaya, "Oomawwùutaqa." Pay antsa pi hopi haqawatuy pan piw piptsanta, nìiqe pàngqawngwu, "Pam pas a'ni yòytuwi'yta," pu' piw, "Pam pas yooyangwuy angwu'yta."*

Ôngtupqa 'the Grand Canyon': *öönga* 'salt' (*òng-*), *tupqa* 'canyon'.

paa'o'oytima 'go along placing water': *paahu* 'water' (*paa-*), *oo'oytima* 'go along placing' (*-'o'oytima*). *Hak hakiy aw paa'oye' qa pas tusoq'ew aw kuuyit wuutangwu. Pay hak hakiy aw, sen hìita aw, wuutangwu, niikyangw pam hapi pas hìita ayawa'ykyangw aw wuutsìltingwu. Hakim tsaatsayomnen hevetotangwu; qa yuwsi'ykyàakyangw hevetawit kitpik tawnumyaqw pu' momoyam, mamant hakimuy amumi paa'o'oyyangwu.*

Yooyangw naap pite' pu' hakimuy mowananiqat pam ayawa'yta.
Yokve' oovi pam aqwhaqami tutskwava sòosok hìita mowani'yme'
pan pam paa'o'oytimangwu.
paaho 'prayer feather(s)': *paahu* 'water' (*paa-*), *hoohu* 'arrow' (*-ho*).
Paakyeletotim 'Killdeer Boys': *paakyele* 'killdeer, *Charadrius vociferous*'; *tootim* 'boys' (*-totim*). *Paakyele* can be analyzed *paahu* 'water' (*paa-*) plus *kyeele* 'sparrow hawk' (*-kyele*), but the word *paakyele* is likely based on the bird's cry, as is English *killdeer*. *Paakyele pay himu masa'ytaqa, it kyelèwyat àasayhaqam, niikyangw yokve' ang paatotiqw pu' pítungwu. Pam himu wupahokya'ytangwunìiqe tutskwava kwangwawarikngwu, töötökiy qa pevewmakyangw. Hópitniqw pam himu yooyangwuy akw enang waynumqw oovi pam ephaqam taawit ep pakiwtangwu.*
paamotoro 'water pillar', a reference to the little pillars of water that appear when raindrops rebound from the surface of a puddle: *paahu* 'water' (*paa-*), *mootoro* 'stalactite' (*-motoro*). (Though a *paamotoro* ascends from below, it is not a "stalagmite"—for which Hopi has no known special word. *Motoro* is used here because a *paamotoro* originates from the surface of a puddle, though upward, much as a stalactite develops from its surface, though downward. A stalagmite builds up gradually by the accumulation of the residue of droplets from above.)
Paamuya, a lunar month that roughly corresponds to January: *paahu* 'water' (*paa-*), *muuyaw* 'moon' (*-muya*).
Paamuynalönangwmomngwit 'the Four-Directional Cloud Chiefs of the month of Paamuya': *Paamuya*, a lunar month (*Paamuy-*); *Nalönangwmomngwit* 'the Four-Directional Cloud Chiefs'.
pàapu'uyi 'pod bean plant(s)': *pàapu* 'pod beans, string beans', *uuyi* 'planted plant(s)' (-*'uyi*).
paasatuwani 'the expanse of all the fields': *paasa* 'field', *tuwani* 'measure'. Compare *pastuwani* 'field measure', which refers to a marked-out area where one intends to work as a field although not necessarily doing so yet. *Paasatuwani* and *pastuwani* are constructed of the same elements but *paasa* appears in unreduced form in the first and is reduced to *pas-* in the second.
paasimasa'am 'their moisture-beaded wings': *paasi-* 'surface moisture', *masa'am* 'their wings'. *Paasi-* has *paahu* 'water' (*paa-*) as its first element but *-si-* remains unidentified.
paatalawinta 'be making it glisten with water': *paahu* 'water' (*paa-*), *taalawinta* 'be making it light, illuminating it' (*-talawinta*).

paatalawna 'make glisten with water': *paahu* 'water' (*paa-*), *taalawna* 'make it light' (*-talawna*). *Yokve' tutskwava paatotiqw put akw aqwhaqami paatalngwuniqw put hapi pàngqawkyangw oo'omawt yooyangwuy akw pang paa'o'yangwuniqw paatalawna.*

paatalawva 'become glistening with water': *paahu* 'water' (*paa-*), *taalawva* 'become light' (*-talawva*).

paatalawyungwni 'will be glistening with water (plural)': *paahu* 'water' (*paa-*); *taala* 'light' (*-tala-*); *-wa*, stative; *-yungwa*, durative plural (*-yungw-*); *-ni*, future. The plural form indicates that it will be glistening in many places.

paatalnawit 'along where it is bright with puddles of rainwater': *paahu* 'water' (*paa-*), *taala* 'light' (*-tal-*), *ánawit* 'along it' (*-nawit*).

paatàlpuva 'along a land glistening with water': *paahu* 'water' (*paa-*), *tàlpuva* 'in a brightened area'. *Yokve' ang paatotiqw put paa'iwyùngqat ang aqwhaqaminìiqat pàngqawe' "paatàlpuva," kítangwu.*

paatayayata 'be trembling with water': *paahu* 'water' (*paa-*), *tayayata* 'be trembling, shaking, quaking'.

paatayayatoyna 'be pouring water while shaking things', literally 'be shaking water', a reference to raining while thunder makes things shake: *paahu* 'water' (*paa-*), *tayayatoyna* 'be shaking something'.

paatsinawta 'be sprouting with moisture': *paahu* 'water' (*paa-*), *tsiinawta* 'be sprouting' (*-tsinawta*). *A'ni yookye' ang pam yeevante' a'ni naanahoy tsinanatangwuniqw oovi ang paatsinawta.*

paatuwatavi 'lay water on the land': *paahu* 'water' (*paa-*), *tuuwa* 'sand' (*-tuwa*), *tavi* 'put'. *Yooyangw tutskwava yòypalay púhikne' pan ang paatuwatavingwu.*

paatuwvota 'rings of ripples in water' ("water shield"): *paahu* 'water' (*paa-*), *tuwvota* 'shield'. *Tuwvota* is from *tuwqa* 'enemy' (*tuw-*), *poota* 'coiled plaque' (*-vota*). *Tuwvota pi hisat pootat an pöqniwtangwunìiqe naanangk angqe pongomvut pe'ytangwu. Oovi hak hìita ówat'ewakw paamiq tuuvaqw pam aqw yeeve' paahut naanahoy mupipitimaqat yukuqw pas pay pootat an sonìltingwu, angqe naanangk pongomvu pe'yvangwu, paniqw oovi paatuwvota.*

paavasnawit 'along the course of the fields': *paavasa* 'fields' (*paavas-*), *ánawit* 'along its course' (*-nawit*).

paavatalawinta 'be making it glisten with puddles of water': *paa-*, reduplication, meaning 'in various locations'; *paahu* 'water' (*-va-*); *taalawinta* 'be making it light, illuminating it' (*-talawinta*).

paavatalawna 'make it glisten with puddles of water': *paa-*, reduplication, meaning 'in various locations'; *paahu* 'water' (*-va-*); *taalawna* 'make it be light, illuminated' (*-talawna*).

paavatalawyungwni 'will be glistening with puddles of water in several places': *paa-*, reduplication, meaning 'in various locations'; *paahu* 'water' (*-va-*); *taalawyungwni* 'will be light, illuminated in several places' (*-talawyungwni*). *Taalawyungwni* is the future (*-ni*) of *taalawyungwa*, whose singular would be *taalawta*. The closest word in everyday language seems to be *taalaw'iwta* 'be light, be daylight'.

paavönmamant 'young corn plants': *paavön-* 'young corn', *mamant* 'maidens'. Though it provides a beautiful image mataphor, evoking the recurrent maiden metaphor, *paavönmamant* is the everyday word for young corn plants. There exists a compound expressing 'young corn plant' more literally, *pavön'uyi* (*paavön-* 'young corn' [*pavön-*], *uuyi* 'plant' [- '*uyi*]), but *pavön'uyi* refers to a corn sprout and is restricted to a ritual context in which it is symbolic of a young corn plant. The 'young corn' element appears only in compounds except for the postpositionalized form *paavönnawit* 'along the young corn plants': *paavön-* 'young corn plant(s)', *-nawit* 'along'.

paavönyevewmamant 'young corn plant maidens': *paavön-* 'young corn plant', *-yevew-* '(?)', *mamant* 'maidens'. The element *-yevew-* seems to serve to differentiate this word for 'young corn plant maidens' from *paavönmamant* 'young corn plants' (see above).

paavönyevewmomngwit 'young corn plant leaders', a reference to the snows of winter: *paavön-* 'young corn plants', *-yevew-* '(?)', *momngwit* 'leaders' (the plural of *mongwi*). The element *-yevew-* seems to contribute to a sense of animacy; compare *paavönmamant* and *paavönyevewmamant*, above.

paavönyevewsonaq 'throughout the midst of the young corn plants': *paavön-* 'young corn plant(s)', *-yevew-* '(?)', *-sona-* 'center; *-q*, diffusive suffix.

paavopkomat 'water creatures', a reference to the creatures of the natural world who depend on water for life: *paahu* 'water' (*paa-*); *po-*, reduplication; *pòoko-* 'possessed animal'; *-m*, plural suffix; *-at*, third person possessive suffix.

paayoyangw 'rainwater': *paahu* 'water' (*paa-*), *yooyangw* 'rain' (*-yoyangw*). There is a homophonous word *paayoyangw*, but with *paa-* 'great', meaning 'rainstorm, heavy rain, a "great rain"'.

paayoynguman'ini 'tray of rainwater cornmeal': *paayoyangw* 'rainwater' (*paayoy-*), *ngumni* 'finely ground cornmeal, corn flour' (*nguman-*), *ini* 'tray of' (- 'ini). *Sukw taawit ep Tukwunangwmamant angqw pew paa-yoynguman 'iniy na 'sasa 'yyùngqat lavàyti. Pam hapi hopimamàntuy novangumantotaqamuy tututskyaynaqe oovi pan Tukwunangwmamàntuy piptsa. Antsa maana, sen wùuti, noovat na 'sastanikt mòoti aqw ngúma-ngwu; pàasat pu' pam noovatat pu' tuunopnangwu. Noqw itam hapi oo 'omàwtuy amumi paalayamuy tungla 'yyungqw pam hapi tsölökye ' pu' nöösiwqat aniwnaqw pu' itam tuwat nöönösangwu. Yan hapi oovi Tukwunangwmamant (oomawmamant) songyawnen tuwat paalay ngumayat pu' put akw nöösiwqat itamungem na 'sastotangwu.*

paayoysingumannayuwsina 'adorn self with rainwater pollen': *paayoysi-ngumni* 'rainwater pollen' (*paayoysinguman-*), *naayuwsina* 'dress one-self' (*-nayuwsina*). *Paayoysingumni* is from *paayoyangw* 'rainwater' (*paayoy-*) plus *síngumni* 'pollen' (*-singumni*). *Naayuwsina* is the reflex-ive of *yuwsina* 'dress, clothe another', the transitivized form of *yuwsi* 'get dressed, put on clothing'.

paayoywuta 'am 'their poured-out rainwater, the rainwater they pour out': *paayoyangw* 'rainwater' (*paayoy-*); *wuuta* 'pour' (*-wuta*); - 'am 'their'.

paho 'ini 'tray of prayer feathers or other ritual objects': *paaho* 'prayer feather' (*paho-*), *ini* 'contents of an open, shallow container, tray of' (- 'ini).

pahomamant 'prayer feather maidens': *paaho* 'prayer feather' (*paho-*), *mamant* 'maidens'.

pahomomngwit 'prayer feather leaders': *paaho* 'prayer feather' (*paho-*), *momngwit* 'leaders' (the plural of *mongwi*).

pahovena 'paint prayer feathers': *paaho* 'prayer feather' (*paho-*), *peena* 'draw, paint' (*-vena*).

pahowuyomomngwit 'elder leaders dealing with prayer feathers': *paaho* 'prayer feather' (*paho-*), *wuy* 'old' (*wuyo-*), *momngwit* 'leaders' (the plural of *mongwi*).

pahoyàwtoyna 'place a prayer feather in a katsina performer's hand during a dance to hold'; *paaho* 'prayer feather' (*paho-*), *yaawitoyna* 'place something customary to hold in a performer's hand during a dance'.

pahoyesiwa 'be sitting and working on prayer feathers (plural)': *paaho* 'prayer feather' (*paho-*), *yeese* 'be sitting (plural)' (*-yes-*), *-iwa* 'stative'. *Yeesiwa* normally means 'be dwelling, living (in a location) (plural)' but in songs the ending *-iwa* is often better understood as an embellishment rather than as a meaningful element.

pala 'omaw 'red cloud': *pala-* 'red', *oomaw* 'cloud' (- 'omaw).

palasowitsmi'ytawi 'Red-Whiskered Long-Hair katsina song': *pala-* 'red', *sowitsmi'yta* 'have a beard, whiskers' (*sowitsmi'y-*), *taawi* 'song' (*-tawi*). The Red-Whiskered Long-Hair katsina is *Palasowitsmi'ytaqa* 'the one that has red whiskers'.

palatalwìipiki 'red lightning': *pala-* 'red', *talwìipiki* 'lightning'.

Palatkwapi 'the Red-Walled City': *pala-* 'red', *tùukwa* 'masonry wall' (*-tkwa*), *-pi* 'place'. Though *Palatkwapi* figures in migration legends, in the songs it is somewhere in the katsina world.

palayoyleki 'red rain lines': *pala-* 'red', *yoyleki* 'rain lines'.

Palhikwmamant 'Moisture-Drinking Maidens': *paala* 'moisture' (*Pal-*), *hiiko* 'drink' (*hikw-*), *mamant* 'maidens', a kind of Butterfly Maiden katsinas. The "moisture" reference has to do with nectar.

Palhikwmanàwyat 'two little Moisture-Drinking Maiden katsinas', a pair of Butterfly Maiden katsina marionettes: *paala* 'moisture' (*Pal-*), *hiiko* 'drink' (*hikw-*), *manàwyat* 'little maidens (dual)'.

pamös'o'omawt 'fog clouds': *pamösi* 'mist, fog' (*pamös-*), *oo'omawt* 'clouds' (*-'o'omawt*).

pamuymomngwit 'Paamuya [cloud] leaders': *Paamuya*, a lunar month corresponding roughly to January (*pamuy-*); *momngwit* 'leaders' (the plural of *mongwi*).

pasnawit 'along the course of the field': *paasa* 'field' (*pas-*), *ánawit* 'along its course' (*-nawit*).

patangsimamant 'squash blossoms' ('squash blossom maidens'): *patangsi* 'squash blossom', *mamant* 'maidens'. *Patangsi* is a compound of *patnga* 'squash' (*patang-*) and *sihu* 'flower' (*-si*).

patsqawuwuta 'be getting spattered with muddy water': *paahu* 'water' (*pa-*), *tsöqa* 'mud' (*-tsqa*), *wúwuta* 'be spilling out' (*-wuwuta*).

Pavawkyàytiyo 'Swallow Boy': *pavawkyaya* 'swallow' (*pavawkyày-*), *tiyo* 'boy'. *Sukw taawit ep i' Pavawkyàytiyo katsinmuy amumi tuu'awvaqe pàngqawu, "... atkya tsootsonglalwa, naa'itnalalwa; noqw nu' Pavawkyàytiyo tunatyayamuy ömàataqe'e, nu' umuy aa'awna." Pay sen pavawkyayat pöhöyat enang nakwakwusi yukiwtaqw pamniikyangw paho'init angqw qatsqe paniqw tunatyat navota. Put sen pàngqàwqe Pavawkyàytiyo, kita. Pu' sen pay pas it masa'ytaqat pavawkyayat yep tungwani'yta. Pavawkyayt pi paahut aqwsa ö'qalyanìiqe pangsoq teevep wuktotangwu. Pay paniqw sen puma hìitu yooyangwuy angwu'yyungqw oovi taawi put tawsomi'yta.*

pàytukwi 'triple peaks', a description of the San Francisco Peaks: *paayom* 'three, three of them' (*pày-*), *tuukwi* 'promontory, peak, butte' (*-tukwi*).

The San Francisco Peaks are usually referred to as *Nuvatukya'ovi* (at Third Mesa) or sometimes as *Nuvatukwi'ovi* (at Second Mesa).

pikmoki 'bundle of piki': *piiki* 'piki' (*pik-*), *mooki* 'bundle' (*-moki*). Piki is a preparation of corn flour cooked in thin sheets on a hot stone and rolled back on itself.

poli'ini 'butterfly whorl hairdo': *povolhoya* 'butterfly' (*poli-*), *ini* 'contents of an open shallow container' (*-'ini*).

poĺiisi 'evening primrose, *Oenothera pallida runcinata*': *povolhoya* 'butterfly' (*poĺi-*); *sihu* 'flower' (*-si*). Note that the evening primrose, a North American plant, is only remotely related to the primrose, which is an introduced plant of European origin. Taxonomically they are in different families, family Onagraceae for the evening primrose, Primulaceae for the primrose.

poĺiisimamant 'evening primrose maidens': *poĺiisi* 'evening primrose'; *mamant* 'maidens'.

powatawi 'curing song': *powata* 'cure, purify' (*powa-*), *taawi* 'song' (*-tawi*). *Powatawi pay himu tuuhikyat pi himu'at. Pam taawit akw enang hakiy tuuyat angqw powatangwu.*

    Pu' taawit ep pakiwte' powatawi pay Honanwùutaqat pas maki'ytangwu. Pam hapi Honanngyamuy wu'ya'amnìiqe hak tuwat ngatwi'yta. Noqw oovi pumuy wiimiyamuy, Powamuyat ep, mong'iwtaqat piw ephaqam pàngqaqwangwu, Honanwùutaqa.

pölöneyang 'mixed with or having ball-shaped things (like nubbins of fruit) all around': *pölö'at* 'its ball- or lump-shaped thing' (*-pölö*), *neeneyang* 'in mixed or various kinds' (*-neyang*).

pòötaplawu 'keep laying out a path': *pöhu* 'road, path' (*pòö-*), *tavilawu* 'keep putting, placing, depositing' (*-taplawu*).

pòötavi 'consecrated path': *pöhu* 'road, path' (*pòö-*), *tavi* 'put, place, deposit' (*-tav-*), *-i* 'noun-forming suffix'.

pòötaviwa 'be laid out as a consecrated path': *pöhu* 'road, path' (*pòö-*), *taviwa* 'get placed, deposited'.

pötskwani 'life plan, plan of life': *pöhu* 'road, path' (*pö-*); *tsìikwa* 'make straight' (*-tskwan-*); *-i*, noun-forming suffix. *Tsìikwa* is derived from *tsìikwi* 'become straight, get resolved' plus the transitive-verb-forming suffix *-a(-)*.

qa'ömamant 'corn maidens', more technically, 'dry-ear-of-corn maidens': *qaa'ö* 'dry ear of corn' (*qa'ö-*), *mamant* 'maidens'. *Taawit ep humi'uyit qa'ömamant kítangwu. Pu' pay piw pas qaa'öt pan ayàwtoynangwu; pay pi hakim sutsep paho'iniy ep put qaa'öt enang tavi'yyungngwu.*

Qa'ömana 'Corn Maiden': *qaa'ö* 'dry ear of corn' (*qa'ö-*), *maana* 'maiden' (*-mana*).

qa'ömomngwit 'corn leaders': *qaa'ö* 'dry ear of corn' (*qa'ö-*), *momngwit* 'leaders' (the plural of *mongwi*).

Qa'ötotim 'Corn Boys', a katsina type: *qaa'ö* 'dry ear of corn' (*Qa'ö-*), *tootim* 'boys' (*-totim*). These katsinas are also called *Ngayayatotaqam.*

qaatsiptu 'lie down': *qaatsi* 'lie', *pitu* 'arrive, come, get there, reach a destination' (*-ptu*). *Puhumuyaw maatsìlte' piw qaatsiptungwu, suupan paatang.wat qatsngwunìiqe oovi.*

qatsi'nangwa 'will to live': *qatsi* 'life', *unangwa* 'heart' (*-'nangwa*). *Ephaqam hak qatsiy ep ókiwte' qa suyan yuumo qatsiy naatniqat ang öqawtangwu. Naamahin sen as himu hakiy unangwayat wílökni'ytaqw pay itam itàaqatsiy ang ö'qalyaniqat it enang katsinam taawiy akw itamuy piw tutuwnaya. It yanwat öqalànpit pàngqawe', "qatsi'nangwa," kítangwu.*

qatsimkiwa 'preordained lifeway, inherited duty': *qatsi* 'life', *makiwa* 'something received or inherited, gift, birthright, duty, allotment'. In the discussions of the songs, this word is also translated as the corn lifeway, the corn-based lifeway, and the Hopi lifeway.

qatsinahuyvaniwa 'be choices made in ways of life': *qatsi* 'life', *naahuy-vaniwa* 'be apportioned' (*-nahuyvaniwa*). *Kurpi qatsiyàyngwaveq hak hìitawat qatsit akw qatsi'àasatimaniqat namortaqw pu' pepeq hak, himu put hakiy maqangwuniqw put pàngqàwqe qatsinahuyvaniwa.*

qatsituvinglawu 'be petitioning for acceptance to join the life of a village': *qatsi* 'life', *tuuvinglawu* 'keep asking for' (*-tuvinglawu*). *Hopit navotiyat ep itam sòosoyam haqaqw ökìiqe mooti tuuvingtotat pu' hu'wanit akw yùngqe pan hopìituy amumi sinototi. Yan yuykiwqat pàngqawe' "qatsituvinglawu," kítangwu.*

qatsivaptsiwta 'have one's turn at life': *qatsi* 'life', *paptsiwta* 'have one's turn' (*-vaptsiwta*). *Hakim haqam nùutum sinoyese' pep yumuy pu' namuy amúngk tuwat paptsiwyungngwu, timu'yvayaniqey, hin pumuy amungem tunös'àasalalwaniqey, pu' hìita mongqeqnit ang tuwat qeniptuye' put ang hongkyangw sinot engem qatsit wuuwantotaniqey. It yantaqat pàngqawe' "qatsivaptsiwta," kítangwu.*

qatsivötskwani 'rules of life to be followed': *qatsi* 'life', *pötskwani* 'life plan' (*-vötskwani*) (see above).

Qatsiyamakiwqa 'the Emergence, that which emerges as life': *qatsi* 'life'; *yámakiwa* 'undergo an emergence' (*-yamakiw-*); *-qa*, relative suffix: 'that which'. *Hopi hapi pay angqaqw yu'a'atima, yaw haqaqw atkya qatsit angqw pew yámakqey. I' hapi pas hopit navoti'at. Noqw oovi hopi* *wiimiy ang yanwat yep qatsi yàyngwa'ytaqat put ang tuvoylatima. Itam yaw pas pangqw atkyaqw pew nöngakqe pep pu' naap qatsit yesniqey put namortota, hìita hopivötskwanit. Itam pepeq sooyat namortotaqe put akw nöösiwqat akw yesniqey àasatiwisni. Yan itam yaw qatsimkiwa'y- kàakyangw hopimatsiwtaniqat it hopi ahoy piptse' pàngqawngwu, "Qatsiyamakiwqa."*

qatsiyàynawisa 'go to begin life (plural)': *qatsi-* 'life', *yàyna* 'start, begin (volitional)', *-wisa* 'go to' (plural of *-to*).

qatuptu 'get into a sitting position; place onself close to something; get up from bed; stop for the night; settle into a lifestyle; marry, settle down with': *qatu* 'sit, dwell, live', *pitu* 'arrive, come, get there, reach a destination' (*-ptu*).

qöqlökatsìntawi 'katsina song of the Qööqöqlöm': *Qööqöqlöm* (*qöqlö-*), *katsina* (*katsìn-*), *taawi* 'song' (*-tawi*). The Qööqöqlöm are the katsinas who open the kivas for katsinas at the time of the Winter Solstice ceremony (*Soyalangw*).

qöya'omaw 'white cloud': *qöya-* 'white', *oomaw* 'cloud' (*-'omaw*). The element *qöya-* refers to natural white, lack of coloring, purity. *Qötsa'o- mawuy pàngqawe' "qöya'omaw," kítangwu. Taawit ep pay sutsep qöya- 'omawuy tungwe' hoopoqwat maamasangwu; pangqw pam tuwat pítu- ngwu. I' oovi hopit wimhimuyat ang lavayi.*

qöya'omawmamant 'white cloud maidens': *qöya'omaw* 'white cloud', *mamant* 'maidens'.

qöya'omawnakwa'am 'their white cloud headdresses': *qöya'omaw* 'white cloud'; *nakwa* 'feather(s) worn as a headdress'; *-'am* 'their'.

Qöyahonaw 'White Bear': *qöya-* 'white, uncolored', *hoonaw* 'bear' (*-honaw*).

qöyangwùntalawkuyva 'for daylight to make its appearance as white dawn', a reference to the first part of dawn: *qöyangnu* or *qöyangwnu* 'be white dawn' (*qöyangwùn-*), *taala* 'light' (*talaw-*), *kuyva* 'appear'. *Qöyang(w)nu* is derived from *qöya-* 'white, uncolored' plus *wunu* 'stand' (*-ng(w)nu*). *Taalaw'iwme' mòoti qöyangnuptungwu, noqw oovi pantaqat akw naat pu' taala hihin maatsìlte' qöyangwùntalawkuyva- ngwu.*

qöyapaw'omaw 'low-lying white cloud(s)': *qöya-* 'white', *heyapaw'omaw* 'low-lying nimbus cloud' (*-paw'omaw*). *Heyapaw'omaw* is from *heehe- yapawt* 'low-lying dark clouds, usually the aftermath of a cloudburst' (*heyapaw-*) plus *oomaw* 'cloud' (*-'omaw*).

qöyapqa'ö 'white corn': *qöya-* 'white', *-p-* (?), *qaa'ö* 'dry ear of corn' (*-qa'ö*).

qöyatalwìipiki 'white lightning': *qöya-* 'white', *talwìipiki* 'lightning'.

qöyawunùuqa 'white dawn' ("the one that stands as white"), a reference to the part of the twilight before sunrise before colors can be discerned: *qöya-* 'white'; *wunu* 'stand' (*-wunùu-*); *-qa,* relative suffix: the one that'. *Qöyangnuptuqat pàngqàwqe qöyawunùuqa.*

qöyayoyleki 'white rain lines': *qöya-* 'white', *yoyleki* 'rain lines'.

Sa'lakwmanat 'two Sa'lako maidens': *Sa'lako* (*Sa'lakw-*), *maanat* '(two) maidens' (*-manat*).

sakwa'omaw 'blue/green cloud': *sakwa* 'blue/green', *oomaw* 'cloud' (*-'omaw*). *Sakwa'omaw hapi tuwat taavang qeni'ytaqe oovi pangqw pítungwu, Hopit wimhimuyat ang lavayit epe'.*

sakwatalwìipiki 'blue/green lightning': *sakwa* 'blue/green', *talwìipiki* 'lightning'.

sakwavaho 'blue/green prayer feather(s)': *sakwa* 'blue/green', *paaho* 'prayer feather(s)' (*-vaho*).

sakwavahomamant 'blue/green prayer feathers' ("blue/green prayer feather maidens"): *sakwa* 'blue/green', *paaho* 'prayer feather(s)' (*-vaho*), *mamant* 'maidens'.

sakwavahomongwi 'blue/green prayer feather leader': *sakwa* 'blue/green', *paaho* 'prayer feather' (*-vaho*), *mongwi* 'leader'.

Sakwavayu'am 'Blue Lake', literally 'their Blue/Green River': *sakwa* 'blue/green', *paayu* 'river' (*-vayu*), *-'am* 'their'. Blue Lake is a location sacred to the people of Taos.

sakwavoli 'blue/green butterfly': *sakwa* 'blue/green', *povolhoya* 'butterfly' (*-voli*).

sakwavolmamant 'blue/green butterfly maidens': *sakwavoli* 'blue/green butterfly' (*sakwavol-*), *mamant* 'maidens'.

sakwayevewmamant 'blue/green young corn(?) plants', literally 'blue/green young corn(?) plant maidens'. *Sikyavavönmamant* 'yellow young corn plants' and *sakwayevewmamant* are a ritual pair: *sakwa* 'blue/green'; *-yevew-*, an unidentified element (seemingly it means 'young corn plant' because of the parallelism in the ritual pair, though elsewhere it seems to contribute a sense of animacy, see *paavönyevewmamant,* above); *mamant* 'maidens'.

sakwayoyleki 'blue/green rain lines': *sakwa* 'blue/green', *yoyleki* 'rain lines'.

Salapmamant 'Douglas Fir maidens': *salavi* 'Douglas fir' (*salap-*), *mamant* 'maidens'.

Sa'lakwmanat '(two) Sa'lako maidens': *Sa'lako* (*Sa'lakw-*); *maana* 'maiden' (*-mana*); *-t*, dual ending.

Sa'lakwmanàwyat '(two) little Sa'lako maidens': *Sa'lako* (*Sa'lakw-*), *manàwyat* 'little maidens (dual)'.

si'ohemiskatsìntawi 'Zuni Hemiskatsina song': *si'o* 'Zuni', *hemis-*, *katsina* (*katsìn-*), *taawi* 'song' (*-tawi*).

sìipölölöta 'be forming buds all over': *sihu* 'flower' (*sìi-*), *pölölöta* 'be forming into spherical things'.

sìipuyayata 'be opening out as flowers': *sihu* 'flower' (*sìi-*), *puyayata* 'be opening out'.

sìiqölnawit 'along the course of the flowery expanse(s)': *sihu* 'flower' (*sìi-*), *-qölö* 'area, expanse' (*-qöl-*), *ánawit* 'along its course' (*-nawit*). *Himu a'ni si'yve' aqwhaqami ang sìiqölòltingwuniqw put ang ánawit himu hinme' sìiqölnawitningwu. Ephaqam himuwa taawi it pas yaavo tungwe' "sìiqölönawit," kítangwu.*

sìiqòlpa 'in, along the flowery expanse(s)': *sihu* 'flower' (*sìi-*), *-qölö* 'area, expanse' (*-qòl-*), *-pa* 'in, along'.

sìitala 'be bright with flowers': *sihu* 'flower' (*sìi-*), *taala* 'be bright'. *Himu si'yve' ang sìitalngwu, sihuy akw pas ang maatsiwtangwu, nìiqe oovi sìitala.*

sìitalawva 'become bright with flowers': *sihu* 'flower' (*sìi-*), *taalawva* 'become light' (*-talawva*). *Himu si'ymakyangw ang sòosoy puyàmte' sìitalawvangwu.*

sìitalawvatay 'after it has become bright with flowers (object form)': *sihu* 'flower' (*sìi-*); *taalawva* 'become light' (*-talawva*); *-t* 'after' (subordinating suffix) (*-ta-*); *-y*, accusative case suffix.

sìitàlpuva 'along a land brightened with flowers': *sihu* 'flower' (*sìi-*), *tàlpuva* 'in light'. *Haqe' sìitàlqat ang hinme', sen ang hintsakme' pu' sìitàlpuvaningwu.*

sikya'omaw 'yellow cloud': *sikyàngpu* 'yellow' (*sikya-*), *oomaw* 'cloud' (*-'omaw*).

Sikyahonawmomngwit 'Yellow Bear leaders': *sikyàngpu* 'yellow' (*Sikya-*), *hoonaw* 'bear' (*-honaw-*), *momngwit* 'leaders' (the plural of *mongwi*).

sikyangwùntalawkuyva 'for daylight to make its appearance as yellow dawn': *sikyangnu* or *sikyangwnu* 'be yellow dawn' (*sikyangwùn-*), *taala* 'light' (*talaw-*), *kuyva* 'appear'. *Sikyang(w)nu* is derived from *sikya-* 'yellow' plus *wunu* 'stand' (*-ng(w)nu*). *Taalaw'iwme' mòoti qöyangnuptungwu, pu' taawa kuyvaniqey aqw hàykyalaqw taavi'at angqe hihin maatsìlte' pam hapi sikyangwùntalawkuyvangwu.*

sikyatalwìipiki 'yellow lightning': *sikya-* 'yellow', *talwìikipi* 'lightning'.

sikyavavönmamant 'yellow young corn plants': *sikya-* 'yellow', *paavönmamant* 'young corn plants' (*-vavönmamant*).

sikyavolim 'yellow butterflies': *sikya-* 'yellow'; *polìit* 'butterflies' (*-voli-*); *-m*, plural.

sikyavolmamant 'yellow butterfly maidens': *sikyavoli* 'yellow butterfly' (*sikyavol-*), *mamant* 'maidens'.

sikyayoyleki 'yellow rain lines': *sikyàngpu* 'yellow' (*sikya-*), *yoyleki* 'rain lines'.

sínevelantoya 'provide with the perfection of something that is another's due': *sihu* 'flower' (*sí-*), *neevelantoy(n)a* 'provide another with what they are due' (*-nevelantoya*). *Hak hìita lolmat neevela'yve', hak hìita maqsoniy akw àasatangwu. Hak hakiy neevelantoyne' yan àasatiyat aw nó'angwu. Taawit ep i' lavayi pakiwte' hìita itam hakiy àasatiyat ep aw antsatsnayaniqat put pàngqawngwu.*

    Pay hopi sutsep pàngqawngwu, naawakìnpit hintsakye' maqsontangwu. I' yan maqsoni'at unangwvàasit akw katsinmuy amumi maataviwngwu, pu' puma katsinam itamumi pas na'okiwvewat angnìiqat itàa-'unangwvàasiy tungla'yyùngqe put itamuy u'nantoynaya. Noqw hopi hapi sihut akw hìita pitsangwayat sus'omiq tsókyangwuniqw oovi sùupan sihut akw itàa'unangwvàasiy pitsàngwtoynayaqat àntotit pu' put katsinmuy amumi maatatveqw pam hapi sínevelantoya.

sínevela'yta 'have perfection as one's due': *sihu* 'flower' (*sí-*), *neevela'yta* 'have as one's due' (*-nevela'yta*). In this and similar words, the incorporated element *sihu* 'flower' refers to ideals of beauty and harmony and of spiritual perfection.

síngumanyuyuwina 'be dancing with pollen': *síngumni* 'pollen' (*sínguman-*) [from *sihu* 'flower' (*sí-*), *ngumni* 'flour, fine-ground cornmeal'], *yuuyuwina* 'be dancing' (*-yuyuwina*).

síqöyavunit 'in adorned white': *sihu* 'flower' (*sí-*); *qöya-* 'white, colorless'; *-vu*, resultative suffix; *-ni* noun-forming suffix; *-t*, adverbializing suffix.

Sivu'ikwiwtaqa 'Pot Carrier katsina, the One that Carries a Vessel on his Back': *siivu* 'vessel, kettle, pot' (*sivu-*); *iikwiwta* 'have on one's back'; *-qa*, relative suffix: 'the one that'.

siwahopmangu'iwta 'be tired of bachelorhood': *siwahova* 'bachelor' (*siwahop-*), *mangu'iwta* 'be tired'.

siwawaytima 'go along in joy, in happiness': perhaps from *sihu* 'flower' (*si-*); *waayaya* 'move to and fro repeatedly' (*-waway-*); *-ta*, repetitive (*-t-*); *-ima* 'go along'.

siwiswukiwta 'have cascading tendrils': *siwi* 'tendrils'; *síwukiwta* 'be cascaded' (*-swukiwta*).

somiviki 'blue corn pudding boiled or steamed in a corn husk wrapper, tied in two places to form three equal sections': *somi* 'something tied', *piiki* 'piki' (*-viki*). Girls make *somiviki* as gifts to give to boys in return for rabbits they kill on the hunt.

Soongwuqa 'the Milky Way': *soohu* 'star' (*soo-*); *wunu* 'stand' (*-ngwu-*); *-qa*, relative suffix: "the one that stands as stars." (The identification of *wunu* 'stand' as the element underlying *-ngwu* is somewhat speculative. *-ngwnu*, which is often reduced to *-ngnu*, is a combining form of *wunu*, cf. *qöyangwnu* or *qöyangnu* 'be white dawn'. It is supposed that in this name, *-ngwnu* has lost its medial *-n-*, resulting in *-ngwu-*.)

Sootukwnangwmomngwit 'Star-Cumulus Cloud katsina leaders': *Sootukwnangw*, *momngwit* 'leaders' (the plural of *mongwi*). Sootukwnangw (from *soohu* 'star' (*soo-*), *tukwnangw* 'cumulus cloud') is a katsina that appears in the Bean dance procession. In everyday language, the singular form *tukwnangw* is not used, only the plural *tùutukwnangwt*.

soyohim'o'omawt 'all kinds of clouds', referring to clouds of different forms: *sòosoy himu* 'all kinds' (*soyohim-*), *oo'omawt* 'clouds' (*-'o'o-mawt*).

soyohìmkatsinam 'mixed katsinas, katsinas of various sorts': *sòosoy himu* 'all kinds' (*soyohìm-*), *katsinam* 'katsinas'.

soyohìmqaqa'ö 'all different kinds of corn': *sòosoy himu* 'all kinds' (*soyohìm-*), *qaaqa'ö* 'different kinds of corn' (*-qaqa'ö*). *Sòosoy himu hinyùngqaniikyangw tungwaniwte' soyohim-matsiwngwu. Oovi pi soyohìmkatsinam. Qaa'öt sòosok hinyùngqat Hopi natwantaqat pàngqàwqe soyohìmqaqa'ö.*

sumi'nangwat 'together in intentions, united in endeavors, in unanimity': *suumi* 'together' (*sumi-*), *unangwa* 'heart' (*-'nangwa*), *-t*, adverb-forming suffix. *Suumi wuwniniikyangw pang tunatyat himu pasìwtiniqat epye' sumi'nangwat epyangwu.*

sunsa'unangway 'with hearts together as one': *sunsa* 'the same way only'; *unangwa* 'heart' (*-'unangwa*); *-y*, adverb-forming suffix.

sustalyokva 'rain all day': *suus taala* 'one day' (*sustal-*), *yokva* 'rain'. *Suus taalat ang teevep yooyokye' sustalyokvangwu.*

suviptuyqa 'sumac point, the point with sumacs', a description of *Kìisiw* (Shadow Springs): *suuvi* 'sumac' (*suvip-*), *tuyqa* 'projecting point of a mesa'. The irregular combining form here (*suuvip-*) of *suuvi* is related somehow to the form *suvipsi* 'sumac berries', from *suuvi* (*suvi-*) plus *poosi* 'seed(s)' (*-psi*).

suvo'oyiwa 'have been united as one': *suuvo* 'toward one purpose, goal' (*suvo-*), *oyiwa* 'get selected' (- *'oyiwa*). *Himu qa suukyaniikyangw suuvo oyiwe' suvo'oyiwngwu. Katsinmuy taawi'am pay it tunatyat, naawakìnpit ep sinmuy amungem lolmat tunatyat, put suvo'oyiwqw pu' pam pankyangw sinot tunatyayat aniwnaniqat pàngqawe' tunatya suvo'oyiwa, kítangwu.*

suvuyoyangw 'steady drizzle, gentle rain, long and steady rain': *suvuvuta* 'be raining gently, drizzling' (*suvu-*), *yooyangw* 'rain' (*-yoyangw*).

suvuyoysonaq 'in the steady drizzle, through the gentle rain': *suvuvuta* 'be raining gently, drizzling' (*suvu-*); *yooyangw* 'rain' (*yoy-*); *-sona-* 'center'; *-q,* diffusive suffix.

suyanis'unangwa 'good-heartedness, a righteous and sincere attitude': *suyan* 'clear' (*suyani-*); *-s-,* an unidentified element; *unangwa* 'heart'.

suyanisqatsi 'life of harmony': *suyan* 'clear' (*suyani-*); *-s-,* an unidentified element; *qatsi* 'life'.

taalaw'omàwki 'dwelling place of the clouds at the place of the sunrise': *taala* 'light, daylight' (*taalaw-*), *oomàwki* 'dwelling place of clouds' (- *'omàwki*).

taalawkuyva 'for daylight to make its appearance': *taala* 'daylight, light' (*taalaw-*), *kuyva* 'appear'.

taalawsiwawayna 'be making delighted at the beginning of the day': *taala* 'light, daylight' (*taalaw-*), *siwawaya* 'be exhibiting happiness, a good feeling' (*siwaway-*), *-ina* 'causative' (*-na*). *Siwawaya* may be from *sihu* 'flower' (*si-*) plus *waayaya* 'move to and fro repeatedly' (*-wawaya*).

Taalawsohu 'Morning Star': *taala* 'light, daylight' (*taalaw-*), *soohu* 'star' (*-sohu*).

taalawsonmi 'toward the center of daylight, of the light of sunrise': *taala* 'light, daylight' (*taalaw-*); *-sona-* 'center' (*-son-*); *-mi* 'toward, to'.

taatawyuyuwintima 'go along dancing and singing songs': *taa-*, reduplication, *taawi* 'song' (*-taw-*), *yuuyuwina* 'be dancing' (*-yuyuwin-*), *-tima* 'go along'.

taawanasave 'at midday, at noon': *taawa* 'sun, day', *naasave* 'at the middle' (*-nasave*).

tal'angwyokva 'rain during the summer': *tal'angw* 'summer', *yokva* 'rain' (verb).

talahoyiwa 'awaken for the new day': *taala* 'light, daylight', *hooyi* 'get fully fledged' (*-hoy-*), *-iwa* 'stative'.

talasi 'pollen': *tala'at* 'its tassel' (*tala-*), *sihu* 'flower' (*-si*). This is the generic word for 'pollen' though it is derived as though referring specifically to the pollen of plants with tassels, especially corn plants. A poetic word for 'pollen', restricted to song contexts, is *síngumni*, from *sihu* 'flower' (*sí-*) plus *ngumni* 'flour, fine-ground cornmeal'.

talasimasa'am 'their pollen-laden wings': *talasi* 'pollen', *masa'am* 'their wings'.

Talasiva 'Pollen Spring': *talasi* 'pollen', *paahu* 'water' (*-va*).

talasiyalaha 'glittering pollen, pollen with sparkles in it': *talasi* 'pollen', *yalaha* 'specular hematite'.

talasiyalaha'iqöma 'my face painted with pollen with sparkles in it': *talasi* 'pollen', *yalaha* 'specular hematite', *i-* 'my' (*-'i-*), *qöma* 'face paint'.

talavàytötöqa 'be giving the calls of the morning': *talavày* 'in the morning' (*talavày-*), *töötöqa* 'be giving calls, shouting' (*-tötöqa*).

talwìipiki 'lightning': *talwìipi(k-)* 'flash as lightning' (*talwìipik-*); *-i*, noun-forming suffix.

talwipi'am 'their lightning': *taala* 'light' (*tal-*); *wìipikma* 'get flung off' (*wipi-*); *-'am* 'their'. *Ephaqam taawit ep qa sòosok lavayit pasiwtaqat akw lavàytingwu. Talwipi'am pay oovi talwìipiki'am asniqw pay pi taawinìiqe hàypo ephaqam lavayit túngwanmangwu.*

talwiptutuveni 'representation of lightning': *talwìipi* 'lightning' (*talwip-*), *tutuveni* 'visual representation, writing'.

taqvahomomngwit 'men who make the prayer feathers': *taaqa* 'man' (*taq-*), *paaho* 'prayer feather' (*-vaho*), *momngwit* 'leaders'(the plural of *mongwi*).

tasaphonaqmomoyam 'women who are crazy for Navajo men': *tasavu* 'Navajo' (*tasap-*), *hoonaqa* 'one who is inclined to become overly silly, excitable' (*honaq-*), *momoyam* 'women'.

tasapkatsìntawi 'Navajo katsina song': *tasavu* 'Navajo' (*tasap-*), *katsina* (*katsìn-*), *taawi* 'song' (*-tawi*). *Tasapkatsinam* 'Navajo katsinas' represent Navajos as perceived by Hopis.

Tatatsiwkiva 'Ball Game kiva': *tatatsiw* 'ball game', *kiva*.

tawaktsi'uyi 'sweet corn plants': *tawaktsi* 'sweet corn', *uuyi* 'planted plant(s)' (*-'uyi*).

tawamanaw 'oriole', a category including Bullock's oriole, the western tanager, and the black-headed grosbeak: *taawa* 'sun' (*tawa-*); *maana* 'girl' (*-mana*); *-w*, noun suffix.

tewaki 'Tanoan country': *teewa* 'Tewa' (*tewa-*), *kiihu* 'house, dwelling place' (*-ki*). *Tewaki* also refers to Hano, the Tewa village at First Mesa. *Teewa* is the Hopi term for any Tanoan group, whether Tewa (Arizona

Tewa, Santa Clara, San Juan, San Ildefonso, Nambe, Tesuque), Tiwa (Taos, Picuris, Sandia, Isleta) or Towa (Jemez).

tiitawi 'in-place song', the middle main song which is sung in place in the kiva or plaza: *tiihu* 'dance' (*tii-*), *taawi* 'song' (*-tawi*).

tiitayawna 'entertain with a performance, gladden with a performance': *tiihu* 'dance' (*tii-*); *tayawna* 'delight, make glad'.

tiiti'ayalawu 'be asking others to perform': *tii-*, reduplication, *tiihu* 'dance' (*-ti-*), *ayalawu* 'be asking one to do something'.

tiiti'ökiwa 'have come in dance (and thereby to soothe)': *tiihu* 'dance (noun)' (*tii-*); *tihu* 'child' (*-ti-*); *öki* 'arrive, come, get there, reach a destination (plural)' (*- 'ök-*); *-iwa*, stative. With its inclusion of two noun roots, 'dance' and 'child', this verb alludes to two other verbs, *tiiva* 'dance' (with *tiihu*) and *tiititapta* 'be babysitting, entertaining' (with *tihu*). *Tiikive 'yyungwniqey oovi ökye' tiiti 'ökiwa.*

tiitiwayakniwa 'have been invited to dance': *tii-*, reduplication; *tiihu* 'dance (noun)' (*-ti-*); *wáyakna* 'ask to do a favor' (*wayakn-*); *-iwa* 'stative'.

tiitiwungwinta 'be nurturing offspring repeatedly': *tii-,* reduplication: 'repeatedly'; *tihu* 'child, offspring' (*ti-*); *wúngwinta* 'be raising, nurturing, making grow' (*-wungwinta*).

tiitiwungwna 'raise children, nurture like children': *tii-*, reduplication; *tihu* 'child' (*ti-*); *wungwna* 'raise, nurture, make grow'.

tiitiwunima 'be dancing in performance' to sooth, ease the mind: *tii-*, reduplication; *tihu* 'child' (*-ti-*); *wunima* 'dance (verb)'. *Tiihuy akw sinmuy tiitapte' tiitiwunimangwu.*

tiitiwuniwa 'have been called upon to (come and) dance in performance': *tii-*, reduplication; *tiihu* 'dance (noun)' (*-ti-*); *wunima* 'dance (verb)' (*wun-*); *-iwa*, stative.

tiitiwunuto 'go/come to stand dancing': *tii-*, reduplication; *tiihu* 'dance' (*-ti-*); *wunu* 'stand'; *-to* 'go/come to'.

timaynànkwusa 'set out on a journey to watch a performance (plural)': *tiimayi* 'watch for the sake of pleasure, especially a dance' (*timay-*), *nànkwusa* 'start on a journey (plural)'.

tímoki 'young corn ear on the stalk': *tihu* 'child' (*tí-*), *mooki* 'bundle' (*-moki*).

tivongyapami 'to the dance-display place', destinative form of *tivongya-pavi*. *Kiisonve tiihu pongya 'iwtangwuniiqe oovi tivongyapavi.*

tivongyapave 'at the dance-display place', punctive form of *tivongyapavi.*

tíwungwnitotim 'boys being raised': *tihu* 'child' (*tí-*), *wungwni* 'something raised', *tootim* 'boys' (*-totim*).

toko'omawtotim 'dark billowing cloud boys': *toko 'omaw* 'dark billowing cloud', *tootim* 'boys' (*-totim*). *Toko'omaw* is from *toko* 'flesh, body' plus *oomaw* 'cloud' (*-'omaw*).

tokotswùuti 'mean, grouchy woman': *tokotsi* 'wildcat' (*tokots-*), *wùuti* 'woman'.

tokyephoyoyota 'be moving all night': *tookyep* 'all night long' (*tokyep-*), *hoyoyota* 'be moving'. *Tookyep himu haqaqw hoyoyote' tokyephoyoyotangwu.*

tokyepyoyangw 'an all-night rain': *tookyep* 'all night long' (*tokyep-*), *yooyangw* 'rain' (*-yoyangw*).

töökiwangwayi 'be shouting of joy': *töötöki'at* 'its characteristic calls, sounds' (*tööki-*), *wángwayi* 'summon, call' (*-wangwayi*).

töökiyuyuwina 'be dancing while making characteristic calls, sounds': *tööki'at* 'its characteristic calls, sounds' (*tööki-*), *yuuyuwina* 'be dancing'.

töökiyuyuwinta 'be dancing while making characteristic calls, sounds': *töötöki'at* 'its characteristic calls, sounds' (*tööki-*), *yuuyuwina* 'be dancing' (*-yuyuwin-*), *-ta* 'repetitive'.

tsa'kwaynakatsìntawi 'Tsa'kwayna katsina song': *Tsa'kwayna* (a katsina), *katsina* (*katsìn-*), *taawi* 'song' (*-tawi*).

tsorosi 'blue aster(s), *Aster* spp.': *tsooro* 'bluebird' (*tsoro-*), *sihu* 'flower' (*-si*).

tsukumana 'coot, American coot, *Fulica americana*', a migrant water bird: *tsuku* 'clown', *maana* 'girl' (*-mana*).

tsukumomngwit 'clown leaders': *tsuku* 'clown', *momngwit* 'leaders'.

tsukutotim 'clown boys': *tsuku* 'clown', *tootim* 'boys' (*-totim*).

tsukuviki 'blue corn pudding wrapped into a crescent shape in a green corn leaf and boiled or steamed': *tsuku* 'point', *piiki* 'piki' (*-viki*). *Tsukuviki* is a festive food; it is made by brides at their weddings for the men who help weave the wedding garments.

tukwi'ova 'up along the mesa(s)': *tuukwi* 'promontory, mesa, butte, peak' (*tukwi-*), *oova* 'in, along, through an area above' (*-'ova*).

tukwunàngwkatsìntawi 'Cumulus Cloud katsina song': *tùutukwnangwt* 'cumulus clouds' (*tukwunàngw-*), *katsina* (*katsìn-*), *taawi* 'song' (*-tawi*).

tukwunangwmamant 'cumulus clouds', literally 'cumulus cloud maidens': *tùutukwnangwt* 'cumulus clouds' (*tukwunangw-*), *mamant* 'maidens'. *Tuukwiwyùngqam oo'omawt pan maamatsiwyangwu, taawit ep, tukwunangwmamant.*

tulakinsivu 'vessel for toasting cornmeal over fire': *tulakna* 'toast coarsely ground cornmeal in a pan over the fire in an oven' (*tulakin-*), *siivu* 'vessel'. This toasting is done in preparation for fine grinding.

túsanmaqtö 'dirty hands': *tusna* 'dirt on the body' (*túsan-*), *maqtö* 'back of the hand, fist'. *Maqtö* is from *maa'at* 'hand' (*ma-*), *qötö'at* 'head' (*-qtö*).

Tuuwanasavi, a reference to all the Hopi lands: *tuuwa* 'land', *naasa-* 'middle' (*-nasa-*), *-vi* 'place'. (A sandy plain south of Orayvi is also known as *Tuuwanasavi*, but *tuuwa-* here is probably for 'sand' rather than 'land', perhaps in origin a play on words.)

tuuwapongya 'earth, the land part of the earth', more literally, 'a display of things set out in place on the land': *tuuwa* 'land/world'; *pongya* 'a display of things in place'. *Tuuwapongya* is often rendered in English as the "sand altar" in an attempt to express the Hopi reverence for the land. Though the independent word *tuuwa* means 'sand' (or 'earth, dirt', especially in a farming context), in many compounds *tuuwa* is conceived as a more abstract, primordial substance, that which constitutes the land portion of the earth. The word *pongya*, which refers to any set of things laid out in a display, including sacred objects, is often translated as "altar" when used in reference to ritual. *Tutskwa aqwhaqami qatsqa hapi tuuwapongya; tutskwa hapi hópitniqw hìita ayawa'ykyangw qatsqe' oovi songyawnen pongya'iwta.*

tuuwaqatsi 'land, world': *tuuwa* 'sand', *qaatsi* 'lie' (*-qats-*), *-i*, noun-forming suffix. Here "sand" is to be conceived as the primordial substance that constitutes the land.

tuuwatavi 'place on the land': *tuuwa* 'land', *tavi* 'put'.

tuuwaytalawvangaqw 'from where the first light of day is still out of sight': *tuuwayi* 'a place out of sight' (*tuuway-*), *taalawva* 'become light' (*-talawva*), *-ngaqw* 'from'.

tuvenangöyta 'be chasing one other about colorfully': *tuve-* 'of various colors'; *naa-*, reflexive (*-na-*); *ngöyta* 'be pursuing, chasing after'.

tuvevakwam 'toads of various colors': *tuve-* 'of various colors'; *paakwa* 'toad' (*-vakwa*); *-m*, plural. See also *mösivakwam* 'food-packet toads'.

tuvevakwamomngwit 'toad leaders of various colors': *tuve-* 'of various colors'; *paakwa* 'toad' (*-vakwa-*); *momngwit* 'leaders' (the plural of *mongwi*).

tuvevolmamant 'butterflies of various colors' ('butterfly maidens of various colors'): *tuvevolìit* 'butterflies of various colors' (*tuvevol-*), *mamant* 'maidens'. The Hopi Dictionary (1998) has *tuvevolmamant* as a song form meaning 'cornstalks', possibly originating as an imaginative extension of the butterfly metaphor to the leaves of the corn plants waving in the breeze.

tuvevolvitsangwa 'countenance of butterflies of various colors': *tuve-* 'of various colors; *poŀiit* 'butterflies' (*-vol-*); *pitsangwa* 'facial appearance, countenance'.

u'nangwvaslawu 'keep praying repeatedly in a heartfelt manner for good results': *u-*, reduplication; *unangwa* 'heart' (*-'nangw-*); *-vàasi* 'wish, desire' (*-vas-*); *-lawu* 'keep on', continuative suffix.

umùu'unangwvàasi 'your heartfelt wish, hope, prayer': *umùu-* 'your (plural), *unangwa* 'heart' (*-'unangw-*), *-vàasi* 'wish, desire'.

umùukisonaq 'through the middle of your (plural) village': *umùu-* 'your (plural)'; *kiihu* 'house, village'; *-sona-* 'center'; *-q,* diffusive suffix.

umùupahoveni 'your (plural) marked prayer feathers, prayer feathers with ritual markings': *umùu-* 'your (plural)', *paaho* 'prayer feather(s)' (*paho-*), *peeni* 'drawing, design, mark' (*-veni*).

umùutuwapongyava 'along your land': *umùu-* 'your (plural)'; *tuuwapongya* 'earth, the land part of the earth' (*-tuwapongya*); *-va*, diffusive suffix: 'along, in an area'. See *tuuwapongya*.

umùutuwaqatsi 'your (plural) land, world'; see *tuuwaqatsi*.

unangwvàasi 'heartfelt wish, hope, prayer': *unangwa* 'heart' (*unangw-*), *-vàasi* 'wish, desire'.

uuyimamant 'plant maidens', a reference to corn plants: *uuyi* 'planted plant(s)', *mamant* 'maidens'.

uymukti 'become thriving in full growth, become plenty of plants in full growth': *uuyi* 'planted plant(s)' (*uy-*), *-mukti* 'become in full growth'.

wakaskatsìntawi 'Cow katsina song': *waakasi* 'cow' (*wakas-*), *katsina* (*katsìn-*), *taawi* 'song' (*-tawi*). *Waakasi* is from Spanish *vaca* 'cow', possibly via a Keresan language, cf. Santa Ana *wá·gaši* (Davis 1964: 182).

wukokuri'am 'their big buttocks': *wuukoq* 'big' (object form of *wuuyoq*) (*wuko-*), *kuri* 'behind, buttocks', *-'am* 'their'.

wukotupqa 'big canyon': *wuukoq* 'big' (object form of *wuuyoq*) (*wuko-*), *tupqa* 'canyon'.

wukwlavayi 'words of wisdom': *wuukw,* object form of *wuy* 'old' (*wukw-*), *lavayi* 'speech'.

wukwnavoti 'oral tradition': *wuukw,* object form of *wuy* 'old' (*wukw-*), *navoti* 'teachings, traditions'.

wukwtuvoyla 'mark of old age', a reference either to commemorative observations of ritual practices of old or to the crook placed atop a kiva at the Winter Solstice ceremony (*Soyalangw*) for people to touch by grasping in prayer for long life and freedom from suffering: *wuukw* 'old' (object form of *wuy*) (*wukw-*), *tuvoyla* 'marker'.

wùutaqharurutiwa 'for men to be getting older and older toward ripe old age': *wùutaqa* 'old man' (*wùutaq-*), *harurutiwa* 'be getting bent over'.

wùutaqkatsìntawi 'Old Man katsina song': *wùutaqa* 'old man' (*wùutaq-*), *katsina* (*katsìn-*), *taawi* 'song' (*-tawi*).

wùutiharurutiwa 'for women to be getting older and older toward ripe old age': *wùuti* 'woman', *harurutiwa* 'be getting bent over'.

wuyolvayi 'recollections, remembrances': *wuy* 'old' (*wuyo-*), *lavayi* 'speech, words' (*-lvayi*).

yongyaywùuti 'adulteress': *yongyaya* 'unvirtuous, adulterous person' (*yongyay-*), *wùuti* 'woman'. (*Yongyaya* also means 'chipmunk', or, more precisely, 'whitetail antelope squirrel, *Ammospermophilus leucurus*'.)

yoniwsonaq 'in the midst of obligations': *yoniwta* 'be indebted to, owe a favor' (*yoniw-*), *àasonaq* 'in the midst of it'.

yoy'öki 'arrive as rain': *yooyangw* 'rain' (*yooya-*), *öki* 'arrive, come, get there, reach a destination (plural)' (*-'öki*). (The plural verb *öki* corresponds to the singular *pitu*; rain, being a liquid, collocates with the plural verb.) *Yooyoktivakyangw ökye' yoy'ökingwu.*

yoy'ökiwa 'have arrived as rain': *yooyangw* 'rain' (*yoy-*), *öki* 'arrive, come, get there, reach a destination (plural)' (*-'ök-*), *-iwa* 'stative'.

yoy'ùmtima 'go along thundering (slowly)': *yooyangw* 'rain' (*yoy-*), *ùmtima* 'go along making booming sounds in slow succession'. *Haqaqw yooyangw ùmtimakyangw hoyoyote' yoy'ùmtimangwu.*

yoy'umuki 'thunder': *yooyangw* 'rain' (*yoy-*), *úmuki* 'booming sound as from an explosion' (*-'umuki*).

yoy'umumuta 'be thundering': *yooyangw* 'rain' (*yoy-*), *umumuta* 'be making booming sounds in rapid succession' (*-'umumuta*).

yoy'umumutima 'go along thundering (rapidly)': *yooyangw* 'rain' (*yoy-*), *umumuta* 'be making booming sounds in rapid succession' (*-'umumut-*), *-ima* 'go along'.

yoy'umumutoyna 'make it be thundering': *yooyangw* 'rain' (*yoy-*), *umumuta* 'be making booming sounds in rapid succession' (*-'umumuto-*); *-ina*, causative (*-yna*).

yoyhahawiwma 'go along descending as rain': *yooyangw* 'rain' (*yoy-*), *haahawi* 'be descending' (*-hahaw-*), *-iwa* 'stative' (*-iw-*), *-ima* 'go along' (*-ma*).

yoyhahawtima 'go along descending as rain': *yooyangw* 'rain' (*yoy-*); *haahawi* 'be descending' (*-hahaw-*); *-ta,* repetitive (*-t-*); *-ima* 'go along'.

yoyhani 'descend as rain': *yooyangw* 'rain' (*yoy-*), *haani* 'descend (plural)' (*-hani*).

yoyhaniwa 'be a descent of rain': *yooyangw* 'rain' (*yoy-*); *haaniwa* 'for there to be a descent' (*-haniwa*), impersonal form of *haani* 'descend (plural)'.

yoyhohonginma 'go along repeatedly making (them) stand in the rain': *yooyangw* 'rain' (*yoy-*), *hoohongna* 'keep erecting, making stand (plural object)' (*-hohongin-*), *-ima* 'go along' (*-ma*). Cf. *hongna* 'erect (plural object), place (them) in an upright position'.

yoyhoyoyotima 'be moving along as rain': *yooyangw* 'rain' (*yoy-*), *hoyoyotima* 'be moving along'.

yoyleki 'rain lines, rain descending in lines as seen from a distance': *yooyangw* 'rain' (*yoy-*), *-leki.* The element *-leki* is unique to this compound and is of unknown origin. *Hak yaavoq yooyangwuy aqw taytaqw oo'omawtuy amutpip angqw atkyamiq susmataq himu siwukiwtaqat an sóniwngwu; pam hapi yoyleki. Pu' oomaw piw peeniwte' angqw atpik atkyamiq tutuwuwvut akw peeniwtaqw, pam piw yoyleki'atningwu.*

yoynanatuwniwa 'be practicing the skill of rain': *yooyangw* (*yoy-*), *nánatuwna* 'be practicing, learning by doing' (*-nanatuwn-*), *-iwa* 'stative'.

yoynànkwusa 'start on a journey as rain': *yooyangw* 'rain' (*yoy-*), *nànkwusa,* the plural of *nakwsu* 'start on a journey'. The verb *nànkwusa* is in the plural form because in Hopi liquids collocate with plural verbs and *yoy-* 'rain' here is an incorporated subject of the verb.

yoynawakna 'pray for rain': *yooyangw* 'rain' (*yoy-*), *naawakna* 'pray, want' (*-nawakna*).

yoyngyàlpuva 'in the postlude of the rain, during the time after it has stopped raining': *yooyangw* 'rain' (*yoy-*); *yaala* 'abate' (*-ngyàl-*), *-pu* 'resultative'; *-va,* diffusive suffix. *Yooyangw ang yàlqw pàasat pu' pan yàlpuva himu hintsakye' yoyngyàlpuva hintsakngwu.*

yòyqóqöngö 'rain racing stones': *yooyangw* 'rain' (*yoy-*), *qööqöngö* 'racing stones' (*-qöqöngö*), the plural of *qööngö.*

yoysingöla 'rain flower-hoop', a ritual object symbolic of rain: *yooyangw* 'rain' (*yoy-*), *sihu* 'flower' (*si-*), *ngöla* 'hoop'.

yòytalwipi 'lightning in the rain': *yooyangw* 'rain' (*yòy-*), *talwìipiki* 'lightning' (*-talwipi*).

yòytalwiptima 'go along flashing as lightning in the rain': *yooyangw* 'rain' (*yòy-*), *talwipta* 'be flashing as lightning' (*talwipt-*), *-ima* 'go along'.

yòytalwiptoyna 'make lightning in the rain': *yooyangw* 'rain' (*yòy-*), *talwiptoyna* 'make lightning'.

yòytatawi 'rain songs': *yooyangw* 'rain' (*yòy-*), *taatawi* 'songs' (*-tatawi*). This is the plural of *yòytawi* (see below).

yòytatawlawu 'keep singing songs for rain': *yooyangw* 'rain' (*yòy-*), *taatawlawu* 'keep singing songs' (*-tatalawu*). Cf. *tawlawu* 'be singing'.

yòytawi 'rain song': *yooyangw* 'rain' (*yòy-*). *taawi* 'song' (*-tawi*). *Yokvaniqat oovi tawlàwqat pàngqawe' yòytawi, kítangwu.*

yòytitiwunuto 'go to stand dancing as rain': *yooyangw* 'rain' (*yòy-*); *tii-*, reduplication (*-ti-*); *tiihu* 'dance' (*-ti-*); *wunu* 'stand'; *-to* 'go to'. *Katsinam pi oo'omawtnìiqe yooyangwuy na'mangwu'ykyàakyangw angqw tiivawise' yòytitiwunutongwu. Hihin yaavo pàngqawe' yòytiitiwunuto, kítangwu.*

yòytokila 'the date set for rain': *yooyangw* 'rain' (*yòy-*), *tokila* 'appointed date, set date'.

yòytötöki'am 'their rain sounds': *yooyangw* 'rain' (*yòy-*), *töötöki'am* 'their characteristic calls' (*-tötöki'am*).

yòytu'awma 'deliver a rain message': *yooyangw* 'rain' (*yòy-*), *tuu'awma* 'go to announce, take a message' (*-tu'awma*). *Hakim tapkiqw tiitso'qw katsinmuy pahomqayaqw pu' puma put akw yòytu'awwisngwu; it taawit ep lavayte' yòytu'awma, kítangwu.*

yòytutuveni 'rain marks': *yooyangw* 'rain' (*yòy-*), *tutuveni* 'visual or written representation'.

yòytuveqöqöngtsongo, a kind of pipe used in ritual smoking as part of praying for rain: *yooyangw* 'rain' (*yòy-*), *tuve-* 'vari-colored, fancy', *qööqöngö* 'racing stones' (*-qöqöng-*), *tsoongo* 'smoking pipe' (*-tsongo*). These pipes are made of the same clays as the racing stones that are moved along by teams of runners in order to metaphorically hurry the coming of rain.

yoyvivìikwam, plural of *yoyvìikwa* 'common nighthawk, *Chordeiles minor*': *yooyangw* 'rain' (*yoy-*), *pìikwa* 'lesser nighthawk, *Ch. acutipennis*' (*-vìikwa*). The plural of *pìikwa* is *piivìikwa* (*-vivìikwa*).

yoywangwaytiwa 'have been earnestly requesting (them) to come as rain': *yooyangw* 'rain' (*yoy-*); *wángwayi* 'summon, call'; *-ta*, repetitive (*-t-*); *-iwa*, stative.

yoywunuto 'go stand as rain': *yooyangw* 'rain' (*yoy-*), *wunu* 'stand', *-to* 'go to'. There is no independent verb *wunuto*; it has been suggested that *-wunuto* here may derive from *wunimato* 'go to dance'.

yöngöson'angaktsìntawi 'Tortoise Long-Hair katsina song': *yöngösona* 'tortoise' (*yöngöson-*), *Angaktsina* 'Long-Hair katsina' (*angaktsìn-*), *taawi* 'song' (*-tawi*).

Yöngösòntotim, the "Turtle Boys," a reference to certain Long-Hair katsinas: *yöngösona* 'tortoise' (*yöngösòn-*), *tootim* 'boys' (*-totim*). For some reason it has become conventional to refer to these song characters in English as "Turtle Boys" rather than "Tortoise Boys." The Hopi language does not distinguish between land-dwelling "tortoises" and water-dwelling "turtles," which are unknown in the Hopi region, and would use *yöngösona* for either; but the word *yöngösona* is from *yöngö* 'prickly pear cactus' plus *-sona* 'craver' and is descriptive specifically of the land-dwelling desert tortoise. *Yöngösòntotim pay katsinam, Pala-sowitsmi'angaktsinmuy amunhaqam titwi'ykyàakyangw taywave alöngöt akw pe'yyungwa.*

yumaki'yta 'have as a ceremonial mother': *yu'at* 'his/her mother' (*yu-*); *maqa* 'give' (*-mak-*); *-i,* noun-forming suffix; *-'y-,* possessive; *-ta,* durative.

yungtawi 'entering song', a song sung as katsinas enter a kiva: *yungta* 'be entering (plural)' (*yung-*), *taawi* 'song' (*-tawi*).

Appendix 3: Glossary of Hopi Words

This glossary lists words found in the songs and in the discussions according to Third Mesa (3M) pronunciation. Where there are pronunciation differences in Musangnuvi (2MM) or Songòopavi (2MS) dialects, they are indicated. "2M" is used when the 2MM and 2MS pronunciations differ from 3M in the same way. 2MS is not indicated when the only difference between it and 3M is the absence of the feature indicated by the grave accent mark. Note that these markings are only to indicate the Second Mesa spellings that correspond to the given Third Mesa forms; with rare exception they offer no information on actual Second Mesa usage.

a'ni 'very (male speaker)'
aa'awna 'inform'
àapiy 'away from it' (2MM *ahpiy*, 2MS *aapiy*)
àasa' 'as much, many as, enough, as often as, the right number of times' (2MM *asa'*, 2MS *aasa'*)
àasatti 'become the appointed time for it' (2MM *ásatti*, 2MS *aasatti*)
ahaw 'isn't it so?'
ahoy 'back to' (2MS *ahwiy*)
ahoy kuk.wuwaya 'reflect or think back on the past (plural)' (2MS *ahwiy kuk.wuwaya*)
akw 'using it, by means of it, with it' (2M *ak*)
alí, exclamation of pleasure
alòngkimi 'to a house belonging to someone who is not a relative' (2MM *alöhngkimi*)
alòngkingaqw 'from or inside a house belonging to someone who is not a relative' (2MM *alöhngkingaq*, 2MS *alöngkingaq*)
alòngkiva 'in/at houses belonging to someone who is not a relative' (2MM *alöhngkiva*)
amum 'with him/her, accompanying, together with'
amumiq 'at them'

amumumyakyangw 'while with them (plural)' (2M *amumumyakyang*)
amunawit 'along them, along their course'
ánan'ivo 'to each side of it'
ánawit 'along its course'
ang 'along it, along there, in that area, in several places'
angqw 'from it, from there' (2M *angq*)
angwu 'in anticipation of, beforehand, ahead of time'
Angwusnasomtaqa 'Crow Mother katsina'
anìwtini 'will develop, grow' (2MM *anihwtini*)
anìwtotani 'will make crop or plant grow (plural)' (2MM *anihwtotani*)
ansa 'constant'
antani 'will be like that, be right'
antaniqa 'that which will be right'
antsa 'truly, really, indeed'
ápi'ewayniikyangw 'while seemingly useful' (2M *ápi'ewayniikyang*)
aqwhaqami 'throughout' (2M *aqhaqami*)
as 'presumably'
askwallawni 'will be thanking' (female speaker)
atkya 'down, down there, down below'
atkyami 'downwards'

atkyaqw 'from below, from down there' (2M *atkyaq*)

atpip 'beneath' (2M *atpiv*)

aw 'to him/her/it, to there'

awya 'go there (plural)'

ayalawu 'be asking someone to do something'

ayám 'over there'

ayángqw 'from over there' (2M *ayángq*)

ayawa 'purpose, reason for being'

ayé' 'along over there'

ayó' 'to, toward over there'

ep 'there, at it' (2M *ev*)

ephaqam 'there, at an unspecified place' (2M *evhaqam*)

ha'o, vocative particle

ha'óo, vocative particle

haa'o, vocative particle

haa'oo, vocative particle

haahannaya 'be moving things down (plural)'

haahawiwmani 'will come/go along descending, will be coming down'

haahawtimani 'will come/go along descending at intervals'

hàalay'unangway 'with happy heart(s), with beneficent intentions' (2MM *hahlay'unangway*)

hàalayi 'be happy' (2MM *hahlayi*)

hàalaykyangw 'while being happy, happily' (2MM *hahlaykyang,* 2MS *haalaykyang*)

hàalàyti 'become happy' (2MM *hahlahyti*)

hàalàytimani 'will go along expressing gladness' (2MM *hahlahytimani*)

hàalaytsotsong.yat 'after smoking the pipe with untroubled minds' (2MM *hahlaytsotsong.yat*)

hàalayya 'be happy (plural)' (2MM *hahlayya*)

hàalayyani 'will be happy (plural)' (2MM *hahlayyani*)

hàalayyaniqat 'that should be happy' (2MM *hahlayyaniqat*)

haani 'descend (plural)'

haaniwa 'for there to be a descent'

haaw, vocative particle

haaya, vocative particle

Hahay'imanat '(two) Hahay'i maidens'

hak 'who'

hakim 'some people, who (plural)'

hakiy viy 'I wonder who'

hakwurkwi 'cornmeal'

hal 'but then, well' (particle of concession)

hantani 'will be descending (plural)'

hapi 'truly, surely, certainly'

hapi me, formulaic expression introducing the song's second part, *oomi* 'upward'

haqaqw 'from/inside somewhere' (2M *haqaq*)

havivokyalyat 'after (you) become wide awake (plural)'

haw, vocative particle

haw'o, vocative particle

heesi 'mariposa lily/lilies'

hekwpa 'white fir' (2M *hekpa*)

hiihimu 'some things, many different things'

hiihin 'in various ways, in all kinds of ways'

hiikyangwintani 'will be vitalizing'

himu, indefinite pronoun: 'something, what, one, you'

himu'yta 'have something, have things' (2MS *himu'ta*)

himùwya'iwnuma 'go around feeling proud' (2MM *himuhwya'iwnuma*)

hin 'in some way, somehow, how'

hin pa 'I wonder how'

hin'eway 'unattractive, plain-looking'

hìngqaqwa 'say something (plural)'

(2MM *hihngqaqwa*)
hìngqawni 'will say something, say what' (2MM *hihngqawni*)
hìngqawkyangw 'while saying' (2MM *hihngqawkyang,* 2MS *hingqawkyang*)
hintani 'will be some way, how will (it) be'
hintiqey 'to happen, occur'
hintiqw 'why, what for, for what purpose' (2M *hintiq*)
hisat 'sometime, when, long ago'
hísathaqam 'sometime long ago'
hísatngaqw 'since an earlier time' (2M *hísatngaq*)
hisnentiqw 'hopefully' (2M *hisnentiq*)
hom'oya 'hand out consecrated cornmeal'
Honanngyam 'Badger clan'
Honànpave 'at Badger Spring' (2MM *Honahnpave*)
Honanwùutaqa 'Old Man Badger' (2MM *Honanwuhtaqa*)
hoohongnani 'will make (them) stand (intermittently)'
hoohongnaya 'keep making (them) stand (plural)'
hoohonginmani 'will go along making stand'
hoohongvani 'will stand up (in several places)'
hoohopaqw 'from places in the northeast'
hooma 'consecrated cornmeal'
hoonat 'after sending away'
hoopaq 'in the northeast'
hoopaqw 'from the northeast' (2M *hoopaq*)
hoopo 'to the northeast'
hopìit 'Hopis' (2MM *hopiht*) (plural of *hopi*)
hopimatsiwta 'have a Hopi identity'
hopiyungta 'be initiated as Hopis'
hotam'iwta 'be spread out, as of run-

ners or vines'
hovalanta 'be disheartening'
hoyoyota 'be moving'
hoyoyotani 'will be moving'
hoyoyotima 'be moving along'
hoyoyotimani 'will be moving along'
hölömnata 'uncover one at a time'
hömsomi 'hairknot'
humi'uyi 'corn plant(s)'
humi'uyimamant 'corn plant maidens' (2MM *humi'uyimamahnt*)
humi'uyisìiqölnawit 'along the flowery expanse(s) of corn plants' (2MM *humi'uyisihqölnawit*)
humi'uysonaq 'throughout the midst the area(s) planted with corn'
humisi'uyi 'blossoming corn plants'
humisimamant 'corn blossom maidens' (2MM *humisimamant*)
humivota 'coiled plaque for shelled corn'
hurusuki, a thick blue cornmeal pudding
huvam, hortative particle

i' 'this'
i'omaw'inakwa 'the down feathers worn on my head'
i'unangwa 'my heart'
i'uyi 'my planted plant(s), planted field'
Ihiwkatsina 'Plain Hehey'a katsina'
ii'its 'promptly, soon, early'
ii'itsyani 'should be prompt (plural)'
iikwilni'at 'his load on the back'
iikwìltota 'put on the back to carry (plural)' (2MM *iikwihltota*)
iingyàlti 'tire of, not want around' (2MM *iingyahlti*)
iits 'soon, early'
iitsyani 'will/should be soon, early (plural)'
ikituwungwnimi 'to my spiritual homeland' (2M *ikituwungnimi*)

ikukunawit 'along my footprints, along my tracks'

ikwatshòoyam 'my little friends' (2MM *ikwatshohyam*)

ikwatsi 'my friend'

ikwatsim 'my friends'

ikwil'a'yat 'hired carriers'

ima 'these'

imànkwatsi 'my girl friend' (2MM *imahnkwatsi*)

imöm 'my grandchildren'

ina 'my father'

ina'mangwu 'my katsina-brought gift(s)'

inam 'my fathers'

ingu 'my mother'

ingum 'my mothers'

inu'ove 'above me'

inumi 'to me'

is, intensifying particle

is haw, an expression indicating admiration or that one is impressed

is uní 'how nice, how delightful'

isiwamniikyangw 'even though they are my younger sisters' (2M *isiwamniikyang*)

isòöqölö 'patch of mustard plants' (2MM *isöhqölö*)

itàakwa 'our grandfather' (2MM *itahkwa*)

itàamö'wim 'our in-married women' (2MM *itamö'wim*)

itàana'mangwu 'our gifts brought by the katsinas' (2MM *itana'mangwu*)

itàapatuwvota 'our water shields, rings of ripples in water' (*itahpatuwvota*)

itàaso 'our grandmother' (2MM *itaso*)

itàatalwiptutuveni 'our depictions of lightning' (2MM *itahtalwiptutuveni*)

itàatawi 'our song' (2MM *itahtawi*)

itàatim 'our children' (2MM *itahtim*)

itàatitwi 'our customary way of dancing' (2MM *itahtitwi*)

itam 'we'

itamu'ova 'along above us'

itamumi 'to us'

itamungem 'for us, for our benefit'

itanam 'our fathers'

itangum 'our mothers'

itim 'my children'

itupko 'my younger brother' (2M *ituvko*)

ivòokom 'my creatures' (2MM *ivohkom*)

ivosmiq 'into my eye'

iwùuti 'my woman, my wife' (2MM *iwuhti*)

iy, an exclamatory element

katsinam 'katsinas'

kawaayo 'watermelon(s)'

kawayo 'watermelon(s)'

kaway'u'uyi 'multiple watermelon plants'

kaway'uyi 'watermelon plant(s)'

kaway'uyi'at 'his watermelon plant(s)'

kaway'uynawit 'along the watermelon plantings'

kaway'uysonaq 'throughout the midst of the area(s) planted with watermelons'

kawayho'i 'load of watermelons'

kawàytanga'yyungwa 'have stored watermelons (plural)' (2MM *kawahytanga'yyungwa*, 2MS *kawaytanga'yungwa*)

kawayvatnga 'watermelon(s)'

kii'am 'their houses'

kii'at 'his/her/its house'

kiinasami 'to the middle of where people live'

kiinasave 'in the middle of where people live'

kìisa 'chicken hawk' (2MM *kisa*)

Kiqötsmovi (Kykotsmovi), a Third Mesa village

Kisiw'omàwkive 'at the Shadow Springs dwelling place of the clouds'

(2MM *Kisiw'omahwkive*)
Kisiwvami 'to Shadow Spring'
Kisiwvangaqw 'from Shadow Spring'
(2M *Kisiwvangaq*)
Kisiwvave 'at Shadow Spring'
kiskya 'passageway'
kiskyava 'along the passageway(s), in the passageways'
kítikyangw 'while saying' (2M *kítikyang*)
kitota 'say (plural)'
kitotani 'will say (plural)'
kitotat 'after saying (plural)'
kitsokikinawit 'throughout the villages'
kitsokiva 'in the villages'
kivanasave 'in the middle of the kiva'
kivaya 'bring many things (plural)'
Kivokvami 'to Kivokva' (Kivokva is an unidentified spring.)
kivung.wùuti 'woman who habitually visits around' (2MM *kivung.wuhti*)
komoma 'dark red corn'
kokom'uyi'at 'his dark red corn plants'
koliyaw 'gossip'
koliyawsi'uyi 'pretentious, flashy talk'
kongtotaniqey 'for them to take husbands'
Kookoyemsim 'Mudhead katsinas'
Kòokyàngwtiyoniikyangw 'while being a Spider Boy' (2MM *Kohkyahngtiyoniikyang*, 2MS *Kookyangtiyoniikyang*)
koona 'tree squirrel'
koongya'at 'her husband'
Kooyemsi 'Mudhead katsina'
Kowawayvami 'to Kowawayva' (a spring)
Kowawayvave 'at Kowawayva' (a spring)
koyaanisqatsi 'life of moral corruption'
Koyemosmongwit or *Koyemsimongwit* '(pair of) Mudhead katsina leaders'
kuk.wuwaya 'retrace steps'
kur, modal of inference

kur hapi 'it turns out that'
kuukuyvakyangw 'while making their appearance' (2M *kuukuyvakyang*)
kuukuyvani 'will appear, come into sight (plural)'
kuukuyvat 'after coming into sight (plural)'
kuwan'ew'unangway 'with beautiful hearts, with beneficent intentions'
kuwan'ewsoniwa 'look invigorated'
kuwantalawvangaqw 'from the colorful beginning of the day (dawn)' (2M *kuwantalawvangaq*)
kuwantimakyangw 'while going along putting color on' (2M *kuwantimakyang*)
kuwanvuyayatani 'will be flapping, fluttering colorfully'
kuyapkuyi'am 'their dippers of water' (2M *kuyavkuyi'am*)
kuysiptoynani 'will provide with water storage vessels' (2M *kuysivtoynani*)
kuyva 'appear, come into sight'
kuyvato 'go check on, get up early to go run and pray'
kuywiki'am 'their container(s) of water carried by a string or bail'
kwaakwap'iwmakyangw 'as (they) go along stacked up in several stacks' (2M *kwaakwav'iwmakyang*)
kwakwhá 'thank you (masculine-speaker form), it's a good thing' (2M *kwakhá*)
kwakwha'unangway 'with tranquil hearts, with beneficent intentions' (2M *kwakha'unangway*)
kwakwháta 'express thanks' (2M *kwakháta*)
kwangwa'iwta 'remain with something that is attractive or irresistible'
kwangwa'iwyungwa 'remain with something that is attractive (plural)'
kwangwahimu'yta 'have something pleasing, useful, convenient, readily accessible' (2MS *kwangwahimu'ta*)

kwangwakwas'ikongya 'my husband with the pleasant penis'

kwangwalöw'inöma 'my wife with the pleasant vulva'

kwangwamö'wi'yyungwa 'have a (as) pleasant in-married woman (plural)' (2MS *kwangwamö'wi'yungwa*)

kwangwamö'wi'yyungwni 'will have (as) a pleasant in-married woman (plural)' (2MM *kwangwamö'wi'yyungni*, 2MS *kwangwamö'wi'yungni*)

kwangwatu'awva 'come with a pleasant message, pleasant news'

kwasi 'penis(es)'

kwèetsikma 'scurry off in all directions' (2MM *kwehtsikma*)

Kwikwilyaqaniikyangw 'while being Stripe Nose'

kwiningya 'in the northwest'

kwiningyaqw 'from the northwest' (2M *kwiningyaq*)

kwiniwi 'toward the northwest'

kwiyavasnawit 'along fields with windbreaks constructed on them'

kyaahisathaqam 'sometime very long ago'

kyapi 'I guess'

kyevelvikyungwa 'be stacked right up to the ceiling (plural)'

lavay'ayamat 'their spokespeople'

lavay'aysakwi 'gossip, one who gossips'

lavayhurusuki 'speech *hurusuki*'

lavayi 'speech, words'

lavaymuyiwa 'be talked about, be talking about, there is talk'

lavaysakwiqatsilvayi'at 'the worn-out words of the language of her way of life'

lavayta 'be talking about, telling about'

lavàyti 'speak' (2MM *lavahyti*)

lavàytit 'after speaking' (2MM *lavahytit*)

lalvaytinuma 'go around talking about'

leekya'yta, an unknown word; it seems to mean 'be respected in what one says'

lolma 'beautiful, good, proper'

lolmani 'will be beautiful, good, proper'

lolmat 'beautifully, well, properly'; *lolmat yeese*, 'live in accord with Hopi teachings (plural)'

lolmata 'beautify, restore beauty, improve the looks'

löhavu 'testicle(s), scrotum(s)'

lööqökni 'will go to the groom's mother's house to begin the wedding ceremony' (2MM *löhqökni*)

löqòmti 'go to begin the weddings' (2MM *löqöhmti*)

löwawaqaqa 'squishy sounds of sexual activity'

maakiw 'the hunt, hunting'

maana 'girl, young unmarried woman, maiden'

màasawtiniqey 'to become a death spirit' (2MM *másawtiniqey*)

mamanhòoyam 'little girls' (2MM *mamanhohyam*)

mamkiwa'am 'their things received, allotments, birthrights, duties'

mansonve 'in the midst of girls, at the center of attention of girls, women'

maphenlawni 'will be doing domestic chores' (2M *mavhenlawni*)

maqasti 'become afraid'

maqsoni 'burdensome task, drudgery'

mataqlöva 'in grinding bins'

me 'listen', a particle to direct the attention

melon'uysonaq 'throughout the midst of the area(s) planted with muskmelons'

melon'uyi 'muskmelon plant(s)'

melonho'i 'load of muskmelons'

melooni 'muskmelon'

momitaviya 'prefer, give preference to, favor (plural)'

momngwit 'leaders'

momortoni 'will/should go swimming'

momoyam 'women'

mongkimi 'to the leadership place'

mongmatsiwtaqam 'those who are known as leaders'

mongsonmiq 'into leadership positions'

mongsungwamat 'their fellow leaders'

Mongvami 'to Leadership Spring'

mongvasya 'be benefiting from (plural)'

mongwi'am 'their leader, leadership'

mongwinahuyvaniwa 'be choices made in ways of leadership'

mong.yesvat 'after (they) sit as leaders'

mookwa 'double-headed ear of corn'

mòotiwa 'previous, last, from the time before' (2MM *mohtiwa*)

mori'uysonaq 'throughout the midst of the area(s) planted with beans'

morisi'uyi 'blossoming bean plants'

morisimamant 'bean blossom maidens' (2MM *morisimamahnt*)

Mowàapi 'Mount Beautiful'

Mowàape 'at Mount Beautiful' (2MM *Mowahpe*)

mö'wi 'in-married woman'

möm 'grandchildren'

mösivakwam 'food-packet toads'

mötsikvu 'trash, garbage, refuse'

möyhoyat 'two little grandchildren'

mumuyi'yyungwa 'have as a front tier of stacked ears of corn (plural)' (2MS *mumuyi'yungwa*)

munlalaytoni 'will/should go to channel runoff water'

Mùnqape 'at Mùnqapi (Moencopi)' (2MM *Muhnqape*)

Musangnuve 'at Musangnuvi (Mishongnovi)'

muumunangwsonaq 'in the midst of streams of runoff water' (2M *muumunangsonaq*)

muumunangwtoti 'become runoff water in several places' (2M *muumunangtoti*)

muunangw 'flowing water, runoff water' (2M *muunang*)

na'mangwu'at 'his gifts (re katsina)'

na'qala 'encourage, hearten each other'

na'qalànpi 'mutual encouragement' (2MM *na'qalahnpi*)

na'qalaya 'encourage selves (plural)'

na'sasa'yyungwa 'be prepared, have things ready (plural)' (2MS *na'sasa'yungwa*)

naa'awintiwa 'be known community-wide'

naa'itnakyàakyangw 'while passing around among selves' (2MM *naa'itnakyahkyang,* 2MS *naa'itnakyaakyang*)

naa'itnalalwa 'keep on passing (a pipe) along from one to another (plural)'

naakopantiwa 'have been leaving to go away voluntarily'

nàakwustani 'will be setting out on a journey (as one group after another)' (2MM *nahkwustani*)

naakyasoniwa 'look reticent, reserved'

naala 'alone'

naamongsungwam 'fellow leaders'

naanami 'to one another'

naanamiq 'behind each other's backs'

naanan'ivaqw 'from the different directions around' (2M *naanan'ivaq*)

naanaqavo 'day after day, every day'

naanatwani 'different sorts of life-promoting practices, practices for the renewal of life'

naanawakna 'pray, want (plural)'

naangemintani 'will be inviting each other'

naangöyma 'go along chasing one another'

naangöymani 'will go along chasing one other'

naangöytiwwisni 'will be going along chasing one other (plural)'

naap 'by oneself' (2M *naav*)

naasami 'to the middle, halfway'

nàasaptimakyangw 'while going along making (it) the same length, height' (2MM *násavtimakyang*, 2MS *naasavtimakyang*)

naasave 'in the middle'

nàasawvantimakyangw 'while going along meeting one another coming and going' (2MM *násawvantimakyang*, 2MS *naasawvantimakyang*)

naasomi 'hairdo with hairbuns on the side'

naasomta 'wear tied on the side of the head'

naatayawnawisa 'go to make selves feel glad'

naatayawnaya 'make feel good about each other (plural)'

naatsopta 'be having sex with each other' (2M *naatsovta*)

naatukwsina 'make self mature' (2M *naatuksina*)

naatukwsintani 'will be making selves mature' (2M *naatuksintani*)

naava'angwa 'assist, help one another'

naavaasi 'caring for one another'

naavaastoti 'become caring of one another (plural)'

naavokyawintani 'there will be enjoyment to the fullest'

naavokyawintiwa 'for fulfillment to be being enjoyed by all'

naavokyawintiwni 'fulfillment will/ should be enjoyed by all'

naavokyawnani 'will experience to the fullest'

naawakna 'pray, want'

naawiki'yma 'go along escorting one another' (2MS *naawiki'ma*)

naawungwna 'make self grow' (2M *naáwungna*)

naawungwnaya 'make selves grow' (2M *naawungnaya*)

naawungwnayani 'will make selves grow' (2M *naawungnayani*)

naawuwayani 'should reflect, think back'

nàayongwani 'will delight in' (2MM *nahyongwani*)

naayuwsina 'clothe oneself, get dressed'

naayuwsinat 'after clothing, adorning selves'

naayuwsinayat 'after clothing, adorning selves'

nakwsu 'start on a journey' (2M *naksu*)

nalönanan'ivaqw 'from the four directions' (2M *nalönanan'ivaq*)

nalönanan'ivo 'to the four directions'

Nalönangwmomngwit 'Four-Directional Cloud Chiefs' (2M *Nalönangmomngwit*)

nalönatsva 'in four places one above the other'

nalqatmomoyam 'single women, women who now live alone'

nalqatsi 'life alone, without a partner'

nam 'may it, let it be so'

nami'nangwa 'mutual concern for one another's welfare'

namikwap'iwta 'be put together'

namitngàlti 'get mixed, mix together' (2MM *namitngahlti*)

namunwanvö 'path for the running of the stone race'

námura 'let it be so'

námusa 'let it be so'

nana'löngö 'different kinds of, of different kinds'

nánàatsovi 'be reluctant because of a feeling of inadequacy for the task, lack self-assurance to act' (2MM *nánahtsovi*)

nanamunwa 'be hurrying as though

racing (plural)'

nanaptiwa 'for some fact(s) to become known' (2M *nanavtiwa*)

nanava'ngwa 'be helping each other'

nanawiniwa 'it is being planned'

nanawinya 'be making plans, plotting (plural)'

nànkwusa 'start on a journey (plural)' (2MM *nahnkwusa*)

nànkwusani 'will start on a journey (plural)' (2MM *nahnkwusani*)

nànkwusiwa 'for a journey by several to have begun' (2MM *nahnkwusiwa*)

nasi'am 'their adornment'

natwani 'life-promoting practices'

natwaniwa 'be undertaken as life-promoting practices, practices related to the rejuvenation of life'

natwanlawu 'keep pursuing life-promoting practices, customs related to the rejuvenation of life'

natwanmumuya 'be repeatedly making efforts in support of life-promoting practices'

natwanta 'pursue life-promoting practices, practice customs related to the rejuvenation of life'

natwantimani 'will go along practicing customs related to the rejuvenation of life, life-promoting practices'

navoti'ymani 'will go along knowing' (2MS *navoti'mani*)

navoti'yta 'know' (2MS *navoti'ta*)

navoti'ytani 'will know' (2MS *navoti'-tani*)

Neelaqw 'from Neela' (an unidentified place) (2M *Neelaq*)

ngasta 'lacking'

ngeeminta 'invite to go/come along'

ngölöshoya'am 'their wooden crook, mark of old age'

ngöyta 'be pursuing, following'

ngúmanta 'be grinding cornmeal into flour'

ngúmantakyangw 'while grinding cornmeal into flour' (2M *ngúmanta-kyang*)

ngúmantani 'will be grinding fine, grinding into flour'

ngúmantotakyangw 'while grinding in-to flour (plural)' (2M *ngúmantota-kyang*)

ngumanvòötaviwa 'be laid out as a path of consecrated cornmeal' (2MM *ngumanvöhtaviwa*)

niikyangw 'however, but' (2M *nii-kyang*)

Nimàntikive 'Home dance' (2MM *Ni-mahntikive*)

noonova 'be eating, eat repetitively (plural)'

noonovani 'will be eating (plural)'

noonove' 'if (they) are eating'

noovata 'prepare food'

noqw 'but, whereas, and so' (2M *noq*)

Nòngakiwqa 'the Emergence'

nöönösa 'eat (plural)'

nùutaylawu 'keep awaiting, be waiting and waiting for' (2MM *nuhtaylawu*)

nùutayta 'be awaiting' (2MM *nuhtayta*)

nùutayyungwa 'be awaiting (plural)' (2MM *nuhtayyungwa*)

nùutum 'with others' (2MM *nuhtum*)

nùutumi 'to others' (2MM *nuhtumi*)

Nuvatukya'ove 'at the San Francisco Peaks' (2MS *Nuvatukwi'ove*)

nuvawvaqòlti 'become an area of mature corn' (2MM *nuvawvaqöhlti*)

nu' 'I'

nuwu 'even now'

nuwu pa 'just think, at last'

núwupi 'it's inevitable, unavoidable'

o'yaqw'ö 'when they receive (us)' (2M *o'yaq'ö*)

okiw 'humbly, pitifully'

okiwlawu 'be humbling oneself, as in prayer'

ókiwni 'will be humble, pitiful'

okiwqawlawu 'be humbly pleading'

oo'omawt 'clouds' (2MM *oo'omahwt*)

oo'omàwkimi 'to the dwelling places of the clouds (in different directions)' (2MM *oo'omahwkimi*)

oomaw 'cloud'

oomaw'inakwa 'the down feathers worn on my head'

oomaw'oya 'place as clouds'

oomàwkiikinawit 'along the dwelling places of the clouds' (2MM *oomahwkiikinawit*)

oomàwkimi 'to the dwelling place of the clouds' (2MM *oomahwkimi*)

oomàwkingaqw 'from the dwelling place of the clouds' (2MM *oomahwkingaq*, 2MS *oomawkingaq*)

oomàwkiva 'along the dwelling place of the clouds' (2MM *oomahwkiva*)

oomàwkive 'at the dwelling place of the clouds' (2MM *oomahwkive*)

oomawnanawakna 'pray for clouds (plural)'

oomawvawikyam 'cloud ducks'

Oomawwùutaqa 'Old Man Cloud' (2MM *Oomawwuhtaqa*)

oomi 'upward'

oongaqw 'from above' (2M *oongaq*)

oove 'up above, at a/the place above'

oovi 'that's why'

Orayve 'at Orayvi'

óvekiniw 'social outing for unmarried girls and boys after a summer katsina dance'

owí 'yes'

oya 'hand (to), hand out, deposit, place, put, set (several) in a particular position'

ö'qalyani 'will be persistent, persevere, keep striving (plural)'

öki 'arrive, come, get there, reach a destination (plural)'

ökinayani 'will make several come (plural)'

ökini 'will arrive, come (plural)'

ömàata 'understand, take in, receive' (2MM *ömahta*)

ömàatotat 'after receiving' (2MM *ömahtotat*)

Òngtupqa 'the Grand Canyon' (2MM *Öhngtuvqa*, 2MS *Öngtuvqa*)

Òngtupqangaqw 'from the Grand Canyon' (2MM *Öhngtuvqangaq*, 2MS *Öngtuvqangaq*)

öö'öyani 'will become satiated with food or drink, get full (plural)'

öqalat 'after encouraging'

öqalaya 'encourage (plural)'

pa, particle used to indicate wonder, awe, surprise, doubt

paa'o'oytimani 'will go along placing water'

paaho 'prayer feather(s)'

paakwa 'toad'

paakyele 'killdeer'

Paakyeletotim 'Killdeer Boys'

paamotoro 'water pillars, splashes of raindrops'

Paamuya, the lunar month that roughly corresponds to January

pamuymomngwit 'Paamuya leaders'

Paamuynalönangwmomngwit 'the Four-Directional Cloud Chiefs of the month of Paamuya' (2M *Paamuynalönangmomngwit*)

paapu 'nowadays, anymore, now'

pàapu'uyi'at 'his pod bean plants' (2MM *pahpu'uyi'at*)

paas 'thoroughly, completely, carefully'

paasanawit 'along the fields'

paasatuwani 'the expanse of all the fields'

paasimasa'am 'their moisture-beaded wings'

paatalawintani 'will be making it glisten with water'

paatalawna 'make it glisten with

water'

paatalawnani 'will make it glisten with water'

paatalawnaya 'make it glisten with water (plural)'

paatalawva 'come to glisten with water'

paatalawyungwni 'will glisten with water in several places' (2M *paatalawyungni*)

paatalnawit 'along where it is glistening with water'

paatayayatani 'will be trembling with water'

paatayayatoyna 'be pouring water while shaking things'

paatoti 'for puddles to form, as from the rain'

paatsinawyungwni 'will be sprouting with moisture (plural)' (2M *paatsinawyungni*)

paatu 'waters' (animate plural)

paatuwatapyani 'will lay water on the land (plural)' (2M *paatuwatavyani*)

paatuwatavini 'will lay water on the land'

paavakwt 'toads' (2M *paavakt*)

paavatalawintani 'will be making it glisten with puddles of water'

paavatalawnani 'will make it glisten with puddles of water'

paavatalawyungwni 'will be glistening with puddles of water in several places' (2M *paavatalawyungni*)

paave 'at the spring'

paavopkomat 'water creatures, the creatures of the natural world who are dependent on water for life' (2M *paavovkomat*)

paavönmamant 'young corn plants' (2MM *paavönmamahnt*)

paavönnawit 'along the young corn plants'

paavönyevewmamant 'young corn plant maidens' (2MM *paavönyevew-*

mamahnt)

paavönyevewmomngwit 'young corn plant leaders'

paavönyevewsonaq 'throughout the midst of the young corn plants'

paayoyangw 'rainwater' (2M *paayoyang*)

paayoynguman'ini'am 'their trays of rainwater cornmeal'

paayoysingumannayuwsina 'adorn self with rainwater pollen'

paayoysingumni 'rainwater pollen'

paayoywuta'am 'their poured-out rainwater, the rainwater they pour out'

pahaananiqw 'according to Anglos'

paho'ini'am 'their tray of prayer feathers'

pahomamant 'prayer feather maidens' (2MM *pahomamahnt*)

pahomomngwit 'prayer feather leaders'

pahovena 'mark (as, with) prayer feathers'

pahovenaya 'mark (as, with) prayer feathers (plural)'

pahowuyomomngwit 'elder prayer feather leaders'

pahoyàwtoyna 'place a prayer feather in a katsina performer's hand during a dance to hold' (2MM *pahoyahwtoyna*)

pahoyesiwa 'be sitting and working on prayer feathers (plural)'

pakima 'sink, go down out of sight, set'

pala'omaw 'red cloud'

palalatoyna 'be patting'

palatalwìipiki'am 'their red lightning' (2MM *palatalwihpiki'am*)

Palatkwape 'at Palatkwapi, the Red-Walled City'

palayoyleki'am 'their red rain lines'

pam (acc. *put*) 'that, that one, he, she, it'

pamniikyangw 'while being that in itself' (2M *pamniikyang*)

pamös'o'omawt 'fog clouds' (2MM
   pamös'o'omahwt)
pangso 'to there'
pankyangw 'while being that way'
   (2M *pankyang*)
pantaqa 'one that is like that'
pantaqat 'in that way, in that circumstance'
pantaqw 'if/when it is that way' (2M
   pantaq)
pantsana 'do that to (it)'
pas 'very'
pasiwnayani 'will set out the intent
   (plural)'
pasìwti 'get planned' (2MM *pasihwti*)
paslawkyangw 'while hoeing a field'
   (2M *paslawkyang*)
pasmi 'to the/his field(s)'
pasve 'at/in the/his field'
patangsimamant 'squash blossom
   maidens' (2MM *patangsimamahnt*)
patsqawuwutani 'will be getting
   spattered with muddy water'
pávanti 'get better, improve'
Pavawkyàytiyo 'Swallow Boy' (2MM
   Pavawkyahytiyo)
pay, expressive particle
paypi, particle indicating resignation:
   'let it be, might as well'
paypi núwupi 'of necessity, it can't be
   helped, it's inevitable'
paypu ókiwa 'let it be so'
paysoq 'just, only, simply'
pàytukwimi 'to the triple peaks' (2MM
   pahytukwimi)
peehu 'some things, some of them'
peevewìnti 'become doubtful, come to
   disbelieve, lose faith' (2MM *peeve-
   wihnti*)
peevewna 'doubt, cast doubt on'
pep 'at that place, there' (2M *pev*)
pew 'toward here, coming this way'
pewya 'come here (plural)'
pi 'truly'
pikmoki'at 'her bundle of piki'

pitsangwa 'countenance'
pitsangwa'am 'their countenance'
pitsangwa'at 'his/her/its countenance'
pitsangwa'ykyangw 'while having a
   countenance' (2MM *pitsangwa'y-
   kyang*, 2MS *pitsangwa'kyang*)
pitsàngwtimakyangw 'while going
   along adorning the face with' (2MM
   pitsahngtimakyang, 2MS *pitsangti-
   makyang*)
pitsina 'get someone to come'
pitu 'arrive, come, get there, reach a
   destination'
pítuni 'will arrive, come, get there,
   reach a destination'
piw 'also, too, again'
pó'o'kyangw 'while bending over'
   (2M *pó'o'kyang*)
pó'o'ta 'be bent over, stooped over in
   a C-shape'
pó'o'tota 'be bent over, stooped over
   in a C-shape (plural)'
polayna, a vocable used to save one
   from the consequences of singing or
   saying something that is taboo
polìisi 'evening primrose'
poli'ini 'butterfly whorl hairdo'
polìisimamant 'evening primrose
   maidens' (2MM *polisimamahnt*)
Powamuya 'the month Powamuya';
   'the Bean dance'
powamuymongwi 'head priest of the
   Bean dance society'
powatawi'at 'his curing song'
powatawisa 'go/come to purify (plural)'
pölöneyang 'mixed with or having
   ball-shaped things (like nubbins of
   fruit) all around'
pöötaplawu 'keep laying out a consecrated path' (2MM *pöhtavlawu*, 2MS
   pöötavlawu)
pöötavi 'consecrated path' (2MM *pöhtavi*)
pöötavi'am 'their consecrated path'

(2MM *pöhtavi'am*)
pöötaviwa 'be laid out as a consecrated path' (2MM *pöhtaviwa*)
pöpsöva 'in corners' (2M *pövsöva*)
pu' 'now, then'
puma 'they'
putakw 'with that, by means of that, using that' (2M *putak*)
puuhuta 'renew'
puuhutiwa 'be renewed'
puyayata 'be flapping, fluttering'
puyayatani 'will be flapping, fluttering'
puyayatota 'be flapping, fluttering (plural)'
puyayatimani 'will go along flapping fluttering'
puye'em, adverb meaning approximately 'have a feeling or hunch, suspect'

qa 'not'
qa'ömamant 'corn maidens' (2MM *qa'ömamahnt*)
qa'ömana 'corn maiden'
qa'ömomngwit 'corn leaders'
Qa'ötiyoniikyangw 'while being a Corn Boy' (2M *Qa'ötiyoniikyang*)
qaa'ö 'corn, dry ear(s) of corn'
qaa'ö'am 'their corn, dry ears of corn'
qaaqa'ö 'different kinds of dry ears of corn'
qaatsiptu 'lie down' (2M *qaatsivtu*)
qaavomi 'toward tomorrow, toward the future'
qalalàykina 'begin clanking' (2MM *qalalahykina*)
qatsi 'life'
qatsi'nangwa 'will to live'
qatsinahuyvaniwa 'be choices made in ways of life'
qátsitniqw 'when life will/should be, so that life will be' (2M *qátsitniq*)
qatsituvinglawu 'be petitioning for acceptance to join the life of a village'
qatsivaptsiwta 'have one's turn at life' (2M *qatsivavtsiwta*)
Qatsiyamakiwqa 'the Emergence, that which emerges as life'
qatuptu 'sit down' (*amum qatuptu* 'marry') (2M *qatuvtu*)
qatuptuni 'will sit down, cohabit' (2M *qatuvtuni*)
qöninita 'be whirling, turning around and around in place'
qööqöngö 'racing stone'
qööqòngpi 'things used as though racing stones' (2MM *qööqöhngpi*)
qööyinta 'be toasting cornmeal in a pot prior to grinding it into flour'
qötsaqa'ö 'white corn'
qöya'o'omawt 'white clouds' (2MM *qöya'o'omahwt*)
qöya'omaw 'white cloud'
qöya'omawmamant 'white cloud maidens' (2MM *qöya'omawmamahnt*)
qöya'omawnakwa'am 'their white down feather headdresses'
Qöyahonaw 'White Bear'
qöyangwùntalawkuyva 'for daylight to make its appearance as white dawn' (2MM *qöyangwuhntalawkuyva*)
qöyapaw'omaw 'low-lying white cloud(s)'
qöyapqa'ö 'corn with glossy kernels' (2M *qöyavqa'ö*)
qöyatalwìipiki'am 'their white lightning' (2MM *qöyatalwihpiki'am*)
qöyavolim 'white butterflies'
qöyavolmamant 'white butterfly maidens' (2MM *qöyavolmamahnt*)
qöyawunùuqa 'one that stands as white, white dawn' (2MM *qöyawunuhqa*)
qöyayoyleki'am 'their white rain lines'

sakwa'o'omawt 'blue/green clouds' (2MM *sakwa'o'omahwt*)
sakwa'omaw 'blue/green cloud'

sakwa'omawmamant 'blue/green cloud maidens' (2MM *sakwa'omawmamahnt*)

sakwapu 'blue corn'

sakwatalwìipiki'am 'their blue/green lightning' (2MM *sakwatalwihpiki-'am*)

sakwavaho'am 'their blue/green prayer feathers'

sakwavahomamant 'blue/green prayer feather maidens' (2MM *sakwavahomamahnt*)

sakwavahomomngwit 'blue/green prayer feather leaders'

sakwavahomongwi 'blue/green prayer feather leader'

sakwavolim 'blue/green butterflies'

sakwavolmamant 'blue/green butterfly maidens' (2MM *sakwavolmamahnt*)

sakwayevewmamant 'blue/green young corn plants' (2MM *sakwayevewmamahnt*)

sakwayoyleki 'blue/green rain lines'

sakwayoyleki'am 'their blue/green rain lines'

Salapmamant 'Douglas Fir maidens' (2MM *Salavmamahnt*, 2MS *Salavmamant*)

sé'elhaqam 'sometime this morning'

sen 'perhaps'

sìipölölötota 'be forming buds all over (plural)' (2MM *sihpölölötota*)

sìipuyayatani 'will be opening out as flowers' (2MM *sihpuyayatani*)

sìiqölnawit 'along the flowery expanse(s)' (2MM *sihqölnawit*)

sìiqölpa 'in, along the flowery expanse(s)' (2MM *sihqöhlpa*)

sìitala 'be bright with flowers' (2MM *sihtala*)

sìitalawva 'become bright with flowers' (2MM *sihtalawva*)

sìitalawvaniqam 'those which will become bright with flowers' (2MM *sihtalawvaniqam*)

sìitalawvatay 'after it has come to be bright with flowers' (object form) (2MM *sihtalawvatay*)

siivutoynat 'after providing with pottery containers'

sikya'o'omawt 'yellow clouds' (2MM *sikya'o'omahwt*)

sikya'omaw 'yellow cloud'

Sikyahonawmomngwit 'Yellow Bear leaders'

sikyangwùntalawkuyva 'for daylight to make its appearance as yellow dawn' (2MM *sikyangwuhntalawkuyva*)

sikyatalwìipiki'am 'their yellow lightning' (2MM *sikyatalwihpiki'am*)

sikyavavönmamant 'yellow young corn plants' (2MM *sikyavavönmamahnt*)

sikyavolim 'yellow butterflies'

sikyavolmamant 'yellow butterfly maidens' (2MM *sikyavolmamahnt*)

sikyavuni 'the yellow one'

sikyavunit 'in yellow'

sikyayoyleki 'yellow rain lines'

sikyayoyleki'am 'their yellow rain lines'

sínevela'ykyangw 'while having perfection as their due' (2MM *sínevela'ykyang*, 2MS *sínevela'kyang*)

síngumanyuyuwinaya 'be dancing with pollen (plural)'

síngumni, 'pollen'

sínevelantoya 'provide with the perfection of something that is owed, due to another'

sinom 'people'

síqöyavuni 'the adorned white one'

síqöyavunit 'in adorned white'

Sivu'ikwiwtaqa '[the katsina] that carries a vessel on the back'

siwahopmangu'iwta 'be tired of bachelorhood' (2M *siwahovmangu'iwta*)

siwamat 'their (males') younger sisters'

siwawaytimakyangw 'while going along in joy, in happiness' (2M *siwa-*

waytimakyang)
siwawaytimani 'will be going along in joy, in happiness'
siwi'am 'their tendrils'
siwi'ytaniqa 'that which will have vitality'
siwi'ytaniqatni 'will have that which will have vitality' (2MS *siwi'taniqatni*)
siwiswukiwyungwa 'have tendrils cascading (plural)'
síwukiwyungwa 'be cascading (plural)'
Siwukvami 'to Siwukva' (a spring on Third Mesa)
so'tini 'will end, will come to an end, will die out'
somiviki'am 'their *somiviki'* (*Somiviki* is blue corn pudding boiled or steamed in a corn husk wrapper, tied at both ends.)
sonkiwa 'sound pleasing, for there to be pleasing sounds'
sonway 'beautiful'
soona'ykyangw 'while having nutriment' (2MM *soona'ykyang,* 2MS *soona'kyang*)
soona'ytaqa 'that which has nutriment' (2MS *soona'taqa*)
Soongwuqa 'the Milky Way'
soosonway 'beautiful (plural)'
Sootukwnangwmomngwit 'Star-Cumulus Cloud katsina leaders' (2M *Sootuknangmomngwit*)
sooya 'planting stick'
sosniwa 'be beautiful (plural)'
sòosoy 'all' (2MM *sosoy*)
sòosoyam 'all, all of them' (2MM *sósoyam*)
sosonkiwa 'be pleasing'
sosonkiwlawu 'keep making it pleasing'
sosonkiwyani 'will be pleasing (plural)'
sosonlavayi'at 'his pleasing speech'
Soyalangw 'Winter Solstice ceremony'

(2M *Soyalang*)
soyohim'o'omawt 'all kinds of clouds' (2MM *soyohim'o'omahwt*)
soyohìmqaqa'ö 'all different kinds of corn' (2MM *soyohihmqaqa'ö*)
su'an 'in just the right way, correctly'
su'its 'early in the day'
su'pa'iwtani 'will be showing kindness, friendship' (2M *su'pa'iwtani*)
súmatsiwyungwa 'be quite visible (plural)'
sumi'nangwat 'together in intentions, united in endeavors, in unanimity'
sunsa 'together as one, in harmony'
sunsa'unangway 'with hearts together as one'
sunsaya 'be together as one, in harmony (plural)'
Supawlave 'at Supawlavi'
suqömkoro 'dark hole'
suqömkoro'ta 'be a dark hole'
sustalyokvaniqa 'an all-day rain', literally, 'that which will rain all day'
suukye' 'along one line, in harmony'
sùutok.ya 'forget (plural)' (2MM *suhtok.ya*)
suvituyqave 'at the point with sumacs'
suvo'oyiwa 'have been united as one'
suvuyoyangw 'long and steady drizzle, gentle rain' (2M *suvuyoyang*)
suvuyoysonaq 'in the steady drizzle, through the gentle rain'
suyanis'unangwa 'good-heartedness'
suyanisqatsi 'life of harmony and tranquility'

ta'a 'okay, all right, I agree'
taaha'am 'their maternal uncle'
taalaw'omàwkiva 'along the dwelling place of the clouds in the direction of the sunrise' (2MM *taalaw'omahwkiva*)
taalawkuyva 'for daylight to make its appearance'
taalawnaya 'make glisten (plural)'

taalawsiwawayna 'be making delighted at the beginning of the day'

Taalawsohu 'Morning Star'

taalawsonmi 'toward the center of daylight, of the light of sunrise'

taalawva 'dawn, become light, a new day'

taaqa 'man'

taatangayt 'yellowjackets' (plural of *taatangaya*) (2MM *taatangahyt*)

tàatapyani 'will be placing deposits (plural)' (2MM *tahtavyani*, 2MS *taatavyani*)

taatawi 'songs'

taatawi'at 'his/her songs'

taatawlawu 'keep singing songs'

taatawtimani 'will go along singing songs'

taatawtinuma 'go around singing songs'

taatawyuyuwinani 'will be dancing and singing songs'

taatawyuyuwintani 'will be dancing and singing songs'

taatawyuyuwintima 'go along dancing and singing songs'

taatawyuyuwmani 'will go along dancing and singing songs'

taatö 'to the southeast'

taavang 'in the southwest'

taavangqw 'from the southwest' (2M *taavangq*)

taawa 'sun, day'

taawakoyongo 'peacock'

taawamanaw 'oriole'

taawanasave 'at midday, at noon'

taawanawit 'all day long'

taawaniikyangw 'the sun/day however' (2M *taawaniikyang*)

taawi'am 'their song'

taawi'yvaya 'learn a song (plural)' (2MS *taawi'vaya*)

taayimuyiwni 'will look in awe'

taayungwa 'look (plural)'

tal'angwnawit 'all summer long' (2M *tal'angnawit*)

tal'angwyokva 'rain during the summer' (2M *tal'angyokva*)

tala'am 'their tassels'

talahoyiwa 'awaken for the new day'

talasi'am 'their pollen'

talasimasa'am 'their pollen-laden wings'

Talasivave 'at Pollen Spring'

talasiyalaha'am 'their pollen with sparkles in it'

talasiyalaha'iqöma 'my face painted with pollen with sparkles in it'

talavay 'in the morning'

talavàytötöqa 'be giving the calls of the morning' (2MM *talavahytötöqa*)

talöngwintota 'be going from day to day (plural)'

tàlti 'become daylight' (2MM *tahlti*)

talvewi 'toward the direction of the sunrise'

talwìipiki 'lightning' (2MM *talwihpiki*)

talwipi'am 'their lightning'

talwiptimakyangw 'while going along with lightning flashing' (2M *talwivtimakyang*)

talwiptoynakyangw 'while making lightning' (2M *talwivtoynakyang*)

tapkinaya 'make it to the end of the day (plural)' (2M *tavkinaya*)

tapkinta 'be doing something to the end of the day' (2M *tavkinta*)

taq 'for, seeing that, since, because, despite the fact, notwithstanding, even though'

taqvahomomngwit 'men who make the prayer feathers'

tarukop'öqaqa '(one) that has an erection as hard as a bone' (2M *tarukov-'öqaqa*)

tasaphonaqmomoyam 'women who are crazy for Navajo men' (2M *tasavhonaqmomoyam*)

tatami, an expression of resignation to a situation

Tatatsiwkiva 'Ball Game kiva'

tatkya 'in the southeast'

tatkyaqw 'from the southeast' (2M *tatkyaq*)

tavilawu, not a recognized word; it may have been intended in the song to mean either bury the dead or appoint or choose herself to die and be buried, i.e., wanting to die from shame

taviyat 'after putting, placing (plural)'

tawaktsi'uyi'at 'his sweet corn plants'

tawamanaw 'oriole'

tawamansi 'bright red kind of Indian paintbrush, *Castilleja linariifolia'*

tawasipmasmi 'wristwatch'

tawlawmumuya 'keep singing extensively'

tawma 'go along singing'

tawmakyangw 'while going along singing' (2M *tawmakyang*)

tawmumuya 'be singing intensively'

tayayatimani 'will go along trembling, shaking, quaking'

tayma 'go along looking, seeing, watching'

taymakyangw 'while going along looking, seeing, watching' (2M *taymakyang*)

taymani 'will go along looking, watching for'

taynuma 'be looking around'

tewaki 'Tanoan country'

tiiti'ayalawu 'be asking others to perform'

tiiti'ökiwa 'have come in dance (and thereby to soothe)'

tiitimuyiwa 'be caught up in dancing'.

tiitiwungwintani 'will be nurturing offspring repeatedly'

tiitiwungwna 'raise children, nurture like children' (2M *tiitiwungna*)

tiitiwunima 'be dancing in performance'

tiitiwuniwa 'have been called upon to (come and) dance'

tiitiwunuto 'go/come to stand dancing'

timaynànkwusani 'will set out on a journey to watch a performance' (2MM *timaynahnkwusani*)

tímokimat 'their young corn ears on the stalk'

tímokimuy 'young corn ears on the stalk (object form)'

titwi'yta 'be adept or skilled at several things' (2MS *titwi'ta*)

tivongyapami 'to the dance-display place'

tivongyapave 'at/in the dance-display place'

tiw'aymat 'his nephews, nieces'

tiyòoya 'little boy' (2MM *tiyohya*)

tokila'am 'their set date, the date they set'

toko'omawtotim 'dark billowing cloud boys'

toko'ykyangw 'while having flesh' (2MM *toko'ykyang,* 2MS *toko'-kyang*)

tokotswùuti 'mean, grouchy woman' (2MM *tokotswuhti*)

tokyephoyoyota 'be moving all night' (2M *tokyevhoyoyota*)

tokyeptatoqa 'one that goes to do s.th. all night' (2M *tokyevtatoqa*)

tokyepyoyangw 'all-night rain' (2M *tokyevyoyang*)

tooki 'last night, last evening'

tookila 'night'

tookyep 'all night long' (2M *tookyev*)

tootim 'boys'

tootsi'ykyangw 'while having shoes' (2MM *tootsi'ykyang,* 2MS *tootsi'-kyang*)

totimhòoyam 'little boys, young boys' (2MM *totimhohyam*)

töökiwangwayni 'there will be shouting of joy'

töökiyuyuwinani 'will be dancing while making characteristic calls, sounds' *töökiyuyuwintani* 'will be dancing while making characteristic call, sounds'

töötökimakyangw 'while going along making characteristic calls, sounds' (2M *töötökimakyang*)

töötöki'am 'their calls, cries, sounds'

töötöqa 'be making characteristic calls, sounds'

töötöqlawni 'will keep making characteristic calls, sounds'

töötöqlawu 'keep making characteristic calls, sounds'

töötöqtimani 'will go along shouting, calling'

töqngwa'at 'its (the song's) "chorus" '

töqtini 'will shout, make a characteristic call'

tsaatsawna 'become afraid, frightened, scared (plural)'

tsómikiwyungwa 'be in bunches'

tsoongo'am 'their smoking pipe(s)'

tsòotsona 'kiss' (2MM *tsohtsona*)

tsootsonglalwa 'keep on smoking (tobacco) (plural)'

tsootsonglawkyàakyangw 'while keeping on smoking (tobacco) (plural)' (2MM *tsootsonglawkyahkyang*, 2MS *tsootsonglawkyaakyang*)

tsootsong.ya 'be smoking (tobacco) (plural)'

tsootsong.yakyangw 'while smoking (tobacco) (plural)' (2M *tsootsong.yakyang*)

tsoova 'have sexual intercourse (male subject)'

tsooviw 'act of sexual intercourse'

tsorosi 'blue aster(s)'

tsotsmingwu 'perfect ear of white corn with kernels all the way to the tip, a "corn mother" '

tsovàlti 'gather, assemble' (2MM *tsovahlti*)

tsukumana 'coot, *Fulica americana*' (a water bird)

tsukumomngwit 'clown leaders'

tsukutotim 'clown boys'

tsukuviki 'blue corn pudding wrapped into a crescent shape in a green corn leaf and boiled or steamed'

tsúyakiwta 'be grateful for being able to enjoy'

tu'awi'yta 'have a message, signify, represent' (2MS *tu'awi'ta*)

tukwi'ova 'up along the mesa(s)'

tukwunangwmamant 'cumulus cloud maidens' (2MM *tukwunangmamahnt*, 2MS *tukwunangmamant*)

tulakinsivu 'vessel for toasting cornmeal over fire'

tulakintota 'be toasting coarsely ground cornmeal (plural)'

tum 'let's, let's go'

tumala 'work'

tumala'at 'his work'

tumasi 'a female entity'

tumsi 'clanswoman'

tunatya'am 'their religious intentions'

tunatyawkyangw 'while nurturing hope' (2M *tunatyawkyang*)

tunatyawma 'go along watching'

tunatyawta 'nurture hope for'

tupkiwta 'be hidden, concealed, kept secret' (2M *tuvkiwta*)

túsanmaqtö'at 'his dirty hands'

tutavo 'advice, instruction, council'

tutkivu 'cut up'

tutu'awnaya 'be informing others of the meaning of something (plural)'

tutuvenaya 'be marking (plural)'

tutuven'iwyungwa 'be marked with lines or notches (plural)'

tutuveni 'markings, visual representation, writing'

tutuvèntota 'make many marks (plural)' (2MM *tutuvehntota*)

tutuwnayakyangw 'while showing how to do something (plural)' (2M *tutuwnayakyang*) *tuu'awinmakyangw* 'while going along informing' (2M *tuu'awinmakyang*)

tuu'awmakyangw 'while taking a message along' (2M *tuu'awmakyang*)

tuu'awva 'come with a message'

tuuhuylawu 'be giving things away to people'

tuukwiva 'along the mesa(s)'

tuungeminta 'be inviting someone else to go/come along'

tuunopna 'feed the spirits' (2M *tuunovna*)

tùupevu'am 'their roasted sweet corn' (2MM *tuhpevu'am*)

tùutukwiwmakyangw 'while going along stacked up in several stacks' (2MM *tuhtukwiwmakyang,* 2MS *tuutukwiwmakyang*)

tuutunopna 'be feeding the spirits' (2M *tuutunovna*)

tùutuwutsi 'tell about, tell a story, narrate historical facts, reporting on factual events and experiences' (2MM *tuhtuwutsi*)

tuutuya 'be sick, ill, aching, hurting, in pain'

tuuvingtinuma 'go around asking'

tuuvoyi 'vanish, disappear, get obliterated'

tuuvoyni 'will vanish, disappear, get obliterated'

tuuwa 'sand' or (in compounds) 'land'

Tuuwanasave 'at Tuuwanasavi'

Tuuwanasavi, the "place in the middle of the land," a reference to all the Hopi lands

tuuwapongya 'the land part of the earth' (the "sand altar")

tuuwapongyanawit 'along (the course of) the land'

tuuwapongyava 'along the land'

tuuwatavini 'will place on the land'

tuuwaytalawvangaqw 'from where the first light of day is still out of sight' (2M *tuuwaytalawvangaq*)

tuuwingaqw 'from the cliff ledge, from the terrace' (2M *tuuwingaq*)

tùuyongwaya 'delight others (plural)' (2MM *tuhyongwaya*)

tuvenangöytani 'will be chasing each other colorfully'

tuvevakwam 'toads of various colors'

tuvevakwamomngwit 'toad leaders of various colors'

tuvevolmamant 'butterfly maidens of various colors' (2MM *tuvevolmamahnt*)

tuvevolvitsangwa 'countenance of butterflies of various colors'

tuwamöyikinta 'be spreading out sand'

tuwat 'in turn, for (one's) part'

tuwi'at 'his practical knowledge, skill'

tuwi'yvaya 'learn (plural)' (2MS *tuwi'-vaya*)

tuyqa 'point, projecting point of a mesa, external corner of a structure'

tuyqawva 'prevail, attain'

tuyqawvani 'will attain'

u'na 'remember'

u'nangwvaslawu 'keep praying repeatedly in a heartfelt manner for good results' (2M *u'nangvaslawu*)

um 'you'

uma 'you (plural)'

ùmtimakyangw 'while going along booming (slowly)' (2MM *uhmtimakyang,* 2MS *umtimakyang*)

ùmtoynakyangw 'while making slow booming sounds' (2MM *uhmtoynakyang,* 2MS *umtoynakyang*)

umu'ova 'along above you'

umumi 'to you (plural)'

umumutima 'go along booming'

umumutimani 'will go along booming'

umuna 'your (plural) father'

umungem 'for you (plural), for your benefit'

umùu'unangwa 'your (plural) hearts' (2MM *umu'unangwa*)

umùu'unangwvàasi 'your heartfelt wish(es), hope(s), prayer(s)' (2MM *umu'unangvasi,* 2MS *umuu'unangvaasi*)

umùu'uyi 'your (plural) planted plants, planted fields' (2MM *umu'uyi*)

umùu'uyimamant 'your (plural) (corn) plant maidens' (2MM *umu'uyimamahnt*)

umùu'uyinawit 'along your (plural) planted fields' (2MM *umu'uyinawit*)

umùuhom'oyi 'your prayer (plural) offering' (2MM *umuhom'oyi*)

umùukaway'uyi 'your (plural) watermelon plants, plantings' (2MM *umuhkaway'uyi*)

umùuki 'your (plural) houses, dwelling places' (2MM *umuhki*)

umùukisonaq 'through the middle of your (plural) village' (2MM *umuhkisonaq*)

umùukiva 'your (plural) kiva' (2MM *umuhkiva*)

umùukwa 'your (plural) grandfather' (2MM *umuhkwa*)

umùulavayi 'your (plural) speech, words' (2MM *umulavayi*)

umùumasa 'your (plural) wings' (2MM *umumasa*)

umùupaho 'your (plural) prayer feathers' (2MM *umuhpaho*)

umùupaho'ini 'your (plural) tray of prayer feathers' (2MM *umuhpaho-'ini*)

umùupahoveni 'your (plural) marked prayer feathers, prayer feathers with ritual markings' (2MM *umuhpahoveni*)

umùupasanawit 'along your (plural) fields' (2MM *umuhpasanawit*)

umùuqatsi 'your lives' (2MM *umuhqatsi*)

umùusakwavaho 'your blue/green prayer feathers' (2MM *umusakwavaho*)

umùutim 'your (plural) children' (2MM *umuhtim*)

umùutokila 'your (plural) set date, the date that you set' (2MM *umuhtokila*)

umùutunatya 'your (plural) religious intentions' (2MM *umuhtunatya*)

umùutuwani 'your (plural) set time, the time that you set' (2MM *umuhtuwani*)

umùutuwapongyava 'along your land' (2MM *umuhtuwapongyava*)

umùutuwaqatsi 'your (plural) land' (2MM *umuhtuwaqatsi*)

umùuvìikya 'your area set aside for a particular use' (2MM *umuvihkya*)

umùuvìikyava 'along your area of use' (2MM *umuvihkyava*)

umùuyoysingöla 'your rain flower-hoops' (ritual objects symbolic of rain) (2MM *umuyoysingöla*)

umùuyòyqöqöngö 'your rain racing stones' (ritual objects symbolic of rain) (2MM *umuyohyqöqöngö*)

umùuyòytuveqöqöngtsongo 'your rain racing-stone pipes' (2MM *umuyohytuveqöqöngtsongo*)

unangwa 'heart'

unangwvàasi 'heartfelt wish, hope, prayer' (2MM *unangvasi,* 2MS *unangvaasi*)

uní 'how delightful, how wonderful'

unisava 'of an ideal short length, height'

ura, modal of recollection

ùu'unangwvàasi 'your heartfelt wish, hope, prayer' (2MM *u'unangvasi,* 2MS *uu'unangvaasi*)

ùukongya 'your husband' (2MM *uhkongya*)

ùuqöyapqa'ö 'your white ear of corn' (2MM *uhqöyavqa'ö,* 2MS *uuqöyavqa'ö*)

uuyi'am 'their planted plant(s), planted fields'

uuyi'at 'his planted plant(s), planted

field'
uuyimamant 'plant maidens' (2MM *uuyimamahnt*)
uuyive 'at the planted field'
uymukti 'become thriving in full growth'
uysonaq 'throughout the midst of the planted area(s)'

waayani 'will move away'
wahima 'go along throwing'
wángwaylawu 'keep summoning, calling for'
wari 'run'
wayma 'walk along'
waymakyangw 'while walking along' (2M *waymakyang*)
waynuma 'be walking around'
Weenima, the southeast katsina home
wikmuyiwa 'have brought'
wikvaniwa 'have brought'
wik.ya 'take/bring along (plural)'
wukokuri'am 'their big buttocks'
wukotupqave 'at the big canyon' (2M *wukotuvqave*)
wukwtuvoyla 'mark of old age' (2M *wuktuvoyla*)
wúngwiwmakyangw 'while growing' (2M *wúngwiwmakyang*)
wunimani 'will be dancing'
wunimantinuma 'be going around dancing'
wutsilawu 'be doing something by artifice, sleight of hand'
wuupa 'long, tall'
wuuta 'pour'
wùutaqharurutiwa 'for men to be getting older and older toward ripe old age' (2MM *wuhtaqharurutiwa*)
wùutiharurutiwa 'for women to be getting older and older toward ripe old age' (2MM *wuhtiharurutiwa*)
wùutimiqsa 'toward married womanhood only' (*wuhtimiqsa*)
wuuvi 'climb up, ascend'

wuuwankyàakyangw 'while thinking, focusing on (plural)' (2MM *wuuwankyahkyang,* 2MS *wuuwankyaakyang*)
wuuwanlawu 'keep thinking, worrying'
wuuwanmaqam 'those that go along thinking, worrying, wondering'
wuuwanta 'be thinking, worrying, wondering'
wuuwuyom 'elders, old ones'
wuyolvayi 'recollections, remembrances, words from long ago'
wuyomihaqami 'all the way towards old age'
wuyomiq 'toward old age'

ya, question particle
yaala 'make abate, put an end to (weather)'
yàasatti 'become this time' (2MM *yásatti*)
yàasavo 'to this length or distance, as far as this; to this present time only, until this time (and no longer)' (2MM *yásavo*)
yaawitoyna 'put something customary to hold in the hand'
yaayan 'in these ways'
yaayanhaqam 'in approximately these ways'
yaayatima 'go along teasing, frolicking'
yaayatimani 'will go along teasing, frolicking'
yàlti 'cease' (2MM *yahlti*)
yan 'like this, in this way, thus, so'
yan'eway 'such as this, like this, being this homely looking'
yang 'here, along here, in these places, in this area'
yangqaqw 'from here somewhere' (2M *yangqaq*)
yangqw 'from here, in here' (2M *yangq*)
yangsava 'this long'

yangsay 'of this size, this big, big like this (plural)'

yanhaqam 'in approximately this way'

yaniwma 'be happening this way'

yaniwmani 'will be happening this way'

yanìwtini 'will happen this way' (2MM *yanihwtini*)

yansa 'only in this way'

yanta 'be this way, be like this'

yantaniqa 'one that will/would be this way'

yaw, quotative particle

yawmani 'will be carrying by hand, taking, bringing'

yawtoyna 'put something in someone's hand to hold'

yeese 'live, dwell (plural)'

yeesiwa 'be in place, exist'

yeesiwva 'begin living (plural)'

yep 'here' (2M *yev*)

yephaqam 'approximately here, around here somewhere' (2M *yevhaqam*)

yesqam 'those who are sitting, residing, living'

yoknawisa 'go to make it rain (plural)'

yoknaya 'make it rain (plural)'

yoknayani 'will make it rain (plural)'

yoknaye' 'if (you/they) make it rain, get rain'

yokva 'rain' (verb)

yokvani 'will rain'

yomimitoyna 'be thrusting the hips rapidly against'

yongyaya 'chipmunk, whitetail antelope squirrel, *Ammospermophilus leucurus*'

yongyaymomoyam 'adulterous women'

yongyaywùuti 'adulterous woman' (2MM *yongyaywuhti*)

yoniwsonaq 'in the midst of obligations'

yooki 'rain' (verb)

yoowi 'corn silk'

yoowi'am 'their corn silk'

yooyangw 'rain' (2M *yooyang*)

yooyàngwtiniqa 'that which will become rain' (2MM *yooyahngtiniqa,* 2MS *yooyangtiniqa*)

yooyokni 'it will be raining'

yooyokpuva 'along the places it rains, has rained'

yooyoktivakyangw 'while beginning to rain repeatedly' (2M *yooyoktivakyang*)

yooyokva 'rain in several places and/or at several times'

yooyokvaniqa 'that it will rain repeatedly'

yortinuma 'be looking about, turning the head so as to see'

yoy'öki 'arrive, come as rain'

yoy'ökini 'will arrive, come as rain'

yoy'ökiwni 'will have come, arrived as rain'

yoy'ùmtimakyangw 'while going along thundering (slowly)' (2MM *yoy-'uhmtimakyang,* 2MS *yoy'ùutimakyang*)

yoy'ùmtimani 'will go along thundering (slowly)' (2MM *yoy'uhmtimani*)

yoy'umuki 'thunder'

yoy'umuki'am 'their thunder'

yoy'umumuta 'be thundering'

yoy'umumutani 'will be thundering'

yoy'umumutimani 'will go along thundering'

yoy'umumutoyna 'make it be thundering'

yoy'umumutoynani 'will make it be thundering'

yoyhahawiwmani 'will have gone along descending as rain'

yoyhahawtima 'go along descending as rain'

yoyhahawtimani 'will go along descending as rain'

yoyhani 'descend as rain'

yoyhaniwa 'be a descent of rain'

yoyhohonginmani 'will go along

repeatedly making (them) stand in the rain'

yoyhoyoyotani 'will be moving as rain'

yoyhoyoyotimani 'will be moving along as rain'

yoyleki'am 'their rain lines'

yoynanatuwniwa 'be practicing the skill of rain'

yoynanawakna 'pray for rain (plural)'

yoynànkwusa 'start on a journey as rain' (2MM *yoynahnkwusa*)

yoynànkwusani 'will start on a journey as rain' (2MM *yoynahnkwusani*)

yoynawakna 'pray for rain'

yoyngyàlpuva 'in the postlude of the rain, during the time after it has stopped raining' (2MM *yoyngyahlpuva*)

yòytalwipi'am 'their lightning in the rain' (2MM *yohytalwipi'am*)

yòytalwiptimani 'will go along as rain with lightning flashing' (2MM *yohytalwivtimani*, 2MS *yoytalwivtimani*)

yòytalwiptoynakyangw 'while making lightning in the rain' (2MM *yohytalwivtoynakyang*, 2MS *yoytalwivtoynakyang*)

yòytatawi'am 'their rain songs' (2MM *yohytatawi'am*)

yòytatawi'at 'his rain songs' (2MM *yohytatawi'at*)

yòytatawlawu 'keep singing songs for rain' (2MM *yohytatawlawu*)

yòytokila'am 'the date they set for rain' (2MM *yohytokila'am*)

yòytötöki'am 'their rain sounds' (2MM *yohytötöki'am*)

yòytu'awmani 'will deliver a rain message' (2MM *yohytu'awmani*)

yòytutuveni'at 'his rain marks' (2MM *yohytutuveni'at*)

yoyvivìikwam 'nighthawks' (2MM *yoyvivihkwam*)

yoywangwaytiwa 'have been earnestly requesting (them) to come as rain'

yoywunuto 'go/come stand as rain'

yumaki'ykyangw 'while having as a ceremonial mother' (2MM *yumaki'ykyang*, 2MS *yumaki'kyang*)

yuuyahinaya 'dress (them) as for a ceremony, adorn (plural)'

yuuyahiwa 'have been dressed as for a ceremony, be adorned (plural)'

yuuyahiwva 'come dressed, adorned, clothed in (plural)'

yuuyahiwvat 'after having come (to be) clothed, adorned (plural)'

yuuyupkyaqe 'in the innermost rooms' (2M *yuuyuvkyaqe*)

yuuyuwinani 'will be making dance'

yuwsinani 'will clothe, adorn'

yuwsina 'clothe, adorn'

yuwsinat 'after dressing, clothing, adorning'

yuwsinaya 'clothe, adorn (plural)'

References Cited

Barrett, Samuel A.
 1946 Notes on Hopi Songs Recorded by S. A. Barrett in 1911 for the Milwaukee Public Museum. San Rafael, California, Feb. 3, 1946. Typescript. Archives of Traditional Music, Indiana University.
Bauman, Richard and Charles Briggs
 1990 Poetics and performance as critical perspectives on language and social life. *Annual Review of Anthropology* 19: 59–88.
Beeman, William O.
 1993 The anthropology of theater and spectacle. *Annual Review of Anthropology* 22: 369–393.
Black, Mary E.
 1984 Maidens and metaphors: an analysis of Hopi corn metaphors. *Ethnology* 23: 279–288.
Black, Robert A.
 1959 Typescript listing of songs recorded. On deposit at the Archive of Traditional Music, Indiana University.
 1965 *A Content Analysis of 81 Hopi Indian Chants.* Ph.D. dissertation, Indiana University.
 1967a Hopi grievance chants: a mechanism of social control. *Studies in Southwestern Ethnolinguistics: Meaning and History in the Languages of the American Southwest,* Dell H. Hymes, ed., with William E. Bittle. The Hague: Mouton. Pp. 54–67.
 1967b Hopi rabbit-hunt chants: a ritualized language. *Essays in the Verbal and Visual Arts,* June Helm, ed. Seattle: University of Washington Press. Pp. 7–11.
Brady, Erika, Maria La Vigna, Dorothy Sara Lee, and Thomas Vennum
 1984 *The Federal Cylinder Project: A Guide to Field Cylinder Collections in Federal Agencies.* 3 vols. Washington: American Folklife Center, Library of Congress.
Clements, William M.
 1996 *Native American Verbal Art: Texts and Contexts.* Tucson: University of Arizona Press.
Comrie, Bernard
 1985 *Tense.* (Cambridge textbooks in linguistics.) Cambridge University Press.

Crystal, David
  2003 *A Dictionary of Linguistics and Phonetics.* Fifth Edition. Malden, MA: Blackwell Publishing.
Curtis, Natalie
  1907 *The Indians' Book: An Offering by the American Indians of Indian Lore, Musical and Narrative, to Form a Record of the Songs and Legends of their Race.* New York: Harper & Bros. Second edition published 1923. (Dover reprint of the second edition, 1968. Reprint of the 1907 edition by Bonanza Books, New York, distributed by Crown, 1987.)
Davis, Irvine
  1964 The Language of Santa Ana Pueblo. *Bureau of American Ethnology Bulletin 191* (Anthropological Paper 69). Smithsonian Institution. Washington: U.S. Government Printing Office. Pp. 53–190.
De Reuse, Willem J.
  2005 Review of *Hopi Traditional Literature,* by David Leedom Shaul. *International Journal of American Linguistics* 71(3): 356–359.
Densmore, Frances
  1943 The use of meaningless syllables in Indian songs. *American Anthropologist* 45: 160–162.
  1950 The words of Indian songs as unwritten literature. *The Journal of American Folklore* 63: 450–458.
Eco, Umberto
  2003 *Mouse or Rat? Translation as Negotiation.* London: Weidenfeld and Nicolson.
Eriacho, Wilfred, Sr.
  1998 Bena:we Dana:we—Word Categories. Draft. Zuni, NM: Zuni Public School District No. 89.
Feld, Steven and Aaron Fox
  1994 Music and language. *Annual Review of Anthropology* 23: 25–53.
Fewkes, Jesse Walter
  1926 Two short articles to accompany Gennett Records 5757–5761: Music of the Hopi Indian *and* The relation of Hopi music to their culture.
Frisbie, Charlotte J.
  1980 Vocables in Navajo ceremonial music. *Ethnomusicology* 24: 347–392.

Gilman, Benjamin Ives
  1908 Hopi songs. *Journal of American Ethnology and Archaeology*
        5: 1–226.
Glowacka, Maria D.
  1998 Ritual knowledge in Hopi tradition. *American Indian Quarterly*
        22(3): 386–392.
Hack, John T.
  1942 *The Changing Physical Environment of the Hopi Indians of
        Arizona.* Papers of the Peabody Museum of American Archae-
        ology and Ethnology, Vol. 35(1). Cambridge, MA: Harvard
        University.
Halpern, Ida
  1976 On the interpretation of "meaningless–nonsensical syllables" in
        the music of the Pacific Northwest Indians. *Ethnomusicology*
        20: 253–271.
Harrington, John Peabody
  1907–1908 The Ethnogeography of the Tewa Indians. *Bureau of
        American Ethnology 29th Annual Report.* Washington: Govern-
        ment Printing Office. Pp. 27–636.
Hill, Jane H.
  1992 The flower world of old Uto-Aztecan. *Journal of Anthropologi-
        cal Research* 48(2): 117–144.
  2001 Proto-Uto-Aztecan: a community of cultivators in central
        Mexico? *American Anthropologist* 103(4): 913–934.
Hinton, Leanne
  1989 Vocables in Havasupai song. *Southwestern Indian Ritual
        Drama.* Charlotte J. Frisbie, ed. Santa Fe, NM: School of
        American Research Press. Pp. 275–305.
Kabotie, Mike
  1978 *Two Hopi Song Poets of Shungopavi: Milland Lomakema and
        Mark Lomayestewa.* Privately printed.
Kaeppler, Adrienne L.
  1978 Dance in anthropological perspective. *Annual Review of
        Anthropology* 7: 31–49.
Kalectaca, Milo
  1978 *Lessons in Hopi.* Ronald W. Langacker, ed. Tucaon: University
        of Arizona Press.
Keane, Webb
  1997 Religious language. *Annual Review of Anthropology* 26: 47–71.
Keeling, Richard
  1991 *A Guide to Early Field Recordings (1900–1949) at the Lowie*

Museum of Anthropology. Berkeley: University of California Publications: Catalogs and Bibliographies 6.

1997 *North American Indian Music: A Guide to Published Sources and Selected Recordings.* New York: Garland.

Kinkade, M. Dale and Anthony Mattina

1996 Discourse. *Handbook of North American Indians, Volume 17, Languages.* Ives Goddard, volume Editor; William C. Sturtevant, general editor. Washington: Smithsonian Institution. Pp. 244–274.

Kroeber, Karl, ed. and compiler

1981 *Traditional Literature of the American Indian: Texts and Interpretation.* Lincoln: University of Nebraska Press.

Krupat, Arnold

1992 On the translation of Native American song and story: a theorized history. *On the Translation of Native American Literature.* Brian Swann, ed. Washington: Smithsonian Institution. Pp. 3–32.

Kurath, Gertrude

1970 *Music and Dance of the Tewa Pueblos.* Museum of New Mexico Research Records No. 8, Santa Fe.

Lee, Dorothy

1979 *Native North American Music and Data: A Catalogue of Sound Recordings 1893–1976.* Bloomington: Indiana University Press.

List, George

1962 Song in Hopi culture, past and present. *Journal of the International Folk Music Council* 14: 30–35.

1985 Hopi melodic concepts. *Journal of the Musicological Society* 38: 143–152.

1987 Stability and variation in a Hopi lullaby. *Ethnomusicology* 31: 18–34.

1993 *Stability and Variation in Hopi Song.* Memoirs, Vol. 204. Philadelphia: American Philosophical Society.

1997 Hopi kachina dance songs: concepts and context. *Ethnomusicology* 41(3): 413–432.

McLeod, Norma

1974 Ethnomusicological research and anthropology. *Annual Review of Anthropology* 3: 99–115.

Merriam, Alan P.

1964 *The Anthropology of Music.* Evanston, IL: Northwestern University Press.

Miller, Wick R.
    1965 *Acoma Grammar and Texts.* University of California Publica-
    tions in Linguistics, Volume 40.
    1996 The ethnography of speaking. *Handbook of North American
    Indians, Volume 17, Languages.* Ives Goddard, volume editor;
    William C. Sturtevant, general editor. Washington: Smithsonian
    Institution. Pp. 222–243.
Miller, Wick R. and Irvine Davis
    1963 Proto-Keresan phonology. *International Journal of American
    Linguistics* 29(4): 310–330.
Murphy, William P.
    1978 Oral literature. *Annual Review of Anthropology* 7: 113–136.
Newman, Stanley
    1958 *Zuni Dictionary.* Indiana University Research Center in Anthro-
    pology, Folklore, and Linguistics, Publication 6. *International
    Journal of American Linguistics* 24.1, part 2.
Powers, William K.
    1992 Translating the untranslatable: the place of the vocable in
    Lakota song. *On the Translation of Native American Literature.*
    Brian Swann, ed. Washington: Smithsonian Institution. Pp.
    293–310.
Reed, Susan A.
    1998 The politics and poetics of dance. *Annual Review of Anthropol-
    ogy* 27: 503–532.
Rhodes, Willard
    1952 North American Indian music: a bibliographical survey of
    anthropological theory. *Notes,* a publication of the Music
    Library Association, 2nd ser., 10: 33–45.
Roberts, Helen H.
    1927 Indian music from the Southwest. *Natural History* 27: 257–265.
    1932 Melodic composition and scale foundations in primitive music.
    American Anthropologist 34: 79–107.
    1933 *Form in Primitive Music.* New York: Norton.
    1936 *Musical Areas in Aboriginal North America.* Yale University
    Publications in Anthropology No. 12.
Seeger, Anthony and Louise S. Spear
    1987 *Early Field Recordings: a Catalogue of Cylinder Collections at
    Indiana University Archives of Traditional Music.* Blooming-
    ton: Indiana University Press.

Sekaquaptewa, Emory and Dorothy Washburn

2004 They go along singing: reconstructing the Hopi past from ritual metaphors in song and image. *American Antiquity* 69: 457–486.

Shaul, David Leedom

1992 A Hopi song-poem in context. *On the Translation of Native American Literatures.* Brian Swann, ed. Washington: Smithsonian Institution. Pp. 228–241.

1994 Two Hopi song poems. *Coming to Light: Contemporary Translations of the Native Literatures of North America.* Brian Swann, ed. New York: Random House. Pp. 679–689.

Smith, Watson

1952 *Kiva Mural Decorations at Awatovi and Kawaika-a, with a Survey of Other Wall Paintings in the Pueblo Southwest.* Cambridge, MA: Peabody Museum. (Peabody Museum of Archaeology and Ethnology, Papers, Volume 37, Awatovi Expedition, Report no. 5.)

Stevenson, Matilda Coxe

1904 The Zuni Indians: their mythology, esoteric fraternities, and ceremonies. *Twenty-third Annual Report of the Bureau of American Ethnology, 1901–1092.* Washington. Pp. 3–634.

Swann, Brian

1987 A note on translation and remarks on collaboration. *Recovering the Word: Essays on Native American Literature.* Brian Swann and Arnold Krupat, eds. Berkeley: University of California Press. Pp. 247–254.

Voth, H. R.

1912 *The Oraibi Marau Ceremony.* Chicago: Field Museum of Natural History, Anthropological Series 11(1): 1–88.

Weigle, Marta, ed.

1989 *Indian Tales from Picuris Pueblo.* Santa Fe: NM: Ancient City Press.

Whorf, Benjamin Lee

1946 The Hopi language, Toreva dialect. *Linguistic Structures of Native America,* by Harry Hoijer et al. Viking Fund Publications in Anthropology, Number 6. Pp. 158–183. (Reissued 1963, 1965, New York: Johnson Reprint Corporation.)

Index

CPSIA information can be obtained at www.ICGtesting.com
Printed in the USA
BVOW03*2358010215

385795BV00002B/91/P